MWAKENYA
THE UNFINISHED REVOLUTION

Selected Documents of the
Mwakenya - December Twelve
Movement (1974-2002)

Compiled and Edited by Maina wa Kĩnyattĩ

MWAKENYA: THE UNFINISHED REVOLUTION
First Published by Mau Mau Research Center
P.O. Box 746-00200
Nairobi, Kenya
Cell phone 0723-911-371
Email: info.mmrc@gmail.com

Copyright ©Mau Mau Research Center, 2014
All rights reserved

ISBN 978-9966-7489-3-5

Copy-edited by Leigh Brownhill & KubeJones-Neill
Proofread by Margaret Gacherũ & J.G.Mũnene
Cover design by Elizabeth Mazrui

Distributed worldwide by Mau Mau Research Center

Printed in Kenya, 2014

Contents

Acronyms 8
Preface...10
Historical Introduction...12

Part One

The Beginning of A New Stage.............................. 36
The Birth of the Underground Movement:Formation
and Early Roots 37

Part Two

WPK/DTM Documents, 1974-1985.....................88
   1. The first Conference of Kenyan Marxist-Leninists...................89
   2. Constitution of the Workers' Party of Kenya............................94
   3. The Need for a Proletarian Party, February 1, 1975. 101
   4. The Nature of a Proletarian Party, February 1, 1975...............104
   5. Guidelines on Cell-Formation, March, 2, 1975 108

Our History Should Not Be Distorted 110
   1. Education and Imperialism. 110
   2. An Extract from Cheche Kenya, 1981.................................151

Mwanguzi Newsletter (1975-1980) 160
   1. Mwanguzi, April 1975 160
   2. Mwanguzi, March 1976...163
   3. Mwanguzi, April 1976 166
   4. Mwanguzi, May 1976 169
   5. The Conditions of the Working Class in Makũyũ
      Plantations..171

Tactics and Strategy 177

    1.   Report of the Central Committee, April 1976 177

    2.   Cell Report for Year 1980 (Nairobi) 180

    3.   Report of the March Second Center 191

The Proletarian Press 197

    1.   Launching a Party Paper 197

    2.   Pambana, No.1, May 1982...200

    3.   Pambana, June 1983. Nairobi...205

    4.   Pambana No. 2, July 1983...207

    5.   Mpatanishi No 7, December 1983..215

    6.   Mpatanishi No. 8, February 1984..217

    7.   Leaflet: J. M. Day of Solidarity 220

    8.   Leaflet: Moi's Divisive Tactics Exposed 222

    9.   Leaflet: What to do when you are arrested 225

Part Three

Mwakenya Documents, 1987-2001 232

    1.   The Fundamental Goals and Objectives of Mwakenya........233

    2.   Kenya Democracy Plank..239

    3.   Mwakenya Purges Factional Clique..250

    4.   Mwakenya Internal Newsletter...256

    5.   The Mwakenya Stand 260

What is to Be Done?..265

    1.   Political Priorities for the 1990s..273

    2.   Charter for Democracy In Kenya...278

    3.   Circular No. 5: On Recruitment 286

    4.   Minutes and Reports 291

    5.   Minutes of Central Committee...291

    6.   From Home Front: Our Response to the CC minutes 299

    7.   Internal Memo 304

Democracy and State Terrorism 306

1. Stop Moi's State Terrorism against the Kenyan People 306
2. Moi: Stop Genocide and Disintegration. 310
3. Assassination of Karĩmi Nduthu 316
4. The Political History of a Patriot. 318
5. Murder of Bishop Muge. 325
6. Ukenya Appeals to the International Community. 328

Study is the Key in the Revolutionary Process 331

1. Levels and Handling of Contradictions 331
2. Liberal Tendency and Its Manifestations 334
3. Theory and Practice 335
4. Study in a Circle 338
5. Conducting a Political Meeting 342
6. Some Basic Principles of Underground 347
7. Cell Study Sheet: A Study of Political Economy 351

Part Four

Ukenya Documents 358

1. The Ukenya Manifesto 359
2. From Kĩmathi to Mwakenya 368
3. Struggle for Democracy in Kenya 382
4. The Struggle Continues 411

Part Five

We March Forward 416

The Harare Declaration 417

Part Six

The Party Study Guide 423

5

6

Dedicated To

Karĩmi wa Nduthu

And all the comrades who struggled and sacrificed for democracy and social justice during the Kenyatta and Moi dictatorships.

Acronyms

CC	Central Committee
CID	Criminal Investigation Department
COTU	Central Organization of Trade Unions
CPK	Communist Party of Kenya
DC	District Commissioner
CRC	Central Revolutionary Council
DMPM	Draft Minimum Programme of Mwakenya
DP	Democratic Party
DTM	December Twelve Movement
FCKML	First Conference of Kenyan Marxist-Leninists
FORD	Forum for Democracy in Kenya
GEMA	Gĩkũyũ, Embu and Mĩĩrũ Association
GCCC	Gĩkũyũ Club Cultural Center
GSU	General Service Unit
IPK	Islamic Party of Kenya
ISU	Indian Special Unit
JM	Josiah Mwangi
KADU	Kenya Democratic Union
KAIF	Kenya Anti-Imperialist Front
KANU	Kenya African National Union
KAU	Kenyan African Union
KDC	Kenya Defense Council
KENDA	Kenya National Democratic Alliance
KES/Ksh	Kenya Shilling
KAR	King's African Rifle
KKM	Kĩama Kĩa Mũingĩ (The People's Party)
KLFA	Kenya Land and Freedom Army

KLFP	Kenya Land and Freedom Party
KNC	Kenya National Congress
KPR	Kenya Police Reserve
KPU	Kenya People's Union
KUC	Kenyatta University College
KWC	Kenya War Council
LDP	Liberal Democratic Party
MEKAREMO	Me Katilili Revolutionary Movement
MK	Mwakenya
MKDTM	Mwakenya-December Twelve Movement
MLM	Marxism-Leninism-Maoism
MMCC	Mau Mau Central Committee
MMDCC	Mau Mau District Central Committee
Mwakenya	Muungano wa Wazalendo wa Kuikomboa Kenya
MP	Member of Parliament
NARC	National Rainbow Coalition
NARCK	National Rainbow Coalition Kenya
NATO	North Atlantic Treaty Organization
NDR	National Democratic Party
PC	Provincial Commissioner
PNU	Party for National Unity
RPP	Release of Political Prisoners
SDP	Social Democratic Party
TP	Tribal Police
TP	Tamaduni Players
UASU	University Academic Staff Union
Ukenya	United Movement for Democracy in Kenya
UWAKE	Umoja wa Wazalendo Kenya
VOK	Voice of Kenya
WAK	Writers Association of Kenya
WPK	Workers' Party of Kenya

PREFACE

This volume represents the development of the WPK/DTM-Mwakenya's anti-imperialist line in Kenya from 1974 to 2002. It is a product of rich collective experience, and we believe it is a powerful political document. The fundamental aim of producing this volume is to: **1)** raise Kenyan people's consciousness and awareness about the recent history of the movement for liberation; **2)** highlight socio-economic issues that the Kenyan ruling class ignores and suppresses; **3)** expose the regime's puppetry to world imperialism; **4)** deepen anti-imperialist, anti-neocolonial resistance amongst the Kenyan people; **5)** and finally, combat the ethnopolitics preached by the reactionary Kenyan intellectuals and the pro-neocolonial members of parliament and their NGO cronies.

We urge Kenyans in factories and on university campuses, in colleges and schools, in the urban centers and the rural areas, to read and discuss the book's political line for it will broaden and deepen the national democratic revolution.

Apart from Preface and Introduction, the volume is divided into six parts. Part I analyzes the historical development of the underground movement from 1974 to 2002. Part II opens with a report of the Conference of the Kenyan Marxist-Leninists secretly held in Nairobi in December of 1974. It also contains underground revolutionary notes, party reports and minutes, leaflets and essays written from 1974 to 1985—a scientific

Mwakenya: The Unfinished Revolution

analysis of Kenya's neocolonial society of that time, a road map for the struggle for new democracy. In this section, we have identified the forces in our country that will make the revolution and create a new society based on egalitarianism. We have also identified the immediate and principal enemies of our people. Part III includes three major party documents: *The Fundamental Goals and Objectives of Mwakenya, Kenya Democracy Plank, The Mwakenya Stand,* and *Study is the Key in the Revolutionary Process.* It also discusses and analyzes how to organize a proletarian party and the role of Marxism in a revolutionary movement. Uncompromisingly, it exposes the brutality and impunity of the Kenyan compradorial regime and its puppetry to the imperialist bourgeoisie. Part IV contains several major documents, including the *Manifesto of Ukenya, Struggle for Democracy,* and *From Kĩmathi to Mwakenya.* The documents in Parts V and VI include two major documents: *The Harare Declaration* and *The Party study Guide.* In summary, this volume demands for the arrest and imprisonment of dictator Moi and his cohorts for crimes committed against humanity. In a similar vein, it urges Kenyans to intensify the struggle for national democratic revolution.

This volume remains incomplete because some revolutionary records, reports and minutes were eaten by termites or lost over the long years of underground resistance. Secondly, it is difficult to include all the party writings and particularly numerous letters to and from the comrades, reports and minutes, leaflets and pamphlets, which form a considerable part of the party archives.

Historical Introduction

Mau Mau: A Lesson of Struggle

In 1885 an imperialist conference was held in Berlin by the European imperialist countries—Britain, Germany, Portugal, Spain, The Netherlands, Italy, and France—to carve up Africa for their own personal use. Kenya found itself under the control of the British, who immediately began seizing land that would be beneficial for the Empire; and in doing so, the construction of a railway system, for trade and military purposes, went into effect immediately; along with the silencing of anyone who challenged their acquisitions or motives. Regard for the homeland, culture and freedom of all Kenyans were not issues of concern. Instead, Kenyans were considered heathens, primitives and savages; the railway would "save them" by spreading "civilization" and "Christianity". In a word, the racist defenders of the baseless Eurocentric theory made insanely unfounded claims that their occupation of our country was "a civilizing mission", "a Christian crusade" that was in our best interest as Kenyans.

In an effort to prevent the imperialist occupation of our homeland, our people vigorously fought the acquisition of our country under British rule. But in the face of superior weapons, organization, and technology, their efforts proved ineffective. By 1920 the British imposed colonial rule over our motherland. We became a conquered people and our country became *de facto* an overseas province of Britain, with all the resources, human included, belonging to the British Empire.

Mwakenya: The Unfinished Revolution

With our people subdued and conquered, Kenya was now ripe, and safe, for white settlers, investors, game hunters, and missionaries, who came in droves. They took land indiscriminately; fully believing that such an act of gross theft was justified by their Christian God, who gave them this right to see to it that their culture, free a *heathen* people, was needed to save the entire population of Kenya. They wanted in Kenya a mirror of themselves, from their attire, to their culture, to their religion and so much more; and those of our people, who resisted imperialist occupation, and total control, were ruthlessly murdered; their homes set on fire; their land taken from them; and their livestock confiscated. The problem of labor was solved by the implementation of a tax system that forced Kenyans to work. A Kipande system (the wearing of a small metal container around the neck, the size of a cigarette pack, that hung from a metal chain; and inside the small metal container was the person's fingerprints, identification, ethnicity, present employer, and employment history) was instituted as a means of controlling the African labor force, requiring any male age 16 and above to wear it around their necks at all times; and in doing so white supremacy was imposed on the entire country, in an effort to control the movement of all Kenyans, and to keep track of the labor pool. Furthermore, our people were prohibited from growing cash crops, owning a business, and keeping dairy cows. Disarmed, oppressed and exploited, our people were restricted to "native reserves", which were governed by colonially appointed chiefs and the police force under British commanders. To leave the reservation one was required to have a road pass, in addition to the kipande, a work card and tax receipts. In a word, Africans could not walk on the streets of their own national capital without identification papers. Racial segregation became the law of the land and Manichaeism was brutally deployed to assault an indigenous culture of inhabitants that had been living in Kenya for thousands of years. By definition, Manichaeism is intrinsically a perverse theory that assumes its anti-African, anti-black ideology just and fair, as it proclaims white supremacy.

The vision of Kenya as *a white man's country* came to fruition by the early 1930s. Our people were excluded from the government, denied their human rights, super-exploited and their traditions and culture ruthlessly eradicated and replaced by Anglo-centric culture. Complete disregard for our people and their culture set the stage for unbearable living conditions, both in the rural area and the urban centers to which many of them flocked to looking for jobs. Starvation forced many to move between dead-end jobs—hustling, prostitution and other illegal activities often ending in prison. Police cells, prisons, and detention camps became homes for many of our compatriots. Uprooted, oppression and exploitation, poverty and misery forced others to become squatters on the European plantations, where they were paid slave wages. They had little food or clothing and were overworked, overtaxed, humiliated and viciously terrorized by their European employers. Many of them were decimated. Under these inhumane, brutal conditions, the stage was set for the development of anti-imperialist nationalist organizations, among them, the Kenya African Union (KAU) with Jomo Kenyatta as the president. The KAU leadership was composed of two groups: the liberal, in which Kenyatta was one, and the militant. The aim of the liberal nationalists was to achieve independence by constitutional means; they argued that the colonial state was all-powerful and, therefore, any direct confrontation to its military forces would have untold repercussions for the oppressed masses. This position was summarily rejected by the militant, anti-imperialist sector of the party led by Bildad Kaggia and Fred Kubai. They forcefully argued that only an armed, revolutionary struggle could force the British occupiers to begin to address the fundamental injustices and social inequalities in the country. The split in the party occurred. Rejecting Kenyatta's non-violent method of struggle, the KAU militants secretly decided to form an anti-imperialist movement underground, which later came to be known as the Mau Mau movement. The Central Committee of the revolutionary movement consisted of twelve members, including Bildad Kaggia, Fred Kubai, Eliud Mũtonyi, Stanley Mathenge, Enoch Mwangi and Maina wa Gathanju. With the support of the working people, the East African Trade Union Congress, under the leadership of Fred Kubai and Makhan Singh, threw its weight on the side of the Mau Mau revolutionary leadership. Central Kenya became the epicenter of the revolution. In this book, Central

Mwakenya: The Unfinished Revolution

Kenya includes Gĩkũyũ, Embu, Mbeere, Mĩĩrũ and Kamba regions and the City of Nairobi.

In order to strengthen and streamline the movement, a Mau Mau administration was setup in Nairobi, with its own central secretariat, police force, revolutionary cultural centers, legal structure and system of taxation, which resulted in the revenues that would sustain the movement. The headquarters of the movement was Kĩburi House on Kĩrĩnyaga Street, Nairobi. In 1952, it was transferred to Mathare, then the citadel of the working class. The fundamental aim of the Mau Mau leadership was to use revolutionary violence to overthrow the colonial regime and establish a democratic society in which people would participate in a decision-making process that would affect their lives. To achieve its ultimate goal, the Mau Mau leadership organized a revolutionary army, the Kenya Land and Freedom Army (KLFA), led first by General Mathenge wa Mĩrũgĩ who was responsible for the active execution of the war.

Members of the Mau Mau were recruited selectively into the revolutionary movement and given an anti-imperialist oath, which was known as the Oath of Unity. This oath was used to unite as well as bind the member to the movement. Specifically, the Mau Mau oath comprised three categories: **1)** the Oath of Unity; **2)** the Mbatũni Oath; and **3)** the leadership Oath. To join the movement one was required to take the Oath of Unity and to pay membership due (Ksh. 60.00) monthly. Cadres and fighters were obligated to take the second oath, the Mbatũni Oath. The third oath was administered to those who were secretly selected to be in the leadership of the anti-imperialist resistance; it was called the Oath of Leadership. Hence, Mau Mau membership was composed of three components: **1)** general membership; **2)** cadreship; and **3)** leadership. The fighting force was selected amongst the party cadres. It is important to mention here that only those possessing patriotic qualities and committed to the cause were admitted into the leadership roles of the revolutionary movement and enrolled in the guerrilla army. The entire underground movement was highly, and secretly, organized. In every region of Central Kenya and in Nairobi city, there were male and female cadres who secretly served the

Mwakenya: The Unfinished Revolution

revolution in a variety of local leadership roles, from village leadership to field commander of the guerrilla army. Underground revolutionary centers were also established in the rural area of Central Kenya, Nairobi and the European-occupied areas of the Rift Valley region. Communication centers and intelligence networks that kept the liberation army functional were secretly constructed. Oral and print media were employed as a mode of mobilizing the revolutionary masses and expressing the ideology of the movement to members. Anti-imperialist songs were created that instilled a sense of national pride and patriotism among the revolutionary masses. Other vehicles used for mass mobilization were traditional institutions, the Karĩng'a independent schools and churches, and anti-imperialist campaign rallies. In addition, Mau Mau secret agents were deployed in the City of Nairobi and other major towns to gather intelligence on the colonial regime strategies. Women cadres in the rural area and the urban centers were strategically important in the movement. One of their many tasks was to carry intelligence, food, and ammunition back and forth across the line. It was a risky, revolutionary, task, which required an extraordinary amount of courage and daring. Many were captured, grisly tortured, sexually assaulted, and then savagely murdered. Others were mowed down by machine-guns as they tried to cross the line in the night.

The Mau Mau revolution was remarkable in the sophistication of its organization and complexity of its military and political tactics and strategies. This greatly increased its revolutionary effectiveness as a force for social change. The movement developed its own war economy, strategies, and tactics; created a strong armed force, established a judicial system, intelligence network, and expanded its base from the urban center to the countryside. In order to strengthen the grassroots supporters, according to Maina wa Kĩnyattĩ (2009: 31), three basic structural levels were created. It consisted of: **1)** the base level structure; **2)** the middle level structure; and **3)** the leadership level structure. The base level structure was the broad worker-peasant base support organized in a cell network at three levels: **a)** sub-locational; **b)** locational; and **c)** divisional. Each level was represented at the level's Central Committee. The middle Level structure was the level above the three sub-levels of the base level structure and was called the Mau Mau District Central Committee (MMDCC). The leadership level structure was at three levels: **a)** Provincial Central committee; **b)** the Supreme People's Court; **c)** the Central Committee (its name was changed to the Kenya War Council in 1952); and **d)** the National Congress. These organizational efficiencies and the revolutionary commitment of the Mau Mau leadership aligned the material and constitutional aspects of the movement with its ideological component, lending the type of synergy necessary for a united struggle against an alien enemy and his indigenous supporters.

The British occupiers had gotten wind of the development of "a secret society" called Mau Mau, which, according to them, was an "irrational" attack against law and order, civilization and Christianity. In a word, Mau Mau was a monster, it was evil and those who led it were "dark and dreadful distortions of the human spirit" (Edgerton, 1989: 145). The British occupiers refused to acknowledge that the oppressive conditions they had created in our country would have to be eradicated if violence was to be avoided. Instead, they took an uncompromising, bigoted, position. They claimed Kenya was theirs; it was nothing before they got there, and they *discovered* the country, "discovered" Kĩrĩnyaga and Nyandarwa Mountains, rivers and lakes. Nobody was going to take what was "rightly" theirs and they would fight to the last drop of their blood to keep it. In response, the Mau Mau Central Committee (MMCC) authorized the extermination of the foreign occupiers and their Kenyan running dogs. To achieve this goal, the Mau Mau leadership adopted a specific strategy. Widespread support and total commitment of members and cadres was ensured. In the urban centers and the rural area of Central Kenya, leaders called on all members and cadres to bring families, relatives and friends into the movement. Mau Mau migrant workers were oathed to spread the membership to even remote rural areas of the Rift Valley region, Western and Nyanza provinces, and see to it that revolutionary centers were established in those regions. Other centers of the movement were established in Ũkambani, Mombasa, Northern Tanzania, Pemba, and Zanzibar. The use of the Oath of Unity was imperative for its continued existence, and its need to reach and bring

Mwakenya: The Unfinished Revolution

more members into the movement from every corner of the country, as well as to ensure loyalty, discipline, and secrecy. Though clearly political in its nature, the Mau Mau anti-imperialist oath was a powerful tool that incorporated traditional rituals with political objectives that reinforced the philosophical and spiritual righteousness of the revolutionary movement.

In an effort to decolonize the minds of the oppressed masses, there was a call for Kenyans to return to the roots of their culture and history, to reject imperialist culture and Eurocentric education, and to resist cultural conquest. In this respect, traditional practices and spirituality were celebrated in Central Kenya and Nairobi City and their sacred connection to the land, given to Kenyans by *Mwene-Nyaga* (God) was emphasized. This had the important effect of revitalizing people, who took strength, courage and purpose from their tradition, culture, philosophy and history. A manifestation of this celebration of tradition was the Karĩng'a independent school and church movement and the Gĩkũyũ Club Cultural Center (GCCC) in Pumwani, Nairobi, which embodied the anti-imperialist ideology of the Mau Mau movement. The revolutionary leadership saw this pro-Kenyan, anti-imperialist, culture as invaluable in teaching and training the youth, particularly those who had been selected to join the liberation army. It is quite apparent in many of mobilization songs of the people, that anti-imperialist education was seen as a potent weapon. Listen to the following stanza:

> This is the time to struggle
> Kenyans come forward
> And build many revolutionary schools
> All over Kenya
> We have suffered long enough
> Now it is time
> To add power of the pen to the gun

Carrying out the overall strategy of the movement required attending to the many ups and downs that the movement faced daily. Faced with a formidable, brutal, foe that had many advantages over them and controlled the state machinery, media, technology and education, the Mau Mau leaders had to dedicate much of their time and effort to matters of organization and communication, secrecy, and discipline. In order to ensure secrecy and discipline, the structure of the movement, which was based on democratic centralism, was such that only the principal leaders in the Central Committee (CC) had full knowledge of the geography and scope of the membership. From the CC there were regional branches which fed into a whole network of lower cells. Members of a particular cell knew nothing of other cells; they gave and received information only through the higher cells. An elaborated underground communication network involving secret codes, newspapers, magazines, books and leaflets, was used to disseminate news and collect intelligence. With so many people playing such vital roles in the movement, precautions against betrayal were necessary. This is, of course, where oathing became crucial. In part, a new recruit was required under oath to pledge:

> I will never reveal the secret of this movement or anything else concerning this movement to the colonial authorities or to any person who is not himself a member. I will obey without question all the rules and regulations of this movement and if I ever transgress against them, I will surrender my life to the movement.

Also, in taking the second oath, the Mbatũni Oath, a cadre was vowed to be faithful to the revolutionary movement and its leadership and to uphold national patriotism regardless of the consequences:

> I swear in the name of our country, the name of this movement, that I shall work with all my power for the total liberation of Kenya from British imperialism, sacrificing for this even my own and my family's lives. I shall never, come what may, reveal the names of this movement, or that of the leader of my unit, even if I am caught, tortured or killed. I shall always be loyal and truthful to the leader of my unit and the entire movement. I shall perform any task, which is assigned to me no matter how difficult it may be. If I betray this vow, this pledge, this commitment, I shall deserve every punishment meted out to me as a traitor.

Mwakenya: The Unfinished Revolution

Whilst administering an oath was no guarantee against treachery or betrayal; it certainly did act to bind members and cadres in such a way that their fate was inextricably interlinked to the fate of the movement and homeland. Fundamentally, the oath was psychologically necessary as a process of re-armament, recharging and re-empowerment of the Mau Mau membership, as well as a tool to unshackle the minds of new recruits.

Discipline, loyalty and moral rectitude were of paramount importance, especially among the cadres, as was clear from the Mau Mau directives that urged them to be truthful, polite, helpful to one another, faithful and loyal to the movement and country, and not to steal from the people or to treat the people like enemies, or to sexually abuse women. Such moral imperatives acted to strengthen the revolutionary movement by avoiding petty squabbles and demanding respect of one's comrades and loyalty to the movement and homeland. Consistent with that, the cadres were instructed to build a ring of sympathizers and collaborators within the colonial system. These patriotic elements (police and army officers and civil servants) within the colonial structure supplied the movement with funds, intelligence, ammunition and weaponry. They formed a secret army within the colonial system; and they paid a hefty price when discovered by the enemy. Equally, every cadre was obligated to build a Mau Mau cell at his workplace and residence and join an anti-imperialist cultural movement in his community.

On the other inspiring side of the daily struggles, there was the need to weed out and expose traitors, spies and turncoats. This task was often complicated as members were oathed to disclose acts of betrayal, even if committed by a family member. Frequently, members proved where the ultimate fidelity lay when they turned in their own parents, spouses, children and relatives. Speaking for the whole movement, Wanja wa Mũgo, a Mau Mau Veteran, told this author in July 1978:

> When I discovered that my husband Mũgo was secretly working against the armed struggle, I surrendered him to the guerrilla army, and he was swiftly liquidated. It was a tough decision to make. I

had to choose between my husband, my children's father, and my country. I chose my country (Maina wa Kĩnyattĩ, 2009:213).

Another important aspect of the daily struggles involved fostering optimism, dedication, courage and commitment among the members and cadres. This is where those who organized the resistance against the white invaders in the 1800s, namely Waiyaki wa Hinga, Gakere wa Ngunju, Koitalel, Mwangeka and others, played the most significant role in the movement as symbols of the anti-imperialist resistance. At the oathing centers and political rallies, the revolutionary masses lavished praises on their heroic ancestors, their courage and love for the homeland. They drew their strength and courage from the well of their patriotism and martyrdom. In addition to symbols, traditional and anti-imperialist songs, as mentioned above, were an essential aspect of morale boosting. They sang about the pre-colonial greatness, of heroic ancestors; they sang about the evil of the British imperialist occupiers, of the past successes of resistance, of the homeland abounded in water, plants, flowers, fruits, birds, bees, animals, thick forests, the abundance of sun, huge trees, and beautiful lustrous mountains that invigorated the heart, mind and soul. They sang about the united people who will overcome foreign domination and win the battle of independence. Fundamentally, the songs served to unite the Mau Mau members and other patriotic Kenyans who could join in the common songs of freedom and love for the homeland. They provided people with a store of hope, courage and commitment; which they could call upon when times were hard. Equally, they provided solace to those in the detention centers and motivation to those at battle, and gave courage to those in torture-chambers and gallows. In a word, the anti-imperialist songs were truly invaluable to the movement; they were the rivers of courage where those who had been chosen by history swam in.

On October 20, 1952 after the Mau Mau gunned down traitor Chief Warũhiũ, the colonial regime savagely retaliated against the nationalist insurgency and this signaled the beginning of the war of independence. A state of war was declared and white settlers were quickly armed and recruited into the swelling ranks of the police and army. Feelings such

Mwakenya: The Unfinished Revolution

as "the only good Gĩkũyũ is a dead one" were rampant in the white community. Some white planters, diseased with hearts full of hate and minds full of racism, went on hunts to find and kill any patriotic Kenyan they came across. Shooting first and asking questions later was a common procedure and many compatriots became victim of this organized genocide. But that was not all. The white settlers called for the extermination of the entire inhabitants of Central Kenya and the white missionaries, armed with the Bible and the Cross, preached obedience and loyalty to the colonial authorities even in the face of barbaric acts of the colonial state. In imperialist newspapers and other pro-colonial media, the Mau Mau leaders were demonized and dismissed as bloodthirsty terrorists who must be stopped at all costs. To strengthen their colonial forces, the British brought tens of thousands of troops and white mercenaries to Kenya equipped with weapons of mass destruction, and organized indigenous traitors into special armies to fight on their side. These counter-insurgent forces included the King's African Rifle (KAR), Indian Special Unit (ISU), Tribal police (TP), *Warũrũngana* (paramilitary police), *hũmungati* (local militia), Kenya Police Reserve (KPR), Tai Tai Special Unit, and murder squads. This was followed by the arrest and imprisonment of the national leaders, including Jomo Kenyatta, the banning of the nationalist, anti-imperialist organizations and newspapers, the closing of the independent nationalist churches, cultural centers and public markets. The anti-imperialist schools, "catering to more than 62, 000 students, which the people of Kenya had patiently built up at the cost of great self-sacrifice to make up for the [colonial] government's neglect of education [for African children,] were forced to close down" (Maina wa Kĩnyattĩ, 2000:18).Since the entire Gĩkũyũ community, according the British occupiers, was Mau Mau; hence, its traditional beliefs—oath system, religion, God, arts, dance, music, marriage system, shrines, circumcision system, political thoughts, philosophy and self-consciousness—were denounced in colonialist literature as the work of terrorists. Even wearing Gĩkũyũ traditional dresses or speaking Gĩkũyũ, Kĩembu or Kĩmĩĩrũ, or worshipping facing Kĩrĩnyaga was considered a crime punishable by imprisonment or death.

Mwakenya: The Unfinished Revolution

The Mũkũrwe wa Nyagathanga Shrine, the most notable cultural and historic landmark in Central Kenya, was demolished, its material culture that held hearts and souls of the inhabitants of Central Kenya together was brutally burned down and the spirit of their heroic ancestors was mutilated. Simultaneously, the Christian colonial churches and schools in Central Kenya were transformed into anti-Mau Mau, military fortresses. The Bible and the gun became weapons of choice against the Mau Mau revolution and the unity of the Kenyan people. As we shall learn below, the British occupiers would act like Nazis when dealing with the Mau Mau movement and its members, supporters and sympathizers.

In the meantime, the KLFA troops entered the Nyandarwa and Kĩrĩnyaga forests to wage a war of national independence. Central Kenya became the revolutionary base of the whole country and Nyandarwa the guerrilla headquarters. As the war raged on in Central Kenya, Nairobi and the European occupied areas of the Rift Valley province, and the colonial regime intensified its repression and viciousness nationwide, the KLFA leadership called for a special congress to discuss the war efforts, strategies and tactics and to consolidate the armed forces. The congress was held at the Mwathe guerrilla camp in Nyandarwa in August 1953 and was attended by more than 5,000 guerrillas, twelve members of the Kenya War Council (KWC) and the representatives of the village central committees, with whom the women were the majority. The Mwathe Congress witnessed the reorganization of the KLFA base. Eight armies charged with operating in specific regions of the country were consolidated. The military and political arms of the KLFA were concentrated into the Kenya Defense Council (KDC) with Dedan Kĩmathi elected as its president. He was also promoted to the post of Field Marshal, the highest military office in the liberation army. He replaced Mathenge who was dropped from the KLFA leadership because of his limited knowledge of guerrilla warfare and his spineless leadership. Kĩmathi's natural simplicity, his extraordinary courage, compassion and love for our people and homeland; his strength of character, his uncompromised leadership and knowledge of guerrilla warfare qualified him to be the commander-in-chief of the liberation army.

It was during the Mwathe Congress, Kĩmathi launched his famous slogan: "It is better to die on our feet than to live on knees", which became the slogan of the armed revolutionary movement. Simultaneously, he declared in combative language, "With our revolutionary movement and our guerrilla army and the support of hundreds of thousands of our compatriots, our homeland can proudly stand on her own feet. With our courage and determination, with our blood and soul, we will sacrifice ourselves for our country" (Source: Major Mũirũrĩ, 2008).

Under Kĩmathi's leadership, the KLFA exhibited great tactical sophistication. Specifically, three distinct guerrilla tactic zones were organized, namely the inner zone, the middle zone, and outer zone from which they operated an elaborate system of agents whose primary task was to infiltrate the colonial war machinery in order to obtain weapons and strategic information, to monitor the movements of the enemy troops and to eliminate the colonial informers, spies and other national traitors. Many of the tactics and strategies developed within the movement developed in contradiction to the tactics and strategies used by the enemy. In a further effort to strengthen the liberation army, Kĩmathi created the Kenya Parliament. It was the KLFA central command. Its fundamental aim was to consolidate the guerrilla leadership and provide a democratic forum for discussing organizational and logistical problems, war tactics and strategies and the political future of the homeland. It is significant to note here that the most successful period in our history was during the armed struggle when our people and their guerrilla army firmly occupied the driver's seat, set agendas and priorities, and decisively acted upon them even when the international community expressed its doubts about our heroic, anti-imperialist, deeds, and our African continent remained passive while the British and their North Atlantic Treaty Organization (NATO) allies savagely continued to slaughter our people in the villages and the urban centers in the name of colonialism and Christianity.

Nazism's Gestapo Tactics

In addition to using cannons, mortars, machine-guns, armored cars, napalm bombs, land-mines and warplanes against the people's army, according to Maina wa Kĩnyattĩ's book, *History of Resistance in Kenya, 1884-2002* (2009), the British employed Nazism's Gestapo tactics in an attempt to break the mass support of the movement for national independence and to exterminate the people's liberation army. Hundreds of thousands of our compatriots were held in the detention centers, prisons, transit centers and screening stations, where they were mercilessly and grisly tortured. Many were hanged from the ceiling by their hands or feet for a prolonged period of time, or a heavy metal chain was fastened to their necks and they were left in that position for hours or days. Others were dismembered, burned alive, hewn in pieces and mutilated; their nails and hair torn out, their bowels crushed, red-hot irons thrust into the rectums of men and women. Many died in suffering, pain and agony, and others were maimed for life. Other methods of torture recommended were: putting a detainee into a dark cramped cage, severely beating him and then unleashing a snake inside in an effort to exploit his fear of snakes, forcing him to sleep naked in a cold, wet cage, treating him like an animal, controlling his use of the latrine, denying him food and using electronic gear such a sealed telephones attached to the man's testicles to shock him into submission. Others were chained in painful positions and then subjected to unspeakable and excruciating abuses until they died. Corpses were sexually assaulted by necrophilia counter-revolutionaries; they were spat on and urinated on, and then mutilated before they were buried in a communal grave. In some instances, the enemy soldiers, smiling, posed with mangled body parts of Mau Mau insurgent corpses.

Further, Mau Mau captives were forced to drink their urine and to eat their feces, to fight each, and then subjected to severe beatings until they died. Male captives were subjected to water-boarding, sodomy and castration before they were shot. Female captives were forced to walk on fire without shoes; their hair burned with butts of cigarettes or savagely pulled out with pliers. They were whipped naked and then gang-raped or

Mwakenya: The Unfinished Revolution

forced to sit on a wire mesh that had been heated red-hot over a charcoal burner. Glass bottles, gun barrels and *mĩrũndo* (spikes) were thrust into their vaginas. Breasts, necks, thighs and buttocks were burned with *njegeni* (a poisonous shrub), their vaginas stuffed with stinging nettles, penetrated by snakes or filled with scalding hot water; their genitals mutilated and much more. Quite often it was a matter of expediency just to eliminate a Mau Mau activist or a guerrilla combatant immediately after he was captured. Many of our compatriots were killed this way. Thousands who were mowed down with machine-guns in the hamlets and villages of Central Kenya and the Rift valley region; hundreds who were gunned down in the city streets, and countless others were savagely murdered in detention centers, screening stations, transit stations, gallows, police cells, *hũmungati* camps and torture-chambers. And that was not all. There were hundreds who disappeared while in police cells and countless others who vanished after their arrest. Even to this day, their fates are unknown. A British colonial police officer, who perhaps speaks for the entire system of imperialism, states:

> At first, they weren't human to me [;] they were black animals who had done inhuman things to women and children. I was bloody well going to beat the Mau Mau poison out of them. At the end of a day my hands would be bruised and arms would ache from smashing the black bastards. I hated them and sometimes I wanted to kill them. A few times I did or we all did together. I never worked alone [;] it was always a whole lot together like a rugger scrum. I screened those bastards for four months, almost five, and only got a handful of confessions out of them. I'd been drinking too much for some time before I really tied on one at Manyani. The next morning I realized that they'd won.
>
> I hated myself for what I was doing more than I hated them. I finally had to admit that they were brave men who believed in what they were doing more than I believed in what I was doing. I resigned and got out of Kenya as quick as I could (Edgerton, 1989: 186-187).

Similarly, another British killer, using racist language, confessed:

Mwakenya: The Unfinished Revolution

I stuck my revolve right in his grinning mouth and I said something. I don't remember what, and I pulled the trigger. His brains went all over the side of the police station. The other two mickeys were standing here looking blank. I said to them that if they didn't tell me where to find the rest of the gang I'd kill them too. They didn't say a word so I shot them both. One was hot dead so I shot him in the ear. When the sub-inspector droveup, I told him that the Mickeys tried to escape. He didn't believe me, but all he said was "bury them and see the wall is cleared up" (Anderson, 2005:179).

The British imperialists went to such extreme and bestial measures in their bellicose efforts to break the revolutionary spirit of the people, to drown the revolution in blood, but they were not successful. The Kenyan people stood firmly behind the national liberation army and Mau Mau members, cadres and combatants preferred death rather than live under colonial barbarianism. By 1957 the British occupiers had learned that there could not be a military victory over a determined, patriotic, insurgency. They released the imprisoned national leaders, including Kenyatta in 1960, and in 1963 they surrendered—handed over the country back to the people of Kenya. This reaffirmed the revolutionary movement's potent power as the ultimate strength that wrenched freedom from the British imperialist occupiers and their NATO allies. But it is important to mention that, even to this day our people have not forgotten the genocide committed by the British imperialist occupiers before and during the Mau Mau war of national independence.

Linked to all of the above, the Mau Mau revolutionary movement laid the cornerstone for *uhuru* in Africa and gave history a shining example of a righteous and tenacious fight against the imperialist forces of occupation. It taught the oppressed masses of Africa that a united and determined people with their revolutionary army can defeat a powerful imperialist army and win the battle of independence; and, that the people's power is not originated in a bourgeois parliament or at a round table conference, it is forced upon the country by the people with the barrel of the gun.

Independence Was Betrayed

When Kenyatta was released from colonial prison and returned to his political life, his release was jubilantly and heroically celebrated nationwide. For the great majority of our compatriots his release was a victory against the evil forces of colonialism—a Mau Mau victory. On December 12, 1964 Kenyatta was overwhelmingly elected the first President of the Republic. Streets and national institutions were named after him, his statue replaced that of the colonial occupiers in our national capital and his face replaced that of the British monarch on the national currency. He became a national icon— the custodian of our national values. Our people, however, did not realize that the man they had selected and trusted to lead the nation to democracy would become a monster, and when they realized whom they had elected to such a key position of democracy and the healing of a nation, it was too late; Kenyatta had already sharpened the tools of repression and was ready to use them against the voices of progress and democracy. At the same time, he formed an alliance with white settlers, British imperialists and *hūmungati* traitors in order to expoit and oppress the Kenyan working people.

In his independence speech, Kenyatta did not suggest any substantial change in the colonial structure. The colonial state and its oppressive machinery would remain intact—despite the fact that the fight for national independence had been dominated by demands for social justice, egalitarian reform, participatory democracy, prosecution of those who had committed genocide and other heinous crimes during the war of independence, and the abolition of the colonial state and its oppressive institutions (Maina wa Kĩnyattĩ, 2009: 363). In addition, Kenyatta never mentioned in his speech the heroism of the Mau Mau or the heroic role Field Marshal Dedan Kĩmathi and the KLFA fighters played in the struggle for independence. He never acknowledged that it was the blood of Kenyans, their courage and determination under brutal conditions, and the enduring sacrifice of the Mau Mau revolutionary movement, that forced the British occupiers to release him from prison, and more importantly, brought him to power. But there is more. During the independence celebrations, no Mau Mau freedom

Mwakenya: The Unfinished Revolution

songs were sung and no KLFA leader was allowed to speak or be officially recognized. In fact, during his rule, Kenyatta unsuccessfully tried to bury the revolutionary history of the Mau Mau; he made sure that Mau Mau history was not taught in schools and universities, and no former Mau Mau fighter would be allowed to serve in the army or police department, or to be in a position of power in his administration. No monument or memorial, statue or plaque, would be built or displayed in honor of Dedan Kĩmathi or other Mau Mau heroes or heroines. He proscribed the Mau Mau as a political party, ruthlessly demolished its institutions and organizations and imprisoned its leadership, whilst consolidating the anti-Mau Mau base in government and state institutions. At the same time, he viciously combatted the anti-imperialist cultural movement and deepened, protected and expanded Eurocentric culture nationwide. The English language, a colonial language, was adopted as the official language. This meant that only those who could speak the colonial language were qualified to be members of parliament or employed as civil servants; and most of them were traitors and killers who had murdered countless numbers of our people during the war of independence. To put it bluntly, the Kenyatta regime was anti-Mau Mau, anti-Kenyans, and anti-democracy. It was a puppet regime that was in a full cooperation and collaboration with Anglo-American imperialism and its NATO allies. While acting as executive agency of Anglo-American imperialism, it consolidated neocolonial dependency and dependent capitalism, deepened foreign domination and cultural imperialism, suppressed national patriotism and anti-imperialist culture; and worked side by side with the Anglo-American imperialists to exploit and oppress the Kenyan workers and peasantry. The society Kenyatta and his henchmen created was a dog-eat-dog- society—a brutal society where only the fittest survived.

In an attempt to prevent the Kenyatta neocolonial regime from derailing the national democratic revolution, the leftwing leadership, with the support of the working class and peasantry, formed an opposition party, the Kenya People's Union (KPU) in 1966. Since it was operating aboveground, it was expeditiously and brutally crushed by the Kenyatta regime. This was

Mwakenya: The Unfinished Revolution

followed by the arrest and imprisonment of the leftwing leaders, among them, Bildad Kaggia, Jaramogi Odinga and Achieng Oneko. Pinto and J.M. Kariũki were not as lucky as their fellow comrades, as Kenyatta ordered both of them to be executed, without due process of the law. In the same period, Tom Mboya, a rightwing, pro-imperialist politician, was assassinated by Kenyatta's secret police.

The brutal murder of Pinto, Mboya and J.M. Kariũki, the suppression and proscription of KPU and the imprisonment of its leadership were a clear indication to the great majority of our people that "the country was under a ruthless blood-thirsty tyrant who would stop at nothing to restrict people's basic freedoms and democratic rights, including their right to life" (Maina wa Kĩnyattĩ, 2009:422). In response to the murderous Kenyatta regime, a Marxist-Leninist party, the Worker's Party of Kenya (WPK), was formed in December of 1974 to lead the struggle for the national democratic revolution. It was underground and its primary goal was to use any means necessary, including revolutionary violence, to overthrow the Kenyatta neocolonial regime and establish a just society based on democracy and egalitarianism.

Mwakenya: The Unfinished Revolution

 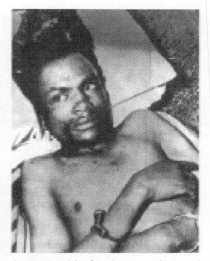

Field Marshal Kĩmathi addressing the Mwathe Congress held in Nyandarwa, August 1953. His leadership embodied Kenya's revolution against the British imperialist occupiers.

Dedan Kĩmathi after he was shot and captured on October 21, 1956. He was executed by the British marauders in February of 1957.

General Kago, Chief Commander of the Mũrang'a KLFA front; he was shot and captured in battle in 1954. The British occupiers savagely burned him alive. Gen. Kago lives.

General Tanganyika was promoted in January of 1954 to the Chief Commander of the Kĩrĩnyaga Front after the capture and betrayal of General China.

General Kariba, Chief Commander of the Levellation army (a section of the KLFA) in Nyĩrĩ County.

Mwakenya: The Unfinished Revolution

Wanjikũ wa Thamweri was a KLFA guerrilla fighter under General Kariba's command. She was captured in battle in November of 1955 and grisly tortured by the British enemy. She refused to surrender or betray the homeland. Consequently, she was dragged to a colonial court and sentenced to life imprisonment. At the time of her sentencing, she was 17 years old. Our women played a central role in fight for national independence.

The dreadlocks of the KLFA guerrillas were a symbol of resistance against foreign, imperialist domination. The youth of the Black World, including the Jamaican Rastas, positively identify with the KLFA's revolutionary image.

Mwakenya: The Unfinished Revolution

General Mũtungi showing Mũnyua Waiyaki (left) how to use a Kenyan-made gun at Rũrĩngũ Stadium, Nyĩrĩ, December 17, 1963. On the right is General Mwariama.

General Mwariama (third from left) inspecting his guerrilla army at Rũrĩngũ Stadium, December 17, 1963. The guerrillas were armed with Gatua-Ũhoro—Kenyan-made guns.

Part One

The Beginning of A New Stage

Kĩmathi once said, "Fighting against oppression is the duty and responsibility of every patriotic Kenyan." He also said, "A revolution starts with you wherever you are." Similarly, Frantz Fanon tells us: "Each generation must, out of relative obscurity, discovers its mission, fulfill it, or betray it."

The Birth of the Underground Movement: Formation and Early Roots

The Workers' Party of Kenya

The roots of the December Twelve Movement (DTM) and Mwakenya go directly back to the formation of a clandestine political party during the First Conference of the Kenyan Marxist-Leninist delegates, which was secretly held in Nairobi on December 22-23, 1974. The conference delegates included Kamoji Wachiira, Maina wa Kĩnyattĩ, Adhu Awiti, Koigi wa Wamwere and Amin Kassam. After scientific analysis of the politics of the neocolonial state, the consolidation of a one party dictatorship and exploitation of the Kenyan working people by the comprador bourgeoisie and its imperialist friends, the Kenyan Marxist-Leninist conference resolved to setup a proletarian center, the Workers' Party of Kenya (WPK), to lead the struggle for democracy and social justice. The Conference resolved that the above-mentioned five delegates be made full members of WPK because of their rich experience in proletarian political work. Further, it resolved that the historic five constitute the party's Central Committee and each contribute five percent of his monthly salary to the party. Finally, the Conference discussed and approved the party constitution and adopted six ideological documents—*The Need for a Proletarian Party, The Nature of a Proletarian Party, The Ideological Nature of our Party, The Need to combat Revision, Outline of Social classes of Kenya* and *Guideline on cell-formation*—which formed the theoretical foundation of the proletarian party and its organizations. The documents clearly stated that the Workers' Party of Kenya was a Marxist-Leninist-Maoist party whose supreme goal was the establishment of a socialist society in Kenya under proletarian leadership. Its immediate task was carrying out the National Democratic Revolution (NDR) by overthrowing the neocolonial system and establishing a national democratic government in the country. The Kenyan Marxist-Leninist conference was convinced that the NDR would be the basis for advancing the national liberation struggle to Socialism and then to Communism. In this case, it was resolved that the WPK should build itself in accordance with MLM principles and that MLM theory, based on our history, culture and traditions, should guide the party cadres in their revolutionary work. And every party cadre and member must engage in criticism and self-criticism in order to advance and deepen the MLM theory in the party and its organizations.

Ngũgĩ wa Thiong'o, Willy Mutunga, al-Amin Mazrui, Edward Oyugi, Shiraz Durrani, Ngũgĩ wa Mĩriĩ, Sultan Somjee, Kũria Mũrĩmi, Kariũki Kĩboi and Ngotho wa Kariũki, among others, were later recruited to the clandestine party and they formed the second ring of the leadership of the movement. The central authority of the party, which was the Central Committee (CC), was referred to as "The Higher", and the party coordinating committee (the Standing Committee) was known as "The March Second". For security reasons, the CC made the decision not to reveal the name of the party to the general members. In fact, very few party cadres knew the "real" name of the party. It was only the CC members and party candidates who knew the party's actual name. Democratic centralism, which was the cornerstone of the WPK, means that party members and cadres only know as much as that which is required for the operations, at the relevant level of their participation, involvement and decision-making. In retrospect, the CC realized that it was ideologically wrong for a communist party to conceal its name from its advanced cadres and from the working class whose support was needed for the party's success.

Theory and Practice

From Independence Day until 1991 the Kenyan neocolonial regime had denied us the right to challenge its interpretation of nation-building. It had denied us a voice in the shaping of our country, the destiny of it, and a dialogue that allowed us the opportunity to engage, ideologically, in independent political and intellectual activity. The freedom to discuss the future of our country, to transmit progressive ideas, and to write our history in our own image and interests was prohibited; it was considered a subversive act—a crime punishable by imprisonment or death.

The formation of the Workers' Party of Kenya was therefore the most significant political event in Kenya, since the Mau Mau resistance movement of the 1950s. Its significance was manifold: First, it was a bold and courageous challenge to the reactionary, pro-imperialist KANU regime; it laid down an alternative, patriotic agenda of revolutionary activism and resistance. Second, it opened a new chapter in a struggle for a new democracy in Kenya. Third, it marked the end of the attempts by liberal, petty-bourgeois forces to form legal opposition parties. Earlier attempts to form anti-imperialist, anti-neocolonial political parties—*Kĩama Kĩa Mũingĩ* (KKM), Kenya Land and Freedom Party (KLFP) and Kenya People's Union (KPU)—were brutally crushed by the comprador-imperialist alliance. Equally, the efforts to regroup within the governing party, KANU, and to make it pro-people, patriotic, democratic, and anti-imperialist, also floundered, reflecting the complete surrender of the Kenyan comprador bourgeoisie to the world imperialists. Hence, it became the historical role of the WPK to articulate a new phase of anti-imperialist, anti-neocolonial politics and to create a revolutionary path for a new democracy.

Initially, it was only possible to map out and deepen the struggle for the national democratic revolution at a clandestine level, under strict discipline and secrecy, determination and dedication, which called for extraordinary courage, daring and an unbending, patriotic spirit. What distinguished the WPK from the KKM, KLFP, KPU and their leaderships was the fact

Mwakenya: The Unfinished Revolution

that for the first time in the history of our country, a written revolutionary programme was boldly presented to the Kenyan people by a MLM party. The programme became an alternative to that of the comprador bourgeoisie, which was, and remains, fundamentally reactionary, pro-capitalist and anti-Kenyan.

The WPK leadership provided an ideological framework—a MLM framework within which Kenyan anti-imperialist forces began to work together and collectively to express their resistance against the Kenyan comprador bourgeois class and their determination to overthrow the neocolonial system. It further provided an organizational framework, which deepened and broadened national, anti-imperialist base, sharpened the contradictions between the forces of reaction and the progressive forces, and created new courage amongst our people. This new courage posed a serious challenge to the comprador ruling class and its imperialist backers. In addition, the WPK and its organizations and supporters played a crucial role in shattering the long period of political passivity and the culture of fear, which followed the crushing of the KKM, KLFP and KPU in the 1960s by the Kenyatta neocolonial regime. The Workers' Party of Kenya was an organization whose cadres and members were wielded together by unity of will, patriotism, action, discipline, commitment and ideology. In other words, it derived much of its determination, enthusiasm and courage from tightly knit and well disciplined cadres.

In 1975 the WPK leadership established an underground proletarian press. The press played an important and decisive role in mobilizing the anti-imperialist forces and the constitutional-democrats in the country. Through its exposure of the endemic corruption in Kenya's neocolonial regime, it revealed the class forces involved in the social struggle, and thus, it educated the masses by exposing the reactionary nature of the system and the need for revolution. It tied together the work of the party and ideologically mapped the path of struggle, defined the basis of the struggle and identified the enemies of the people. Moreover, it battled the ruling comprador bourgeoisie on the idea front and combated bourgeois,

Mwakenya: The Unfinished Revolution

capitalist propaganda amongst the people using the science of Marxism-Leninism-Maoism. According to Lenin:

> The construction of a vanguard party depends greatly on its publications. A party is built, other considerations aside for the moment, through a center, which, acting as a kind of scaffolding, provides a structure around which ideas are disseminated, agitation is carried out and cadres are trained and brought into a coherent, tight, systematic network of agents. This network acquires all the skills necessary to mobilize the working class and assume the reins of government when the time comes.

In the process of educating the masses and exposing the regime's puppetry to the global imperialists, the party press secretly printed and distributed several anti-imperialist, anti-neocolonial documents and leaflets nationwide, including *Mwanguzi* (a monthly newsletter), and *Cheche Kenya* (which was reprinted under a new title, *InDependent Kenya,* by Zed Press, London, 1982). In addition, the party printed anti-imperialist leaflets and pamphlets and distributed them in the major towns and on the university campuses of the country. The fundamental aim of producing these publications was to inculcate Kenyan students, militant youth, workers, peasants and progressive petty-bourgeois intellectuals with patriotic consciousness and the MLM ideology. It was also to clarify for them the hard reality that only through hard struggle, dedication, commitment, and sacrifice, could we free the country from the vicious claws of imperialism and its native agents. In this respect, the WPK leadership strongly believed that the dissemination of progressive ideas amongst the working class, peasantry, pastoralists, militant youth and patriotic petty-bourgeoisie, was a task that had to be uncompromisingly undertaken by the party cadres, regardless of the ruthlessness and viciousness of the Kenyatta and Moi regimes.

Another important area of WPK's activity was theater. The party played a central role in organizing the performances of anti-imperialist plays. These included *Ngaahika Ndeenda,* co-authored by Ngũgĩ wa Thiong'o and Ngũgĩ wa Mĩriĩ, which took place at Kamĩrĩthũ village, Limuru, in

Mwakenya: The Unfinished Revolution

1977 and *The Trial of Dedan Kĩmathi*, written by Ngũgĩ wa Thiong'o and Micere Gĩthae Mũgo, which was first staged at the Kenya National Theater in 1976 followed by performances in 1977 at the Second World Black and African Festival of Culture and Civilization (FESTAC) in Lagos, Nigeria, and in 1980 at the University of Nairobi theater under the direction of the Tamaduni Players, which was led by Mũmbi wa Maina and Janet Young. These patriotic performances exposed the dog-eat-dog leadership of the comprador bourgeoisie, explained the revolutionary line of the party, and called the Kenyan people to unite against the forces of the comprador-imperialist alliance. The performances attracted thousands of Kenyan working people, petty-bourgeoisie, high school youth and university students. They constituted a huge victory for the underground movement. In response, the KANU repressive regime proscribed the people's theater, intimidated the actors, physically destroyed the Kamĩrĩthũ people's center; and then arrested Ngũgĩ wa Thiong'o in 1977 and subsequently imprisoned him for one year without trial. The imprisonment of Ngũgĩ was followed by the death of dictator Kenyatta. Whilst the Kenyan ruling class and its imperialist friends were moaning for his death and shedding rivers of tears at the burial site, our party's remark was loud, clear and historic: Kenyatta is dead long live the revolution! To retain control of the state and government, the ruling party, KANU, selected Daniel Moi to replace him. Moi had no passion, no idealism, no philosophy. As we shall see later, he would transform the entire apparatus of the state into centralized dictatorship.

Concurrently, the party organized public lectures and debates in the universities, colleges and schools in its efforts to popularize socialist ideas and to win the support of progressive petty-bourgeoisie and militant students on its side. These anti-imperialist lectures were well attended. They influenced the thinking of many students, exposed the political indecisiveness and reactionary stand of the liberal academics and created sharp contradictions between the rightwing and leftwing academics. These contradictions were healthy; they deepened the anti-imperialist struggle on the university campuses and, more importantly, made it easier for the party

Mwakenya: The Unfinished Revolution

to win new members and to create anti-imperialist centers on the university campuses.

In 1979 the party took over the leadership of the Writers Association of Kenya (WAK). Its attempt to revitalize it and to make it an anti-imperialist cultural force was not successful because the bulk of its membership was liberal petty-bourgeoisie who expressed, in theory and practice, their readiness to cooperate with the neocolonial state. The WPK's effort to organize an anti-imperialist trade union on campus was exemplified by the struggle the party waged around the University Academic Staff Union (UASU), which became an anti-neocolonial, radical labor movement, until it was proscribed by dictator Moi in 1982. The regime's anti-people stand and its comprador bourgeois puppetry enacted at the behest of the imperialist bourgeoisie was reflected by this venomous, anti-patriotic deed.

On the idea front, the WPK leadership insisted that the party members, particularly the university academic party members, should write revolutionary books in a bid to counter the reactionary efforts of the Kenyan rightwing academics and their imperialist academic friends whose aim was, and is, to demoralize our people and instill in them a sense of hopelessness. The goal of the reactionary academics was further to disarm the people politically and to weaken their patriotic resolve and anti-imperialist spirit. In response to the call of the party, books such as *Thunder from the Mountains; Kenya's Freedom Struggle; Petals of Blood; Devil on the Cross; Ngaahika Ndeenda; Kilio cha Haki, Cheche Kenya* and many more were produced. The main themes of these books were anti-imperialist fervor and nationalist spirit of patriotism and democracy, the struggle against neocolonialism and for social justice, and the defense of the rights of Kenyans. In addition, the WPK leadership demanded that the party cadres should study the MLM theory, understand it and be able to apply it, in theory and practice, in their revolutionary work. The clandestine, inner-party studies were organized by the party cell leaderships and were secretly held at homes of party cadres. The party required every member and cadre to be faithful to the cause of the party, to be polite to each other,

43

Mwakenya: The Unfinished Revolution

to participate fully in all its struggles and strives, and to firmly uphold communist values.

Pambana and the December Twelve Movement

In January of 1982 the WPK leadership made the decision to launch an underground newspaper to openly challenge the neocolonial state and its imperialist backers. The paper was also meant to serve as an instrument to consolidate the party's political base amongst the working class and peasantry and to be the voice of the silent majority. The rationale for setting up a clandestine party newspaper was contained in an internal document entitled, *Launching of a Party Paper* and was adopted by the Central Committee and the party in January 1982. In part, the CC leadership asserted:

> We have long wished to affect the launching of a consistent and regular propaganda organ as a crucial aspect of our general political work. Along with that, we always maintained that such a publication or organ is absolutely necessary for the purpose of extending and hopefully consolidating a thoroughly Bolshevized Marxist-Leninist center—a center towards which the Kenyan masses can systematically gravitate. Such a center, we have always felt must aspire to be national in scale and have a broad mass character. It must be a center which is not only fully consolidated ideologically and organizationally, but one which also commands a unified and systematic approach to its general and specific political tasks.

The name of the paper was *Pambana, The Organ of the December Twelve Movement*. The name *December Twelve Movement* (DTM) was meant to be a front name for the Workers' Party of Kenya. The CC leadership felt that the time was *not* ripe to publicly expose the *real* name of the clandestine party to the neocolonial security agents, spies and informers. However, that decision turned out to be a political error, for the name DTM became popular among university students, workers and the patriotic petty-bourgeoisie, and they identified with it. Within the party and the entire anti-

Mwakenya: The Unfinished Revolution

imperialist movement, the name DTM became the symbol of resistance against the comprador-imperialist alliance. The Kenyan anti-imperialist forces rallied around the name and its mass organ; hence, it was difficult for the party leadership to reverse the decision and change the name to WPK, because it would have confused the party cadres and largely created sectarianism within the Kenyan anti-imperialist movement.

The first issue of *Pambana* was printed in May of 1982 and was heavily distributed nationwide. Copies were mailed to fraternal organizations and newspapers abroad, to the Kenyan rightwing newspapers (*Daily Nation* and *The Standard*), to international friends of Kenya, and members of the National Assembly including dictator Moi. Many more were secretly distributed on the university campuses, in colleges and schools. It was also serialized by the Tanzanian newspaper, *The Nationalist*; but the Kenyan rightwing newspapers refused to serialize the document. Instead, they took their copies to the police headquarters. The Kenyan media was, and still is, an extension of world imperialism.

Pambana was the first underground anti-imperialist, anti-neocolonial newspaper since Independence; the first mass paper to publicly denounce the puppetry of the Kenyan ruling class and call for its overthrow; the first mass paper in the history of our country to use the science of MLM to analyze class forces in our society and diagnose the sickness of the neocolonial society. Indeed, it was the first newspaper in Kenyan history to declare openly that its ideology was based on scientific socialism and dialectical materialism. Fundamentally, it committed itself to defend the interests of the majority of Kenyans and to lead the people in overthrowing the neocolonial system and creating a just society based on equalitarianism. In its editorial page, it boldly stated:

Pambana is neither free nor neutral. It will accept no apologies for oppression or thievery and will forcefully represent the truth as seen from the viewpoint of the majority poor, dispossessed Kenyans who have hitherto been so fully ignored. The KANU government has looted unspeakable sums of money and national wealth. They have

Mwakenya: The Unfinished Revolution

finally given our entire country over to the U.S. imperialists to use as a political and military base. This is not independence. Kenyans, therefore, have no alternatives, but to begin anew in order to continue the revolution that was diverted. We are once again called upon to marshal our forces and prepare for a protracted counter-attack in order to salvage and reconstruct our nation. This is war. We must have no illusions.

In the first place, *Pambana* represented a significant ideological phase in understanding and analyzing the political and economic realities of neocolonialism in our country. Secondly, it "placed on the political scene in our country a set of demands and a vision by which unfolding political resistances could be analyzed and judged". Thirdly, it nourished a broad rebirth of anti-imperialist nationalism among Kenyans, contributed to the breakdown of a culture of silence and old patterns of neocolonial politics, and more importantly, it opened the gate to the pro-democracy movement. Fourthly, it interlinked our struggle for a new democracy with those of Latin America, the Caribbean and Asia. Fifthly, it struck terror in the ruling comprador class and its foreign imperialist allies, provoking a national debate on the university and college campuses, in parliament and factories, and among the people in the city streets, villages and hamlets. Its forceful argument brought about a qualitative change in the anti-imperialist resistance in the country by defining the path of the struggle, identifying the enemy of the people and more fundamentally, introducing and popularizing Marxism in the country, particularly on university campuses, in colleges and schools. Under its influence, the militant opposition movement of students against the reactionary KANU regime assumed greater intensity and boldness. In retaliation, the regime reacted violently. It brought its security forces into the city streets to look for copies of *Pambana* and to arrest anyone caught reading or distributing it. A secret police force was deployed on the Nairobi and Kenyatta University campuses to hunt down what the dictator Moi termed "Marxist academics." Anti-*Pambana*, anti-DTM rallies were organized by the vile dictator and his cronies throughout the country, and a special session of parliament was held to denounce the

Mwakenya: The Unfinished Revolution

"communist conspiracy." Not a single member of parlaiment had the guts to declare his support for the DTM revolutionary programme, or even try to defend the people against the viciousness and brutality of the neocolonial regime. With their tails between their legs and their fat tummies hanging almost to the ground, they left the Parliament Building singing: *Kanu yajenga nchi. Baba Moi tawala, tawala. Moi juu! Nyayo juu!* They were dictator Moi's puppies.

Dictatorship Consolidated

The year 1982 witnessed the acceleration of neocolonial repression in the country. The Moi regime consolidated its dictatorship—silenced an already sodomized parliament, created a more subservient judiciary, closed down public universities indefinitely, built torture-chambers and ordered the arrest of militant students, Marxist university academics, and the anti-imperialist elements in the ruling party and parliament. Never before had the police force been granted such immense powers, and never before had censorship of thought been so strictly tightened and brutally reinforced. But that was not all. Moi and his rightwing nuts used state power to combat progressive ideas and promote backward, ethnic politics, and loot the country's resources. Meanwhile, the great majority of our people lived on the margins, without access to decent housing, schools, healthcare or portable water. Weighed down by oppression and exploitation, degradation and poverty, their children ate from garbage cans and slept on verandahs and under the bridges in our capital city.

As the underground opposition gained strength and boldly challenged the puppet regime, the bloodthirsty dictator responded by sharpening instruments of repression. Persecution of patriotic Kenyans broke out nationwide, spreading across the country at an alarming rate that shocked everyone. In June of 1982, six university academics—Maina wa Kĩnyattĩ, Kamoji Wachiira, al-Amin Mazrui, Willy Mutunga, Edward Oyugi and Mũkarũ Ng'ang'a—were arrested, accused of teaching revolutionary violence and imprisoned. In prison they were physically and psychologically

Mwakenya: The Unfinished Revolution

tortured.Since five of them—Kamoji, Maina, Mutunga, al-Amin and Oyugi—were the key leaders of the underground movement, their imprisonment was a serious blow to the struggle for a new democracy in Kenya. Meanwhile, many other university academics that endorsed DTM's anti-imperialist programme were targeted. Mũmbi wa Maina, a Kenyatta University academic, was arrested and released, but only after three days of brutal interrogation and humiliation. Ngũgĩ wa Thiong'o escaped arrest and imprisonment because he was out of the country at the time and would remain in exile for more than ten years. Ngũgĩ wa Mĩriĩ, Kĩmani Gĩcaũ, Shiraz Durrani, Shadrack Gutto, Kũria Mũrĩmi and Micere Mũgo, among others, were forced to go into exile. Wangondu wa Kariũki (journalist) was arrested, charged with sedition and imprisoned, and Salim Lone, editor-in-chief of the *Viva Magazine*, was stripped of his citizenship by the Moi gangster regime and expelled from Kenya—his country of birth. Militant parliamentarians and patriotic lawyers were also arrested and imprisoned without trial. Prisons and detention centers filled with patriots.

The majority of university academics renounced the revolutionary struggle against the repressive Moi regime from fear of being arrested. They began preaching the policies of reconciliation and appeasement with the dictator. Some rightwing academics even regarded the regime's punitive measures, including censorship of thought, justified. Others organized groups of students and faculty who went to the State House to plead loyalty to the nefarious dictator. Liberals who previously had considered themselves "Marxist scholars", but who had never held firmly to Marxist convictions, strategies and tactics, bent over backwards to avoid imprisonment. They burned their Marxist texts and research papers, denounced the anti-imperialist resistance, and began singing Nyayo songs loud and clear, and calling the vile dictator, *Baba Moi.* Some of these sycophantic traitors were systematically placed in strategic administrative positions in the ruling party and the government. Others were appointed heads of institutions of higher learning. Still others became sweethearts of the wicked dictator. A selected few became agent-provocateurs on university campuses and speechwriters of the dictator and were amply rewarded monetarily. In our

48

country, there are two types of intellectuals: patriotic, revolutionary, anti-imperialist ones and the servile, pro-imperialist, anti-Kenyan ones.

In spite of the viciousness of the Moi regime and the imprisonment of the party leadership, the anti-imperialist center survived the brutal attempts to strangle it. With the support of the people and its revolutionary cadres, it remained effectively underground. Without any compromise it boldly persisted in producing *Pambana* and other anti-imperialist literature. Covertly, it continued to organize the working class, peasantry and the patriotic petty-bourgeoisie against the repressive regime and for the national democratic revolution. In July of 1983, *Pambana* declared:

> We cannot remain silent when our rights to good housing, adequate food, decent clothing and education have been denied us by the oppressive regime...Compatriots, let us unite and defeat the comprador ruling class and its imperialist allies. As long as imperialism reigns over us, it's our right and responsibility to liberate our country. Our hope for our future lies in our history of struggle, in our patriotism and in the unity of all exploited and oppressed. The fire has been lit, the oppressed will burn the enemy to ashes and we shall march in unity singing: Pambana, Pambana, Pambana. Victory is ours.

The DTM leadership strongly argued and insisted that no coercive and oppressive system, however brutal and complex its mechanism of repression, ever succeeded in crushing an organized and united people led by a proletarian party. In truth, the Kenyan compradorial rulers will never voluntarily surrender state power. Like other bourgeois ruling classes, they will clutch their *panga* until they are taken out of the State House by violent revolution. In 1950 the Mau Mau leadership made the same scientific observation. Hence, it armed its forces and mobilized the popular masses against the British imperialist occupiers.

Mwakenya: The Unfinished Revolution

The Central Revolutionary Council of DTM

With the imprisonment of a section of the DTM leadership in June of 1982, the movement then led by *The Provisional Committee for December Twelve Movement*. Shortly, the name was changed to *The Central Revolutionary Council of December Twelve Movement*. The new leadership appointed new editorial staff that continued to produce *Pambana* and other anti-imperialist literature. In July of 1983, the Central Revolutionary Council leadership launched a party journal, *Mpatanishi*. It was an internal organ of the movement whose primary task, according to the Central Revolutionary Council (CRC), was to shape, sharpen and deepen the science of Marxism-Leninism-Maoism among the party cadres, the working class, and the progressive petty-bourgeoisie. The journal was to be an ideological link between the center and the rank and file members of the movement. It was secretly distributed among the rank and file and the patriotic Kenyans. In *Mpatanishi*, Number 8, February 1984, the CRC wrote:

> Our journal Mpatanishi continues to be the Central organ linking all our forces both internally and externally. But our Pambana newspaper remains a mass paper…We must use our central organ, Mpatanishi as an organizer if we have to be highly organized; our level of commitment should be raised and our discipline tightened. All the Marxist principles of absolute secrecy and strictest selection of members must be observed if our organization is to have firm roots among the workers, peasants and the progressive petty-bourgeoisie.

In *Mpatanishi*, Number 9, 1984, the DTM leadership refuted Moi's claim that *Pambana* was produced and distributed in the country by a foreign embassy. It stated:

> The Central Committee of DTM released a press statement as a reaction to Moi's allegations that Pambana is a foreign embassy's affair. The statement refuted Moi's allegations and strongly stated that Pambana is published and distributed in Kenya and abroad by Kenyans. Probably the quality of a translated Kiswahili to English

issue of Pambana No. 2 (which is still circulating in the country) could have confused Moi and his security forces, to drive them to make such allegations. It is now an open secret that Moi has lost direction and definitely fears the organization of DTM and its tactics of preparing the masses for revolution...The DTM is still gaining momentum nationwide.

Pambana and *Mpatanishi* set out the strategy of achieving a broad unity of all democratic forces, including the progressive petty-bourgeoisie and the workers and peasantry. Simultaneously, the CRC urged the party cadres and members to embrace socialist ideas and to organize and mobilize for socialism. In *Mpatanishi,* Number 8, February 1984, the CRC leadership clearly explained:

> Many comrades are aware that we have intensified our political activities throughout the country and in particular the major urban areas of Kenya. Our movement has grown and continues to expand both locally and abroad. We know victory is certain, but we can not ignore the fact that our aims, goals and objectives can only be achieved if we are thoroughly organized throughout the [country].

> An examination of revolutionary movements reveals that we had for long acted as isolated groups, study circles, etc., until we organized ourselves as the December Twelve Movement (DTM) in the 1970s. The DTM is a united, anti-imperialist, anti-fascist front that aims at bringing together all democratic forces as a first phase of the general struggle towards Socialism. In the process, the democratic forces, mainly the workers, peasantry and progressive intellectuals are to be trained and prepared for a future communist party.

Similarly, a leaflet secretly distributed by the DTM cadres in the City of Nairobi on March 2, 1984 reads:

> Our organizational ability in publishing and distributing revolutionary literature throughout the country within a short notice has caused worries to the puppet government of dictator Moi and his

foreign imperialist masters...Although the dogs of the dictator are everywhere, it is our national responsibility to bring new democracy in the country or die in trying.

In 1983 and 1984 the CRC leadership consolidated its political base in the country, recruited new members, and constructed more anti-imperialist cells, particularly in the urban centers and on the university campuses, in colleges and schools. The bulk of its membership, however, was militant university students, primary and high school teachers and the lower petty-bourgeoisie in government departments. Most of them were not serious; they were flirting with the revolution. As the democratic struggle deepened and the repression intensified, some of these elements slipped into the morass of petty-bourgeois opportunism, vacillation, inconsistency, falsification and cowardice. The party had not succeeded in building a mass base amongst the workers and peasantry. In truth, no revolution can succeed in Kenya without the massive involvement of the working class and its peasantry ally.

Besides printing and distributing *Pambana* and *Mpatanishi*, ideological classes were held in the party cells to educate the cadres in the MLM science and to study the history of our people as well as the natural sciences and geography of our country. In addition, the CRC leadership forcefully campaigned for the release of the DTM Five, university students and other political prisoners, whilst members of parliament, petty-bourgeois trade union leaders, the majority of university academics, Christian and Muslim leaders, and leaders of professional organizations (the Kenya Medical Association, the Kenya National Union of Teachers, the Law Society of Kenya, the Historical Association of Kenya, etc.), remained silent from fear of the dictator's brutal security forces. Publishers, editors and reporters of the mainstream rightwing newspapers, journals and magazines—*Daily Nation*, *The Standard*, *The Kenya Times*, and *The Weekly Review*—collaborated fully with dictator Moi as he bestially continued to demolish democratic platforms countrywide and to arrest, torture, imprison and kill party cadres and other patriotic dissidents.

Mwakenya: The Unfinished Revolution

While we are on the subject, it is worth mentioning that the CRC leadership stemmed from one of the sparks of DTM in Nairobi, which was led by Kĩbacia Gatũ and Chitechi Osundwa. They were young patriotic intellectuals who had little knowledge of Kenya's history. They were weak in revolutionary theory and inexperienced in political organization, and had a vague idea of the MLM philosophy. As a result of their ideological limitations and political inexperience, they threw the door of the party wide open to petty-bourgeois opportunists, pretenders, self-seekers and other unstable elements. Many of us in prison and in exile expected that Adhu Awiti, the CC member, and Sultan Somjee, the Nairobi party branch representative, would coordinate the party activities, reorganize the Central Committee and lead it, but this did not happen. From fear of being arrested, they abandoned the revolution and went into hiding, leaving the party without a central leadership despite the fact that Maina wa Kĩnyattĩ had secretly written both of them from Kamĩtĩ maximum security prison and urged them to take up the party leadership and continue with the struggle. With concern for the continuity of DTM leadership, Kĩbacia contacted Sultan and a delegation from the DTM Nakuru branch went to see Awiti, but both men were determined to keep out of the movement. Consequently, the party's central authority degenerated, and some of the weak party cells collapsed. But thanks to their excessive courage and daring, complete contempt for danger, torture and imprisonment, Kĩbacia and Chitechi, despite their ideological limitations, saved the movement from total degeneration and annihilation. But as we shall later learn, lack of a strong center would result in the weakening of the political and theoretical position of DTM. It further led to an infiltration of petty-bourgeois opportunists, and the aggravation of organizational chaos and ideological confusion. In short, a weakened center would sow the seeds of opportunism, liberalism, dogmatism, subjectivism and sectarianism in the party.

Anti-Imperialist Center in Prison

An anti-imperialist center was constructed in Kamĩtĩ maximum security prison in 1982, which played a pivotal role in exposing the cruelty of Kenya's penal system internationally through smuggled letters and annual reports on prison conditions. The center was composed of four people: Maina wa Kĩnyattĩ, and three militant university students—Mwangi wa Kwĩrĩkia, Onyango Oloo and Peter R. Ogego. Later Mwandawiro Mghangha, who was imprisoned for being a member of Mwakenya in 1986, joined the group. Ogego, Onyango and Mwangi were not officially members of DTM, but they played a key role in constructing the revolutionary front in prison. Overall, they identified with the underground movement and courageously and fearlessly defended the DTM revolutionary line. Despite the brutality of prison guards, the center organized weekend political study sessions. The imprisoned comrades used these political study sessions to clarify their ideas and strengthen their determination. The center was also involved in politicizing the other imprisoned Kenyans and the prison guards. The Center organized a ring of politicized prison guards whose duty was to smuggle reports on prison conditions and revolutionary writings out of the prison. The politicized prison guards took these documents to Mũmbi wa Maina who, in return, gave them books, newspapers, party reading material and personal items, including letters from families, relatives, friends and comrades, to bring to the imprisoned comrades. Reports on the prison conditions and other political writings were secretly shipped to Ngũgĩ wa Thiong'o in London by Mũmbi. From London, the imprisoned cadres received political literature, including *Kenya News, Moi's Reign of Terror, University Destroyed: Moi Crowns Ten Years of Government Terror in Kenya, Repression Intensified in Kenya Since the August 1st Coup Attempt, Struggle for Democracy in Kenya and Draft Minimum Programme of Mwakenya,* among others. Parallel with this, the prison center established underground communications with the detained comrades as well as the imprisoned Air Force rebels in the condemned cells. Kamoji Wachiira (DTM) was the main contact in the detention center and Oshuka (Air Force) was the contact in the gallows. Between 1985 and

Mwakenya: The Unfinished Revolution

1988 more revolutionary centers were organized in Kenya's maximum-security prisons where imprisoned patriots were held. In prison, exile, and underground, the revolutionary cadres played a vital role in mobilizing the Kenyan and international communities against the KANU dictatorship.

With the encouragement of the party and the revolutionary commitment of the Kamĩtĩ political group, the following books—*Kenya: A Prison Notebook, Mother Kenya, A Season of Blood* and *Mwaki Ũtangĩhoreka*—were secretly written, and secretly smuggled out of prison by a patriotic prison officer and taken to Mũmbi wa Maina. Their publication proves that prison walls, chains and guards with guns, cannot dampen the revolutionary process, and can serve to organize new revolutionary cells for transformational ideas and practice.

The Communist Party of Kenya

The debate to change the name of the movement, to transform it into a political party, became a major issue within the CRC leadership and among the rank and file members in 1984. Some members argued and claimed that the name DTM was "abstract" and was not forceful enough or emotionally appealing to the great majority of the Kenyan working class and peasants. They wanted a name that was "more definitive, scientifically correct, and one which does not give room to opportunistic deviations from Marxism." In October of 1984 the CRC leadership, after consulting the rank and file and the DTM cell coordinators within the country, made the decision to change the name of the movement to the Communist Party of Kenya (CPK). In the process, the DTM main center, the CRC, was transformed into a Central Committee of the CPK. The rationale for choosing the name CPK is printed in *Mpatanishi,* Number 7. October 1984. In part it reads:

> Now that the time has come when all the Kenyan progressives must address themselves to the question of the Party programme; it is becoming necessary to have a name for our movement. We cannot indefinitely refer to ourselves as the "movement", the "progressive", or just the "revolutionaries". We are not suggesting that these terms

Mwakenya: The Unfinished Revolution

should not be used; however, we believe that a name that is more definite, scientifically correct and one which does not give room to opportunistic deviations from Marxism should be adopted.

Our name, all by itself, must reflect our aims. It must also correspond to the nature of the struggle we are involved in at this point in time of our history. That name is the "Communist Party". It is the name that would terrify the international capitalist-imperialists and their Kenyan comprador allies, and be capable of leading the Kenyan working masses along a socialist path. It is the name that places Scientific Socialism as the basis of our movement. For that fundamental reason, we are proud to call ourselves, Communists and our movement, the Communist Party of Kenya (CPK).

In the same issue of *Mpatanishi,* the CRC leadership printed the draft programme of the Communist Party of Kenya and circulated it to the party cells and branches for discussion and adoption. It was unanimously adopted. In the process, *Pambana* and *Mpatanishi* became the central organs of the proposed Communist Party of Kenya. To be more precise, the three issues of *Mpatanishi* (Numbers 10, 11 and 12) were produced under the red banner of the CPK. However, as the following pages shall demonstrate, the effort to convert DTM into a communist party would be aborted and the ideological path of the movement diverted once more.

In the process of transforming the DTM into the Communist Party, the CRC leadership intensified its recruitment of militant youth and patriotic petty-bourgeoisie to the movement; Simultaneously, it exposed the undemocratic character of the Moi-Kanu regime amongst the toiling masses. It produced several anti-imperialist, ideological documents, including "A *Major Task on our Ideological Path"* (*Mpatanishi,* No. 8, February 1984), *"On our Organization, Strategy and Tactics"* (*Mpatanishi,* No.12, December 1984), *"On Recruitment"* (*Mpatanish*i, No.11, November 1984) and countless leaflets which called for the overthrow of dictator Moi's anti-people regime and the release of the DTM Five. In *Mpatanishi,* No. 8, February 1984 the following is recorded:

56

The DTM served President Moi with an open letter, which was also distributed to the Kenyan masses and to friends and fraternal organizations abroad. Some of our demands were the release of the DTM leaders—Maina wa Kĩnyattĩ, Kamoji Wachiira, Willy Mutunga, al-Amin Mazrui and Edward Oyugi—and other political prisoners, and the removal of all foreign forces from the soil of Kenya.

As the campaign for the release of political prisoners was intensified at home and abroad, Moi was forced to release some political detainees by the end of 1984, including al-Amin, Mutunga, Kamoji, Oyugi, Mũkarũ, Koigi, and George Anyona. Maina wa Kĩnyattĩ was not released until October 1988. Unlike South Africa where Mandela, Sisulu and other ANC leaders, who resumed the party leadership immediately after their release, the released DTM leaders, citing security, did not resume the party leadership until four years later. Had the party resumed its leadership, immediately after the release of the leaders, it would have prevented the petty-bourgeois opportunists and other reactionary elements from hijacking the revolutionary movement.

Opportunism, Subjectivism and Sectarianism

The period between 1984 and 1987 was one of increased organizational looseness and ideological confusion within the movement. In February of 1985 the CRC leadership once again changed the name of the movement from the Communist Party of Kenya to Mwakenya (a Kiswahili acronym for *Muungano wa Wazalendo wa Kuikomboa Kenya*), forming an alliance with other anti-imperialist forces in the process. The alliance was dominated by petty-bourgeois opportunists, pretenders, ultra-left adventurists, and other bellicose reactionaries. It was some of these elements who, in turn, took over the Mwakenya leadership. David Kĩnyua, who had not been schooled in the ideological traditions of the December Twelve Movement, was elected Mwakenya's General Secretary. With the exception of Kĩbacia and Chitechi who were elected to the Central Committee of Mwakenya, the rest of the CRC members were dropped from the leadership of the movement.

Mwakenya: The Unfinished Revolution

The DTM's political documents and files, and the entire party archives were handed over by the CRC leadership to the newly appointed Central Committee under the leadership of the General Secretary. The power to run the new party was vested in the office of the General Secretary. Under these new developments, the name of the DTM mass paper, *Pambana,* was changed to *Mzalendo Pambana* and then to *Mzalendo Mwakenya.* The DTM ideological organ, *Mpatanishi,* was adopted as the central organ of Mwakenya (MK) and the DTM Editorial Board was converted into the MK editorial board under Chitechi's leadership. The printing press and its equipment were made the property of Mwakenya. The main effort of the new leadership, however, was to purport that there was no organic link between DTM and Mwakenya, that Mwakenya was a new movement with a new leadership and a new programme. In this effort, the Mwakenya liquidators, with the collaboration of Kĩbacia and Chitechi, doctored the DTM documents and files. The name DTM was erased from the party documents and files, and then the name Mwakenya was imposed on them. They backdated the first issue of *Mpatanishi* to 1982, removed the name of DTM from the cover pages of the old issues of the journal, reprinted new covers and then imposed the name Mwakenya on them. In the process of this falsification of the history of the movement, many documents and files were destroyed and names of the DTM leaders, cadres and members erased from the documents and files. Once in their hands, *Mpatanishi* became a weapon in the fight against the DTM ideological line and an instrument for the propaganda of petty-bourgeois opportunism and ultra-left adventurism.

But there was more. The MK liquidators set the movement on fire. They changed the structure and political philosophy of the movement, including the criteria of recruitment, the principles of democratic centralism, the mechanisms of collective responsibility, and the principled policy of criticism and self-criticism, secrecy, discipline, sincerity and trust. They dismissed the study of revolutionary theories, strategies and tactics as a waste of time, introducing the traditional oath-taking as criteria of recruitment for the movement. Insidiously, the liquidators argued and insisted that the time for guerrilla welfare was ripe, hence the party members and cadres

Mwakenya: The Unfinished Revolution

should prepare for a bloody confrontation with the neocolonial state and its imperialist backers. By distorting the DTM mass line, dogmatism, petty-bourgeois opportunism and ultra-leftism caused the movement to lose its most important features as a revolutionary communist movement closely linked with the popular masses.

Let us now discuss some of these issues and their negative impacts on the movement for a new democracy.

1. Transformation and Alliance: Alliance, coalition, or merger of MLM parties must be based on ideological principles. This in turn demands a broad consensus within a revolutionary movement through deep and critical discussion and scientific analysis of the nature of the alliance before such a fundamental and ideological decision is taken. Democratic centralism explicitly demands that party members and cadres are entitled to know specifically the organization or group they are aligning or merging with and why; they are entitled to discuss and approve the decision made by the Central Committee, or to reject it if they can prove it is a deviation from the ideological line of the party. In this respect, the transformation of DTM into a mass organization (Mwakenya) was contrary to the principles of democratic centralism and the MLM ideological line. It resulted in the creation of sectarianism within the party, in the undermining of ideological unity, and in the setting up of the party cadres against each other. It was a plan the liquidators cleverly masked by ultra-left phraseology and self-righteousness.

2. The Oath: In principle, we find nothing wrong with an oath pledge in a revolutionary movement; what is wrong and unacceptable is to use an oath pledge to distort the ideological line of the movement. The WPK/DTM leadership from December 1974 to June 1982 had particular regulations, rules and policies pertaining to defining, identifying, preparing and recruiting new cadres into the movement. These regulations, rules and policies, were derived from well-thought-out, tried and tested, MLM methods of recruitment. With the transformation of DTM and its organizations into Mwakenya, the MK liquidators rejected DTM's recruitment policy and

Mwakenya: The Unfinished Revolution

insisted that the effective and quick method of membership recruitment was the administration of an oath of loyalty and unity to new recruits as it was done in the Mau Mau movement, forgetting that Mau Mau took place in different historical circumstances and in a different epoch of our country's history. They failed to scientifically study the historical and political context of the Mau Mau anti-imperialist oath and the history of the Mau Mau movement in general. If they had critically read the history of the Mau Mau movement, they would have learned that the Mau Mau leadership combined the aboveground and underground politics and strategically built a firm foundation amongst the workers and peasantry before launching the armed struggle. In addition, the MK liquidators disregarded and ignored the present day sociopolitical and cultural forces of our multiethnic nation, which militate against the revolutionary effectiveness and efficacy of the traditional oath as an instrument of recruiting patriotic Kenyans into a revolutionary party. This method of recruitment tends to organize the people on ethnic lines instead of across ethnic lines.

Despite their failure to consult with the rank and file members, and their disregard of the party's core principle of collective responsibility and collective decision-making, the MK liquidators insisted that party members, including the former DTM members, must take an oath of loyalty and unity in order to qualify to be members of Mwakenya. Yet oath-taking was not voluntary; force was utilized to bring party members and new recruits to the oath-taking ceremony. Compatriots were actually captured, forcefully dragged to a house where, with *panga,* daggers and swords brandishing, they were forced to take the oath and to declare that they were now "members" of Mwakenya and they would never betray the "secrets" of the movement to the enemy. Those who hesitated to take the "patriotic oath" were humiliated, vilified, slapped and kicked; they were treated like enemies. Recruitment was also done in restaurants and bars. Anti-Moi comments over a bottle of beer in a crowded city-slum bar were considered "revolutionary" and led some to bring their drunkard friends to the movement, force them to take the oath of loyalty, unity and commitment, and then enroll them in the "MK armed wing". The manifestation of oath-

Mwakenya: The Unfinished Revolution

taking was an ideologial deviation from the MLM path and was concrete and clear proof that the CRC leadership and its reactionary alliances had become the gravediggers of the patriotic, revolutionary movement that DTM had been.

The repercussions of oath-taking were sixfold: **1)** since it was violently administered, it brought into the party undesirable and dangerous elements, including liberals of every hue, self-seekers, pretenders and opportunists; **2)** it opened the door for the government security agents to infiltrate the central organs of the movement. In fact, several police informers who pretended to be anti-Moi in order to gather intelligence were *captured*, given the oath of unity, and made members of Mwakenya; **3)** it demolished the structure of the party, transformed the party into a loose coalition of liberal petty-bourgeoisie, reactionary nationalists and pretenders; **4)** it undermined the movement's principles of democratic centralism, criticism and self-criticism and collective responsibility and collective decision-making; **5)** it created distrust and suspicion among the rank and file, making it difficult for them to work as a collective force; and finally, **6)** it dismissed the revolutionary vision of the movement, disregarded the MLM revolutionary theory and distorted the role of DTM as a communist vanguard party. Lenin forcefully argues that, "without a revolutionary theory, there can be no revolutionary movement. The role of vanguard can be fulfilled only by a party that is guided by the most advanced theory and has the support of the proletariat." Fidel Castro and Mao Tse-tung say the same.

3. Democratic Centralism: The organization and operation of WPK/DTM were based on the democratic centralism which constitutes the following Leninist precepts: **1)** the individual is subordinate to the party; **2)** the minority is subordinate to majority; **3)** the lower level is subordinate to the higher level; **4)** the entire party membership is subordinate to the Central Committee and the National Congress; **5)** party decisions, discipline and secrecy must be strictly observed. With democratic centralism, a strong party emerges capable of planning and coordinating of the activities and ideology of the party. Without democratic centralism, the party would not achieve its fundamental aims and objectives; liberalism would creep

Mwakenya: The Unfinished Revolution

in, opening the party gate wide to class enemies. Monsters, freaks and cockroaches would get the opportunity to seize control of the party leadership.

As noted earlier, after the transformation of DTM into Mwakenya, democratic centralism was replaced with commandism. According to Mao Tse-tung, "Commandism can ruin a revolution; leave it in isolation, denying it the indispensable nourishment of the people support." Whereas before cadres were used to democratic methods of work and strictly adhered to the party secrecy and discipline, observed party rules and regulations because they strongly and sincerely believed in the party leadership and had faith in its MLM orientation, now the demolition of the party structure and the distortion of its MLM line made it difficult for the party cadres to work as a cogent team or to have faith in the Mwakenya leadership. Under these new developments, the Mwakenya Central Committee refused to be accountable to party membership or listen to members' objections, criticisms or personal complaints. There was no room for dissenters, criticism, collective responsibility and collective decision-making. Commandism became the ideology of the Mwakenya Central committee. Abuse of power, intimidation, threats, favoritism, nepotism and corruption became the policy of the party. This ideological deviation from the DTM's Marxist line greatly affected party methods of work and psychologically demoralized the party cadres, weakened their tenacity and resolve, and undermined their fighting spirit and ideological conviction. Overall, it seriously distorted the MLM theory which had imbued the DTM cadres with patriotism, courage, and communist values, and instilled in them a strong sense of comradeship and revolutionary consciousness. But there is more. Using decrees, the Mwakenya Central Committee transferred cell members from one cell to another and replaced cell leadership without consulting cell members or taking into consideration the security risks involved in such a decision that would, inevitably, question the role of its leadership and weaken its position. It also prohibited intraparty struggles despite the fact that the main purpose of "intraparty struggles was not to destroy the party, but to increase its unity, improve its discipline",

Mwakenya: The Unfinished Revolution

deepen its ideology and weed out undesirable elements who might have sneaked into the party. Furthermore, since cadres were oathed to give all—their lives, wealth and property—to the party, demands for financial contributions increased and vultures multiplied as cadres were coerced to withdraw, nay, to empty their bank accounts for the best interest of the party and country in spite the fact that some members had families—wives and children to feed and rent to pay. Recalcitrant members were warned: either withdraw the money from their bank accounts and hand it over to the party or be expelled from the party. The Mwakenya Central Committee was operating like a militia crip of thugs; its reactionary acts demolished the party structure, derailed its fundamental aims and objectives, and crippled its ideological development. As a result, the party degenerated into opportunism and ultra-leftism. In organizational terms, this was no longer a proletarian center, but a petty-bourgeois party, led by an insecure and dangerous clique of petty-bourgeois liquidators.

4. Criticism and Self-Criticism are the most important tools for resolving contradictions within the MLM party, between the leadership and the rank and file, and among the cadres. Extensive criticism and self-criticism are needed for consolidation of the party unity and discipline, and for discovery and removal of dangerous and reactionary recalcitrant elements from the party. They purify the party's ideological conviction and deepen its commitment to national liberation and socialism. If a revolutionary party refuses to adopt criticism and self-criticism as instruments for sharpening contradictions within its ranks and amongst the masses, it sinks into the bag of ideological confusion and organizational looseness.

5. Guerrilla Warfare*:* Our party has never denied the role and importance of armed resistance in the national liberation movement. In fact, since 1974 the WPK/DTM believed that armed struggle may be necessary to remove the KANU puppet regime from power, but never advocated it as the *only* way forward. In other words, the WPK/DTM leadership believed that the party commands the gun and never does the gun command the party. The questions before us, therefore, are: Was the party and its revolutionary cadres prepared to wage an armed struggle against a well-armed comprador

Mwakenya: The Unfinished Revolution

bourgeois regime in league with the imperialist bourgeoisie? Was the majority of our people –peasantry and workers alike—ready at that historical period to support the revolution and massively and colossally participate in protracted guerrilla warfare? The answer to both questions was: No. Firstly, the party could not possibly launch an armed struggle before it had solidly consolidated its revolutionary base amongst the proletarians, peasantry and pastoralists and had a strong, ideological network with a core of tested and unshakeable, committed MLM revolutionaries. Secondly, a scientific analysis of the social contradictions, class alliances and political consciousness of the Kenyan working class, at that period of time ruled out the advisability of launching a guerrilla war.

In spite of the fact that the subjective and objective conditions in the country were not ripe for armed resistance, and the party did not have its own armed forces, the MK liquidators went ahead to prepare for what they termed "patriotic war against the reactionary KANU regime and its foreign allies". Subjectively, they argued that all peaceful means and democratic platforms had been dismantled by the repressive regime, and, therefore, the only method of struggle left was the armed, revolutionary, struggle whereby the party and its organizations would mobilize the oppressed masses and arm the militant youth, as was done during the Mau Mau war, to respond to state terrorism with organized revolutionary violence. They insisted that a revolution, by its very nature, employed violence, blood and death, and the sooner the party cadres become aware of it and prepared for it, the better. Their slogans were: "Blood for Blood" and "Death for Death". To defeat the neocolonial forces, the MK liquidators claimed they would use the same military tactics and strategies Dedan Kĩmathi had used against the British imperialist occupiers. They would drink from the same cup of courage that Kĩmathi drank and sing the same freedom songs the KLFA guerrillas had sung and follow the Kĩmathist revolutionary line to the letter. Such pretentious claims revealed their flagrant ignorance of the scientific principles of revolution. Their sloganeering vividly demonstrated that the MK liquidators "were carried away by subjective wishes" and were not informed by a concrete, ideological analysis of the situation on the ground; it was clear proof of their intellectual sterility, ideological penury and backwardness.

In preparation for war, the party leadership, without consulting the cell representatives and the rank and file, converted the underground political cells into "guerrilla units" and appointed the party General Secretary—who not only was ideologically and morally bankrupt, but also had no military training or experience in handling firearms—the commander-in-chief of the Mwakenya "Liberation Army." Correspondingly, each "guerrilla unit" was falsely made to believe that it was a section of a huge people's army— hundreds of whom were safely and firmly entrenched in the Kĩrĩnyaga and Nyandarwa forests waiting for the order from the "commander-in-chief" to assail the enemy forces. Such naked and callous deceitfulness is simply criminal in a revolutionary movement. According to the MLM discipline, it is punishable by death.

Miscalculating the strength, ruthlessness and viciousness of the Moi neocolonial regime, the MK General Secretary publicly issued a leaflet on April 3, 1986, entitled, *"It Is Now Guerrilla Warfare In Kenya"*, announcing the beginning of the armed resistance. And yet, ironically, the party had not made preparations for war; it had no armed forces, no weapons, and no support from the workers and peasantry in the country. The compradorial regime responded to the challenge with an iron fist. A large number of "suspect MK guerrillas" were captured before they entered Nyandarwa or Kĩrĩnyaga forest, viciously tortured and then imprisoned. Many of them, including Oyangi Mbaja and Peter Young Kĩhara, broke down during the bestial interrogation and surrendered vital information to the police. Others, after their surrender, agreed to join the secret police unit to hunt down their comrades, friends and relatives on the city streets. The oath, which was *supposed* to steel party members and deepen their convictions and harden their courage, did not prevent them from surrendering secrets of the movement to the police. Furthermore, as a consequence of its unscientific methods of recruitment, the party was heavily infiltrated by state secret agents, informers, agent provocateurs and other monsters. With most of its leaders and cadres imprisoned, Mwakenya was reduced to a skeletal

Mwakenya: The Unfinished Revolution

movement and was unable to operate effectively within the country. Its center of operation shifted outside of Kenya. Those who were lucky enough to escape arrest, including David Kĩnyua, Kĩbacia wa Gatũ and Kaara wa Macaria, to name a few, crossed into Tanzania. They reconstructed their political base in Dar es Salaam under the watchful eye of the Tanzanian secret police.

The Height of State Terrorism

The year 1986 marked the height of state terrorism. Any Kenyan identified as a Mwakenya, a Communist, or a Marxist, was arrested, grisly tortured, including bestial sexual assaults, and then imprisoned in a desperate attempt by the dictator and his sycophants to uproot the seeds of the anti-imperialist national resistance. Many more were driven underground and others into exile. Once again, the national universities were shut down and hundreds of students were flung into prison. The attacks on the civilian population, including gang rapes, torture, collective punishment, unlawful imprisonment and murder, were aggressively and ruthlessly accelerated. To create fear among the people, censorship of thought was viciously and callously tightened nationwide and reinforced with impunity. What people read and wrote, the organizations they belonged to, the play they performed in and the theatre they attended, the movies they saw, what they heard on the radio and television, where they lived and the schools they went to, who they married and slept with, what jobs they held and the salaries they earned—everything was under dictator Moi's scrutiny and control. Moi was a megalomaniac dictator; he maintained himself in power through institutionalized state violence and with the economic, political and military support of the Western imperialist democracies. His rule was a time of total subjugation of the Kenyan society. And yet reverent tales were retold on the state controlled radio and in the rightist bourgeois newspapers in which Moi was praised, hailed and portrayed as a champion of democracy, a freedom fighter, a father of the nation, a first class patriot.

Mwakenya: The Unfinished Revolution

Whilst it was true that the police infiltration of the anti-imperialist movement had tremendously weakened it and caused distrust and suspicion amongst the rank and file, the Kenyan masses remained united against the comprador-imperialist alliance. However, to justify his reign of terror, dictator Moi capitalized on the use of the state radio, conservative, religious institutions and the bourgeois rightwing mainstream newspapers, journals and magazines, and the party machinery. At KANU rallies, he frenetically attacked Marxist university academics and militant students and at the same time implored Kenyans to report those who were distributing anti-government leaflets in the country. The sodomized KANU branch leaders and members of cabinet, to demonstrate their loyalty to the vile dictator, tried to outdo each in using the filthiest epithets to characterize, define and describe the "communist agitators". Others used bellicose, anti-communist rhetoric in order to be on the same page with the dictator. The Moi regime was hated by the people, therefore, by orchestrating anti-communist demonstrations and rallies, dictator Moi popularized the underground movement amongst the popular masses; he also confirmed what the majority of Kenyans had suspected since 1970 that there was, in fact, an underground revolutionary movement within the country organizing the overthrow of the KANU dictatorship and aiming at replacing it with a new democracy.

Globally, the inhumanity and impunity, the brutality and viciousness, of the Moi regime further shattered to shards the false belief of many people in the world, particularly the liberals in the imperialist countries, that Kenya was a paradise—an island of peace, democracy and socio-economic stability in Africa in a sea of ethnic wars. This also deepened and expanded democratic struggle waged by progressive Kenyans in exile and those in prison and detention centers. Equally, it hardened the position of the clandestine movement both at home and abroad. In this respect, many in the movement believed that the socialist revolution was the only just cause, the only cause worth dying for.

Mwakenya in Exile

The first months of Mwakenya in exile, according to Kaara wa Macaria (1990), were characterized by bitter intraparty struggles. Out of these intraparty struggles, two factions emerged. One was led by Kĩnyua and Kĩbacia, and the other one by Kaara. Kĩnyua and Kĩbacia were members of the MK Central Committee, hence, the principal leaders of Mwakenya in exile. The Kaara faction consisted of the rank and file; it was the majority faction—loosely organized, undisciplined and lacked the MLM spirit of criticism and firmness. The sectarianism emerged during the intraparty struggles. The Kaara faction demanded reorganization of the party from top to bottom. It insisted that in order to return the party to the ideological path of the December Twelve Movement as well as to make the party democratic and responsive to the needs of the rank and file members and the people of Kenya in general, Kĩnyua must be removed from position of General Secretary. In his place, a special party committee should be organized to lead the party and to investigate his abuse of power and endemic corruption in the Party. The Kĩnyua-Kĩbacia faction rejected the call for reorganization of the party, and despite its minority position within the party, accused the Kaara faction of deviation and expelled it from the party. Instead of waging an intraparty struggle, with an unflinching and unbending patriotic spirit and unified discipline, the expelled faction took a reactionary line. It walked out of the party, and together with some other Kenyan exiles in Tanzania, formed the Me Katilili Revolutionary Movement (MEKAREMO), whose main base was in Dar es Salaam. Shortly after that, MEKAREMO merged with another little-known, political group, the Kenya Anti-Imperialist Front (KAIF), which was led by Shadrack Gutto and Micere Mũgo and was operating in Harare, Zimbabwe; the new party was named the *Umoja wa Wazalendo Kenya* (UWAKE). In the meantime, the Kĩnyua-Kĩbacia faction seized the central organs of the party. They turned the party into an army barrack where conscious party discipline was transformed into a mechanical discipline based on intimidation and on mercenary methods of political work. Criticism and self-criticism were replaced by coercion. While consolidating the party

Mwakenya: The Unfinished Revolution

power in their hands, they officially contacted Ngũgĩ wa Thiong'o, DTM representative in Europe, and in the course of discussion agreed to re-unite the party. The name Mwakenya was officially formalized as the name of the party and Ngũgĩ was appointed the leader and spokesman of the party. The appointment of Ngũgĩ the party spokesman legitimized the Kĩnyua-Kĩbacia leadership in the party. Despite the appointment of Ngũgĩ the party spokesman, control of the movement and the party leadership remained under the Dar clique until 1991.

In September of 1987 a party programme, *Draft Minimum Programme of Mwakenya* (DMPM), was adopted. The DMPM was not, and is not, a socialist programme; it is an anti-imperialist, nationalist programme like the South African's ANC Freedom Charter. It degraded the party to a national, patriotic alliance of all classes. This change weakened further the MLM line in the party. Despite its ideological defect, the new Mwakenya leadership was somehow convinced that its tactics and strategies, aims and objectives, would answer the basic needs of the great majority of the Kenyan people and lay a firm, patriotic, foundation for the advancement of the country to a new democracy. At a more general level, the DMPM reunited the party, formalized the party's united front line, defined the aims and strategy of Kenya's anti-neocolonial struggle nationwide and prompted its further anti-imperialist development. The fundamental questions that were not discussed during the drafting of the party programme in Harare, Zimbabwe, were: **1)** Why the name of the movement was changed and what was the rationale of changing it? **2)** What were the names of the organizations that merged with DTM and who were the leaders of the "organizations" that supposedly to have merged with DTM? **3)** Who introduced oath-taking into the movement and what ideological justification prompted this drastic, reactionary decision? **4)** Why did the CRC leadership deviate from the Marxist methods of struggle? A critical analysis of the history of the movement from June 1982 to 1987 could have answered the above fundamental questions and also exposed the ultra-left elements and other undesirable characters in the party.

The London Unity Conference, 1987

Another crucial development during this period was the search for unity with other externally based Kenyan democratic organizations. For this purpose, a unity conference, sponsored by Mwakenya under Ngũgĩ's leadership was held in London on October 16-19, 1987.and was attended by seven externally based democratic organizations, including UKENYA (an acronym for: United Movement for Democracy in Kenya). UKENYA was a broad front for Mwakenya abroad and its central secretariat was based in London. Its leadership consisted of seven members: Wanjirũ Kĩhoro, Naila Durrani, Nish Matenjwa, Wangũi wa Goro, Abdilatif Abdalla, Shiraz Durrani, Yusuf Hassan and Ngũgĩ wa Thiong'o. Yusuf was the first chairperson of the front; he was replaced by Abdilatif after moving to New York City to work for the United Nations.

Although the conference floundered because of the political disagreement among the participants, it hightened the deveolopment of the struggle for democracy in Kenya. Apart from that, it produced, monumental historical documents, which enriched the collected history of Kenya and contributed to the cultural liberation of our people. These documents include: **1)** Women in Kenya People's Resistance; **2)** Pambana Legacy of Resistance; **3)** The Heritage of Armed Resistance in the Northern Kenya, 1880-1963; **4)** Unity in Resistance; **5)** Legacy of Resistance at the Coast; **6)** Resistance in Central and Rift Valley; **7)** Kenya Asians Participation in Kenya People's Resistance Against Imperialism (1884-1963); and **8)** Resistance to Imperialism by the People of Nyanza and Western Provinces of Kenya. In brief, the documents denounced in strong language the Eurocentric theory of African history, condemned anti-Mau Mau, imperialist scholarship and rejected the reactionary, neocolonial, anti-Mau Mau arguments prescribed by Kenyan rightwing scholars and their foreign academic friends.

The Nineties

The 1990s saw the monstrous intensification of state terrorism

Mwakenya: The Unfinished Revolution

countrywide: pro-democracy political organizers, liberal parliamentarians and lawyers were arrested and imprisoned, their homes and families attacked, newspapers banned, patriotic journalists, editors and printers terrorized, militant students, progressive schoolteachers and university academics hunted down by the vicious state police; and thousands of homes of the working class in Nairobi city razed to the ground by the regime. In the Rift Valley region, a ruthless, ethnic war was engineered by dictator Moi—women brutally raped, hundreds of people murdered with impunity, their homes destroyed and their livestock and land confiscated; and on top of that, official corruption tripled nationwide, while poverty and unspeakable misery among the Kenyan poor increased tenfold. But in spite of the acceleration of institutionalized state violence and official corruption, the pro-democracy movement continued to deepen and widen, forcing the wicked dictator in 1991 to reinstate the multiparty system in the country and release all political prisoners. Indeed, the reinstatement of the multiparty system broadened and deepened the struggle for the national democratic struggle, which opened the gate for freedom of speech, press and association, and for human rights movement.

Among the most important developments of the '90s were: **1)** The DTM-Mwakenya leadership conference; **2)** Multiparty electoral politics and Mwakenya's Stance; **3)** The expulsion of the Dar clique of liquidators; and finally **4)** Revival and rejuvenation of the party within the country.

The DTM-Mwakenya Conference

After the release of the remaining leader of DTM from prison in 1988, there was an urgent need for the movement to meet, assess and review the situation, and draw up new tactics and strategies. But where could the meeting take place? Certainly not in Kenya where the ban on meetings of more than three persons was still enforced; where the arrest, torture and imprisonment of patriotic Kenyans were still the order of the day, and where convict prisons and detention centers were full-to-overflowing with patriots. Since the majority of the DTM-Mwakenya leadership was in exile

Mwakenya: The Unfinished Revolution

in Europe and North America, New York City was chosen as a venue. The conference took place on October 20-22, 1991 at Maina wa Kĩnyattĩ's residence.

The majority of delegates who attended the conference were members of DTM, including Shiraz Durrani, Ngũgĩ wa Thiong'o, Kamoji Wachiira, al-Amin Mazrui and Maina wa Kĩnyattĩ. Willy Mutunga (now Kenya's Chief Justice) was in Canada and was invited, but indicated that he belonged to another third force, the Law Society of Kenya. Shortly after that, he and others formed the Kenya Human Rights Commission—a liberal, petty-bourgeois organization heavily funded by the Western financial institutions, among them Ford Foundation. The Dar delegates, Kĩbacia and Kĩnyua, were expected to attend the conference, but instead, they emailed their ideas. Edward Oyugi (now member of the Orange Democracy Movement) did not attend the conference; he was in Africa and could not be reached. Koigi wa Wamwere, Sultan Somjee, and Amin Kassam were not invited to the conference because they had been expelled from the party for failing to follow the party's discipline, rules and regulations. Koigi formed his own underground party, the Kenya Patriotic Front, and then in 2002 dissolved it. Next, he joined a liberal petty-bourgeois party, the Kenya National Democratic Alliance (KENDA), and unsuccessfully ran for the Office of President. Likewise, Adhu Awiti was not invited to the conference because he had joined the UWAKE, which remained in its formative stages and finally withered. He then crossed to the rightwing side; he and Raila and their followers joined Moi's anti-Kenyan regime in 1991. Awiti was appointed a government minister and Raila the KANU General Secretary and minister for Energy. As the KANU General Secretary, he became the mouthpiece of the murderous dictator. In 2001, a bunch of these rightwing compromisers and opportunists were kicked out of KANU by dictator Moi. They formed the Liberal Democratic Party (LDP), a rightwing bourgeois party, with Raila Odinga as the party spokesman. But Awiti and Koigi were not the only ones who crossed to the Right. Many leftwing intellectuals, some of them who were our comrades underground and in prison, began to consider ways of attempting to get themselves back into the neocolonial

Mwakenya: The Unfinished Revolution

system. Some of them became NGO activists sponsored by the imperialist democracies. They were, and are, unabashedly in the business of promoting imperialist's political and cultural agenda in our country. Others joined the newly formed rightwing political parties and were elected to the reactionary, anti-Kenyan parliament. Still others, wrapping themselves in the national flag, became loudspeakers for imperialist democracy and leaders of the pro-imperialist human rights movement. In a word, they were, and are, the fifth columnists for Anglo-American imperialism in our country. There were others—opportunists and pretenders—who, even to this day, continue to claim that they are members of Mwakenya-DTM despite the fact that they do not participate in the party activities or pay their membership dues. Our party rule is very clear: a party member who fails to take part in regular party activities, fails to attend party meetings, fails to pay membership dues or fails to do work assigned by the party for six successive months without good reasons is regarded as having given up his party membership.

The conference took place as scheduled. Most of us had not seen each other since June 1982, so we embraced each other, shook hands and shared the joy of comradeship and the dream of a socialist fatherland. Ngũgĩ chaired the conference and Maina was the recorder. Mũmbi wa Maina was the hostess. The conference deliberations were constructive and businesslike. After analyzing the world situation in general and the Kenyan people's struggle for democracy in particular, the conference delegates decided that in order to strengthen the party and its organizations, there was a need to reorganize the party anew, including the Central Committee. For that purpose, the conference resolved that Ngũgĩ, Maina, Kamoji, al-Amin, Shiraz, Kĩbacia, Kĩnyua, Mwangi Thuo and Warũirũ Mũngai be members of the MK Central Committee. The conference resolved that the party would have three main centers. **1)** the externally-based center, which would be the central authority of the party and would consisted of five members—Kamoji, Maina, Ngũgĩ, al-Amin and Shiraz; **2)** the Dar Center under the leadership of Kĩnyua and Kĩbacia, which would form the bridge between the central authority and the home front, and **3)** the Home Front

Mwakenya: The Unfinished Revolution

Center, which was under the leadership of Mwangi Thuo and Warũirũ Mũngai and which had as its main task to coordinate the activities of the party within the country. In the party files and documents, the home front is referred to as the "Inside," the Dar center as the "Outside" and the central authority as the "External."

Parallel with the reorganization of the Central Committee, the Central Secretariat of the party was transferred from Dar to New York City under Maina wa Kĩnyattĩ's directorship. Simultaneously, Shiraz was appointed the Publicity and Information Secretary of the party. His main task was to produce the Party journal, *Mpatanishi*. Ngũgĩ was re-appointed as the party's spokesperson, and Maina the Party Administration Secretary. In the process, Ukenya was dissolved and its members and branches incorporated into Mwakenya. Abdilatif Abdalla, who was the Ukenya chairperson at the time, was appointed to the MK Central Committee. These changes were intended to invigorate and strengthen the party leadership and its organizations and, more importantly, to return the party to the MLM line. The new leadership was assigned the responsibility of preparing the party for the armed struggle, drafting a workable and scientific method of recruitment; writing a MLM party constitution and a political, educational, manual for the party cadres.

The issue of changing the name of the movement back to its original name, DTM, was raised by Kamoji. It was collectively agreed that in order to avoid sectarianism and unnecessary intraparty struggles in the party, Mwakenya should remain the official name of the party until a national congress was held to discuss the issue. Apart from that, the conference did not critically review, examine, discuss or analyze the history of the party from 1974 to 1990. As a result, some rogue cadres remained in the party and this led to further damage, weakening the foundation of the party. The party conference also failed to scientifically review and revise the party minimum programme so that it could reflect the political economy of the country, concretize the demands of the oppressed masses of our people, uncompromisingly denounce the politics of ethnicity, and ideologically articulate the basic principles of the national democratic revolution and the MLM theory.

Electoral Politics and the Mwakenya Stand

The '90s also witnessed the formation of the new rightwing bourgeois parties (LDP, DP, FORD, FP, Safina, Sisi Kwa Sisi, KNC, SDP, KENDA, etc.) after dictator Moi reinstated the multiparty political system in the country in a bid to counter the efforts of the national democratic revolution. In 1991, it was officially announced that the 1992 general election would be "open", "democratic" and "fair" and those Kenyans who wanted to run for parliamentary seats should register their parties and follow the rules of the game that the dictator had drawn up. Nothing else was changed. The state remained under the tight control of the KANU dictatorship, whilst ethnic cleansing in the Rift Valley province viciously intensified and patriots were hunted down, put in prison on trumped-up charges and their families disrupted and/or destroyed.

The new parties were no different ideologically from their mother KANU. They were not even able to create the lowest form of bourgeois parliamentary democracy. They were neocolonial parties, ready and willing to serve global imperialism. The imperialist bourgeoisie provided substantial financial and political support to these neocolonial parties, objectively making them, like the KANU party, middlemen, commission agents and junior partners of international capital. Through their backward, narrow nationalism and ethnic affinities, they splintered the ranks of the anti-imperialist, anti-neocolonial movement, imprisoned national consciousness and paralyzed people's will to struggle for the new democracy and against foreign domination. Their main aim was to weaken and divide Kenyans ethnically so that they could hold them in subjection to and exploited by global imperialism.

In addition to the formation of the rightwing political parties, there was a parallel formation of liberal human rights organizations and non-government organizations funded by the imperialist bourgeoisie, the same imperialists who funded and supported the Moi dictatorship to rape, oppress and exploit our people. These liberal, petty-bourgeois organizations, as mentioned earlier, serve the imperialists in our country by supporting

Mwakenya: The Unfinished Revolution

neocolonial policies and developing rightwing arguments against working class people, class struggle, social revolution and Marxism-Leninism-Maoism. Their ideological platforms are similar to, if not the same as that of, the imperialist U.S. Peace Corps. To put it bluntly, the NGO activists and the human rights advocates are grandchildren of the world imperialists; the imperialists feed them, pay their rents and provide them with anti-Kenyan ideas, which they use to sabotage the national democratic revolution and, above all, to deepen neocolonial culture and foreign domination in our country in the name of human rights. In short, they are running dogs of world imperialism—traitors and betrayers of the homeland.

Whilst the rightwing petty-bourgeois political parties, the human rights advocates and the NGO activists embraced the reinstatement of the multiparty system, the Mwakenya leadership dismissed it as "cosmetic change" and called for the dismantlement of the neocolonial state and the arrest and imprisonment of dictator Moi and his cronies for their crimes against humanity. Correspondingly, the Mwakenya leadership argued that to register the party as an official opposition party would legitimize and strengthen the KANU dictatorship, even as it would weaken the national democratic revolution. The Mwakenya leadership also pointed out that because of the contradictory and conflicting tendencies within the newly-formed rightwing parties—their ethnic chauvinism and neocolonial outlook—the party and its organizations would not establish any working links with them. However, the revolutionary leadership left the door open for future cooperation or alliance with progressive democratic forces within the country and the rest of East Africa. Furthermore, the party leadership made the decision not to participate in the bourgeois electoral politics, but declared that it would continue to operate underground and operate legally through concrete projects, institutions and linkages that allowed establishing extensive and strong roots among the people. It made clear that its programme and goals were, and still are, the creation of a democratic government based on egalitarianism

76

We Failed To Take a Correct Line

There were heated arguments that took place at the party's Central Committee meetings between those who, on the one hand, felt and forcefully argued that we should pack up our political bags and go home, not to register our party, but to campaign for the national democratic revolution and to popularize our party programme among the toiling masses, and, on the other hand, those who strongly felt that we should not participate in bourgeois electoral politics. The bottom line is that, we finally decided not to go home, not to participate in the bourgeois parliamentary elections and not to register our party as an official leftwing opposition party. In short, we stepped aside to let history pass by. To justify our position, we issued two pamphlets: *Kenya Democracy Plank* (1991) and *The Mwakenya Stand* (1992) and secretly shipped hundreds of them to the home front center for distribution amongst the popular masses and party members. We only found out later that the documents were never distributed, since there was no organization to carry out the task. Instead of doing political work, Mwangi Thuo and Warũirũ Mũngai were in the bar lavishing. It was also found out later that there were zero cadres recruited, but Mwangi and Warũirũ would send letters and reports to the party Central Secretariat claiming that they had more than a hundred cadres in the party and had established new party cells in Nairobi and other major towns in the country and would demand more money for the recruitment project, food, rent and transport. During the Mau Mau movement cadres who were involved in embezzlement and diversion of party funds or in politics of falsification were liquidated once they were discovered.

At any event, did the party leadership take a correct line by refusing to participate in the bourgeois parliamentary politics? Was it ideologically and strategically correct to abandon the democratic movement that our party had given birth to, leaving it to the reactionary, pro-imperialist bourgeois parties and their NGO allies? After rigorously studying our party documents, will the next generation of Kenyan revolutionaries dismiss us as "Leftwing doctrinaires" and dump our party documents into the garbage can of history? Looking back now, our refusal to participate in electoral politics only isolated our party from the great majority of our people, confused and disoriented the party cadres, members, supporters, and sympathizers, and made it easier for national reactionaries, liberal compromisers, NGOist flunkeys and other pro-imperialist elements to take over the democratic movement and use it to push their bourgeois, pro-imperialist agenda. Lenin forcefully argues:

> When the opportunity arises and the struggle has not reached the stage of armed confrontation, the revolutionary party of the working class is obliged to make use of bourgeois parliament in order to become better organized to build a firm foundation among the working class, and progressive petty-bourgeoisie, to unite its forces for overthrow of the bourgeois state. If the proletarian party rejects parliamentary politics, it isolates itself, it restricts its opportunities, and it paralyzes the revolutionary process and makes the struggle for national liberation more difficult, if not impossible. Only after the bourgeois parliament is weakened by its contradictions, the proletarian party can now organize its forces for the armed struggle.

Again Lenin explains,

> A party which shuts itself up in its own shell, isolates itself from the masses, and loses, or even relaxes, its connections which its class is bound to lose the confidence and support of the masses, and, consequently, is surely bound to perish.

It is a fact of history that the proletarian center cannot tail in the wake of the revolutionary process and seriously call itself a communist vanguard party.

The Dar Liquidator Clique Expelled

Despite the reorganization of the party and its organs, the Dar center violated, on several counts, its assigned role of coordinating activities between the central authority and the home front. In the first place, the Dar center, without consulting the central secretariat, continued issuing reckless, anti-Moi pamphlets, publicly attacking other externally-based

Mwakenya: The Unfinished Revolution

Kenyan democratic organizations and individuals, misleading the party cadres and misrepresenting the party to friendly foreign embassies, fraternal organizations and friends. Second, the Dar center had a history of corruption and prevarication. This included: **a)** embezzlement and diversion of party funds; **b)** nepotism and extensive dependence on money for political work; **c)** lack of accountability of expenditure, fake investments and conduits for funds; **d)** lavish living, prostitution and heavy drinking; **e)** disbursement and extensive misuse of funds; and **f)** practice of the politics of deception and falsification. Third, the center General Secretary Kĩnyua and his accomplice Kĩbacia behaved like common sergeant-majors when dealing with the rank and file members of the party. Cadres and members who opposed their undemocratic practices, deviations and corruption were expelled from the party; others, frustrated by the deviation line taken by the center leadership, cancelled their party membership and walked away, never to return. As a result, the party membership in Dar center shrank from 20 in 1987 to 3 in 1990. In spite of the decline of membership, the center leaders continued to claim a large membership. Like their home front accomplices, they would send fake names of members to the Central Secretariat and demand more money for running the center. This devious and reactionary trend was not discovered until 1991 and by then, it was too late to repair the damage done to the party or cure the psychological pain inflicted on many comrades by the reactionary clique. In concrete terms, the rule of the party was, and still is: that one should not tell lies or distort the truth; that one should respect other comrades; that one should not mislead the people of Kenya; and that one should not use the party as a vehicle for self-enrichment.

Whilst it would be untrue and dishonest to suggest that the Dar clique in any way was on the payroll of the enemy, the information the clique printed and publicly distributed without consulting the central authority was rather disturbing. For instance, on July 1, 1990, the Dar clique printed a leaflet, *"Moi must be Overthrown Violently"*, and secretly distributed it in Kenya and to foreign embassies in Dar es Salaam, including the Embassy of the United States. The leaflet was nothing but demagoguery, posturing, and

Mwakenya: The Unfinished Revolution

ultra-left phraseology. Again on July 17, 1990, without authorization, the Dar ultra-left clique, with the collaboration of the home front leadership, printed and distributed another leaflet in Nairobi, entitled, *"It is Armed Insurrection"*. The leaflet, which had no support of the working class in the city or the country at large, called the unarmed and unorganized population to kill government security forces, despite the fact that between the people and the government stood the army of the dictator, armed with the best weapons supplied by the NATO countries. In brief, the leaflet reads:

> Attack the enemy using stones, bows and arrows, pangas and simis, guns and petrol bombs...kill chiefs, Kanu youthwingers, Special Branch and CID officers. Grab by force their guns, seize military hardware and equipment from security forces to be used by our armed groups...Confront authorities everywhere and make towns and country ungovernable. Defy all orders and directives from the government officials.

Further defying the authority of the Central Committee, the Dar clique in August 1991 printed and distributed another pamphlet, entitled, *"Mkombozi-Mwakenya"*, which was intended to create sectarianism and factionalism within the party and disunite the externally based Kenyan anti-imperialist front. The pamphlet leveled an unprincipled attack on some progressive and patriotic Kenyans living in exile, dismissing them as reactionaries who "are alienated from the political realities of our country." Simultaneously, it tried to devalue the Mau Mau movement by claiming that it lacked scientific revolutionary theory, organization and leadership. Moreover, its claim that *Mkombozi-Mwakenya* was the organ of the Defense Forces of Mwakenya was a complete fallacy; the party did not have such a component.

These ultra leftist tactics not only isolated the party from the progressive petty-bourgeoisie, workers and peasants, it also undermined inner party secrecy, unity and discipline, made it hard for cadres do the party work in the country, exposed the internal weaknesses of the party and made the work of dictator Moi's secret police easier. Further, it made it very

Mwakenya: The Unfinished Revolution

difficult to convince many of our supporters, friends and the people of Kenya in general that the party was not infiltrated by dictator Moi's secret police. Indeed, the language of violence used by the Dar clique helped the dictator to justify his bestial cruelty against the captured "Mwakenya terrorists" and "Marxists" and to harass and terrorize the working class people in their homes and on city streets. This resulted in strengthening the neocolonial regime and its imperialist allies, even as it weakened the anti-imperialist, democratic movement. In October 1991, the Dar liquidator clique was expelled from the party and the center was closed down. After the expulsion of the Dar clique, the Central Committee found out that the home front leadership was not only a replica of the Dar clique, but its caricature. The home front leadership, like the Dar clique, thrived on falsehood, corruption, deception, debauchery and prostitution. To avoid being investigated by the party leadership for their showy style of life and the extensive misuse of the party funds, Mwangi and Warũirũ cancelled their party memberships, refused to handover party documents and files, closed down the party business (electrical store in Nairobi), divided the cash and the remaining stock among themselves and disappeared, leaving the party within the country in such a deplorable state, that to rebuild it was an immensely difficult task.

Revival and Rejuvenation of Home Front, 1992-1996

The party, within the country was restored to the ideological path and methods of the parent body, the December Twelve Movement, after the expulsion of the Dar clique and the cancellation of the party memberships by Mwangi and Warũirũ. This was followed by the appointment of Karĩmi Nduthu the national coordinator of the home front. Under Karĩmi's leadership, the party inside the country was revived and rejuvenated; the communications between the home center and the Central Secretariat was increasingly improved, the recruitment of new members was intensified, old party cells were revived and restructured, and new party centers were constructed in Nairobi shantytowns and in the rural areas of the Rift Valley and central Kenya. In a report Karĩmi sent to the party Central Secretariat

Mwakenya: The Unfinished Revolution

in August 1995, he pointed out that,

> To grow we must recruit. We must bring new blood in the organization. It is therefore the duty and responsibility of every member to bring a new member in the organization. Some members don't recruit because they don't think that is their jobs. This elitist behaviour must be stopped...We must have two types of membership: Core membership and general membership. The core membership (cadreship) should always be strong, committed and ideologically clear; it is the engine of MK. General Membership is our training ground for party cadres. The masses are the sea where we fish for new members.

Karĩmi made political education the centerpiece of the party programme. Constantly, he urged party cadres to combine theory and practice in their political work, to read and understand the history of our people and the geography of our country and to comprehend the global politics. He pointed out that in order to bring about the revolution there must be an ideological leadership at its center. Simultaneously, he insisted that before a new recruit was made a full member of the party, he must read and clearly understand the seven fundamental goals and objectives of MK as defined in its *Draft Minimum Programme*, pp. 21-25. In order to understand Mwakenya's stance on the electoral politics and multiparty system, he organized weekend study sessions of the party cadres to read, discuss and analyze party documents (*Pambana, Cheche Kenya, Kenya Democracy Plank* and *The Mwakenya Stand*). Since Marxism-Leninism-Maoism is the most scientific and revolutionary truth, Karĩmi instructed party cadres to read Marxist books, particularly the works of Marx, Lenin, Mao, Che, Castro and Cabral. On the issue of coalition and alliance, Karĩmi argued that,

> We have to form a united front with other Kenyan progressive and patriotic organizations and movements in order to defeat Moism and to neutralize the reactionary opposition parties and the imperialist-sponsored human rights organizations. But we can only form a united front with other Kenyan progressive movements if we are strong

Mwakenya: The Unfinished Revolution

to define and defend our party's ideological tactics and strategies, otherwise we would lose our ideological identity and character and compromise our basic programme. We have made it very clear that our party will never change its colour; it will remain red.

Correspondingly, Karĩmi stressed the importance of discipline and secrecy, respect and honesty, collective responsibility and moral cultivation of the party member, self-sacrifice and hard work in the party. He vehemently opposed the extensive dependence on money for political work and the misuse of party funds, nepotism and ethnic politics. In fact, during Karĩmi's leadership, corruption, prostitution, debauchery and prevarication in the party were things of the past.

Apart from rebuilding the party, Karĩmi was compiling reports for the party on the government sponsored ethnic violence in the Rift Valley and on the strikes by tea farmers, protesting the failure of the regime to remit their pay for the crop. In addition, he was doing research on the role of women in Kenya's war of independence for which he had been commissioned by the Mau Mau Research Center in the United States, and was working fulltime as the Secretary General of the Release of Political Prisoners (RPP), a human rights organization. Without exaggeration, he was the most active cadre of the party in the country and his courage was second to none. His passion, his commitment and dedication, his energy and courage, deepened the party's revolutionary spirit. However, his movement and activity did not escape the evil eye of the dictator's secret police. On March 7, 1996 he wrote to Maina wa Kĩnyattĩ in the United States:

> Recently, the secret police have been following me. I think they want to harass me to weaken my resolve. It is certainly psychological warfare. I suspect the regime has never forgiven me for my MK membership. They know that I have always stood firmly behind the party's agenda, a clear focus, and a courageous membership that is always ready to confront the regime over human and democratic rights! They can follow me as much as they want, but they underestimate me if they think they can intimidate me and force me

Mwakenya: The Unfinished Revolution

to abandon the struggle for democracy and social justice. But let this not worry you, I can handle it.

These were Karĩmi's last words. On March 23, 1996 at midnight, they came for him, broke his apartment door, went straight to his bedroom and savagely struck him on the head with an iron bar while asleep. He did not have a chance to defend himself. It was a painful death. They took nothing from his apartment. As the killers were leaving, with Karĩmi's blood dipping from their hands, they told a neighbor who witnessed the monstrous killing that they had to kill Karĩmi because he was an enemy of dictator Moi and the government. These savage monsters are still at large, working in the police department, their wages paid from Kenyan taxpayers' money.

Karĩmi's death was enormously felt in the entire anti-imperialist movement in Kenya. Many painful tears were shed. By killing Karĩmi, the enemy robbed the party of one of its most active, committed, and courageous cadres. He was preparing to go abroad to study the science of guerrilla warfare and the philosophy of dialectical materialism when the enemy assassinated him. *Karĩmi Nduthu: A Life in the Struggle,* published by the party in 1998, "is a celebration of the immortality of Karĩmi's selfless dedication and the strongly held convictions of this truly remarkable Kenyan patriot". Kenyan revolutionary youth should read this book. Karĩmi lives.

The death of Karĩmi was followed by the resignation of al-Amin Mazrui from the party. In a brief note he sent to the party Central Secretariat, al-Amin stated that he was unable to devote any time to the party duties because of his heavy academic responsibility. Shortly after that, he joined the Kenya Human Rights Commission. Njenga wa Gĩkang'a, MK representative in Sweden, replaced al-Amin in the party Central Committee. Simultanously, he was appointed the party Finance Secretary. In 2000 a new, youthful leadership was elected to the Central Committee.The change of the leadership injected youthful blood into the party leadership and gave the party fresh oxygen. Parallel with that, the name of the party was changed

Mwakenya: The Unfinished Revolution

to Mwakenya-December Twelve Movement (Mwakenya-DTM) "so as to reflect correctly the history, continuity and the mainstreams that have gone into making it". It is important to mention here that the change of the party leadership witnessed the resignation of Abdilatif Abdalla and Shiraz Durrani from the party. According to chateaubriand, "There are men associated with every phase of a revolution; some follow it through to the end, and others begin it but do not finish it."

The Path to Power

The Moi-KANU repressive regime, which for years bragged that it would rule the country for the next hundred years, was finally removed from power by the people through electoral politics in 2002. The people elected Mwai Kĩbaki, a spineless, center-right bourgeois politician, to run the Second Republic. Kĩbaki took over the government when everyone in the country was scared and worried. The future of our country looked bleak. The economy was imploding. Harvests were catastrophic and nationwide peasants and pastoralists were starving and dying.There was no jobs for millions of the working people and the corruption was the official policy of the ruling class, while poverty and misery were rampart among the great majority of our people. On top of that, the ethnic politics was on the rise and reactionary politicians were calling for war against the "enemy tribe" (meaning 41 tribes against one), whilst Moi and his men were conducting ethnic cleansing in the Rift Valley region. Yet the eyes were on the new president. He would turn the country around, the people said.

The people expected that the Kĩbaki administration would put the country out of its economic crisis—initiate land reform, create jobs for the working class, arrest and imprison dictator Moi and his cronies for looting the country's wealth, order the arrest of corrupt politicians and have them imprisoned, overhaul the corrupt state bureaucracy, provide clean water and healthcare to the people, combat foreign domination and, most significantly, empower the people by giving the country back to them. This did not happen, and the people nationwide were angered; they felt

Mwakenya: The Unfinished Revolution

betrayed. At the same time, the ethnic struggles for seats in parliament and State House have been intensified, ethnic hatred and backward politics escalated and the contradictions among the rightwing, ethnic political parties dangerously sharpened. But as these backward, ethnic struggles for power intensify, as the bourgeois contradictions become more apparent; it will become more succinctly clear that nothing has changed in Kenya since the removal of dictator Moi from the State House. Nothing is new. So long as any of the rightwing political parties occupy leading positions in parliament and the State House, so long as their ideological outlook holds political leadership, the fundamental interests of the Kenyan working people will be increasingly compromised, and betrayed. What's more, the country, particularly the Kenyan economy, will remain under the imperialist tyranny of Bretton Wood institutions—the World Bank (WB), the International Monetary Fund (IMF), and the World Trade Organization (WTO). Fundamental changes are what our people are demanding, not handouts from the imperialist democracies.They want revolution and not imperialist, neocolonial democracy.

On balance then, the Mwakenya-DTM leadership believes that only a truly revolutionary democratic system controlled by Kenyans, guided by MLM and guarded by a proletarian army can bring fundamental changes in the country—liberate the people from foreign domination and national oppression, overhaul the corrupt neocolonial system, combat ethnic and chauvinist nationalism, and establish an egalitarian system. This means class warfare. We, the people, must be prepared.

Part Two

WPK/DTM Documents, 1974-1985

Some men are more dangerous dead than alive, even when those who fear them cut the hands from their corpses, burn their bodies and hide their ashes.

Fidel Castro.

The first Conference of Kenyan Marxist-Leninists, Nairobi, 1974

The First Conference of Kenyan Marxist-Leninists was held in Nairobi on December 22-23, 1974. The following delegates were present: Comrade Kamau, Comrade Kiprono, Comrade Makau, Comrade Ochieng' and Comrade Wasige. Comrade Kamau chaired the meeting. After vigorous discussion of the neocolonialist oppression imposed upon the Kenyan people by the imperialists through a handful of lackeys and the glorious history of the Kenyan people's struggle against colonialism and imperialism, the Conference made the following resolutions and recommendations:

I. Setting up a Proletarian Center

After an analysis of world revolutions, in general, and the Kenyan people's struggle for freedom in particular, the Conference came to the conclusion that emancipation from imperialism was impossible under the bourgeoisie. It hailed the National Democratic Revolution (NDR) begun by the Kenyan people after the Second World War and condemned the Kenyan neocolonial rulers for betraying the people. The Conference concluded that the NDR could only be completed by the proletariat, led by its own party, in alliance with the peasantry, and with the support of other revolutionary sections of the people. The experience of the delegates also pointed to the necessity for a center to coordinate the movement against the imperialists and their local agents.

The First Conference of Kenyan Marxist-Leninists, therefore, resolved to set up a proletarian center to be called the Workers' Party of Kenya (WPK). The Conference resolved that Comrade Kamau, Comrade Ochieng', Comrade Wasige, comrade Kiprono and Comrade Makau be made full members of the WPK because of their rich experience in proletarian political work.

The conference further resolved that the above-mentioned five comrades be members of the Party's Central Committee. Comrade Wasige was elected interim chairperson of the Central Committee; Comrade Kamua, the General Secretary; and Comrade Makau, the Party Treasurer. The Conference resolved to defer other nominations for membership and candidate membership to the first meeting of the Central Committee.

II. Constitution

The First Conference of Kenyan Marxist-Leninists discussed the Draft Constitution of the WPK and, after some amendments, recommended it for adoption.

The Conference resolved that the word "communist" should be avoided in mass propaganda because bourgeois propaganda has distorted its meaning and it creates a negative response among the middle class and backward sections of the working class. But the Conference stressed that the Party should never deny that its ideology is communist. If Party members or candidate members captured by the neocolonial security agents, should fearlessly declare their commitment to communism and loyalty to the WPK without betraying the Party's secrets.

III. Membership

The First Conference of Kenyan Marxist-Leninists recommended that members of Party units to be placed in one of four categories:

A. Supporter: A supporter of the party should be a progressive person who sympathizes with the aims of the party and does not engage in such action as would be prejudicial to the party.

Mwakenya: The Unfinished Revolution

B. Friend: A friend of the party should have, in addition to the above, participated actively in promoting the party's aims. Wherever a specific party unit has engaged in mass work, a friend of the party should also have participated in such work.

C. Candidate Member: A candidate member of the party should have worked actively in setting up and expanding a party unit. His commitment to communism should have been proved in the courage of this activity. He should have shown willingness and ability to work under communist discipline. He must be a member of one of the party organizations.

D. Member: A member of the party should have served at least a year as a candidate member. His commitment to communism and loyalty to the party should be beyond question. He should be capable of applying the party's general line to specific concrete conditions without the necessity of constant supervision.

The First Conference of Kenyan Marxist-Leninists noted that candidate members and party members should both be subject to the conditions for membership laid down in the party's constitution.

The Conference further recommended that only full members should be given the right to vote and the right of access to the contents of all party documents. Candidate members should have no right to vote, but should have restricted access to documents at the discretion of the Central Committee. Both candidate members and party members should pay monthly dues. The Conference recommended that these should be at least five per cent of net revenue. The Conference delegates recommended that such dues should be waived or reduced in specific cases where a candidate member or member is unable to pay them.

IV. Setting up of Party Organization

The First Conference of Kenyan Marxist-Leninists (FCKML) recommended the setting up of party branches. The delegates also discussed and resolved to set up units through study groups based on specific concrete conditions.

Mwakenya: The Unfinished Revolution

The Conference analyzed the classes in Kenya and resolved that an investigation be carried out into the working and living conditions of the following sections of the people, as a first step towards mobilization of the revolutionary elements in Kenya: workers on tea, sisal, sugar, coffee and pineapple plantations; forest workers and rural intellectuals.

The FCKML concluded that these sections represented the points at which the bourgeoisie was weakest and, therefore, most vulnerable to attack. The Conference decided that while some sections of the people were receptive to revolutionary propaganda, conditions were as yet unfavorable for their mobilization. The Conference worked out specific mobilization tasks for the immediate future. The tasks included: **a)** recruitment of new members; **b)** set up a Party center in every province; and **c)** constructing underground Party Headquarters in Nairobi.

V. Propaganda

The FCKML resolved on printing arrangements for the production of party propaganda. It recommended that an internal newspaper be produced as soon as possible. It recommended that the Central Committee discuss the question of an external newspaper when the party had developed to a level where underground distribution became possible or the political situation changed so that a newspaper could be distributed openly. Further, it recommended that, in the meantime, party branches carry out propaganda among units under them and that leaflets be used for this purpose. The FCKML also recommended that the Central Committee arrange for the production of documents, which could be used as a basis for discussion and mobilization in the party's study groups.

VI. Working Documents

The First Conference of Kenyan Marxist-Leninists discussed the following working documents:

Mwakenya: The Unfinished Revolution

a. The Need for a Proletarian Party
b. The Nature of a Proletarian Party
c. The Ideological Nature of our Party
d. The Need to combat revisionism
e. Outline of social classes of Kenya
f. Guideline on cell-formation

All the documents were recommended for adoption as Party documents for distribution to candidate members and members. Documents (c, d and e) are not included in this volume because they were eaten by termites in underground party archives.

VII. Secrecy

The First Conference of Kenyan Marxist-Leninists resolved that conditions were not ripe for publicizing the formation of the Workers' Party of Kenya. It, therefore, resolved that the existence of the Party be made known only to candidate members and Party leadership until the Central Committee decided otherwise.

VIII. Adoption of the Minutes

The FCKML resolved that the documents and minutes containing resolutions and recommendations of the Conference should be brought up at the first meeting of the Central Committee for approval. The documents and minutes containing the conference resolutions and recommendations were approved by the Central Committee of the Workers' Party of Kenya at a meeting on February 1, 1975.

Note: To avoid being identified by the secret police, those who attended the Conference used cover names: Comrade Kamau (Amin Kassam), Comrade Kiprono (Koigi wa Wamwere), Comrade Makau (Kamoji Wachiira), Comrade Ochieng' (Maina wa Kĩnyattĩ), and Comrade Wasige (Adhu Awiti).

Constitution of the Workers' Party of Kenya
December, 1974

General Line of the Workers' Party of Kenya

The Workers' Party of Kenya is the political party of the Kenyan proletariat. The basic programme of the WPK is the complete overthrow of the neocolonial regime and its exploiting classes, the establishment of the dictatorship of the proletariat in place of the dictatorship of the bourgeoisie, and the triumph of socialism over capitalism. The ultimate aim of the party is the realization of a classless society—a communist society.

The WPK is composed of the advanced elements of the proletariat and other revolutionary elements in society. It is a rigorous vanguard organization leading the proletariat and the revolutionary masses in the fight against the class enemy.

The Independence for which our people shed blood has been betrayed by a handful of compradors that now oppress every section of our society. They are responsible for the increasing rape of our resources by the imperialists. They have enabled the imperialists to make huge profits by keeping down the wages of workers. They have imposed considerable hardship and misery on the peasantry by letting them suffer the brunt of imperialist-induced inflation. They have further oppressed the peasants directly by seizure of their land, leaving many of them landless. The manipulation

Mwakenya: The Unfinished Revolution

of cooperatives, that are only beneficial to the bourgeoisie, and forced donations to various projects, from which the money is drained off and solely used for the benefit of the ruling compradors and their imperialist allies, is not what will save the Kenyan working people and their need to rid itself of neocolonial exploitation and oppression.The immediate task of the WPK is therefore to complete the national democratic revolution, which the compradors betrayed. To achieve this, the WPK will mobilize and unite with all anti-imperialist forces in the country and abroad.

The compradors have deliberately sharpened contradictions among the people in order to carry out their exploitation. Our people have been divided into nationalities, gender, races, and regionally, in order to hide the economic contradiction, which is the principal contradiction in our country. The WPK opposes all attempts to create such divisions. Our people have a common enemy in the imperialists and their agents in Kenya. The party's task is to unite revolutionary and progressive elements into the movement and lead the struggle against all forms of exploitation, if a national democratic revolution is to ever come to fruition.

The WPK upholds proletarian internationalism; it firmly unites with genuine Marxist-Leninist parties and groups the world over, unites with the proletariat, the oppressed people and nations of the whole world, and fights together with them to overthrow imperialism headed by the United States as well as modern revisionism with the Soviet revisionist renegade clique as its center, and the reactionaries of all countries, and the abolishment of the system of exploitation of human by human around the globe. Our goal is the emancipation of all humanity.Members of the WPK, who dedicate their lives to the struggle for a classless society, must be resolute, fear no sacrifice, and surmount every difficulty to win victory.

For this fundamental aim, the WPK is constituted and has established the basic rules of its organization in the following Constitution:

Name

Article I: The Name of party shall be the Workers' Party of Kenya (WPK)

Membership

Article II: Any Kenyan worker, poor peasant, lower-middle peasant, petty-bourgeois revolutionary intellectual, or other revolutionary element who has reached the age of eighteen and accepts the constitution of the party, joins a party organization and works actively in it, carries out the party's decisions, observes party discipline and pays membership dues, may become a member of the Workers' Party of Kenya. Before an applicant is considered for party membership, he/she should have worked, at least one year as a candidate member of the party, supported the party financially, and belonged to one of its organizations.

Article III: Applicants for party membership, or candidate membership, must go through a highly selective procedure for admission, individually. An applicant must be recommended by a member of the Central Committee (CC) and be examined by a representative of the CC, who must seek the opinions of the masses whenever possible. An applicant's application is subject to acceptance by the party branch and approval by the Central Committee.

Article IV: Members and candidate members of the WPK must:

a)   Study and apply Marxism-Leninism-Maoism in a living way.

b)   Work for the interests of the majority of the people of Kenya and the rest of the world.

c)   Be able to unite with the great majority of our people on a principled basis.

d)   Consult with the masses when matters arise.

e)   Be bold in making criticism and self-criticism.

Article V: When party or candidate members violate party discipline, the party organization at the level concerned shall, within its functions

Mwakenya: The Unfinished Revolution

and powers and on the merits of each case, take appropriate disciplinary measures—warning, serious warning, removal from the posts in the party, placing on probation within the party, or expulsion from the party, and, where necessary, each matter shall be taken up by the Central Committee. The period for which a party or candidate member is placed on probation shall not exceed six months. During this period he/she has no right to vote or elect or be elected.

If a party or candidate member asks to withdraw from the party; the party branch concerned shall remove his name from the party roster and report the matter to the Central Committee after ascertaining the legitimacy, or lack thereof, of the withdraw. Proven renegades, enemy agents, and opportunist elements must be cleared out of the party and not be readmitted under any circumstances, once such has been proven.

Organizational Principle

Article VI: The organizational principle of the party is democratic centralism. This principle combines centralized leadership and the greatest degree of discipline with the fullest discussion and struggle over line and policy within the Party and the selection and political supervision of party members on the basis of MLM.

The leading bodies of the party, at all levels, are elected through democratic consultation. The whole party must observe unified discipline—the individual is subordinate to the organization; the minority is subordinate to the majority; the lower level is subordinate to the higher level; and the entire party is subordinate to the National Party Congress or to the Central Committee chosen by it when this Party Congress is not in session.Party members have the right to criticize party organizations and leading members at all levels and make proposals to them. However, such criticism should be voiced, or documented, only within the party through proper channels. No party matters shall be disclosed to non-party members. Leading members of the party have the responsibility to ensure that all such criticisms are considered carefully and, where true, mistakes rectified.

Mwakenya: The Unfinished Revolution

It is essential to create a political climate in which there are centralism and democracy, discipline and freedom, both unity of will and personal ease of mind and liveliness.

Article VII: The leading bodies of party organizations at various levels are membership meetings of the party branches at these respective levels. When these cannot be held, the working committee elected by them has the authority to make party decisions. Meeting concerns, between party branches, are subject to approval by the Central Committee.

Central Organs

Article VIII: The highest leading body of the party is the National Party Congress, which is authorized to make political and organizational decisions that are based upon the entire party and its membership. When it is not in session, the Central Committee, chosen by it, has the authority to make party decisions and lead the party. Regular National Party Congress shall be held every five years. Under special circumstances it may be postponed or convened before it is due.

The National Party Congress delegates are chosen by their respective units under the careful guidance of the party. The following powers and functions are assigned to the National Party Congress:

- To hear and examine the reports of the Central Committee and central organs.
- To determine the party's line and policy.
- To amend the party constitution.
- To elect the Central Committee members.

Article IX: Between National Party Congress, the Central Committee is the highest authority of the party, representing the party as a whole, and as such has the authority to make decisions and take actions necessary for the welfare of the entire party and to act upon all problems and developments occurring between the National Party Congress. Furthermore, it is

Mwakenya: The Unfinished Revolution

responsible for the enforcement of the constitution and execution of the general line adopted by the National Party Congress. The decisions of the Central Committee shall be binding on all party branches, organizations, and members.

Primary Organizations of the Party

Article X: Party branches must hold high the great red banner of Marxism-Leninism-Maoism, give prominence to proletarian politics, and develop the style of integrating theory with practice, maintaining close ties with the masses of the people, and practicing criticism and self-criticism. Their main tasks are:

1. To lead the proletariat in alliance with the peasantry and revolutionary and progressive sections of the people in the struggle against exploitation and for socialism.

2. To give constant education to the party members and the broad revolutionary masses concerning class struggle, and lead them in fighting resolutely against the class enemy.

3. To propagate and carry out the policy of the party, implement its decisions, and fulfill every task assigned by the party.

4. To maintain close ties with the masses, constantly listen to their opinions and demands, and wage an active ideological struggle within the party so as to keep the party life rigorous.

5. To take in new party members, enforce party discipline, and constantly consolidate the party organizations.

Party and Mass Organizations

Article XI: A party member working in mass organizations—trade unions, co-operative society, community or professional associations, etc.—must promote and strengthen the unity of workers and peasantry, distribute party literature and should not compromise the party ideological line.

Mwakenya: The Unfinished Revolution

Authority

Article XII: The Workers' Party of Kenya and its organizations and branches are not responsible for any expressions of political opinion, written or verbal, except such as issued by the authority and approval of the National Party Congress.

The Need for a Proletarian Party
February 1, 1975

We have agreed on the need to set up a central organization of Marxist-Leninist-Maoists to lead the Kenyan revolution. But what sort of an organization should we build, which will survive all attempts of the bourgeoisie to destroy it, while mobilizing the revolutionary and progressive sections of our people around it? Historical experience shows clearly that the organization must be a communist party constructed on Marxist-Leninist-Maoist (MLM) line. This party must conform to several basic principles:

Firstly, it must be a party of the proletariat, prepared to lead the proletariat in alliance with the peasantry and other revolutionary sections of our people in seizing power from the bourgeoisie and creating a socialist and, ultimately, a classless society.

Secondly, Marxism-Leninism-Maoism should guide the party in all its policies and actions. Its basic programme should be of MLM revolution. This programme should be based on the concrete conditions of our country and not on mere dogma picked up from books. But the party should be prepared to learn from, and apply, the experience of other revolutionary movements. We should remember that only a party which has a truly revolutionary theory based on the conditions in Kenya will be able to lead the Kenyan revolution to victory.

Mwakenya: The Unfinished Revolution

Thirdly, the party of the proletariat must also have a method of work that is Marxist-Leninist-Maoist. It should practice the mass line by maintaining links with the revolutionary masses, learning from them and serving them, and it should adopt an internal policy of criticism and self-criticism by which it corrects wrong tendencies and exposes alien class elements within itself.

Fourthly, the party should integrate theory with practice. Its theory should be based on a summing up of practice and should be tested in practice. Thus, if a theory is incorrect, practice will show this and the party will be able to correct its policies and develop the revolution to a higher stage. On no account should the party be built on the basis of intellectual theories formulated in isolation from the historical reality of our society. It is only the party built on the basis of integrating theory with practice that it will be able to mobilize the advanced sections of the proletariat and earn the trust of the broad masses of the people. Fifthly, the party must have a programme of political action on which tactics can be based. The programme must set out the changing immediate tasks in the context of constant long-term aims. In this way, a consistently revolutionary line will be maintained and the danger of an opportunistic short-term outlook will be lessened. If we maintain a constant revolutionary line, the broad masses of the people are bound to be attracted to the party because it will be the only organization standing like a rock in the stormy seas of class struggle.

Sixthly, the party's actions should be based on MLM analysis and its methods of class struggle be determined by this analysis. The party must struggle against all opportunistic theories within itself and outside, which threaten to divert the revolutionary movement. This truth has been born out by the experience of all communist parties. While engaging in struggle against opportunism, however, the party should be careful not to succumb to ultra-left tendencies and doctrinairism. Criticism should be based on the stage of revolution and its purpose should be to advance the revolution, not to establish party members as experts on Marxism-Leninism-Maoism. Seventhly, the party should train its members to make the revolution their very life and subordinate their interests to those of the revolution. Members should be trained to regard the party as supreme and to put the interests of the party and the masses above those of any individual. They should be trained to wage a tireless struggle against incorrect ideas and actions. Only then will the party be able to lead the revolutionary masses while serving them and not become an overlord over them. Lastly, the party of the proletariat should be prepared to seize power from the comprador bourgeoisie whenever the opportunity occurs. Lenin said on the matter: "I continue to maintain that any political party generally, and the party of the advanced class in particular, would forfeit its right to exist, would be unworthy of being regarded as a party, would be a wretched cipher in all respects, were it to refuse to assume power when it had the opportunity to do so."

Comrades, these are basic principles that a party of the proletariat has to conform to if it is to lead the revolution successfully. Let us build the party along these lines and the comprador bourgeoisie and their imperialist allies will never be able to stop the revolution.

The Nature of a Proletarian Party
February 1, 1975

The Workers' Party of Kenya (WPK) is a Leninist vanguard party. It is organized on the principles of *democratic centralism*. Democratic Centralism is fundamentally aimed and intended to combine the fullest discussion of and struggle over the party's ideological line, with firmest and most disciplined implementation of that line. In essence, the principles of democratic centralism include, first and foremost, the subordination of the individual to the party as a whole, of lower party levels to higher ones and, finally, of the entire party and its organizations to the National Party Congress, or to the Central Committee chosen by the National Congress, when it is not in session.

A centralized party—organizationally *tight* while flexible and supple—is absolutely necessary if we are to carry through the national democratic revolution. But remember democratic centralism embodies and reflects more than just the political necessity facing the party and oppressed millions of our people; it also reflects the MLM theory of knowledge and understanding, and the correct relation between *knowing* and *doing*. It must be based on historical reality of our country. If this is downplayed or incorrectly interpreted, understood or applied, the political and ideological character of our party will change and eventually will be turned into a bourgeois party. Our ability to combat opportunists and crooks, liberals and reactionaries, pretenders and agents provocateurs, to recruit the most

Mwakenya: The Unfinished Revolution

progressive and advanced Kenyans, to formulate and implement a correct line based on our party constitution, pivots on our party's democratic centralist form of organization.

Our party must concentrate and correctly synthesize the experience gained by the membership overall in struggle, in other aspects of practical work among the masses and in the theoretical struggle within and outside the party. Its organizational structure must serve that process. This is the key in enabling our party as a whole to forge a political and ideological line reflecting our anti-imperialist, anti-neocolonial stance. It is for this fundamental purpose that inner-party democracy and struggle over the correct line are encouraged. Democratic centralism therefore is a means for developing the most correct possible concentration of the broadest experience and struggle, and a correct political line which to guide the party cadres. Such democracy is dialectically linked to party discipline, secrecy and commitment. Once the line is collectively determined, the party's cadres must unite as tightly as possible in carrying it out—and this is for two basic reasons. First, because the struggle in which we are involved is deadly serious, and once a particular initiative is decided upon by the party, *steel-like unity and courage* are necessary to see it through. More fundamentally, centralism is necessary to give the party ideological direction and discipline, to combat liberalism among the membership and within the party leadership. In other words, the centralized leadership of the party is necessary to really making the party line a material force and deepening and developing its ideological line. Through this process, democracy and centralism are not walled off from each other—there is democracy in centralism and centralism is democracy. The party ideological line is the key link in their strength, interpenetration and mutual transformation. For instance, struggle over line throughout the party—an aspect of democracy—cannot be anarchic but must itself be led, if it is to actually contribute to developing and deepening an ideological line of the party. There has to be central guidance within the party to figure out what path to take, what the terms of the struggle are, where knowledge must be advanced to deepen the ideological line (or programme) without

Mwakenya: The Unfinished Revolution

consistently and constantly summing up experience gained from applying that line to practice through its cadres. The new line must collectively be discussed and accepted by the majority in the party.

Fundamentally, this takes on a concentrated expression in the dialectical relationship between higher and lower levels of the party and the principles of top-down leadership. While the basic units/cells of the party are critical to the overall formulation and implementation of the line (or the programme), no single unit/cell can develop or formulate the overall line. That is the responsibility of the Central committee. The CC is dialectically linked to the ideological development of the party cells and branches. We believe that collective, concentrated party, leadership based on democracy and comradeship gives the party strength; it also prevents the party goal from being derailed or betrayed by opportunists, reactionaries, turncoats, or sheer human weakness of the party cadres. The central bodies of the party are most able to develop a correct line not only because their members are most advanced ideologically, and not only because the division of labor within the party demands that they devote more time to studying major theoretical and political questions, but also because the party's highest bodies are in a position to synthesize and sum-up the experience of the entire party. The line struggled out there and within the party concentrates the struggle at every level on the highest possible plane. Here then is the ideological basis for the subordination of lower to higher levels.

At the same time (and this is an important point), none of this *guarantees* that the party leadership will always be correct; that too would provide a mechanical view in which truth could be ensured merely by organizational structure. Obviously, it can't, and there is a danger to create a *dictatorship* in the party. For that reason, party members when in opposition to the party as a whole and its leadership, are not only allowed to reserve their opinions and appeal to higher bodies (including the Central Committee itself). But if convinced of the rightness of their opposition, the urgency of the matter and that an opportunist line has been consolidated, they also have the duty and responsibility to come out and oppose the incorrect line. In fact, going against the tide of an opportunist line and respecting the discipline and

Mwakenya: The Unfinished Revolution

secrecy of the party are themselves dialectically linked. Both are aimed at preserving the correctness of the party line. Both of them formed the ideological frame of the party. The basic and underlying principle involved here is the responsibility of every member of the party to pay attention to the party programme, to struggle as vigorously as possible for what they understand to be correct, and to carry out that struggle with the object of a deeper party unity and discipline around the correct line, and of hardening the party cadres. Struggle and contradiction are the lifeblood of the party. Mao teaches us that opposition and struggle between ideas of different kinds constantly occur within the party; this is a reflection within the party of contradictions between classes, and between the new and the old in society. If there were no contradictions within the party and no ideological instrument to resolve them, the party's life would wither.

In essence, the contradictions between the party and masses, and the intraparty struggles against subjectivism and sectarianism, push forward the development of the party line throughout its existence and deepen the discipline and commitment of its members. But the ways in which these contradictions express themselves change radically as the struggle is intensified, and when the party seizes state power and becomes the leading force in society as a whole. This is a crucial stage, when every member must be a party watchdog to make sure that the revolution is not derailed, compromised or betrayed.

Guidelines on Cell-Formation
March 2, 1975

The primary aim of our work at this stage is to work towards a strong people's organization, to guide and direct the anti-imperialist struggle on a correct line. Cells are an important first stage towards party building. Such cells should be built among workers, peasants, pastoralists and other progressive sections of population. The immediate aim is to propagate correct political orientation, to popularize our party and Marxism-Leninism-Maoism and develop proletarian cadres who can carry out revolutionary work in all areas of our country.

Membership: The first important requirement is that prospective individuals recognize as a result of their political and conscious experience in our society and their understanding that there is need for revolutionary change in the country if the Kenyan people are to be liberated from the forces of neocolonialism. Such an individual must therefore be basically anti-imperialist, anti-capitalist, and patriotic, genuinely committed to change, and willing to take part in committing to change. Thus racists, tribalists, ethnic chauvinists, opportunists, comprador agents and other reactionary elements in our society cannot be allowed membership. Degenerates and elements hostile to the proletarian revolution must have their membership terminated and physically expelled.

Incorrect ideological orientation, lack of clarity on some political issues should not stop a patriotic individual from being considered as long as he has the

Mwakenya: The Unfinished Revolution

honesty to exchange ideas democratically and learn. In no circumstances should an anti-communist be considered. It must be established (through rigorous investigation and observation) that the prospective candidate is not a police agent. Individuals who have participated in any leadership or organizational capacity in progressive practical situation, e.g., strike, demonstration, merits consideration if such an individual fulfills the other requirements. In all cases, the particular individual must be such as to be trusted to maintain complete secrecy of organizational and membership details.

Recruitment: A member of a party branch having spotted a possible recruit should seek to establish acquaintance and friendship on political basis but simply as individuals. During such period the above-mentioned membership requirements can be established. It will be clear if the individual is reliable or frivolous, if his social practice is compatible with serious political work. Obviously, an individual with such bourgeois excesses as over-drinking and partying, prostituting, male chauvinism and misogyny should be encouraged to transform himself first. The member will report on the prospective candidate and keep the party branch up to date on his/her progress. After a period of at least 4-6 months of such observations, the party branch will, after examining the candidate's practice and development, as reported, approve or otherwise. After this, the party branch member concerned will then seek approval in his own cell. The party branch leader, after the approval of his own cell, will forward the name and history of the new recruit to the Central Committee of the party.

Leadership: The Communist cadre will be the overall leader of the cell or party organization. He must struggle for the party's ideological line and ensure that the cell or branch is subordinate to the party. Through him/her the party can encourage political development of the entire unit and the individuals by ensuring struggle against incorrect and harmful tendencies. He is the model to be emulated by the newer recruits. As such, he/she must lead the entire unit to aspire towards Marxism-Leninism-Maoism by first practicing it himself or herself. He must report on all activities, development, and change in the cell or branch to the central organ of the party. The party branch leaders are approved and chosen by the Central Committee.

Our History Should Not Be Distorted

EDUCATION AND IMPERIALISM

Education and University must serve the majority of Kenyans: A Preliminary Critique of the University, Education, Culture and Writers in Kenya, October 20, 1976

Editor's note: This publication was first printed by *Utafiti*, Vol. II, No. 2 (Dar es Salaam, 1977) and serialized by Tanzania's newspaper, *The Nationalist* (1977). The same document was reproduced by *Maji Maji, No. 32*. University of Dar es Salaam, January, 1978. Because of its historical importance, we have decided to reprint it in this book.

Preface

Between 1973 and 1975 it gradually occurred to a group of us university students that there was a serious academic disease spreading rapidly in the university lecture-rooms, seminar-rooms and auditoriums. The carriers of this disease, we felt, were some lecturers and professors who were supposedly "educating" us and dishing out "knowledge" to us. The disease they were spreading, under cover of "learnedness" and "academic authority", was definite servility and continuation of foreign, even anti-Kenyan styles and materials. Apparently convinced that the best concepts are foreign ones (from USA, UK, etc) and only occasionally paying lip service to the initiative and needs of the 15

Mwakenya: The Unfinished Revolution

million "other" Kenyans, these gentlemen of learning perverted the truth about Kenya's past, present and future potential. Many even announced to us in various classrooms that Kenya's salvation lay in becoming more and more dependent on the imperialist masters "because we have no skills, no capital, no wealth". They called this higher education. We knew it was wrong, because it did not agree with what we saw everyday with our own eyes in Kenyan society.

We asked ourselves many questions; we found out that we were ignorant of the real answers regarding our society's problems. Our 12-plus years of *education* had provided little basis for the real knowledge or truth. We practically had to start from zero. We started during serious investigation as to the nature of the university as an instrument of learning and social development in a neo-colony. We assigned serious work to students both at Nairobi University and Kenyatta University College. We have researched a great deal; we have obviously missed much, especially the innermost secrets that are locked in the imperialist controlled guardrooms and safes to be made available only to the select, trusted few. We have confined ourselves to published material—there for everyone to see and evaluate.

We had to restrict our work to local academics and artists and avoid foreign ones because our findings are that the latter are generally outright perpetrators of imperialist thought. One or two may be liberal or even anti-imperialist, but these are the rare exception. Most of the foreign academics, it is our experience, are racist in addition to their other imperialist functions. Indeed, some departments are nothing more than an extension of bigger ones in the USA or UK. No research needed. Our concern was the local collaborators. They are more devious, more difficult to grasp; hence they need deeper investigation. It is now clearer to us that under the difficult undemocratic conditions, such as lack of basic freedoms (speech, association, etc.) prevailing in Kenya today, most Kenyan academics and artists have, albeit individually, upheld a fairly correct political stance. Others may have minor weakness, but are generally pro-Kenyan. We therefore isolated the extreme ones in order to strengthen the better ones. All along, as is made clear in the introduction we have used one guideline

111

Mwakenya: The Unfinished Revolution

and one standard of judgment; who is the audience? Foreign (imperialist) oriented or Kenyan (patriotic) oriented? Who are the main enemies of the Kenyan people? Who are their friends? Where is the dividing line? How do we unite the allies in order to isolate and attack the enemy?

We all agreed that we must lay no claim to being "objective" without purpose. We are partisans. We are shamelessly biased towards the Kenyan people according to above guidelines. Our learned "teachers" will accuse us of "academic infidelity". We have already accused some of them of treason. We have chosen only some sections of learning. Many other areas remain. This is just an example of what we should be doing. These other areas and individuals should be researched and similarly exposed. This is not a private document with "rights reserved". Use it, copy it, enlarge on it as long as your aim is clear—to defend Kenyans, to unite them, to expose their enemies, to learn from facts in order to find truth, use truth to help advance the people's cause, to oppose imperialist propaganda disguised as education, to make every single classroom a forum (a mini-Kamũkũnji) for trying these anti-Kenyan, untouchable academic barons.

Introduction

The entire world is in a state of great turmoil. Everywhere one looks on the globe and sees eruptions of mass discontent and social upheaval as people violently fight old corrupt and oppressive social orders. In the main these eruptions, rebellions and revolutions are most intense here in Africa, in Asia and in Latin America—the neo-colonies. Enraged peoples have militantly risen up, taken up the gun and set about to regain their national destiny, to reshape their history. Vietnam, South Africa, Angola, Guinea-Bissau, Congo, Djibouti, Cambodia, Zimbabwe, Ethiopia, Namibia, Palestine, Mozambique, and Laos, are a few examples that come to mind. Their principal enemy is the imperialist superpowers, particularly the treacherous U.S. imperialists.

Many lessons are to be learned from these glorious victories in the flames of armed national liberation struggles in Indochina and Southern

Mwakenya: The Unfinished Revolution

Africa. The greatest lesson is that it is not the one or two imperialist superpowers, aggressors armed to the teeth that matter. Rather it is a determined, united, politically aroused people—no matter how small, no matter how poor. This is now a simple fact of modern history. This fact disturbs imperialists. Mortally scared U.S. imperialist messenger Henry Kissinger and his friends—Smith and Vorster frantically dash back and forth to try and buy time, protect their loot and install puppets in order to delay history. Fearlessly, Africans rise up even more fiercely from Umtali to Windhoek to Cape Town, from Pretoria to Soweto through to Salisbury and back again to Soweto—an irresistible and inevitable historical trend.It is in this light, in this context of historic revolutionary change, that our own country, Kenya, must be seen.

Kenya is a neocolonial state. Our tremendous natural wealth, our vast labor might are all *completely* controlled by an alliance of foreign capitalist interests and their faithful local assistants (i.e., comprador bourgeoisie). This evil alliance is Kenya's number *One* enemy. Up to a few years ago, British imperialism was our principal enemy. Due to the rapid decline of British imperialism, U.S. imperialism has taken over control and even assigned warplanes, warship "loans", fresh large-scale student airlifts out, and professors and spy airlifts in. All in a grand effort to ensure a permanent lease here. Our prostitute comprador class, anxious to get a little wealth out of it has jubilantly obliged and even gone out of its way to assist in the takeover, and ensure a happy homecoming for the new imperialist grand master. "We recognize the need for protection by a strong democratic, friendly power . . ." they shamelessly proclaim. Protection from whom? We ask. "Communists are all around us, they want our land". "The communist threat", the comprador controlled newspaper reply. Now the imperialist U.S., UK, West Germany, France, and Japan rejoice. Their comprador agents are singing their songs and profits are high and rising— Lonrho records 12 million pounds net profits. Shell, Esso, Inchape, and E.A. Industries, similarly.

Protection from whom? From angry Kenyans tired of landlessness when compradors grab all the land, tired of rising prices and static wages, sick of corruption by big government and cabinet officials, tired of unemployment and endless lies about development and progress when all around blatant evidence abounds to show how we are sinking deeper and deeper in wretchedness. "Stay calm; love each other; obey the law, the Provincial Commissioner, the district commissioner, and your chief, contribute everything to harambee projects, go to church daily; don't rumor-monger (i.e., don't think); leave all politics to us (means shut-up); go back to the land (any land but our huge estates). The compradors repeat and repeat endlessly. In the end if people angrily rise up, if they speak up, the comprador government jails them on false charges; they are detained; they are killed or tortured brutally in Patrick Shaw's Torture Chambers. Police and the General Service Unit (GSU) are unleashed and best to blood entire villages. Today Kisumu, Nakuru, Eldoret, Nairobi, Mombasa, etc. are police states—martial law, state of emergency.

There is democracy at its best wisest leadership in Africa. Aren't you happy you are not in Chad or Tanzania?" Scream the imperialist owned comprador newspapers.

Only by you staying peaceful and submissive", the imperialist owned newspapers advise the Kenyans, "will foreign investors, foreign tourists, foreign experts bring us wealth and develop to our country so we have pipelines brimming with oil, smooth roads to nowhere, shiny new skyscrapers filled with big officials, new hotels, new churches and new exotic religions, this is progress. Foreign investors are welcome.

This is what we mean by neocolonialism in Kenya. This is social reality on which this document is based and which forms the basis of reference. This is the point of departure for serious discussion of Kenyan society, especially discussion regarding answers to the following questions:

6. How did we get to this?

7. How shall we get out of it?

Mwakenya: The Unfinished Revolution

In order to create confusion regarding the above questions, the British colonialists designed a useless educational system. Their curriculum sought: **1)** to isolate educated Kenyans from the rest of the "uncivilized" population; and **2)** to spread lies and falsifications about our history and our future in the form of higher education. After 1963 when the current comprador class took over, they continued the same enemy teaching and called it "education". Now the U.S. imperialists have helped them to design new modernized (i.e., servile to the American system) curriculum and provided "assistance" in the form of books, professors, dormitories, etc. Why? In order to create new diversions and confusion among Kenyans seeking answers to: **1)** how did we get to this and **2)** how shall we get out of this?

Education is in the realm of ideas—thought control. It is an important aspect of a people's culture. As oppressed, occupied people cannot change their condition by using enemy ideas, enemy thought, enemy education, and enemy culture. U.S. imperialists know this and have decided to mount a major onslaught or invasion on the ideas front, i.e., on the cultural front. If they succeed, they think, if we are so confused, misdirected, cowed and depoliticized then they hope they won't have to use guns and bullets as in Vietnam [and now in Iraq] to protect their profits and their faithful comprador assistants.

Nairobi in 1976 is Saigon in 1962, complete with local Ngo Diem, Cao Ky and Van Thieu puppets. That is how the U.S. imperialists have done.

Culture, of which education is an inseparable part, is a reflection of the economic and political order. It is dependent on the social order and in return influences the social order. *There is no culture or education independent of economic and political situation in a country.* In neocolonial Kenya, oppressed and dominated economically, the dominant culture and education is equally neocolonial, dominated by U.S. imperialist culture, but having its own comprador cultural agents.

In these oppressive circumstances what should all genuinely patriotic Kenyan intellectuals be doing? The answer is clear: *rejecting*. Rejecting in total imperialist culture and miseducation, leading to exposing the lies and

Mwakenya: The Unfinished Revolution

falsehoods, fighting weapon for weapon relentlessly to oppose enemy ideas that keep our people and nation shackled to foreign parasites, *representing correctly, militantly, uncompromisingly* the objective political, economic, historical and social *realities*; representing firmly our people's demands for complete democracy, complete national self-reliance, employment, higher wages, lower prices and rents, an end to imperialist exploitation and oppression. To represent our people's demand for complete democracy is our role as patriotic Kenyan intellectuals.The other part of our role is to create a fighting culture in defense of our country, our future, our national wealth, and our people—a new literature and art of the people. A fighting culture that sings praises of the national struggle of all-Kenyan people against foreign domination and against comprador oppression. A culture of our own national forms cherished by the Kenyan people, with a view to promoting national self-respect and self-confidence, enhancing their fighting will and strengthening their conviction of sure victory. To persist against imperialist cultural oppression, to combat ideological infiltration and spiritual subversion, to carry out a long fight against servile, slavish neocolonial culture, which paralyzes the will of the people, drains their self-confidence and leaves them vulnerable. Finally, to take all necessary steps to thoroughly eliminate the harmful influence already wrought.

Many people have dared and have stood firm. Much has been disseminated to expose and to urge on. We hail this and happily join hands. We especially hail the nine university students from Nyĩrĩ, Embu, Kĩrĩnyaga, Mũrang'a, Nyandarwa, Nakuru and Kĩambu who as early as 1973 exposed GEMA as a *hũmungaati* clique of anti-Mau Mau, anti-Kenyan elements; and also *Mwanguzi* (Number 2, May 1975) for showing the correct nature of KANU and GEMA as dangerous pro-imperialist organs. However, we notice that indeed many intellectuals have accepted their imperialist assignments slavishly. Some have stood aloof, indifferent and sneering while many others have plunged right into defending, spreading and apologizing for imperialism. There are therefore *two* types of intellectual—patriotic, revolutionary anti-imperialist ones and the servile, pro-imperialist anti-Kenyan ones.

We direct most of this document against a few fairly typical representatives of the latter group. They are the foreign agents who have believed the imperialist message written on the baccalaureate degrees. This message reads:

Now dear native, you are educated—very educated. You are at the zenith of achievement. Run fast and leave far behind you the dirt and the mud of the illiterate, the hunger, the disease of your rural unlettered kith. Join the world that we shall allow you into, be comfortable, seek pleasure and fame, be content and never oppose us.

Demand from your rural kith the best of life and give nothing in return, instead demand yet more. Remember to insult them, they stink of sweat, mock their suffering, they look sickly and underfed. Deride them for their children, then at the end demand that they worship you, that they respect you and that they seek your learned advice. Then confuse them, hound them, shout them down, impress and awe them, cow them and make sure they never so much as question your authority or your right to be on their backs or our right to be on all of you—this is the natural order of things, this is human nature, willed by gods and sanctified in both the Bible and the Constitution that we kindly gave you and both of which are protected, along with us, by your wise government.

These anti-Kenyan intellectuals serve U.S. imperialists well. They are told that they are the cream of their society. To carry their *dairy* metaphor further, the majority of Kenyans is therefore skimmed milk and when capitalism churns the cream a bit, out comes *butter* that is the fat, greedily big bourgeois that rules with the imperialists. The majority Kenyans is to them *manure* to thrive on. These anti-Kenyan, pro-imperialist intellectuals who arrogantly declare they must be maintained comfortably, paid highly and must do little or no useful work to benefit anyone, are the cultural agents of imperialism—our great enemies.

Now let us look at what these agents of imperialism write about us in Literature and History.

Literature

Writing is an important aspect of a people's culture. Stories, poems, plays, essays can very effectively carry messages and redirect thought and hence action. Having defined Kenya's current social reality, our point of departure in looking at Kenyan writing is: Who is the audience? This is a fundamental question. For whom is a literary author writing? For what purpose is he writing? Whom does it serve? During British occupation aspiring Kenyan writers were aping European literature. Their audience was European intellectuals. To be the "African James Joyce" was the ultimate recognition. Many rejected this and started portraying African situations, patriotic, anti-colonialism and nationalism and later after 1963 even opposed neocolonial subordination. This was one type of socially conscious, committed writer. The other type was the opportunist, get-famous-quick type who found easy employment from foreign anti-African intrigues. For this type, writing was simply on abstraction, uncommitted to reality and requiring complete disengagement from the majority of the people "in order to be objective". We have chosen three such authors: Taban Lo Liyong, Charles Mangua, and David Maillu.

These three individuals represent fairly typically the two general forms of dangerous writing in our society: **1)** outright worship of imperialism and fascism by Taban Lo Liyong and **2)** despondency, sexual vulgarity, aimlessness, unquestioning by Mangua and Maillu. We shall look at them in that order.

Taban Lo Liyong

Taban is the literary version of Ali Mazrui, Gibson Mutiso and William Ochieng'. He is one of those African intellectuals who bask in the sunshine of the applause they get in the West for constantly abusing themselves and the African people. But Taban, who since 1969 has vomited over ten volumes of literary exercises denigrating the liberation efforts of millions of African people, has outstripped even the most enthusiastic defenders of imperialism by calling for the end of African people as a race. In his book, *The Last Word* (1969), he defines the hundred per cent African as the one who has in fact ceased to be African:

Mwakenya: The Unfinished Revolution

A racially and culturally mixed person is the universal man: All is in him: he identifies with all: he is kith and kin to all other Homo sapiens. This leads us to a super-Brazil. He will have slant eyes, kinky hair, Roman nose. Red Indian knight-errantry, democratic folly, dictatorial changeability, Maori tattoos, uses English as a toll for rebuilding Babel tower. All these (and more) will make the hundreds per cent African: the descendant of Zinjanthropus, the culturally and racially mixed man of the future.

Behind the verbiage is a race death wish, a call for race suicide. He also has a deep hatred of his own father presumably because his father was not white or at the very least did not absorb imperialist white culture by going through Gulu High School, Sir Samuel Barker School, the National Teachers' College, Kampala, Harvard University (USA), Knoxville College and the University of Iowa. So, unlike his son Taban, the old man never read Homer, never appreciated Western abstract art, never listened to classical Western music and, of course, never made love to a white woman. In the same book, *The Last Word*, this is how he greeted the news of his father's death:

> *The news of my father's death reached me in North Carolina. I had finished the first session of summer school, subject: European systems of government and cultural anthropology (my minor was to be Sociology).When I enrolled for the second session, I took a graduate course in Shakespeare, taught by the Harvard-trained professor they have down there; and the first part of American Literature—that intellectually richest period comprising the puritans, the metaphysicians, the transcendentalists and such figures as Emerson, Thoreau, Whitman, Hawthorne, Melville.*

> *Hip hip hip! Hurray! Hurray! Three cheers! For dad is dead. And with his death is removed that ruling against my studying art.*

Thus the death of his peasant father who must have scratched the earth hard or sold his last remaining cows to pay fees for Taban can only bring cheers from our *famous* artist to be. What was this art apart from dabbling in paint?

119

*English was thenceforth my major. Written English is art. My long
time aim was to go back to art.*

Through all his utterances, Taban has a pathetic Mazrui-like faith in
the "civilizing" capacity of European languages, hence, according to
him, the need for upgrading local speech into English:

*We are also the people to create new African English and African
French. These will give us the facility we need for transmitting our
culture and wisdom.*

Thus, for the sake of the freedom to study English Literature, Taban
celebrates the death of his own father! What he was really celebrating
was the death of his African parentage, which must also have carried the
symbolic death of the African world from which Taban so desperately
longed to be freed from.

In all his books (vomit because they are not even well written), the
universe is divided into *two:* there is the "civilized" developed Western
world with its enviable technology and culture and music and literature
and women. Then there is the "primitive" under-developed world of
African peoples recently emerged from the dark ages (no doubt because of
colonialism). In 1969, he wrote:

*Those ages were really dark—that is a fact of history; it can't be
denied. But we don't celebrate the skull-hunting days anymore, just as
Hawthorne would not like to see witch-burning days at Salem glorified.*

In 1971, recalling the image of his father also symbolizing pre-colonial Africa. He wrote:

My father's image is abroad. The skull-hunters are here.

This juxtaposition of his civilized imperialist west and the primitive
peasant African world forms the philosophical base and framework of all
Taban's abuses and utterances and sick solutions for Africa's problems and
all parroted out of his racist and fascist Western intellectual mentors.

Mwakenya: The Unfinished Revolution

He never lets us forget how "highly developed" the imperialist countries are in *everything*. He does not, of course, ever stop to wonder which classes in the imperialist countries have pocketed the wealth generated by this development in science and technology. If he does, it obviously does not worry this *famous* artist of the English language. He does not stop to analyze how this wealth was obtained. It does not seem to worry him that this so-called development was a result of the exploitation, oppression and suppression of African, Asian and Latin American peoples. It does not seem to worry this artist that by the same token Africa which in the 14th Century was more highly developed than most parts of Europe (except in gun-power) has remained poor because its human resources (slaves), its natural resources and the fruits of the labor of her people have all been going to enrich Europe, the United States and Japan. For our sage and artist there is no dialectical connection between the wealth of imperialist Europe and the U.S. and the poverty of Africa. For him USA, Europe and Japan are developed, no doubt because they have higher cultures and languages, and what Africa can do to develop is to sell herself even more firmly to USA, Western European and Japanese imperialisms. This is the advice he gives us in his book, *13 Offensive against Our Enemies* (1973). Enslave yourselves to imperialism, and the imperialist, your masters, will help you to develop. Let us quote a few examples from the book:

1. *Say you want to affect political changes in Southern Africa. We would choose a white party (Vorster's party) to groom. We would work hand in hand with that party;*

2. *Say again you want to affect changes in Angola and Mozambique. We would work hand in hand with Portuguese politicians in Portugal;*

3. *Say again British is being troublesome . . . We would work through the ex-colonial servants. Capture the Labour government preferential treatment if they strangled Enoch Powell, if they will be good to Africans, Asians, West Indies . . .*

Following in the footsteps of such spokesman of colonialism as Elspeth Huxley, Robert Ruark, Karen Blixen, Taban Lo Liyong

121

Mwakenya: The Unfinished Revolution

can never see African people as being able to do anything on their own, for themselves, despite the historical evidence of victorious African people's revolutionary struggles against slavery, against colonialism and even despite the glorious, triumphs of armed Africans in Mozambique, Angola, Guinea-Bissau, Sao Tome, etc., it is Taban's bootlicking admiration for, and identification with USA, Western Europe and Japanese imperialisms that makes him advise Africans to yoke themselves even more firmly to Western imperialism including Zionist Israel. It is this identification with imperialism that makes him in his latest book, *Ballads of Under-development,* praise white South Africa:

> *South Africa will be great*
> *for the sake of contrast.*

His admiration for imperialist robbery of Africa and of the Third World is only matched by his even more fervent admiration for and complete identification with the culture of imperialism.

When Taban was in the USA as a student he used to write for CIA publications like *Africa Report.* It was then in 1968 that he first published an article in which he abused other African students and called them culturally deprived because they did not seem as mesmerized by imperialist culture as Taban had been. He must have liked the article because in 1969 he reproduced it in his book, *The Last Word,* apparently to ensure that history records his love of USA bourgeois capitalists. He writes:

> *Africans are the most culturally deprived students in the United States. In the first place, they lack an active classical culture of their own. Then political nationalistically inspired slogans... block their participation in other people's cultures. Opposition to things American and Western is another reason that keeps them from exposures to cultural activities in this country. Indifference or apathy or lack of curiosity, and plain laziness makes deprivation total.*

He was horrified that they danced to Highlife and listened to Miriam

Makeba and read Chinua Achebe, Ngũgĩ wa Thiong'o and Cyprian Ekwensi instead of listening to Beethoven and Mozart and reading Homer and Sartre and attending lectures on Cybernetics. He goes on:

The African is only proud of the drums and heartbeats . . . [He] is never tired of the monotony of the Bongo drums, the Kwela Whistles, the sweet voice of the Congolese vocalist Rossignol. So he keeps his mind functioning strictly by arithmetical progression. To elevate it to this geometrical level of functioning he never cares to do. Simplicity.

He called upon the African geniuses (the small elect like Taban himself) to lengthen their necks (giraffe-wise) and taste the fruits of the higher culture of Western imperialism:

We also need higher things beyond the reach or experience of the vulgar and average.

Obviously, Highlife and Miriam Makeba, Chinua Achebe and Ngũgĩ wa Thiong'o and Kwela music were things vulgar and average; for he asks rhetorically:

You, Sir, swaying to your Kwela music in your Harvard dormitory, are you better culturally than your brother in Kilembe mines?

Thus, he ended his famous article by abusing oppressed African workers just as he had abused his peasant father. It is not for nothing then that Taban quotes European racist commentaries on Africa (see *The Last Word*) with approval. He has imbibed imperialist culture in total including imperialist racist distortion of African history and African pre-colonial, pre-capitalist feudal and communal cultures. He hates Africa and African peoples. In *The Last Word*, he writes:

Most Africans have been and still are, as plebeian as Luther was, with well-marked distaste for what they did or what are above them.

His advice is the oppressed African-American nationality in thus for them to turn away from solidarity with "primitive Africa" where only the other day people were skull hunting. He tells them to look up to European achievements for their cultural heritage. To him, does not seem to matter that African-Americans have been in that U.S imperialist culture for more than 400 years without any improvement of their lot; that it was their labor, blood and sweat which built America; that for more than 400 years the African-American working class has been the most exploited and oppressed by the white American ruling class; now the progressive African-Americans are realizing that the only way is for them to join hands with African, Asian and Latin American peoples and all other oppressed peoples in resolutely opposing U.S. imperialism and racism. He tells the African-Americans:

> *Rather than go to the Motherland (means Africa) go to Library, New York Library . . . to look for your African heritage . . . is it not more worthwhile for you to find out who your European fore-parents were? There might be a family legacy somewhere for you or one the state took away on grounds for intestacy.*

Here Taban comes across very well as one of those spokesmen of the African bourgeois intellectuals who have a permanent incurable wish for identification with bourgeois Europe. When Taban tells African-Americans to look for their European forefathers, he is serious, for that is exactly what he himself would have liked to have been—a European child of feudal or bourgeois parentage pickled soft in imperialism.

Further that biological link to bourgeois Europe, Taban tries to become a European child through total uncritical absorption of every aspect of imperialist culture and claim it for his heritage. In the same book, he writes:

> *In the final analysis, after you have stripped the African of his acquired Africanness, you are left with an individual who ticks the way all other human organisms the world over tick.*

To this great artist-intellectual-cum-philosopher, Africanness is an acquired thing. Strip the African, divest him of his skin, and maybe underneath you will find the *universal man* who, of course, is *European*. That is why in the academic debate initiated and vigorously led by Okot P'Bitek's *Song of Lawino,* Taban took Ocol's and Clementine's sides. If you remember

Ocol and Clementine in the poem are the two characters who have taken imperialist culture. Ocol is the one who asks: "Mother, Mother why was I born Black?" And Clementine is the one who tries to rub her black skin off so that she can be a European lady. Ocol is the one who wants to burn all the village poets, who wants to exterminate rural peasant culture root and branch. Taban says about Ocol:

> He [Ocol] says: 'Black people are primitive and their ways are utterly harmful, their dances are mortal sins, they are ignorant, poor, diseased'. Yes, Ocol, Black people are primitive, their ways are harmful; they are ignorant, poor and diseased.

Indeed, Taban can never see the way out for Africa except through African's acquisition of imperialist culture. Again in *The Last Word*, he writes:

> The African who would like to make his mark in this world has to study the American music, the English novel, the European Theatre or the Japanese Noh theatre and their developments.

Africans too give up their jungle talk and rule their countries according to the ways the white bourgeoisie brought.

In his latest pronouncements under the title *Ballads of Underdevelopment*, Taban compares Africa to the five blind men who went to touch the Elephant to find out what it was. His advice is for Africans to touch the Elephant of European imperialist culture, learn from it, and therefore grow. He writes:

> For this world we live in
> We need native exploiters than declaimers
> For this world we live in
> We need native millionaires
> For this world we live in
> We need more Europeans than natives
> For this world we live in
> We need more Jews than Arabs
> For this world live in
> We need more knowledge than ignorance

Mwakenya: The Unfinished Revolution

But we have seen that Taban equates knowledge with imperialism, oppression and exploitation of Africans and the other peoples of the Third World. We should copy imperialism and learn how to exploit and oppress our people even more. He advises us:

The Germans grow by blood and iron. The Japs (Japanese) bloom by trade and atom. The Americans masquerade by trade and subversion. . . No sacrifice is therefore big enough.

In the same book, he writes of his undying admiration of these that grab without fear—like the current greedy native exploiting ruling class here in Kenya, for instance.A common feature of Taban's writing in his identification of the writer with a social dictator. On other words, he sees the role of the writer as one of subjective dictatorship. He writes:

Isn't each writer an arbitrary maker, ordering or reordering the world? Isn't each reader a naturalized subject who submits to each author's dictatorship?

This is not accidental. It reflects the kind of society, the kind of social relationships he would like to see in real life. For Taban, there is no coherence, no sense in this world. There are no laws governing social development. Everything is arbitrary, accidental, isolated. In *The Uniformed Man* (1971), this *famous* artist-cum-intellectual, tells us that order and coherence, ended with Greeks and Romans. Since then, we live in a world of fragments. He writes:

Nature and culture are broken; art which mirrors them can only correctly register broken images.

So since the world is in chaos, the only people who can hold it together are neocolonial elites, exploiters and feudal dictators. Hence, Taban's fanatical salivating admiration for the Elites, the select few, those "fated" to rule, the U.S., Japan, West Germany, and especially the fascists in these countries. This is scattered in all his writings, but summarized in so-called aphorism 320 in *Ballads:*

Dogs love those who beat and feed them. Beating is recognition of their existence.

He identifies imperialism, racism, fascism, exploitation, and oppression with manhood. In an attempt reminiscent of his kind, Eldridge Cleaver, who reduced oppression to vulgar sexuality. Again in *Ballads of Underdevelopment,* he pronounces:

> *Hear the ballad of those born is rule*
> *The huge black rising Gods*
> *They have huge manhood in their trousers*
> *And when their manhood rises*
> *All other men's shrink up*
> *In limpness of all*
> *The hero's manhood dominates the scene*
> *For the will to power lies in the middle region*
> *Upstairs we have calculating machines*
> *Downstairs we always have had*
> *The forces that drives the hammer*
> *Egyptian Pharaohs measured manhood in pillars*
> *The Empire state building made Americans go to*
> *the moon*
> *Only those born to rule*
> *Have manhood big and strong.*

Not surprisingly Taban admires Nietzsche, the German philosopher of Nazi fascism, and, of course, admires Hitler, Nixon and Amin. Every other line is full of Nietzsche. He invokes Nietzsche in every other paragraph. His own writing is molded on that of Nietzsche. In "aphorism" 416 this identity with Nazism becomes complete:

416 last words (Two Versions) Nietzsche: I attack only causes which are victorious—and at times I wait until they are victorious. (1888). Taban: I attack only causes which are victorious—and at times I wait till they are victotious. Year 1968.

Mwakenya: The Unfinished Revolution

A few later, in the same book of Ballads, he writes:

If Hitler read Nietzsche, he understood him.

Maybe Taban is waiting for his Hitler. Or maybe Taban has found one in Amin who incidentally was placed in power by the very people Taban admires and worships: Golda Meir of Zionist Israel, the British regime and the French regime with the blessing of U.S. imperialism. And no doubt Taban will find symbolic parallel in the fact that it was another Taban, Amin's son, who led in the massacre of hundreds of Makerere University students recently.

Taban's complete identification with imperialism, fascism, oppression, the dictatorship of the bourgeoisie over the majority of humanity, the suppression of Africans and African-Americans comes in "aphorism" 495 of his Ballads. He writes:

I wish I were a Ku Klux Klan.

The Ku Klux Klan is an American white fascist terrorist organization responsible for lynching and murdering thousands and thousands of African-Americans since 1865. Taban's books of poems, stories, e.g., *Fixions, Meditations in Limbs, Frantz Fanon's Uneven Ribs, Another Nigger Dead*, etc., emptied of their wise nothing but subjective mysticism, witticism and desperate efforts to appear original through obscurity and sheer bad writing.

But his writings are dangerous because they are peddled in our bookshops, libraries and classrooms. Again Taban is no exception: he is the spokesman of the class in Kenya and Africa that identifies with imperialism. We as students must oppose imperialism in the classroom and in our university curricula. It does not matter if imperialism and imperialist culture are being sold to us by European neocolonialist writers or by African paid intellectual agents. It is all the same cultural imperialism. University departments and teachers and publishers who peddle Taban should explain to us whose agents they themselves are. We must ask them: "On whose

Mwakenya: The Unfinished Revolution

side are you?" on the side of the majority of the Kenyans or on the side of their enemy-imperialism?" To teach us, Taban Lo Liyong and his ilk, without exposing his imperialist connections, which started when he was an undergraduate in the United States, is to support imperialism in Kenya as whole. Taban and writers like him are enemies of Kenyans and African people in general and of all oppressed people of the world.

Charles Mangua

Charles Mangua in 1971 and 1972 published *Son of Woman* and *A Tail in the Mouth*. The late 1960s and early 1970s were momentous years in the world's history. Internationally, the U.S. aggressor in Vietnam, Cambodia and Laos was losing every battle. Her Portuguese ally in NATO was also suffering defeat after defeat in Africa. The capitalist economies were showing the first signal of a disease afflicting them up to this date—thus in 1967 the British pound was devalued by 15 per cent and later the U.S. dollar was also devalued. Internally, all the imperialist countries, especially the United States were faced with massive popular anger against racism, foreign aggression, inflation and unemployment. In Kenya, being directly connected with the U.S. and British economies, the compradors found themselves in a key position, with more power at their disposal, that allowed them to keep the people down—oaths, fake tripartite agreements, assassinations and the formation of GEMA as a grouping of the ruling class, pro-imperialist and anti-Kenyan elements from all sections of Kenya led by the old anti-Mau Mau, and settler assistants of the central Kenya, were key in the appetite of the Western world to keep a tight grip on Kenya as a country, as a strategic position in the world of a continued, but concealed, highly effective colonial agenda. Everywhere Kenyans were asking: What went wrong, after almost ten years of Uhuru? Why are we galloping backwards in every sector of our society? University students were holding demonstrations; workers were striking, etc.

Mangua trying to ignore all this and obviously waiting to make money and fame out of it, came out preaching "you can do nothing—drink, make

Mwakenya: The Unfinished Revolution

more love, steal, kill, laugh at yourself, hate yourself and all the suffering people, be aimless, but do not question. His language and writing style reflect the source of his training—a mumbo-jumbo of U.S. ghetto jive, British cockney, Australian out-back, South African Boer talk; Cowboy and hippy slang all spouting incongruously out of his characters who unbelievably are largely Kenyans in various Kenyan towns. Sound tough; care never—that is life for Mangua in both books.

Basically, Mangua deals with the dispossessed Kenyans whose lives have been disrupted first by the British colonialism and aggression in the fifties and then by the U.S. take-over in the late sixties. Their lives are described as aimless, self-destructive and anti-social. It is on this detailed cataloguing of suffering that Mangua and his publishers base their literary justification that "this prize winning novel is one of the finest and most entertaining piece of writing about contemporary Africa, yet published, a humorous but yet profoundly disturbing commentary on the seamy side of rapid social change".

The two main characters in these books are Dodge (Dad) Kiunyu and Samson Moira. They are essentially identical in their role in Kenyan society despite such details as the former being a Makerere graduate, orphaned son of a prostitute in colonial Nairobi, while the latter is a rural-Catholic trained priest drop-out, who settles into a shady city existence. The time period for both books spans the socially tumultuous decades of the forties, fifties, sixties and early seventies. At no time is it clear what forces are at work in society. We quote the less vulgar passage to show Mangua's general stance and approach:

In my dingy office the most intelligent companions were evil-smelling, cheating bums bothering me for jobs.

I started feeling sorry for myself . . . I hated myself. . . there was something wrong with me . . .

I started to hit the bottle . . . I mean hit the bottle. No half measure. I simply drank myself silly.

I spat on the floor and walked out. That's me I simply can't stand women hissing at me. Women should not hiss at all. I wouldn't be bothered if they spent their whole goddam life hissing at each other—but at me Oh No . . . That is why I spat.

My shoes are number ten . . . I notice with disgust the red familiar dust on them as I walk towards Eastleigh. They are dusty, my shoes. I can't afford shoes polish and the shoeshine boys wouldn't lend me their brush . . . wet pus is making the inside (of the shoe) slippery. God! I hate myself at times. I hate pus. Ruins my appetite, it does . . . I am all confused.

That's me. Plain broke. Broke as a dry twig. Broke as hell. Not a thing. Damn it. And I am a graduate. That is what I am, a graduate . . . that is how helpful education is. Very helpful. Gosh! I am hungry. My name is Dodge . . . and I like your life.

I started dressing smart and what have you. I did not behave like a goddamn taxi-driver. I behave like a gentleman in her presence... Trouble is that I can't help lying sometimes.

One thing led to another. Movies, game parks, picnics, night-clubs and all expensive things that a man resorts when he is trying to impress a woman.

One day we went to the Swiss Grill . . . there was dancing and lots of girls. Three of them were French whores. George told me that they were easy. You got them drinking and dancing and the rest followed.

And on, and on, and on, purposeless obscenity, self-pity, alcoholism, social disorder. Imperialist laud this trash as literary realism. Had Mangua simply stopped there we would have dismissed him as simply capitalizing on the government's "Africanization scheme of removing one top foreigner and replacing him with an African with a similar outlook". In this Mangua was the local pornographic back in a "Buy Kenyan" obscenity campaign. But no! Mangua went on to denounce and abuse our heroes, the anti-colonial Mau Mau guerrilla fighters and the Mau Mau movement of the fifties:

I hated the Mau Mau all along. They are a murderous lot. They are terrible. They hate the Church. I have a lot of confidence in the [colonial] government. . . We had one thing in common though. We hated the Mau Mau. The village is guarded day and night but terrorists still manage to get in.

Describing a guerrilla fighter, Mangua says:

His ears are hidden behind a mass of knotted hair that is the same black-brown colour as his beard. It makes him look as if he were trying to imitate a gorilla . . . and he smells like an oiled goat skin. It is written all over him.

Imperialists say that a writer should be free to write what his genius tells him. They separate the motive of writing from the effect. We reject this. When Mangua insults oppressed Kenyans, then insults their defenders, he is in *effect,* no matter what the motive, declaring his enmity to us. Our concern is effect; we cannot ignore political and social effect. Mangua's literary trash has the direct objective effect of prolonging the life of imperialism in Kenya.

David G. Maillu

David Maillu started writing in the late 1960s. Now he has his own publishing house—Comb Books Publishing Press. This has enabled this writer to produce many books and get wealthy within a very short time. Among his books are such notorious works as *My Dear Bottle, After 4:30, Unfit for Human Consumption* and the recent *No!* Maillu in all his works attacks Kenyans; he uses vulgar language against them and discourages them from struggling for their liberation. He generally portrays people as helpless, incapable of liberating themselves and advocates that they should maintain the status quo and let things go. He writes:

There are no more great thinkers left to show the people the way, all is in chaos. Then I would say let us all share this chaos and bitterness.

Mwakenya: The Unfinished Revolution

Here Maillu advocates that those masses of the people who have the bitterness of the whole unjust system stick to it and those who delight in the chaos (the thieving, smuggling) should be left to enjoy this privilege.

Maillu using his vulgar language attacks woman more particularly Kenyan African women and portrays them as merely men's tools who cannot serve any useful purpose in this society other than satisfying men's sexual lust. He portrays African women as "sex maniacs" whose desire for sex is uncontrollable. Further, he attacks and abuses the African men as devils. He writes:

Lili, this is Africa. If you invite devils to your home, you must give them what they eat.

This pornography writer portrays the whole African people as being savage and unsympathetic:

But some men laughed, not the usual laughter, but the African laughter, which may even come when looking at a dead body.

This "great" and "famous" writer is not concerned with the problems that our people are facing, and the causes of such problems. He simply shies way away from addressing his mind to the root causes of these problems and he simply declares:

Then sins are not yours.

Maillu does not go forward to tell us who is responsible for the suffering of the masses. He only goes further to justify the status quo by declaring:

You know when you are rich; you want all the good things to come to you. This is human course.

In *After 4:30*, Maillu sees the suffering of women as engendered by men. He attributes the suffering of the women to male domination and goes further to advocate that if the men were to be fair then everything would be all right for women. This is obviously wrong. It shows lack of elementary understanding of the cause of the problem. Maillu tells us that it is human to need more when you are rich. This, of course, is the basis of bourgeois exploitation of the world's people. It amounts to the same thing as telling the people to be submissive and not to struggle for their rights, lest they upset the order of God as predestined.

Recently, Tanzania banned Maillu's trash. When a local newspaper sought Maillu's reaction over the banning, all he had to say was that he realized that Tanzania has a different social system and that is the reason why his books had been banned there. This shows us two things about the "great" author: **i)** that Maillu is writing for a definite class in a rotten political system, that he is representing the Kenyan bourgeoisie and imperialists, and that **ii)** Maillu realizes the destructive role he is playing in our society. And for these reasons it would be dangerous for our people and the progressive peoples of the world to attack this writer's works.

In conclusion about these two writers (Mangua/Maillu) we must say that what causes the misery narrated in their books is *not matter of cheap laughter and jokes but national destiny.* Mangua and Maillu want us to laugh at the violence, the vulgarity, obscenity, the alcoholism, and the lust for money. They want no question as to:

What is the root cause of all this? and What is the solution?

According to these two anti-Kenyan writers, the many victims of oppression are themselves to blame for their condition. They are helpless to change their lives for the better—individually or collectively, as they are innately incapable of serious, dedicated collective struggle. All they can do is chase round in circles like a cat after its tail as Mangua eloquently concludes in *Tail in the Mouth.* Who are these miserable people? These are 90-95 per cent of our people. We cannot afford to laugh.

Mwakenya: The Unfinished Revolution

History

For an oppressed people determined to liberate themselves, the study of the correct history of their society is of primary importance to their struggle for liberation. Incorrect, distorted, history is one trick used by oppressors to prolong a people's suffering. What has the recent role of Kenyan historians been?

We have chosen to examine the work of three university historians—William Robert Ochieng', Atieno-Odhiambo, and Godfrey Mũriũki.

William Robert Ochieng'

Our investigations have revealed this man to be an ambitious academic who cares little where his ideas come from or what damage they do to this country's future as long as they serve to disunite Kenyans, confuse issues, apologize for colonizers and all other foreign devils, and in the process ensure his career security by publishing many, many worthless little books. Ochieng's road to the intellectual camp of neocolonialism and imperialism has been smooth, short and straight. He started his academic career as a relatively pro-African liberal intellectual apparently recognizing the need for some revolutionary changes in our country. He provided liberal, unworkable solutions to the questions, which were raised by the social reality of these revolutionary changes. As neocolonialism deepened its hold on Kenya in the late 1960s Ochieng' moved on to an openly opportunist platform, and by 1975 had become a well-finished agent of the full scale U.S. imperialist offensive in Kenya. Of his many publications, we shall largely deal with two: *The First Word* (1975) and *Eastern Kenya and Its Invaders* (1975) in which his political character is typically portrayed.

The First Word

This is Ochieng's most comprehensive statement of his political stand. In it he gives his unqualified support to the phenomenon of "tribalism" and describes its evil practice as: "a healthy psycho-cultural (sic) aspect of our

Mwakenya: The Unfinished Revolution

people". Instead of seeing how our enemies use the politics of tribalism to divide and disunite us, he approves of it as "a very healthy trend" in our country today.

On the issue of nationalism, Ochieng' has given his name to a very anti-African trend by denying that any genuine attempt had ever been made by the Kenyan masses to resist imperialist settlement in our country. Mau Mau, a valiant resistance against British imperialism in the 1950s which was betrayed by the Kanu neocolonial regime, is reduced by Ochieng' to a "mere Kikuyu chauvinist affair". Since, according to him, other nationalities did not fully participate in that phase of Kenya's nationalist struggle, Ochieng' denies the movement its nationalist character. Again, because of the predominant Gĩkũyũ participation and leadership in Kenya African Union (KAU), this "wise" and "famous" historian denies it a nationalist character. On KAU, Ochieng' argues:

> *It is important to correctly evaluate KAU as primarily a Kikuyu political Union, since only among the Kikuyu did the requisites of leadership and social communication exist to the extent needed to support a mass movement. . .in fact they [Kikuyu] were more concerned with the defense of their land than with wider nationalist issues.*

According to Ochieng', KAU's non-Gĩkũyũ members such as Achieng' Oneko, Oginga Odinga, Tom Mbotela, Ngei, Kali, Khamisi, Ofafa, Awori, etc., were Gĩkũyũ puppets. We feel that it is only a shallow pro-imperialist historian who would describe the Mau Mau guerrillas as *terrorists* and KAU as "Kikuyu chauvinist organization".

In an essay copying the style of Martin Luther King, *Towards African Revolution,* Ochieng' pretends to see the need for revolutionary changes in Africa. But goes on to say that revolutionaries who should affect these changes "are as rare as green-eyed Chinese". But even if we had "a few committed African revolutionaries", Ochieng' would still doubt their revolutionary intentions. First, they must obtain Ochieng's clearance because he is not sure whether such revolutionaries would be "committed

Mwakenya: The Unfinished Revolution

to the welfare of the individual". This is the reasoning U.S. bourgeois professors use to oppose Third World Liberation struggles. For Ochieng' a genuine revolution must involve "spiritual love" and change "human values". Love is a class love and not a love transcending classes—that is abstract love. What Ochieng' calls "human values" are in essence nothing more than the illusory, selfish values which are upheld by imperialists and their comprador agents.

Ochieng' attacks, without specifying all "those African revolutionaries who have been brainwashed by leftist communist ideas". Their revolution scares Ochieng' for it would lead to communism like the one practiced "in Communist China has often reduced men to mere cogs in the wheel of the state". This argument reveals Ochieng' as standing on the side of the enemies of the African people and the entire oppressed masses of the world in general.

It is true that if we as Kenyans want to grasp the process of the African Revolution and have a deep understanding of the class forces involved, we should have a certain amount of knowledge of the international situation and the conditions in the imperialist countries, which are contending for the control of our country. To study the African Revolution in isolation and to overlook class struggle as the key link, like Ochieng', is to assist Kenya's enemies—the imperialists and their Kenyan friends.

Ocheing's pro-imperialist world outlook does not allow him to understand the dialectical connection between *Public* and *Self*. He fails to see that communism does not refute the existence of the Self. All it does, and Ochieng' masks this, is to make it possible for people to subordinate their personal interests to the public interests, consequently to bring the collective and the Self into harmony. To conceal his true colors, Ochieng' tries to make a tactical concession by pointing at some obvious defects in capitalism so that he might appear as the neutral objective, know-it-all academic. Phony neutrality (actually spineless opportunism), as has been proved time and again, is the most outstanding characteristic of neocolonial intellectuals like Ochieng'.

Mwakenya: The Unfinished Revolution

Ochieng's analysis of the historical role played by Kenyan colonial chiefs also lays open his political and academic stance regarding major historical events of our country. He writes that:

Throughout the colonial period, especially up to the beginning of the Second World War, African colonial chiefs led the way in radicalism—call it progressivism if you like.

Clearly, Ochieng' wishes to cover up the collaborationist role played by Kenyan colonial chiefs. A modern Kenyan collaborator shamelessly defending his predecessors!

Thus Ochieng' claims that a well-known traitor like Chief Karūri wa Gakure was a nationalist! Yet it has been proved again and again that Karūri, because of his traitorous acts against our people was handsomely rewarded and was eventually made a paramount chief in Mūrang'a. Richard Meinertzhagen an imperialist chieftain and one who was responsible for killing thousands (and thousands) of our people in Mūrang'a, Nyīrī and the Rift Valley province has this to say about Karūri:

As time went on Karūri was to become my friend and right-hand collaborator, while I, in turn was to raise him to the position of a great chief and myself to supreme power in the country—a virtual king of the Kikuyus(sic).

And Ochieng' considers Karūri as "radical nationalist!"

It was Karūri who encouraged British imperialism to settle in Mūrang'a; it was Karūri who led the colonial forces under Colonel Richard Meinertzhagen in an attempt to subdue our people's resistance against British invasion in central Kenya. In short, what we are trying to say is that such Kenyan chiefs as Mumia, Mwendwa of Kitui, Masaakū, Wambūgū wa Mathangani, Ole Lenana, Nderi wa Wang'ombe, Musa Nyandusi, Kĩnyanyui wa Gathirimū, Wangū, Warūhiū, Njiiri, Magūgū, Gūtū (kutus), Rūnyeje, Mūhoya, etc., were colonial collaborators and outright traitors. All of them played key roles in the colonial regime's efforts to subdue and defeat our people's resistance against foreign occupation and domination.

Mwakenya: The Unfinished Revolution

Like the present comprador class in our country today, the aims of these chiefs, apart from being traitors, were mainly selfish and greedy at the expenses of our people. A.W. McGregor, a white liberal missionary, states:

The chiefs had all the power, wherever they went, they commandeered; whatever they fancied—food, livestock or women. They went to the extent of killing people and if anyone protested, their village would suffer.

Again:

The chiefs enriched themselves by taking other people's wives and property by force.

These individuals were not radical nationalists, as our "great" historian would have us believe. They were anti-Kenyan colonial mercenaries and murderers in the real sense of the word. In Chapter One of the book, Ochieng' dishes out another argument that the European slave trade, imperialism and capitalism were not the root causes of Africa's underdevelopment. He quotes racist historians like Trevor-Roper to support his arguments. Only Henry Kissinger, John Vorster or Ian Smith can put ridiculous arguments such as these. Ochieng' join them in spirit and indeed.

At any rate, studying world history, we would know that as a result of Western European invasion, after the second half of the 16th century, vast areas of Africa were reduced to colonies or semi-colonies and subjected to ruthless exploitation and enslavement. The vicious slave trade and slavery and various forms of cruel plunder and killings by western imperialists changed Africa from a land of wealth, beauty, freedom and progress to a pariah continent. But that is not all. Four centuries of imperialist killings and plunder reduced the African population by 100 million, as civilization and technology were destroyed.

Eastern Kenyan and Its Invaders

This booklet is Ochieng's effort at what colonial historians call "ethnographic history". Ethnography is the European study of "primitive native" customs.

139

Mwakenya: The Unfinished Revolution

Ochieng' under the pretext of writing Eastern Kenyan history, copies the works of early racist European anthropologists and adventurers. He therefore approves of the racist ideas of these anti-Africans. Of the five chapters in this most unoriginal work, the first four contribute nothing new to what has already been written by such racist authors as Coupland, Ingharm, Reusch, Hatch, M.W.H. Beech, H.E. Lambert, J.F. Munro, G. Matthews, Freeman-Grenville and liberal ones like Basil Davidson, R.H. Oliver, etc. Ochieng's job was to collect and compile from them and stick on a likely title and his own *learned* name.

First, the book is based on Eurocentric stereotyped interpretation of African history. He accepts such European labels as "bantu", "nilotic", "bushmen", "pigmy", "man-eating Ethiopians", "negroland", "wazimba cannibalists", etc. It does not bother this "learned" scholar that what has been written by European bourgeois historians on us is pure racist dogma, in both content and form. His aim seems to provide "African" evidence to back these insults especially this "wazimba cannibalistic" myth. On page 5, Ochieng' writes:

> *Meanwhile a peculiar situation had risen at Mombasa owing to the arrival of a horde of savages called the Wazimba. The Wazimba were a black race of cannibals who had come from the interior of Africa . . .In 1587 they had captured Kilwa and after destroying the town, had eaten most of their prisoners.*

Ochieng' has shamelessly copied this passage, word for word, from R. Coupland, a British racist historian. This book shows clearly that it is influenced by colonial European writings. The book is full of supportive quotations from such enemies of Africa as Cecil Rhodes. Of all people Cecil Rhodes!

On the question of the Indian Ocean slave trade, Ochieng' distorts the real conflict of economic interests, especially as concerns African slave-sellers. First it is clear to all, but our *wise scholar,* that European and Asian traders were the major undertakers in this monstrous business; Africans were the victims. A few Africans (traitors) undertook forwarding and hunting duties for minor payment. Politically, there were the forefathers of the present sellout compradors. But to Ochieng' these were the major force. He brands *all* the Wakamba and Waswahili people as slave-hunters and, by so doing shallowly dismisses important distinctions and creates divisions among Kenyans. Ochieng' cannot hide the great historical importance of the slave trade in Africa. This major event brought Africa into conflict with foreign, especially Western imperialists who plundered and unleashed the still continuing class struggle between imperialism and its local running dogs on the one hand and the majority of Africans on the other. On page 83, he writes:

> *This final stage in the slavery and anti-slave trade campaign came in 1897 when a decree was passed entirely abolishing the legal status of slavery in (East Africa) . . . Kenya was thus saved from the worst effects of the slave trade by Britain. Instead of being marched abroad to be enslaved, the British now enslaved Kenyans in their country. It was at least better to be enslaved at home, among one's people than abroad in a foreign and hostile environment.*

Sounds like David Livingstone, Henry Stanley, Krapf or Colonel Richard Meinertzhagen writing to the colonial office in London! Only a true imperialist historian would gloss over the question of slavery by favorably contrasting it to colonial occupation. Neither colonialism nor slave abolition was humanitarian. The basis of slave abolition was economic not humanitarian. The British bourgeoisie argued that the eastern region of Africa offered far greater economic opportunities than man stealing. Ochieng's "better enslavement at home" theory does not seem to include the annihilation and displacement of entire populations and the stealing of land. Extended further, this piece of Ochieng's apologia clears Hitlerite Vorster of much wrong doing since he does it all to Africans among their own.

One might say Ochieng' has a right to produce such claptrap of academic excreta. But we students and others should not be forced to study it as worthy knowledge thus poisoning inquisitive minds and derailing our

Mwakenya: The Unfinished Revolution

patriotic consciousness. In our opinion the most insidious crime to Kenya's history and people is his distortion of the true political nature of GEMA. Naively and shallowly this "great" scholar refers to the Gĩkũyũ, Embu, Mbeere and Mĩĩrũ nationalities as "the GEMA people of Mt. Kenya". This shows the pettiness, the chauvinist-tribalist interpretation of our history. It has been shown and proven, especially since J. M. Kariũki's assassination, that GEMA is *not* a welfare organization in the lines of Luo Union, New Akamba Union, Abaluhya Union and the like, GEMA (as the nine gallant students of the University of Nairobi referred to in the introduction showed us as early as 1975) is an alliance of the richest, the most reactionary wing of the Kenyan comprador bourgeoisie. Their history is one of settler-loving, *hũmungaati*, etc. Most importantly, they are not Gĩkũyũ, Embu and Mĩĩrũ elements only but included too are such other ruling class elements from other nationalities as Okiki Amayo, Nyamweya, Matano, Munoko, Ngei, Towett, Cheluget, etc. GEMA is the executive wing of the minority ruling party KANU and wants to use the Mau Mau heroism to give legitimacy to its comprador activities. Is this too scientific for our "great" scholar to perceive or is this too scary for him to contemplate?

Three other books by Ochieng' deserve mention: *A Precolonial History of the Gusii of Western Kenya, A.D.1500-1914; An Outline History of Nyanza Up to 1914* and *History of Rift Valley.* Although these have the same subjectivist, stereotyped interpretations they are "important" because of another important theme in Ochieng's outlook. He consistently views African people as drifting overland as if they are phantoms in a dream— aimlessly, unexplained, they keep moving now migrating south, now suddenly north, then back south but a bit to the west, etc., endlessly, page after page, no depth, no substance just trivial travelogues of whole populations. People never, never just move.There are always *economic* and *historical* explanations in one form or another: bad weather, deteriorating pasture, therefore declining food and welfare. Perhaps exploitation or threat of war, which may of led to poorer economic welfare for the conquered and better welfare for the conquerors. For Ochieng', people move like ghosts.

Mwakenya: The Unfinished Revolution

In *Nyanza Up to 1914*, Ochieng' goes out of his way to provide a redundant postscript to Ogot's *A History of the Southern Lou*. In *History of Rift Valley*, he again refuses to knowledge the traitorous role-played by colonial chief Lenana. Instead he praises him as a nationalist. His analysis of the conflict between the Nandi and British imperialism is very one-sided, on the British side. Everybody knows that the Nandi under Koitalel's leadership fought the British very fiercely. A.T. Matson's *Nandi Resistance to British Rule* honestly represents this. Honourable Dr. Professor William Robert Ochieng' who are you serving?

Atieno-Odhiambo

On the surface Atieno-Odhiambo seems to disagree, but on examination actually agrees with Ochieng' on major issues about Kenya's history. He differs essentially only in his use of Marxism to cover his anti-Marxist theories and analysis—whereas Ochieng' openly attacks Marxism and Scientific Socialism, Atieno-Odhiambo uses it to cleverly oppose it. We have called him a shrewd twister of Marxism for being an opportunist and tricky.

Atieno-Odhiambo talks eloquently about the "need for a coherent ideology" that will recapitulate an intelligent national programme for development; but not having specified to whom such ideology and programme should be directed or by whom it should be executed. He casually leaves the stage open for foreigners or the local selfish ruling class to run it and benefit from it. He might protest "but I have all along implied that the oppressed Kenyans should benefit". What kind of Marxism is this, so tame and impotent that it does not boldly state, but merely satisfies itself with merely a guide to action based on *living and real* social conditions and not a dead pile of dogma. Dogmatists like Atieno-Odhiambo fail to see that neocolonial Kenya today has a political and economic and cultural framework based on a most "coherent ideology that recapitulates intelligent national programme for development" of Kenya compradors and foreign imperialists. For a true Marxist the fundamental question is "for whom and by whom?"

Mwakenya: The Unfinished Revolution

Only pseudo-Marxists would fabricate such Freudian garbage as Atieno-Odhiambo's theory of "peasant inferiority complex". He uses this theory to explain the alleged historical decline of this vast class. Psychiatrist "Marxist" Atieno-Odhiambo diagnosed this mass psychopathology recently and announced in his book that about the year 1922 this epidemic killed the Kenyan peasantry! If there are any peasants today, one might conclude they are chronically sick at Mathare hospital, their death 54 years over-due! And then strangely he asserts that the peasant class (even in rudimentary form) did not exist anywhere in Kenya before 1888. The wretched class was hatched in 1888 and died prematurely of a serious psychological malady in 1922 after a life of 34 years! This is the "Marxist" history of a university professor. How the peasantry was suddenly formed? Atieno-Adhiambo tells us:

The creation (sic) of an African [Kenyan] peasantry was primarily the result of the interaction between an international capitalist settler economic system and traditional socio-economic systems.

Profound! After this incorrect statement he deliberately omits any analysis of what he calls "traditional socio-economic systems". Who does not know that Kenyan nationalities towards the end of 19th century were developing feudalist tendencies? He, moreover, demonstrates a serious ignorance when he makes the existence of peasantry as a class dependent upon the parallel (or simultaneous) presence of a working class. This is dogma borrowed from the Harvard/Cambridge type of pseudo-Marxist, anti-communist professors! In short, Atieno-Odhiambo denies the existence today of the class that is numerically the most powerful in Kenya and mistakes its historically conditioned backwardness for inherent weakness, non-existence or even sickness.

We stated above that Ochieng's major crime is his glossing over of the nature and role of GEMA. Atieno-Odhiambo avoids this question altogether. That is perhaps better than sowing confusion. He however out does Ochieng' in denouncing and insulting, without exception, all historical incidences of Kenyan people's resistance to colonialism and neocolonialism.

Mwakenya: The Unfinished Revolution

According to him, "Everybody in his book, *Paradox of Collaboration*, one sees in one evil collaborationist basket such as patriots as Kĩmathi, Pinto, Oneko, Me Katilili, Mũthoni Nyanjirũ, Samoei, etc., rubbing shoulders with such bootlicking sellout scum as Karũri, Lenana, Mumia, Ofafa, Tom Mbotela, Rawson Macaria, Mahĩhu, Njonjo, Kĩmeendero John Mĩchuki, Chief Magũgũ, Chief Njiiri, Chief Nderi, Kĩnyanjui, Mũchohi Gĩkonyo, Masaakũ, etc., all of them collaborated with foreign interests. One must quickly conclude that Atieno-Odhiambo is describing his own paradoxical role as a "Marxist" collaborator. Kenyans have a shining revolutionary history. True Kenyan intellectuals would attempt to analyze the past, to illuminate the future, to differentiate the good from the bad in order to enrich and heighten people's revolutionary awareness. What manner of *Marxism* is this professed by this *great Marxist* scholar if not mere anti-Kenyan imperialist trash?

From specific cases of sellout politics of particular comprador elements in colon-ial Kenya, Atieno-Odhiambo makes a general law applying to all African peoples. It is on the basis of this anti-Kenyan line that he revealingly dismisses "the pursuit of the origins of mass nationalism [as] an irrelevant pursuit for historians of Kenya". Here is a "Marxist" who believes that people just rise up on their own, spontaneously, and subsequently affect revolutions without any vanguard or organizational basis. It is not un-marxist that such a vanguard may come from one nationality or more. If nationalism does not address itself to the problems affecting the people concerned, what kinds of political content will it have? On the whole Atieno-Odhiambo is a dangerous pen-wielding academic who is paid handsomely to smuggle pro-imperialist ideas into the Kenyan university classrooms and elsewhere. True Kenyans must, take an antagonistic position against him. He must be exposed and opposed as an intellectual puppet of the imperialists.

Godfrey Mũriũki

One important difference between Mũriũki and the intellectual twin above is that he at times seems to attempt to abandon imperialist-based "academic

Mwakenya: The Unfinished Revolution

objectivity" and occasionally sides with Kenyans. Of course, like them he lacks the requisite uncompromising, pro-Kenyan, anti-imperialist world outlook so that he will accusingly refer to such things as Kenyans committing "grisly massacre" in their self-defense against European invasion.

His book, *A History of the Kikuyu* (1974), is the latest in a series fathered by Ogot's *Southern Luo* attempt. He, like his predecessors, delight in recording a chronology of events. Lacking in the living core of "why societies change?" such chronologies are dead and pointless. The first five chapters add nothing new as, for example, the Gĩkũyũ-Gumba-Aathi relationship tells us nothing we did not know before. The last two chapters Muriuki's fails to grasp the Kenya-wide impact of British colonialism and post 1963 neocolonialism, as well as the worldwide conflict of which Kenya is a part of. In a departure from Ochieng'and Atieno-Odhiambo pro-colonial theories, Mũriũki bravely shows the anti-nationalist traitorous nature of most colonial chiefs. But again, he fails to see the connection between the British colonial policies and the gradual development and differentiation of the current comprador ruling class. Again, like his two friends, Ochieng' and Atieno-Odhiambo, he does not see that the colonial collaborator chiefs, like Karũri, Nderi wa Wang'ombe, Lenana, Gĩoko wa Njega, Wambũgũ wa Mathangania, Mumia, Kĩnyanyui, Mwendwa, Gũtũ, Rũnyeje, Masaakũ, etc., were the political forefathers of today's Kenyatta, Ngei, Moi, Koinange, Njonjo, Towett, Omamo, Angaine, Matano, Oloitipitip, Mahĩhu, Mĩchuki, Mathenge, Mboya, Kĩano, Mũngai Njoroge, Charles Njonjo, G.G. Kariũki, Kamotho, among others. He sees chiefs as individuals doing bad things to Africans, not in their class context. As if the current anti-Kenyan, pro-imperialist comprador ruling class emerged overnight, Mũriũki having failed to give historical underpinnings, whispers:

Even today, it is discernible that some of the early chiefly families are some of the largest landowners.

Just early families owning much land and presumably recent families owning none, "objectivity" has led him to these glib bland, tame

Mwakenya: The Unfinished Revolution

pronouncements on current Kenya lest he be accused of being an agitator, a non-academic or a communist! For Mūriūki, dealing as he seems to with the Central province and its neighbors, the question of GEMA should have been thoroughly discussed. The excuse that his research was done before GEMA was set up is not enough since his publication gave him the chance to add to it or revise it. It is true that GEMA, as their lie goes, is a Gĩkũyũ, Embu, and Mĩĩrũ welfare [social] non-political organization or is the disguise, the cover under which it masquerades? Who are the leaders? Were they not the very *hũmungaati* and anti-Kenyans like Kĩhĩka Kĩmani, Charles Njonjo, Peter Mũigai, Njoroge Mũngai, Angaine, Mahĩhu, Mĩchuki, Mathenge, Magũgũ, Duncan Ndegwa, Kĩereinĩ and many others? Are the other non-Gĩkũyũ, Embu, Mĩĩrũ compradors (i.e., Omamo, Ngei, Amayo, Towett, etc.), not GEMA in essence, in objective political effect? Mūriūki's position on Mau Mau is similarly to that of Ochieng', Otieno-Odhiambo and the British imperialist bourgeoisie.

Perhaps Mūriūki feels that this particular book is not the place for this critical issue, but he should know that this important issue will not go away simply because he has cowardly shied away from it. The book keeps completely silent on the question of exploitation and oppression of our people. His silence on this issue in our country's history today would only mean that he is indifferent to the forces of reaction against the great masses of Kenyans. Dead history, dead facts are of little benefit for us. Mūriūki and his *learned* colleagues refuse to face up to the living reality of today's Kenyan society and their implication to future history.

Further Investigations

In the future, other subjects, other academic departments in universities and other individual academics will need intensive investigation. For instance, Ali Mazrui, a renowned apologist for imperialism in Africa, must be thoroughly exposed . . . He has already been well described as "an ideologist of the ruling class in Africa". He has achieved notoriety internationally by his use of bombastic oratory and false eloquence to

Mwakenya: The Unfinished Revolution

explain away Africans' oppression by imperialism and capitalism. In this he has outdone most neocolonial Third World intellectuals. In reviewing Colin Leys' fairly objective book, *Underdevelopment in Kenya: The Political Economy of Neo-colonialism 1964-71,* Mazrui accused Leys of "symptoms of Kenya-phobia and sheer prejudice against Kenya" (see "Transition", p.46). Marzui opposes any form of national liberation and adores Euro American imperialism prescriptions on development. He even called Amin (a murderous dictator!) "the common man's president". Mazrui, viewed by some as a rightwing intellectual, is now opposed wherever he goes.

Professor G. Mũtiso of the Department of Government, University of Nairobi seems to aspire to Mazrui's style and notoriety. He outdoes Mazrui in abstraction, metaphysics and sheer incomprehensibility. Of late he has been advertising himself as a "specialist" in African Literature, African thought and African politics. In 1975 he advertised himself in one of the imperialist journals, *Africa Today,* vol. 2, No. 4 (p.104). The advertisement reads:

Dr. G.S. Mutiso, Department of Government, University of Nairobi, is in United States through February, and he is prepared to lecture on African Literature and Kenya Politics. Scheduled arrangements are being handled by Alice R. Morton, Social Sciences Research Council, 605 Third Avenue, New York, New York 10016.

The Department of Government, like other foreign extension departments in the University of Nairobi, is well known for opposing a free exchange of ideas, especially Marxist teachings and relying on American government interpretation of the world. Just look at the many shallow treatises on politics and "modernization" that are produced by the *honorable professors* there.

These are just some areas for further work. But at the same time we must be on guard to defeat fake or sham shifts in position by these intellectuals. As they become known as enemies they will attempt to hide and change superficially while deep down they are the same. They will deck themselves out in Marxist attire, support Kenyans and even socialism in words while serving U.S. imperialism in deeds. This is especially so

Mwakenya: The Unfinished Revolution

since some of their foreign mentors are already taking a more scientific and objective stand in their writings—e.g., Colin Ley's book above. This will be a signal for the local ones to cover up a bit and follow suit, at least for academic fashion and respectability!

This is important because up to now imperialists and their servants have always taught us that African societies are exceptional in world history since "in Africa there are no classes". Africa is classless, so class analysis and class consciousness is "foreign ideology!" now is proved wrong here in Kenya by the obvious daily fact of class conflict, but our neocolonial scholars will attempt to explain away classes by lying that "our classes here are exceptional and unimportant politically!

Investigate and be on guard.

Conclusion

This is partly the disease we referred to in the preface. A parasitic and decadent culture and education is fostered by some writers and lecturers/professors who glorify imperialist concepts of freedom, selfish individualism, cynicism, and greed: who exalt pleasurable idleness, commodities and money, which represent imperialism as an irreplaceable system. They want us to believe that there is something eternal and insoluble about the human situation, since they say that human beings are enigmatic and mysterious and that nobody understands how they became what they are.

A great deal has happened in our society since we started this research. Most particularly is the growing awareness about the real nature of GEMA as an inter-ethnic, comprador organization, which is posing great danger to the unity of the Kenyan people. University students have, militantly resisted unwarranted police and General Service Unit (GSU) attacks and held many patriotic demonstrations. We learned a lot from them as well as from the numerous people's newspapers (so-called seditious pamphlets) particularly *Mwanguzi*. We in this document have contributed a small

Mwakenya: The Unfinished Revolution

part toward combating the imperialist, cultural disease, by diagnosing *some* of its carriers. The disease is spreading. We have just learned of the proposed Ford/Rockefeller/UN project to install an Institute of Population Studies and Control to study "objectively" such "relevant topics as "The Comparative Decline of Rural Maasai Fertility in contrast to urban, middle-aged, unemployed Luo males in Kisumu". The Institute of Development Studies "revolutionary" project may study school leaders who never found jobs and blame it on their psychology! And the most learned of them, is a study of Turkana participation in Democracy as adjudged by the 1974 General elections. This is "learning (neocolonial US/UK-controlled learning) totally useless to Kenya and parasiting on Kenyans. The political function of it is to prolong imperialism's lease on us by making us students, supposedly learned, carry out foreigner's wishes against our people.

We must oppose this role. Out of our opposition and work along with all Kenya-ns' struggle, will arise a new fighting culture developed in heated confrontations by a reawakened people made keenly aware of their strength and potential. Out of that will rise proud, fighting intellectuals, writers, and other cultural workers inseparable from their people and nation's history.

An Extract from Cheche Kenya, 1981
Zed Press (London) reprinted this document in 1982
under a new title: *InDependent Kenya*

KANU and Kenyatta: Independence for sale

Kenya has never achieved true independence. Full independence can only be brought about by revolution. It is the culmination of popular, protracted revolutionary change, during which the people seize control of the instruments of power under the leadership of a party dedicated to the eradication of the institutions and forms of the colonial state. In Amilcar Cabral's words, 'It is necessary to totally destroy, to break to ash all aspects of colonial state' before independence can be achieved. Colonial domination must be demolished through active popular struggle. No colonial ruling power has ever voluntarily relinquished hegemony at a negotiating table. It will only consent to negotiate if it can, in the long term, either preserve or even extend its position of privilege through bargaining. Such was the intention of the British when they prepared to hand over nominal power to Kenyatta at the Lancaster House Conference. The terms on which they handed over *power* demonstrated that in one guise or other, they intended to stay in Kenya.

Independence means self-determination and self-government. An independent nation is one with the autonomy to make decisions, which will advance the welfare of its people. It is a nation that controls its own resources, and has the political and economic scope to utilize these resources, human and natural, free of foreign interference.

Independence in this sense has little relevance to our current situation. We find ourselves in a dependent country, wholly subservient to foreign interests. Our economy is geared to the needs of foreigners—both of our ex-colonial masters and other Western capitalist nations. In order to keep things that way our people are deprived of vital human freedoms, including the right of political self-expression and association. 'Neo-colonialism' is not merely a matter of academic debate (and in any case there is very little of that) in Kenya. It is a condition, which our people live with day by day: a form of oppression every bit as effective as that practiced by the British colonialists. In the last 20 years, our aspirations for political redress and economic reconstruction have been strangled. The sense of power we possessed when we took up arms against colonialism in the 1950s has been undermined and stifled. We are told that 'politics' came to an end in 1963. Now that we have our *uhuru,* we must 'forget the past'. We have no need to discuss issues—discussion is dangerous 'rumor-mongering'. All we need is unquestioned loyalty to our gang of leaders, and a mute faith in their ritual incantation of *peace, love and unity.*

Big Boss Politics

As the gulf between the minority rich and the mass of poor continues to widen, we are told that there are no divisions in our country which cannot be healed by "peace, love and unity", a tame obedience and silence on our part. What passes for 'political' life revolves entirely around personalities who serve as our bosses, our patrons. They are far representing our true interests. Instead, they represent, at the local level, the power of the *big boss,* the all-powerful sun of the system around which the politicians rotate like planets. All powers radiate from the center of the system, from our imperial President. Political success and personal enrichment depend on the positions held by the different planets as they circulate around the sun-king. Since the President, through his control of the state apparatus,

Mwakenya: The Unfinished Revolution

bestows access to our country's increasingly scarce resources, the closer the politician planet to the center, the more power he can trap and reflect on down to his own satellites and flunkeys. As our politicians orbit endlessly around the President they compete with each other to sing his praises loudly and attract his favor. Obsequious loyalty brings its own reward—a position closer to the warming power of the sun with all the economic privileges that go with membership of the inner circles. A loss of favor could put the politician out of orbit altogether, into limbo or extinction.

Such is the nature of Kenyan 'politics' today. Like an earlier Sun-king, this President professes to rule by divine right, as the chosen of God. He, too, has his court and jesters. He exercises supreme authority by mumbled decree, his every murmur being sacrosanct until it is found to be unworkable, ruinous, or both. Politicians and appointed officials carry out the imperial will. Their chief function is to smother all debate, and to link the people firmly into a boss-servant chain of relationships, which constitutes our permitted political life. The keys to the chain are the district officials, district commissioners and provincial commissioners: they operate a rigid licensing system through which the government controls all gatherings of the people—no license, no meeting, no matter how innocent. Surveillance practiced by the Special Branch, C.I.D, and General Service Unit (GSU) destroys not only any vestige of 'participatory democracy', but also, we shall see late, our people's own initiative to better their condition. In Kenya today any such initiative is always deemed subversive.

Of course, as in other repressive regimes these are, from time to time, elections of a sort, which allow 'friendly' foreign nations the opportunity to hold Kenya up as the showpiece of 'democracy' in Africa. These elections are totally devoid of debate on issues. Instead, all campaigning centers upon weak, generally corrupt, safe personalities who have the KANU seal of approval. The winners are usually those most adept at the intimidation and/or bribery of voters. Elections do, however, fulfill a useful function as far as the government is concerned; they provide it with fresh packs of *eaters* willing to carry out government policy against the interests of their constituents if necessary.

Mwakenya: The Unfinished Revolution

These victorious politicians are, in practice, accountable to the President alone that has various methods of keeping them in line. Elected MPs who attempt to represent the wishes of their constituents against government policy find that parliamentary immunity is an empty concept in Kenya. Parliament itself is a joker' forum, which can be ignored, ridiculed or dismissed out of hand if 'unruly'.

As for our one official party, the party, which supposedly won us 'independence', it has long been in a stupor. No political initiative or policy-making emanates from the Kenya African Union (KANU), a 'party' without regular party machinery or even functioning local branches. KANU today fulfills two functions, neither reputable. Since only those Kenyans wealthy enough to afford to buy life membership can be elected party officials, it serves as a rich man's club, whose members are dedicated to making themselves even richer. From time to time, party branches are resuscitated in order to counter moves made by political dissidents or those slow in expressing their loyalty to the President and his clique. To further confound those who believed that parties like KANU should represent and respond to the needs of the people, KANU in 1979 was declared to be 'above the law'. It thus became a tool of a President himself 'above the law' and beyond all criticism, even by elected representatives of the people. The President and his closed associates can—and do—indulge in any kind of skullduggery without fear of the courts. With party functions reduced to 'eating' and arm-twisting, with a legislature and judiciary whose autonomy and integrity have been subverted, with a President who rules as a kind of sultan, political life in Kenya today is a complete negation of what we fought to attain. The rulers of 'independent' Kenya could have taught their colonial predecessors a thing or two about how to keep down the *natives*.

Did we fight for *uhuru* in order to be politically silenced in a supposedly *free* Kenya? To be intimidated, detained, and even eliminated for reminding our so-called leaders that they are there to represent *our* interests and not merely their own? To be ruled by a virtual king and his gang of favorites, all above the law and beyond the reach of principle and

Mwakenya: The Unfinished Revolution

social responsibility? At what point did the party in which we once vested our hopes for the future in become little more than a source of jobs and loot for politicians and their hangers-on? An empty office in the Kenyatta Conference Center symbolizes KANU's failure to function, as a forum for political expression—was it a pseudo-party from the beginning?

Enter KANU

The idea of forming the Kenya African National Union was born at the 1960 Lancaster House Conference in London on the prospects for majority rule in Kenya. In the turbulent 1950s, Kenyans had been allowed district, but not nationwide political associations, with all political parties being banned between June 1953 and June 1955. In an effort to overcome the divide-and-rule tactics deployed by the British in their support for the Kenya African Democratic Union (KADU), the originators of KANU, in May of 1960, combined district associations into a national party. KANU promised to usher in full independence for the peoples of Kenya.

The party seemed to be off to a rousing start. It had leaders: Kenyatta, languishing in detention, was surrounded by an almost mythical aura. It had branches: the old district associations. More crucially, it had the enthusiastic support of people who believed to be the vehicle for bringing home independence. And finally, it had a stirring party program. Delivered in the form of a political 'manifesto' to a huge rally at Thĩka on November 20, 1960, the *KANU Manifesto for Independence, Social Democracy and Stability* makes instructive, and ironic, reading today. Before the jubilant crowd the party proclaimed that:

All privileges and vestiges of colonialism will be swept away.
Freedom has no meaning without the provision of the means
for the vast majority of the people to enjoy that freedom.

KANU promised to replace the colonial regime with a 'political democracy', which was concerned with safeguarding the 'good of the country as a whole and not merely the interests of a few'. Such a 'political democracy' would,

155

Mwakenya: The Unfinished Revolution

the party affirmed, always seek to mobilize 'the greatest possible element of consent' and support from below.

Which Kenyans can read the *Manifesto* today without a bitter laugh? How mocking seem the firm pledges made by KANU 20 years ago; how swiftly the pledges were broken! For instance, in 1960 the party vowed always to be dynamic—a promise which it kept perhaps until 1963 when it practically ceased to function as anything other than a tool to be used to remove the politically undesirable. It made a number of other pledges equally ironic in retrospect. Thus, it promised to work for 'the good of the country as a whole and not merely the interests of a few'. It vowed to have nothing to do with the 1959 Detention Act, and other 'undemocratic, unjust and arbitrary practices'. It declared its intention to do away with PCs, DCs and chiefs, and replace their rule by institutions through which the people could exercise the 'right of self-government'. It pledged itself to end the racist practice whereby Africans were stopped on the streets and asked to produce their identity cards (kipande), and it attacked 'artificial restrictions on the movement of produce from district to district coupled with monopolistic control exercised over them' which, in its view, caused 'sky-rocketing prices of the commodities which are the staple food of the African people'. It took a populist line on housing as well as food distribution, maintaining that 'before citizen E has 20 rooms to protect him from rain, citizen A must have shelter'. In short, through its *Manifesto,* KANU expressed its firm intention to develop Kenya 'into a prosperous welfare state', an intention which, like so many others, is further away from realization than ever. Today the document appears as a testament to what might have been a *Manifesto* for a stillborn party, which for most of its official life has been little more than a corpse.

The founders of KANU seem to have been blinded by the fact that there is more to the formation of a party than the adoption of a name. A party is really only worthy of the name 'party' if it acts to animate and then channel popular expression at all levels of society. Despite its appearance of health and a certain measure of unanimity in1960, KANU was never, in fact, a vertically integrated party tapping and giving voice to grassroots interests.

Mwakenya: The Unfinished Revolution

Instead, in Odinga's words, it remained an 'amalgam of many diverse tendencies and policies', a mere 'union of different and even antagonistic interests'. In the *Manifesto* of 1960, KANU acknowledges that it is more of a coalition by implication, temporary, than anything else—it presents itself as a 'united front' composed of Kenyans joined together by the one common goal of working for independence. As our country was shortly to discover, there could be many different things meant by *independence.*

Militants and Moderates

At the risk of some over-simplification, we can say that the 'amalgam', which was KANU, contained two broadly different groups. On one side were people who believed that 'independence' necessitated a total break with the colonial system and a new beginning. They realized that a new beginning was only possible if Kenyans themselves had control of the country's resources and political destiny. For our purposes here we can call this group of radicals the militant nationalists. Their voice set the tone of the 1960 KANU manifesto, demanding a clean break with the past and the creation of a more egalitarian society in the future through such devices as free education for all and a ceiling on how much private property one individual can own. Despite the attempt made by the colonial regime— and later by the 'independent' government—to label them as such, these nationalists were by no means socialists. Nowhere did they speak out against the institution of private property, but they did maintain that a certain amount of nationalization of the country's resources and the serious encouragement of cooperative farming would benefit the Kenyan people as a whole. Their message presented in the *Manifesto* was that wealth and power in Kenya should not be monopolized by the few, as under the colonial regime. The new beginning, demanded by independence, should widen opportunities for all Kenyans, and give the people as a whole a meaningful political role.

But the other broad group within the 'amalgam' was ultimately to win the day. These were the moderate nationalists, who stressed *continuity*

Mwakenya: The Unfinished Revolution

with the past, and not a complete break with the colonial system. They wanted to be well placed to take over positions vacated by the *departing* British, and to maintain the pattern and direction of colonial rule. Early in 1960 they were willing to allow the radicals to set the rhetorical tone of the *Manifesto* in order to win widespread popular support, making sure, however, that the 'Kenya for Kenyans' style of rhetoric were confined to what were essentially *secondary* issues. On the vitally important *primary* issues—of the land and of foreign investment—they were determined to push through their own policies.

Land was the touchstone of new government policy. It was the means of production for the vast majority of our people, and the source of a bitter sense of grievance during the colonial period. With the nearing of 'independence', the people demanded the return of the stolen land as a matter of justice. They saw no need to pay compensation to settlers who had come as thieves. In Kaggia's words, 'It looks very absurd for Africans to buy land that was rightly theirs'. But the moderates felt otherwise, and significantly, wrote their view into the *Manifesto*. KANU as a party accepted 'the principle of fair and just compensation'; despite the fact that such a principle ran directly counter to the needs and interests of the people. There would be no 'free things' in an African-run Kenya.

Nor would there be any radical departure in economic thinking. The moderates asserted in the *Manifesto* that 'development' would continue along the *same line,* making the implicit assumption that colonial style 'development' was in fact the real thing. The *Manifesto* voiced the radical pledge to resettle landless Africans, but 'not at the cost of the high standard of agriculture already attained, and which must continue'. A KANU government would continue to approach economic matters in much the same old way, heavily emphasizing the dubious benefits of large mixed farming. Continuity was not to be confined to agriculture. The *Manifesto* also reassured agents of international capital that there would be no change at 'independence', but 'both public and private enterprise, local or from overseas, have a sure place in Kenya's development'. Investment from all sources would be encouraged and protected.

Mwakenya: The Unfinished Revolution

What conclusions can we draw from the evidence offered by the 1960 KANU Manifesto? We can say that as early as 1960 the group, which was subsequently to inherit the trappings of political power—the moderates—outflanked the militant nationalists. The militants had on their side a strong commitment to the independence of our country, which won them the support of most Kenyans. They had a populist rhetoric, and a sense of indignation, at the way Kenyans were exploited by foreign interests, which enabled them to sway crowds.

Furthermore, they had the support of a grassroots organization, the *Kĩama Kĩa Mũingĩ* (KKM), which was a regrouping of former members of the Kenya Land Freedom Army (KLFA). The KKM was committed to 'free land', through active seizure if necessary. It planned to capture political control of KANU's rural branches, and also to collect arms as insurance against a 'sellout' at 'independence'. The great weakness of the KKM was organizational. When Kenyatta chose to move against its members in 1961, he easily isolated the leaders, and detained key cadres. The decapitation of KKM left the militant nationalists without an organizational base. They remained a minority faction within KANU, having failed to create their own sources of funds, their own propaganda organs, and institutionalized popular support. Their programme won majority favor, but they had no ability to carry it out. Kenya's radicals on the verge of 'independence', therefore, suffered from the same near-sightedness, which has afflicted all opposition spokesmen since. They displayed a lack of political judgment, and ignorance of the nature of political struggle. They were easily isolated and neutralized; and, as the mainstream of Kenya's political history passed them by, made to seem irrelevant.

In 1960 the mainstream within KANU was flowing strongly towards the shores of neo-colonialism. The moderates, therefore, had their say on the primary economic issues, this committed Kenya to continuity, not to change. The colonial model, minus such irritants as the legal color bar and white racism, would be preserved in 'independent' Kenya.

Mwanguzi Newsletter (1975-1980)

(*Mwanguzi* was an underground newsletter produced monthly by *Kamati ya Ukombozi wa Kenya*, a front for the Workers' Party of Kenya. The following are a few selected copies).

MWANGUZI, APRIL 1975

Kenyans are United for Change

Recent events here in Kenya ending with the death of patriotic, poor people's fighter J.M. Kariũki have shown that the minority ruling clique will stop at nothing to protect their big estates, their stolen businesses, their Benzes, their wheat fields, their many mansions and buildings, their fleets of buses and tankers, their directorships and other positions.

Since the assassination, Kenyans have overwhelmingly condemned this puppet government and especially the handful of criminals heading it. Many revolutionary statements, mass leaflets, songs and circulars by various patriotic groups clearly show that the Kenyan people are united on these basic national issues: 1) The rich, ruling class headed by the Kenyatta group, murdered J.M. 2) Government is responsible for continued cover-up and obstruction of evidence. 3) The Parliamentary Select Committee has the people's support, but on condition that its findings show clearly the link between the ruling clique and JM assassination. The people of Kenya

Mwakenya: The Unfinished Revolution

have no doubts about who the murderers are. **4)** The entire question of land ownership and distribution has not been settled. Landlessness continues when the Kenyattas and the Delameres continue grabbing large estates. These estates lie idle while millions and millions of Kenyans starve or remain squatters in their own country. **5)** The Kenyatta puppet regime has denied Kenyans their elementary democratic rights—the right to dissent and freely air views, the right to security and protection of life, the right to employment, food and other welfare, the right to freely assemble and associate with friends, family, and community members alike, and the right to read any and all books one wishes. Kenyans were constantly misled to believe that they must have no rights in order for their country to be stable for foreigners to invest in. Who gains? Not us. **6)** Kenyatta's criminally undemocratic regime relies entirely on British mercenary troops, imperialist loans that burden our future development, and imperialist advisers and experts (the Shaw murderers). This is proof of the regime's fear and distrust of Kenyans. This is a puppet, neocolonial regime of national betrayal, and dissent or opposition is punished by detention or death without trial. This is fascism! This ruling clique has not done anything about unemployment in the country. Instead, they have increased prices of all basic everyday necessities, including rent. **7)** Kenyans are now fully aware that the ruling few have been dividing and disuniting us by nationalities regions and even districts. This helps no one but them. GEMA, for example, is one instrument of division.

Kamati ya Ukombozi wa Kenya firmly supports the above sentiments of our people. We note at the same time that in the past the government appointed Central Organization of Trade Unions (COTU) leadership has often betrayed the workers' demands for fair wages. The COTU leaders have misrepresented and cheated us on many occasions. They have conspired with the government to enforce the "no-strike, no-raise" policies. Therefore, the call for a general strike on May 5, 1975 is good and should be supported. If COTU betrays us again on May 5th, then COTU will be considered *dead* for our purposes.

Mwakenya: The Unfinished Revolution

Where Do We Go From Here?

Kamati ya Ukombozi wa Kenya call for: **1)** Immediate follow-up of Parliamentary Select Committee Report by a vote of no confidence in and resignation of the Kenyatta regime followed by a public trial; **2)** All Kenyan people to remain watchful and vigilant against a fascist, rightwing coup by the ruling clique, e.g., suspension of parliament, constitution, mass detentions, more murders, etc.; **3)** Parliament to militantly take back its rightful constitutional powers and proceed to **(a)** enact laws for prompt redistribution of land to the poor and the landless and renunciation of illegal British "settler land compensation loans"; and **b)** to insist that uncompromising freedom fighter Achieng' Oneko and all other political prisoners be released now; **4)** Salaries and wages to be raised to a minimum of Ksh. 600.000, and for government's COTU to be disbanded and replaced by a true workers' body with worker's control; **5)** The Kenyan people to continue to maintain their unity in opposing oppression, exploitation and foreign domination.

Power to the workers and peasants of Kenya!

Down with the KANU Puppets and their Foreign Masters!

Issued by Kamati ya Ukombozi wa Kenya
Nairobi, Mombasa, Nakuru and Kisumu

(It is available in Kiswahili and English. Watch for future issues. Circulate the document to friends and patriots).

Mwanguzi, March 1976

Kenyatta Government Unleashes Greater Suffering to the Poor

Kenyatta's traitorous government has finally declared itself bankrupt, thus admitting what many Kenyans have known for a long time. While Kenyan workers and peasants have been slaving and getting overtaxed and overcharged for everything, *where has all the money gone? Who will suffer and what now must all patriotic Kenyans do?*

First the bankruptcy was not a sudden thing; it is the end of "ten great years" of theft, corruption and mismanagement by the traitorous Kenyan comprador bourgeoisie. Soon after 1963, when KANU was taken over and changed from a majority patriotic, anti-imperialist instrument into a minority, neocolonial anti-Kenyan clique controlled by Kenyatta, the imperialist countries (Britain, USA, Japan and West Germany) teamed up with big officials in the cabinet and civil servants in order to deepen and to extend the exploitation of our resources and labor. The result was an evil alliance of foreign devils with local comprador lackeys led by KANU and Kenyatta. The imperialists were promised a freeze on workers' wages and banning of strikes to ensure them high profits. In return the compradors got directorships in the imperialist multinational corporations and were also allowed great wealth and assistance to bank it abroad. This was only the beginning with their greed thus aroused, this evil class of traitors went on to rob us Kenyans of our land and to create bogus "public" companies (e.g., the useless Pipeline Corporation) to milk even more money from

Mwakenya: The Unfinished Revolution

us. Ndegwa's Commission in 1970 officially sealed this comprador trick. There followed extreme corruption by big government officials, smuggling of natural and trade commodities (ivory, rice, rubies, etc.), open theft of public money and extortion of bribes from Kenyans to perform even minor official work. Why, they even stole famine relief money and supplies.

Whenever they are in trouble or when they suck the treasury dry, they then run abroad to their masters and beg for more loans. They praise and congratulate each other and then happily commit our future to endless debts. It is now known that little of these loans get here; it will be divided among them and banked in foreign banks and safes. All we get are the bills, plus interest. Kĩbaki just borrowed Ksh. 2,040,000,000 last week. Britain unashamedly ordered that their money must remain in Britain and must be used to buy our own stolen land from their colonial settlers. Kĩbaki smilingly complied then came to announce to us to rejoice for being so loved abroad.

Since Kenyans recognized the real sellout, thieving nature of the comprador Kenyatta government, much anger, opposition and even uprisings have been mounted throughout the country and in all sections of our society—workers, peasants, small businessmen, students and pupils. It is because of mounting military that police, GSU and SB (Special Branch) harassment and repression have been multiplied many times over. In addition, the so-called "law and justice" are daily used to silence any patriotic voice raised against traitorous comprador policies. To keep us confused and weak, they then divide us by nationalities and regions.

This is class war. The compradors have declared war on the peasants, workers and all the poor of our country. They have increased our suffering by raising the prices, taxes and denied us even the already poor services— education, health care, information, etc. and now has started firing people from their jobs thus increasing unemployment.

It is now the duty of all genuinely patriotic Kenyans to *cast out all doubts* and oppose this misrule and mismanagement and to expose completely, and by all means available, the fact that our country cannot possibly develop under comprador imperialist alliance. We can only sink deeper and deeper into misery, international indebtedness and national bankruptcy. Only a truly revolutionary socialist system, controlled and guarded by Kenyans can bring about useful progressive change for all the poor, the peasants, the workers and other exploited classes. We must seriously begin creating and supporting anti-imperialist organizations, which will carry our struggle forward to victory.

Down with Traitorous Compradors!
Down with Neocolonialism!
Build all Kenyan People's Unity!

Issued by Kamati ya Ukombozi wa Kenya
Nairobi, Mombasa, Nakuru, Kisumu.

Mwanguzi, April 1976

KANU is Alive and Working for the Rich Natives and Foreigners

KANU has never died. In fact, it has continued to serve the corrupt rich class of landed influential Kenyans and their foreign friends. KANU has completely given up the interests of the majority of Kenya's people who are generally poor and landless. KANU is therefore an instrument of oppression against Kenyans. This is contrary to our great expectations in 1963 that KANU could lead us from colonial misery to political and economic independence, to prosperity and happiness. How has KANU been turned from a patriotic party to a minority, rightwing, anti-Kenyan party?

In 1963 KANU stood for much that Kenyans desired. The KANU Manifesto correctly called for land reform and redistribution, free education and health, nationalization of major industries, opposition to, and removal of, foreign imperialist domination of the economy and culture, firm material support to all anti-imperialist liberation movements in Africa and elsewhere, and most of all the Manifesto promised to watch for the rights and interests of all our people here in Kenya and abroad. These were good positions and the majority of the Kenyan people supported them and voted KANU to power against all the other pro-colonialist organizations (e.g. KADU).

Mwakenya: The Unfinished Revolution

What has the KANU Government Done Since 1963?

Land was not redistributed. Instead, it was bought from Britain and sold dearly to Kenyans. Most of the land in Kenya is in the hands of big government and KANU officials. A little of it is in the hands of cooperatives where big KANU and government officials again are the bosses. As an example, Kĩhĩka Kĩmani, KANU chairman of Nakuru District and GEMA national organizer, is head of Ngwatanĩro, while a recently proven criminal, Wanyoike Thũngũ is chairman of NDEFFO in Nakuru. Primary education everywhere despite lies about free education is more expensive than ever before. Higher education is now for those with a lot of money. The result of this is that education is for the rich people's children. Health is free in words, but in fact we find that it is inaccessible and often non-existent. Many poor Kenyans are forced to go to costly private clinics, while wealthy influential families easily get free health care. Imperialist interests now control the entire economy, instead of Kenyans slowly building their own enterprises independently. All sugar processing, mining, textile and financial concerns are owned by such foreign monopolies as Lonrho, Booker, Tate and Lyle, Barclays Bank, etc. The fighting blood-unity of Kenyans and all anti-imperialist movements has been betrayed and replaced by occasional empty words by the KANU government promising the obvious of services, but rarely ever delivering on their promise to do right by all Kenyans.

In other words, KANU has criminally betrayed the wishes and basic needs of all Kenyans. Starting in 1964 the pro-imperialist rightwing minority in KANU, headed by Jomo Kenyatta, grabbed party power and started purging and eliminating (detention or killing) all the honestly patriotic members of KANU who stood firm by the party manifesto, i.e., land redistribution, economic independence, etc. KANU stopped being for Kenyans' interests and became an instrument for a small minority of lackeys or puppets of the British, American and other imperialist financial interests. The bogus "African Socialism" (Sessional Paper No. 10) replaced the KANU Manifesto written by an imperialist professor from the United States. This anti-socialist paper was KANU's new policy to turn

Mwakenya: The Unfinished Revolution

Kenya into a neocolony. This process was completed and rubberstamped in Nakuru last month by the so-called KANU chairmen's conference. These unelected chairmen represented only themselves and had no mandate from any section of the people. They were under strict orders to comply or be punished. This joke of a conference was called "Reorganization of KANU". We are not fooled. What they mean by "reorganization" is that KANU has officially become a minority party for the oppression of Kenyans. KANU is not dead; it is alive and working for Kenya's non-development. It is no accident that during their meeting in Nakuru, landless victims of KANU's policies were being attacked for rightfully demanding their share of land!

Being so recognized by all Kenyans as political bankrupt, this reactionary organization of Kenya's wealthy class has been rejected over the years. In desperation the rulers therefore have to force people to join it. But being in the hands of the enemy, KANU cannot change for the better.

We must continue to reject it and oppose it and the evil sellout class it represents. In its place we must organize a revolutionary people's party which will kick the imperialists out the country, and stop the KANU comprador clique from exploiting the majority of Kenyans.

Down with imperialism and neocolonialism!
Down with KANU!
Long live Mau Mau!

Issued by Kamati ya Ukombozi wa Kenya
Nairobi, Mombasa, Nakuru, Kisumu

Mwanguzi, May 1976

Oppose Government Attack Against the Poor

This week Waiyaki called a meeting of the poor people of Mathare. He abused them and all other poor people of Kenya. He obviously did this on behalf of his government and his class friends. He made it clear that the Kenyatta regime wants to blame and attack us for our poverty—that is it our fault that we live in slums covered with mud of poverty and daily misery. But we know you, Waiyaki, and your class friends. Do you think we have forgotten your lies since 1963 that change and betterment were just around the corner? We have finally realized your promises for what they are—Lies! While we watch life around us getting worse every day, you bring us new promises of skyscrapers. When one or two houses are built, you and your class friends own them and charge us outrageous rent.

Kenya's comprador bourgeoisie, which Waiyaki represents, headed by Kenyatta's sellout government, is now noticing our great anger. So they have to come to insult us and to threaten us with their GSU. This shows that they recognize their coming downfall and our growing strength; they are afraid and desperate. They should know that their threats and show of force would not stop us from demanding our rights and social justice.

Who does not know why shanties and slums are coming up in every town in Kenya? The Kenyatta reactionary, anti-Kenyan regime has done

Mwakenya: The Unfinished Revolution

everything possible to make sure that rural Kenya remains undeveloped, weak and apolitical so they can exploit the peasants and rural workers with little resistance. Land, which used to be our means of livelihood, is now entirely in their control while the whole country is under control of world imperialisms. Landlessness and daily poverty force us to move to towns to seek employment. We are not in these slum-towns because we enjoy the smell of rotting garbage and dead cats and dogs, the Kenyatta neocolonial regime forced us to come here. The comprador regime knows very well that when we get to these towns there are no jobs for us. The few that are there are paying slave wages or salaries, and one cannot afford the overpriced food or rent; nor can one afford to pay school tuitions for his children. But that is not all. The government attacks us—burn down our slum houses, destroy our kiosks, arrest and imprison us.

In the last few months, the government, using police dogs and GSU, has attacked us and destroyed our dwellings in Nyalenda in Kisumu, Bondeni and Bahati in Nakuru, Gĩkomba and Mathare in Nairobi, in Nyĩrĩ and in Mombasa. They have jailed us for trespassing in our own country when we seek employment; they call us vagrants. They have collected our children from city streets for the "crime" of having nothing to eat. This is not independence. It is neocolonialism under the *wise* leadership of Jomo Kenyatta and KANU.

How do we get out of this oppression? We must unite and organize—organize a revolutionary party to overthrow this neocolonial regime and its imperialist supporters. Our fundamental aim is to create a just society, a socialist society. Join us.

Down with Kenyatta and KANU!
Smash foreign domination!
Power to the People!

Issued by Kamati ya Ukombozi wa Kenya
Nairobi, Mombasa, Nakuru, Kisumu.

MAKŨYŨ
The Conditions of the Working Class in Makŭyŭ Plantations, January 1975

Makŭyŭ area in Mũrang'a County is essentially what used to be the old Thĩka District. It formed part of the former white highlands (special area) reserved exclusively for British colonialist settlers. The area is very productive with good soils, but unreliable rainfall. A good supply of water from rivers (Thĩka and Cania) makes the area very useful for large-scale irrigation and dry-farming. Towards the end of the 1950s much foreign finance capital (British, French, West Germany, North America, etc.) was poured into area in order to acquire massive tracts of land for growing sisal, pineapple, coffee and cattle ranching. This reflected the changeover from small family estates to giant operations dialectically attached to foreign monopoly imperialist finance.

This preliminary investigation deals, therefore, with the conditions of workers and their families on three plantations: Pineapple, Sisal and Coffee.

Pineapple Plantation Workers

Kenya Canners Ltd. is the name under which a conglomeration of North American and British finance covers itself in pineapple production and processing near Thĩka Township. California Packers (Calpak)—a fully owned subsidiary of Del Monte has all managing rights. Their 200 Sq.

miles plantation, like many others in the area is like an autonomous self-governing state, and is virtually self-sufficient in power, water, roads and labor. There are about 2,000 workers of 3 grades. Grades 3, the lowest, along with *Kibarua* get 0.70 cents an hour or a total of Ksh. 5.60 maximum a day. The average income is about Ksh. 120 a month. These constitute 90% of the labor force, and an area of an extremely oppressed lot. They have their families living on the plantation and from their little pay they have to provide for all of life's basic necessities, including paying for Harambee school fees in some cases. The conditions of workers continue to be as miserable as they were before independence, if not worse. Chronic hunger, depoliticization, powerless, lack of an effective trade union, hard manual labor, and no social amenities are as rampart as they ever were. Housing provided is wretched and shared between many families. They are allowed a little *shamba* for subsistence.

All workers are bitter, angry and strongly curse the "Kaburũ boss", the African comprador managers, *Nyapara*, their MP Representative and most of all the union, "iko mfukoni mwa Kaburũ". One elderly worker said, "In my four years here there has been no union meeting." In essence, the union leaders are comprador agents of the *Kaburũ*. Their job is to keep the "niggers" in their place. In return, they get crumbs. The union in question is the Plantation Workers Union (PWU) centered in Nakuru with a local branch at Thĩka.

Sisal Plantation Workers

Kakuzi Fibrelands and Sisal Ltd. have one of the largest chunks of land in the entire country. In the Makũyũ area, Kakuzi specializes in sisal, coffee and beef. Unlike the outright international monopoly financing of Kenya Canners Ltd., Kakuzi is the continuation of old British colonial settler-type of financing. In Kakuzi the situation has continued to be run under the same colonial system as before, with very minor concessions to the workers, but some of the same colonial and oppressive treatments. The workers reflect this by saying that they feel they are in "Southern Rhodesia". While Kenya

Mwakenya: The Unfinished Revolution

Canners make minor tokenist benefits in the American racist fashion of tricking workers, Kakuzi is blatant and indifferent. One young man, a worker, told us, "You see, Uhuru did not come to the poor people, it came to the rich. See our condition, we are still oppressed and exploited by the same forces as before. We think that our brothers who run the government betrayed us to the imperialists."

There can be no bitterness as deep as that which the Kakuzi workers hold. Most workers make less than Ksh. 80.00 a month and work all day and weekends in hot dry fields doing backbreaking and irritating labor. The whole population is underfed, aged before their time, and is sickly and no longer able bodied as their peers who are employed elsewhere. The children are either bloated with malnourishment or sickly with diseases common with poverty in a country that does not prioritize its biggest investment— their human capitals that will either propel the country forward, or take it backwards. In Kakuzi, misery, sufferings and poverty are the workers' permanent guests.

The colonialist Kakuzi management uses African puppet managers and foreman in its exploitation of the workers. For example, little huts made of grass and bushes are huddled close together ("to save plantation space"). In the long dry season whole villages burn down causing untold misery and suffering to workers' families. There is no water to put out the fire and the managers blame the workers for the fire. Management also allows cattle to feed on the gardens of the workers' patches, and then divides the workers' up by accusing the shepherds of feeding off of the gardens. This question of water is also an important one. Workers use stagnant brackish water, which is contaminated, while clean river water is used to sprinkle coffee plants and given to the cattle. This brackish water has spread deadly diseases such as bilharzia to about 60% of the worker population and their families. There are no medical facilities accessible to these workers, nothing at all!

Extreme misery and great sufferings have driven many workers and their entire families to drink alcohol, *karũbũ*, resulting in further ruin of an already ruined family. Big civil servants, ministers and the local MPs are all big shareholders in Kakuzi and because of them the management feels

Mwakenya: The Unfinished Revolution

secure in oppressing and exploiting the workers and their families.

Everyone we talked to, denounced the plantation union bitterly, and proudly said that they had "suspended" or "banned" the union from there. "There is no difference between the union and Kakuzi", they said. This was the typical comment we got from the workers. The union back in Thĩka is renowned for conniving with the management and has even acquired great wealth that way. The union leadership is known to embezzle union funds and engage in corrupt capitalist activities. Some own big shops, others own public buses (matatũ).

Coffee Plantation Workers

Coffee is grown in the higher wetter areas west of Thĩka. Here there are many medium size plantations—except for minor exceptions—all are foreign-owned. By far the largest is Socfinaf Ltd., own by Anglo-French capitalist. An aura of great wealth is evident in all Socfinaf operations except their vicious treatments of workers. There are so many workers that no one knows the number exactly, but it is well over 10,000. They are divided into "work camps". These camps are concentrations of small round rat-holed houses shared by several families. The average wages are Ksh.105.00 a month, except during harvest season when any debe (a 4 gallon tin) above 3 is considered a "bonus". Women get Ksh. 3.85 a day and are required to be "smart" if they are grading the coffee-cherry. In spite of the increasing number of women in the ranks of the employed working class, they are underpaid and ruthlessly mistreated and sexually abused by their bosses. On all levels of our national economy they still do equal work for unequal pay. In our country, women are the most exploited group of the working class. Consistent with that, Socfinaf shamelessly lures child-laborers from school and pays them less. A good portion of picking-time labor force is under 14 years old.

The only things that workers and their families get are firewood and water, but they insist that their pay accounts partly for the price of both. They know that "Kaburũ" does not give anything for nothing. He is a blood-

Mwakenya: The Unfinished Revolution

sucker. Workers said that for them there are two governments: the national and Socfinaf. Socfinaf has more power according to the workers because it controls their very life and it has power to decide the fate of any worker. It has, in fact, denied the workers many holidays off. The national government is like a paid agent of the powerful Socfinaf. One worker said angrily that workers are forgotten "like children without a father in a wilderness". This remark was repeated many times by workers.

The population immediately next to the plantation is the "reserve", which wonders why it cannot acquire parts of these plantations by Hire Purchase. The people have attempted to do this, but the local MP chump, or his bigger friends beat them to it. One MP lies, stating that he will buy the land now so that "Kĩambu people may not grab it; when people have money I will gladly give it to them." Another big lie!

Conclusion

These are preliminary observations in a vast area with many workers. The uniformity of the oppressive conditions in the three cases indicates that there is much suffering—misery, poverty and untold exploitation caused by these profit-hungry international monopoly corporations. Apart from failing to protect the plantation workers from daily brutality inflicted on them by their plantation capitalist employers, the government of the *"wananchi"* also has failed to be concerned with the slave-wages given to the workers. While some workers continue to earn Ksh.70.00 a month, the government does absolutely nothing to rectify the situation. Yet we are all equal in the eyes of the government. But is this not the government that perpetuates exploitation of man by man; the government that supports the oppressors against the oppressed masses of our people?

The workers are intensely aware of this and wish to see some change. They know very well that the union is in the *"mfuko mwa Kaburũ"* and the government cares very little about their social improvement. A few though believe mistakenly that the MP can tell the government about their suffering, if he is a good man. If he is a bad man then they believe that the

Mwakenya: The Unfinished Revolution

MP is less likely to speak to the government on behalf of their suffering, and this is why government does not know about it. Yet they have tried to send delegations to Gatũndũ with no results. In desperation, families turn to religion and alcohol to ease their pains and daily sufferings. In all this misery, pain and suffering the union is the chief criminal and is a recognized and hated by every worker. This situation seemed insurrectionary. It is clear that the great unity of all the nationalities has been maintained despite divisive practices by corrupt petty politicians. At no place was KANU mentioned indicating its defunct status in living experience.

The entire situation could not be better for scientific revolutionary work, but more specific work and serious investigation would have to be done to discover particular contradictions as a scientific basis of our political work.

Struggle however continues.

Notes:

1. There is the possibility that the government subsidizes the plantation corporation by charging ridiculously little for land lease, and nothing for massive irrigation of water from rivers that dry up before reaching the dry peasant areas in the Masaakũ plains; an irrigation system that is allowed to pollute rivers, destroys the soil, and poisons the air.

2. This preliminary investigation was done by Kamoji Wachiira and Maina wa Kĩnyattĩ in January 1975. A task they were assigned by the WPK Central Committee.

3. Kenya Canner Ltd is owned by Del Monte, a U.S. multinational corporation.

Tactics and Strategy, 1976-1981

The WPK Central Committee Report
April 1976

Let Us Sum Up Our Experiences and Move Forward

Marxist-Leninists must constantly evaluate their work in order to move ahead. This is done by regular summing up of their real-world experiences in political work, by criticism and self-criticism followed by new methods of work aimed at rectifying errors and strengthening gains. This way vitality and success are assured. Herein lays a fundamental difference What has our experience been in the past few years and what can we learn from it? In only a few years those who have submitted themselves to Marxist-Leninist discipline have accumulated rich and useful experience. Method of organization and work, which were correct and successful at an earlier time are now clearly inadequate and sometimes even unworkable. The situation in Kenya, as a whole, is constantly changing, and so is our strength. Failure to adjust and modify tactics in view of new contradictions will surely lead to stagnation and backsliding at the very moment when conditions call for the exact opposite. The nature of revolutionary work is such that without constant evaluation of, and response to, changing conditions setbacks are inevitable.

Our work has centered on *Organization*. It must be clear to all those involved in our work, from the start, that the ultimate aim is to form a

Mwakenya: The Unfinished Revolution

communist party. This is of basic importance. Marxism-Leninism holds that there can be no revolutionary change whatsoever without a rock-solid, disciplined, vanguard. Experience from all socialist revolutions bears this out.

Our primary task now and for a considerable time to come remains to work towards that aim. All our work must be geared single-mindedly to strengthening the center. The backward line of the spontaneous change is possible and must be fought hard. Some among us accept in mere theory that organization is important, but we fail to see the importance of carrying out *practically* those tasks that nourish and expand the party.

With this in mind, the following points need to be renewed, thoroughgoing study and discussion with constant reference to living examples and experiences of each respective unit.

1. The need for Marxist-Leninist organization to lead the Kenyan revolution particularly as seen from other socialist revolutions.

2. The need for building and strengthening the Marxist-Leninist Center; and in the process of doing so, producing proven communist cadres, capable of carrying out correctly (and if need be independently) the tasks of pushing the struggle forward. Their world outlook and lifestyle will be communist.

3. Insisting on rigorous discipline at all times, especially being careful to make it clear to new individuals that entering a unit calls for collective discipline, sub-mitting oneself totally to the unit and placing politics first at all times. The tendency to recruit new members by sometimes seeming to "trap" them into groups and hoping that they will somehow change only leads to groups becoming soft and liberal over the crucial question of struggle because they fear splits. This is extremely serious and can only result in ineffective work, erroneous and harmful lines and can never develop Marxist-Leninist cadres. Instead, it creates yet more bourgeois liberals.

4. Only with such discipline and struggle will serious, committed, individuals change not just their world outlook but their very lifestyles and social practices.

Mwakenya: The Unfinished Revolution

5. We currently find individuals who profess to submit to Marxist-Leninist discipline but have kept much of their bourgeois outlook and practice under the guise that "it is not interfering with organizational work".

6. Secrecy of work and security consciousness at all times is most essential and must be cultivated. But the situation whereby "over-caution" leads to doing nothing in the name of "security" is harmful because it stifles initiative and brings about stagnation. Security to protest the organization and its work is important. Security to protest individuals is a cover for "do-nothing" attitude. We must be more daring in order to break new ground and achieve victory.

7. Group discussions should allow for full participation by, and encouragement for, all members. The aim of discussion is to develop the ability of all members to analyze situations from a Marxist-Leninist point of view. In this context, discussion of current issues and those revolving around the members' places of work should be stressed. Discussion of Marxism-Leninism should not be carried out as an academic exercise merely to give knowledge.

8. Most important is the question of leadership. Building an organization means also seeking to build the correct type of leadership and revolutionary authority. Some groups have failed to see the need for higher or older, more experienced, groups exercising overall authority. There can be no proper development if this "our-small-group is supreme" mentality is not fought. The discipline of Marxist-Leninist democratic centralism must be accepted without question.

These eight points are simply guidelines. Each unit has had some experience and should draw from such an experience to highlight these points and to examine possible ways of rectifying its mistakes and struggling for a new vigorous method of work. It also brings about thorough consolidation of our gains so far and creates conditions for a more unified approach to work. Carried out to its conclusion, this will propel us to even higher levels of achievement, towards fulfilling our immediate goal of building the revolutionary vanguard party.

Cell Report for Year 1980 (Nairobi)

I. Introduction

The Unit has noted with regards to political developments within its region of operation that: **1)** As a result of the increasing dominance of finance capital over Kenya's economy—a trend of maldevelopment in which the ruling clique has been a full participant—the country is sinking deeper and deeper into an economic recession, and the destitution among its workers is intensifying. In part, due to an international market oriented agricultural interests of the multinationals, this sector of the economy has experienced a lopsided development, causing constant shortages in basic food commodities. **2)** The continuance of competing (yet mutually supporting) economic interests of different imperialist countries in Kenya—USA's hegemony in running this show notwithstanding—is directly reflected, in a representational form, in the schism and struggle within Kenya's political elite, as the different sections align themselves with different imperialist countries. The Unit also notes that contrary to popular belief, the "Kĩbaki group" within this ruling clique seems quite incapable of undertaking a bourgeois democratic leadership; a leadership that is progressively responding to the whims and caprices of the "Moi group" in an attempt to regain its favor. **3)** Due to the military and economic interests of the imperialist countries in African states, neighboring Kenya, the latter has been forced to establish rather odd alliances with Ethiopia, the Sudan, and Uganda.

Mwakenya: The Unfinished Revolution

The Unit further notes that as a result of: **1)** The inception of the Moi dictatorship in the country—as evidenced of the banning of trade unions and welfare organizations, and the apparently high degree of intolerance to and personalization of any kind of peaceful dissent; **2)** The politico-economic eclecticism and buffoonery of the leadership; **3)** The failing popularization of a false image of benevolence on the part of the leadership that is replete with anti-democratic practices all of which, in the long run, act against the interests of finance capital and of imperialism at large, the imperialist countries and their multinational corporations in Kenya: **a)** are becoming increasingly concerned about a leadership that is capable of promoting and protecting their interests in Kenya; and **b)** are threatening to divert (in preference for investment in Zimbabwe with its more developed infrastructure).

The Kenya government's reaction to these "threats," in an attempt to reassure the imperialists, has been to adopt a policy which will allow for a greater repatriation of profits on the part of multinationals—a reaction that is necessarily bound to land the country in yet deeper economic problems, and intensifies the development of dictatorship.

Given this perspective of the political situation in Kenya, then how has the party branch responded both in terms of its theoretical and political activities?

II. Unit Activities

A. Background:

i) Theoretical Work.

While every Unit meeting has touched upon some theoretical issue of organizational and/or operational significance, only two sessions were devoted to thorough theoretical study on: 1) The history of the Communist Party of the Soviet Union; and 2) The class basis of Kenyan law—a project of one of the Unit members. No serious attempt was made, however, to

Mwakenya: The Unfinished Revolution

directly link these studies to the more practical aspects of the Unit's present tasks and its future development.

The "National Question" was proposed for study, but there was absolutely no follow up to this proposal, thereby leaving the issue lingering without being subjected to rigorous, theoretical study.

ii) Practical Work

1. ***Recruitment*:** A new member was recruited in the Unit in March of 1980, raising the number of Unit membership to four. Six other potential recruits were observed in the course of the year, but a decision was taken to drop them on the basis of lack of discipline and adventurism. In the case of at least one of these people the Unit's observations have been correct to the extent that he, using an ally who is either politically naïve or an agent provocateur, adventurously disregarded some of the most obvious security measures to engage in the production and distribution of a "manifesto" calling for a nationwide formation of a Marxist-Leninist political party.

2. ***The University Academic Staff Union (UASU):*** This was the most important project of the Unit and as such, it formed the core of the Unit operations in 1980. The election of one of the Unit members for the strategic position of UASU's Secretary-General, and the representation of two Unit members in UASU's executive committee and its steering CORE (organized by the Unit) ensured a strong Unit control of UASU's general direction.

No doubt, trade unions have their limitations and pitfalls as platforms of political work, mainly due to their economist orientation. As Lenin pointed out the rise of Economism in the Soviet Union could actually be traced to the activities of the Social Democratic Party itself, to the party's limiting its sphere of activities in the initial stage to "mere" economist activities among the workers. However, the Unit was able to avoid this pitfall by linking the political issues to the economic issues. Hence, by presenting the political annihilation of Ngũgĩ wa Thiong'o as an economic issue in the form of "tenure of service", and the political solidarity forum on the assassination

Mwakenya: The Unfinished Revolution

of Walter Rodney as a question of professional freedom, popular support, in the midst of much opposition, for these political-cum-economic issues was generated without allowing cause for alarm on the part of the government. In other words, to the extent that the political was directly connected to the immediate economic and professional conditions of the union members, government backlash as well as the possible recoiling of the conservatives within the union membership was successfully avoided.

UASU started getting into problems, however, when its activities became overtly political. This came in the form of UASU-student demonstration against "imperialism" as an offshoot of the UASU forum on Walter Rodney. The Unit line, which was accepted by the UASU Core Committee, was opposed to the demonstration—especially when the government granted a permit for the demonstration at *its own initiative* after refusing to do so a couple of days earlier at the initiative of UASU. However, the Unit failed to carry this line through to the executive committee. The opportunist-adventurers usurped the leadership in favor of the demonstration, which was held the following day. A week later the Union was banned, and the Unit holds this overtly political activity the anti-imperialist demonstration—as responsible for this anti-UASU presidential decree.

Why did the Unit fail to carry its line through in the UASU's Executive Committee? Despite the agreed Unit line the two members of the Unit represented in the Executive Committee (EC) were "divided" on the issue in the EC meeting. And while the Unit did not come up with a concrete analysis of the basis of this division, it was strongly felt that it was due to liberalism on the part of one of the Unit members as a direct product of his socio-personal relation with a non-Unit member represented in the EC and who was in favor of the demonstration. The Unit called for an immediate termination of this relationship.

The strong pro-demonstration force in the executive committee with which the Unit had to contend with was also a product of UASU membership being taken in by the few gains it was making or had made in its struggles. And against such a force, the Unit failed to engage UASU in a tactical retreat when the political conditions demanded one.

Mwakenya: The Unfinished Revolution

Most members of the EC recoiled completely at the banning of UASU, and Unit effort to get the EC members to meet and discuss the Union's future form and direction failed completely. But, since by the end of 1980, no official word has reached UASU to effect its proscription, the Unit has continued to discuss and investigate the possibilities of its revival in some form or another.

Alongside with that, two Unit meetings were cancelled after the banning of UASU due to security fears. However, the way these meetings were cancelled was very un-satisfactory indeed, which led the Unit to re-emphasize that the cancellation of any meeting on the basis of security reasons should lead to the dispersion rather than the concentration of Unit members.

The period immediately following the banning of the Academic Staff Union was one of an extended inactivity on the part of the party unit, and liberalism was actually beginning to set in, but only to be combated by the consciousness of the party unit.

3. *Tamaduni Players:* Another mass-oriented project of the Unit has been the theater group, Tamanduni Players (TP). In 1980 it invited a number of people to participate in organizing and staging the Kiswahili version of Ngũgĩ's and Mĩcere's *Mzalendo Kĩmathi*, which responded positively to the political message. However, there were two destructive developments: **a)** in the initial staging of the play a few politicians took over the platform and, speaking to the audience, completely distorted the political message and used it in their favor; and **b)** opportunists among the invited members, realizing the personal (financial and professional) gains that they could weed out of the theater group, attempted to capture the leadership. This move led to a total disruption of the play and consequently to a withdrawal of the TP group from the general "Mzalendo cast". The previous organizational looseness of TP seemed to have left room for the emergency of precisely these kinds of problems. To ensure a greater control of its own direction, therefore, the group had formed a steering Core Committee, which is under the direction of a member of the party unit.

Mwakenya: The Unfinished Revolution

4. *The Legal Advice Central (LAC):* Though not the direct initiative of the Unit, this bourgeois charity institution, intended to make legal advice easily accessible to the common Kenyan, has a Unit member as its chairman. It was hoped that since the LAC has a number of contacts with trade union movement it would help the Unit's work in directing and strengthening UASU. The Unit member represented in the LAC was required to form a steering core committee, but due to his other heavy engagements in UASU and other duties, the Core Committee did not materialize. Nonetheless, under the chairmanship of the Unit member, the LAC managed: **a)** to issue a newsletter, being, in essence, a politically patriotic stand of Kenyan lawyers against foreign domination, which castigated and opposed an American attempt at pouring money into the center with the ultimate aim of exercising control over it; and **b)** to issue a petition on the Sandstorm case which, in effect, questioned the justice of Kenyan law and therefore, indirectly of justice under comprador law.

5. *Pamphleteering/Leafleting*: In response to continuing efforts by the reactionary regime to perpetuate its neocolonial rule via divisive politics, among other tactics, the party unit issued an underground leaflet entitled *Moi's Divisive Tactics Exposed*. While exposing specific divisive instances within the university, the leaflet had a wider application and essence to the extent that the specifics were so presented and related to the general political scene as to reveal one dimension in the development of dictatorship in Kenya. The leaflet was very well formulated and the issues raised were concretely expository. The production and distribution of the leaflet was well-organized and executed without the slightest security problem. The general feedback received by the party unit indicates that: **i)** the content was received with a lot of enthusiasm and the leaflet was quickly passed around and duplicated to reach a number of members of parliament within a relatively short period of time; **ii)** however, a section of the student-left at KUC felt left out and reacted by exploring the idea of issuing a counter-leaflet. This reactionary move, however, was thwarted by the sheer absence of counter-arguments to the party unit leaflet; and **iii)** the popular explanation from the Moi-Njonjo-GG Kariũki clique was that the

185

Mwakenya: The Unfinished Revolution

leaflet was engineered from, without the university, an anti-Moi group of politicians in alliance with some university student elements. There was an extended period of party unit inactivity for security reasons immediately after the leaflet.

6. *Petitioning*: Taking advantage of the expulsion of some 38 Kenyatta University students following a three days student demonstration in December 1980, the party unit produced a petition addressed to the councils of University of Nairobi and Kenyatta University, castigating the undemocratic manner in which the university is run and holding this responsible for the periodic disruptions caused by student demonstrations and expulsions. At Kenyatta University (KU) there was a strong campaign against the petition from some reactionary academics and from a section of the Christian community. Despite this, however, the party unit managed to solicit some 105 signatures, mostly from KU, and to popularize its cause in the media.

It was felt, nonetheless, that a lot more signatures could have been solicited especially from the main campus of the University of Nairobi. That the end result did not meet the party unit expectations was attributed to liberalism based, essentially, on the above-ground nature of the task, and which was reflected in two ways: **a)** the questions of timing and distribution of manpower in soliciting signatures was so loosely discussed that the party unit ended up being completely divided on what was actually agreed on; and **b)** given that there was a possibility—expressed in the party unit meeting—of authorities associating the petition with the engineers of underground leaflet on Moi's divisive tactics, the security question was naively handled. (While the very act of party unit members openly soliciting for signatures was the element more likely to lead to this association—between the petition and the leaflet—the mere rearrangement of signatures was somehow taken to be an adequate security measure).

This pitfall, to which the party unit had fallen prey to, led to a severe introspection, which touched upon such fundamental issues as commitment and trust, and to avoid some such pitfalls in the future it was agreed that: **i)** the party unit should be more wary of its decisions in its aboveground tasks; **ii)** discussions during party unit meetings should focus more restrictively on the issue in question; and iii) every party unit meeting should be followed by a resume of the proceedings.

B. Achievements

Our achievements in the course of the year have been rather modest, and a number of these apply specifically to the party unit's work in UASU. These include: **i)** to revive UASU as a political transmission belt for party unit activities and develop it into a force of concern in national political circles; **ii)** to mobilize the university staff to make a stand on its economic and professional interests in a politicized manner; and **iii)** to counter government agents and bourgeois media at an attempt at dividing staff and students by promoting staff-student solidarity on a number of issues. Another set of achievements relates specifically to party unit sessions, including: **a)** except in a couple of instances there has always been good and thorough follow up and feedback on every party unit activity (and its broader ties and implications); **b)** there was frequent, open and at times intense, introspection and self-criticism which provoked some moments of strong tension within the party unit; **c)** but despite this, the party unit managed to stick together very well, which in essence means that the party unit stood and survived the test of liberalism.

C. Failures

From a general point of view, and for all practical purposes, it seems that, given the observations on Kenya noted in the introduction of this report, the situation in the country is, both politically and economically, set for some extensive *agitation* work. Yet, clearly, the party unit has done very little in this direction in the course of the year 1980. This situation has to do with a number of specific weaknesses among which are: **1)** the party unit size is so small that it necessarily limits the scope of its work. This then boils down to the question of recruitment, the rate of which has been terribly slow; **2)**

Mwakenya: The Unfinished Revolution

another issue, which may have stultified greater activity of the party unit is the implicit assumption that the party unit may engage in activities of agitation nature which may arouse popular discontent (in a revolutionary manner), it is in no numerical position to direct that expressed mood of agitation to productive ends. Yet, it is also probably true that every instance in which people are politically aroused—whether the party unit is capable of taking that political arousal a stage higher or not—contributes to arise in political consciousness (dormant as it may be at this point); **3)** given the long periods of inactivity after the pamphleteering and the banning of UASU, and the way the security issue was handled during the petitioning, there seems to have been a tendency to use the security as a pretext for laxity; **4)** theoretical study has lagged far behind and has been treated with some degree of indifference. There has also been a total lack of effort to prioritize our theoretical work in terms of, and relate it concretely to, our practical tasks and objectives; **5)** except in the case of the Kĩmathi Play staged by the Tamaduni Players, the party unit has been unable to take the initiative to extend its operations (e.g., distribution of leaflets) outside the university campus; **6)** in the specific case of UASU, the party unit was able to demonstrate mobilization capability, but its capability to control (in a tactical sense) was proved to be rather weak. While this issue may be quite ad hoc, its experiential value requires our reflection in more general terms.

D. Lessons

The following are the lessons that the party unit has experientially derived from its activities in the course of the year: **1)** that, while bourgeois institutions (like UASU) can be successfully used as transmission belts for political work, the moment the party unit's work transcends the boundaries which are "traditionally" associated with such bourgeois institutions, it has laid itself prey to all sorts of internal and external counter revolutionary forces; **2)** our recruitment efforts have persistently shown that the intellectual profession is replete with adventurists and opportunists who have discovered in Marxism-Leninism-Maoism a tool for self-popularization and, for some, a cover for counter revolutionary

Mwakenya: The Unfinished Revolution

work; **3)** that, without consistent effort to relate revolutionary theory to revolutionary practice, theoretical work can recede into the background, be deprived of its significance and essentiality, thereby leading the party unit into an intellectual liberalism; **4)** that aboveground work, by virtue of its very nature, can easily invite *liberalism* in the form of organizational and communicational looseness; **5)** that organizational and communicational looseness, through the party unit experiences in UASU and Tamaduni Players, can be one of the most dangerous weaknesses of any political party unit and a very potent exposure to all sorts of counter-revolutionary forces of sabotage; **6)** that a political cell-unit must always be weary of being carried away by its gains in its political work which may easily distract it form a thorough assessment of the opportune moments for action and tactical retreat in relation to each activity and at each point in time; and finally, **7)** that socio-personal relation can be a strong yet unconscious, and therefore dangerous, source of liberalism, which may severely impair intra-cell unit communication and adherence to the cell-unit line on specific issues.

E. Future Tasks

1. To the extent that the party unit size is a serious limitation to the scope of its work, more active and diversified recruiting which should extend beyond the university and indeed beyond Nairobi city is one of the most pressing immediate tasks of the party unit and no effort should be spared towards the achievement of this objective. (**Note**: one party unit member had a job offer outside Nairobi, which would have helped to extend the party unit's work, but the party unit decided against his accepting it since no party unit existed there to which he could be transferred, and his organizational ability to independently establish another unit has been largely undemonstrated).

2. To continue focusing on the development of mass projects and engage in them more aggressively for agitation purposes as well as to stimulate the exposure of disciplined and committed individuals for recruitment.

3. To intensify, and extensively, theoretical study, especially on the question of mass work, in order to facilitate the promotion and maintenance of *praxis* in party unit activities.

4. In the meantime, the possibility of reactivating UASU in a form more acceptable to the government authorities and under a greater control of the party unit with a unit-controlled regular newsletter should be extensively pursued.

Note: This party unit was operating mainly in the city of Nairobi. In 1981 it was given the task of producing the party organ, *Pambana.* It consisted of five members: Willy Mutunga, Maina wa Kĩnyattĩ, Sultan Somjee, al-Amin Mazrui and Edward Oyugi.

Report of the March Second Center
March 1980-March 1981

A. Introduction

1. Every summing up of our work must be seen against the background of both the international and the national situations.

2. On the international scene, the period saw major ideological setbacks for the world revolutionary movement. In this respect, the death of Mao, the succession to power in China by a gang of capitalist roaders, and the subsequent attack on Marxism-Leninism-Maoism (MLM) were all a blow to the movement. In the United States, the Carter regime with its emphasis on human rights to cover up imperialist domination tended to blunt the edges of anti-imperialist offensives in the Third World. The Carter era has given way to the even more rightwing era of Reaganites. Although there were a few gains (e.g., in Zimbabwe, Nicaragua and el Salvador) the world experienced doldrums in the revolutionary movement and Kenya was part and parcel of that trend,

3. On the national situation, the Kenyatta rightwing era with lip service to a nationalist past died with Kenyatta to be replaced by the Moi era without even a lip service to any nationalist past. The trend is summed up by the change of slogans: From *Harambeeism* to *Nyayoism*, that is from the notion of pulling together to the following the trodden path. But the Nyayo era was a creation of the Kenyatta era. The Kenyatta succession took place without violence because it was virtually the same group succeeding itself. What happened was merely a matter of filling up the vacancies with the next in line.

Mwakenya: The Unfinished Revolution

4. This summing up of our work is based on the two areas of our operations: **a)** above ground and **b)** underground. In turn, each area has two aspects: **i)** practical **ii)** ideological. But the aim is one: the overthrow of imperialism and the struggle for national democratic liberation as a transition towards socialism.

5. Just to remind ourselves: while (a) and (b) are dialectically related, (b) is primary. Also while i) and ii) are dialectically related, i) is primary.

6. In our summing up of 1979 we saw that many gains of 1977, and after, were the result of intensive underground work of the earlier years coupled with the historic decision to move away from the immediate university constituencies.

7. For the eighties, we decided that consolidation of present cells and continued recruitment was our main tasks. But we also decide that we could take more risks in penetrating democratic organization, so as to advance our work aboveground. To create a democratic organization, however weak, was an important thing in view of the systematic suppression of democratic organization by the Moi regime. We also decided on a low profile in the issuing of pamphlets.

B. Gains

i) *Underground:*

1. More cells and units were created.

2. Recruitment is still going on.

3. There was improvement in disbanding and regrouping: the democratic centrist command structure is working better.

4. Though still on a low profile in the issuing of pamphlets, we had two huge successes in two pamphlets: the analysis of Moi regime in terms of a KADU takeover of the KANU of the early sixties, and the exposure of Moiism.

ii) *Aboveground:*

1. The biggest success story was the formation and the growth of the University Academic Staff Union (UASU) to virtually become a

Mwakenya: The Unfinished Revolution

powerful national organization being looked up to by the people for an alternative voice.

2. The virtual reopening and the revitalization of the Writers Association of Kenya (WAK) was our work. In this respect, the Seminar on The Freedom of the Artist early in 1980 was an important result of that revitalization.

3. The struggles against cultural imperialism went on taking various forms from individual articles to organized efforts.

4. We have virtually won the national languages issue. Our previous opponents are advocating our line. Those still opposing it tend to react to initiatives.

5. The play Mzalendo Kĩmaathi by the Tamaduni Players was a huge success once again victorious in our attempts to reassert the reactionary anti-Kenyan line through theater.

6. Books like *Ngaahika Ndeenda, Caitaani Mũtharaba-inĩ* and *Thunder From the Mountains* carried our ideological line and their very popularity among the people shows on the whole the correctness of our line. These were part of the ideological offensive above ground.

C. Weaknesses and Losses

i) *Underground:*

1. There was a virtual neglect of organized studies in theory. Compare this to 1975/76 when an intense theoretical work combined with intense practical work.

2. Though the command structure is working, the discipline was often not as tight leading to some spectacular losses: e.g., the banning of the Academic Staff Union. In the same way the Tamaduni Players production of Mzalendo Kĩmaathi was almost marred by this lack of discipline in obeying orders or in passing instructions through the right communicational channels and structure.

3. We have not yet been able to gain from our successes or to follow up on our successes, and this has been often resulted in opportunist elements or others taking the credit, e.g., the "spokesmen" for the union, etc.

Mwakenya: The Unfinished Revolution

4. We have also been weak in the development of qualities of leadership and authority in broad democratic forms.
5. We have been lax in following up initial contacts for the purposes of recruitment.

ii) Aboveground:

1. Items (3) and (4) above also apply here.
2. Loss of the Union.
3. We could do with more penetrations into democratic organizations. In this respect, our jobs, professions, history, background are often a handicap.

D. Overall

1. We were virtually the only consistent and organized resistance to the Moi dictatorship.
2. We were the first to expose it nationally, not only through underground pamphlets, but also through practical struggle for Ngũgĩ's reinstatement at the University.
3. Our contact with the countryside is still very weak. But it is the only way to go: painful but there is no alternative.
4. Rightists are reacting against our initiatives, e.g., the Ogot/Ochieng'/ Kipkorir/Atieno-Adhiambo reaction to *Thunder From the Mountains* by implication endorsing Mau Mau as a national patriotic movement, a position they had previously rejected.

E. The Future

i) Underground:

1. We must intensify our recruitment work. It might be slow and painful, but there is no other way.
2. We must have more organized theoretical study, e.g., the study of other revolutionary movements like that of Vietnam, Albania, Cambodia, Cuba, etc. We could also revisit some other theoretical issues, e.g.,

Mwakenya: The Unfinished Revolution

the national question, democratic centralism, a study of Marxism-Leninism-Maoism.

3. We must tighten discipline and channel of communications and vigorously combat liberalism within us, in the party and outside the party.

ii) *Aboveground:*

1. There will be continued suppression of democratic organizations. But we must continue trying to create a few where there are none, e.g., among theater workers and to penetrate existing ones, however few. These are other areas we can look into: a) Trade unionism: can we make alliances with individuals or groups? b) universities, colleges and schools, clubs and student organizations; c) churches: e.g. NCCK and progressive individuals within the church leadership. We should try to penetrate the Muslim community; and d) Parliament: try to make friends and alliances with progressive parliamentarians. We can look into possibilities of organizing a loose leftwing alliance or caucus.

2. Overall, we should utilize any openings: cultural, funeral, marriage, ceremonies, and cooperative organizations. In fact, any opening that brings us to where people are.

3. We should continue with a vigorous ideological offensive.

4. We should aim to have a few more public plays rejected or banned, as this will create awareness that it is not right.

5. The ideological offensive both underground and aboveground should be aimed at steering ourselves and at creating the necessary conditions for a higher practical work, i.e., something more than just pamphlets.

6. We must strive to analyze and understand the present post Kenyatta era, the class forces at work—their strength and weaknesses and their practical concrete manifestations in order to really know who the enemy really is so as to fight him better. If we do not recognize the enemy and the concrete form he takes culturally, politically and economically, i.e., the concrete organizational form he takes, we might end up shadow-blocking ourselves to exhaustion.

Mwakenya: The Unfinished Revolution

Note: The March Second Center was the coordinating committee of the movement. Its base was in Nairobi. It consisted of four members, namely, Kamoji Wachiira, Maina wa Kĩnyattĩ, Ngũgĩ wa Thiong'o, Edward Oyugi and Kariuki Forest. In 1981, Kariũki was suspended from the Center for his sluggishness and petty-bourgeois social behavior. Those who do not know the truth write and argue that the March Second Center was an independent movement outside the WPK and DTM.

The Proletarian Press
Launching the Party Newspaper

January 1982

We have long wished to effect the launching of a consistent and regular propaganda organ as a crucial aspect of our general political work. Along with that we have always maintained that such a publication or organ is absolutely necessary for the purpose of extending and hopefully consolidating a thoroughly Bolshevized Marxist-Leninist center—a center towards which the Kenyan masses can systematically gravitate. Such a center, we have always felt must aspire to be national in scale and must have a broad mass character. It must be a center which is not only fully consolidated ideologically and organizationally, but one which also commands a unified and systematic approach to its general and specific political tasks. Concretely, the duty of such a center is to mobilize the masses of the people to overcome the dangers of political inaction and thereby to create appropriate conditions for a militant preparedness of the Kenyan people for the eventual overthrow of the comprador, neocolonial regime. A mass propaganda organ is indeed most necessary at a time like this.

Conditions in Kenya today are characterized by a relatively passive anti-imperialist stance on the part of the mass of the people. Such a situation calls for the revolutionary initiative and leadership of the working class in

Mwakenya: The Unfinished Revolution

alliance with other progressive classes and sub-classes. The main target of such a revolutionary alliance and action is imperialism and capitalism. The success of such a revolutionary strategy will rest heavily on the capacity of the revolutionary movement to appeal to the broad-democratic sensibilities of the popular masses and to rally their democratic behind issues and political-economic interests which enjoy common appeal to all the progressive strata of Kenya's neocolonial society.

Correspondingly, a propaganda organ, which such a movement requires for the fulfillment of its historical mission, must be: **1)** pro-Kenyans both in content and style; **2)** anti-imperialism and anti-capitalism in content and function; **3)** anti-all brands of reactionary socialist trash, peddled by imperialist agent in neocolonial Kenya devoid of any unnecessary far-fetched theoretical antagonism with social-imperialism; **4)** national social-democratic in content, but communist in its systematically concealed long-term functions; **5)** short-term in its political action, yet long-term in its revolutionary vision and anticipation: **6)** "live" in its agitation content, and broad in its political appeal and influence; **7)** devoid of "unnecessarily excessive" Marxist vocabulary, the purpose being to effectively use the broad democratic platform for communist intentions without alerting our deadly enemies, particularly during our incipient stages of development; and finally, **8)** written in the languages that are understood by the great majority of the Kenyan people—in this case, mainly Kiswahili and English, but under special circumstances other national languages may also be used.

The Format

The layout of the organ will be as follows:

1. **Editorial:** Its content will be general and analytical. Its function will be to expose the Kenyan masses to the correct analysis of broadly based ideological and political issues, which are of crucial importance to the development of their political consciousness.

2. **Analysis of Current and Topical Events and Issues:** In this section topical national and international events and issues will be subjected

Mwakenya: The Unfinished Revolution

to a dialectical-materialist analysis—always making the revolutionary interests of the Kenyan people the point of reference. The presentation must be simple, clear and using local imageries, idioms and expressions, i.e., relying on the concrete experiences of our people. It must avoid stereotype and worn out expressions.

3. **Expose Report/Inside Report:** This should be the result of thoroughly carried out investigations into the various aspects of imperialist, neocolonial, and comprador misdeeds against the people of Kenya. First and foremost such reports should aim at muckraking the neocolonial filth concealed under the thin veneer of capitalist pretensions. In order to generate militant opposition within the ranks of the people against imperialism and its local agents they should be subjected to heavy doses of agitation sensationalized. This should also include reports about heroic anti-imperialist (and even anti-intimidation) deeds of Kenyans.

4. **Letters to the Editorial Committee:** Letters bearing faked authorship should always beef up popular stands.

The *first* issue should be a proto-type of the future format of the organ. However, its editorial should contain a condensed version of *Cheche*—adding to it the goals and objectives of the organ and something amounting to "What is to be done?" i.e., a revolut-ionary "Way out" of the impasse. The remaining sections of the first issue should be as suggested in the format above, i.e., News analysis and inside reports, accepting letters to the editorial committee (which should not appear at all.

Name: The name of the party organ is **Pambana.** It will be a mass newspaper.

Pambana, No.1, May 1982
Organ of the December Twelve Movement

Editorial

Cheche: A Park Can Light a Prairie Fire.

This is a historical moment. Today we celebrate: The challenge and spirit of Cheche Kenya.

This first issue of *Pambana* marks a major milestone, indeed even a turning point in our country's history. It is the first truly people's newspaper. It constitutes a stop towards creating our people's own voice and institutions. The government-controlled, foreign owned press, as well as the laughable Voice of Kenya (VOK), lies to us always. They misrepresent Kenya's reality and praise every crime and evil act the ruling class commits. They apologize for them and continually attack our people's struggles or at best ignore them. These newspapers sow confusion and disunity in their attempts to put "a lid on trouble" and stop the wheel of history. Our people want change, revolutionary changes. The government and its mouthpieces want to keep Kenyans down. Just as these government controlled, foreign owned newspapers cannot be free, they cannot be neutral. In many real ways they support our enemies.

Pambana is similarly neither free nor neural. It will accept no apologies for oppression or thievery and will forcefully represent the truth as seen from the majority poor, dispossessed Kenyans who have hitherto been so

Mwakenya: The Unfinished Revolution

fully ignored. Pambana will therefore be militantly and proudly partisan. *Pambana* could not have come at a better time. The current regime, like the last one, is fully exposed as unable to solve the political and economic problems facing us.

During colonialism, there were two types of newspapers representing two fundamentally opposed interests. There were those, like the *East African standard* (now it's named *The Standard*), *The Daily Nation* and *Kenya Weekly*, which represented foreign and white settler interests. Then there were others like *Mũigwithania*, *Mũmenyereri*, *Mũramati*, *Sauti ya KAU*, *Ramogi* and *Mwalimu*, which represented the Kenyan people's aspirations for freedom. The people's press was harassed and finally banned by the colonial regime in the 1950s.

The story did not change after 1963. The two main newspapers are still foreign owned: *The Daily Nation* by the Aga Khan Syndicate and the *East African Standard* by Lonrho. A true people's press has been suppressed. KANU regimes have only allowed newspapers that defend foreign interests; even modest attempts by Kenyans to found a liberal press have been suppressed or discouraged. Thus, the people's press has been pushed underground.

As in order similar situations elsewhere the underground press has been the only truly free press in both colonial and neocolonial Kenya. The existence does not depend on the goodwill of the foreign controlled-KANU regime. It does not depend on the goodwill of advertisers.

Indeed in all modern societies which have made revolution, newspapers have always played a vital part in awakening, mobilizing and unifying them. We quote Lenin who founded *Iskar* in Old Russia and declared prophetically, "A Spark Can Light a Prairie Fire".

Long Live Pambana!

Our Stand

Kenyans have been massively betrayed. The revolution we launched with blood has been arrested and derailed. Today more than 22 years after KANU

Mwakenya: The Unfinished Revolution

was formed, almost 29 years after a fake independence was *negotiated*, the broad masses of Kenya are materially and politically worse off than ever before. The criminally corrupt ruling clique, sanctioned by KANU has isolated itself from the concerns of our daily life and has committed a crime among many others, more brutal than any that British colonialism ever did: they have silenced all opposition and deprived us, forcibly and otherwise, of the very right to participate in Kenya's national affairs. The sacred rights of expression and association have been cast aside.

KANU and its government have disorganized all spheres of economic production, have scattered all communal efforts at organization, have sowed unprincipled discord and enmity among our peoples, and have looted unspeakable sums of money and national wealth. They have finally given our entire country over to U.S. imperialism to use as a political and military base. All these crimes have been wrought in the name of "progress and prosperity" and inane smatterings of "love, peace and unity".

This is *not* independence. This is neocolonialism in its worst form. Kenyans have fought many battles in order precisely to put an end to a similar situation in the past. They did not wage war in order to end up worse off than before. Clearly, serious errors were made in the past— particularly the error not to thoroughly cleanse the people's ranks of pro-colonial elements that later regrouped, took over leadership, and derailed the struggle to where it is today. This is a most important point and we intend to dwell on it at length in the future. We must build on past experiences, avoid mistakes, and not repeat them. The cost has already been too great.

True independence is a *sacred* thing. It is revolutionary. It means a clean break, a new start with no fetters from the past oppressive machinery. It means a fiercely vigilant nation led by a strong people's organization, which works with the people's initiative in building a new society, with new forms and new modes of thought. True independence releases vast new energy and creativity. Kenya has no independence.

Kenya is more dependent today than it was before 1963. Despite her considerable wealth she is starving, in debt and bankrupt. Kenyans,

Mwakenya: The Unfinished Revolution

therefore, have no alternative but to begin anew in order to continue the revolution that was diverted. We are once again called upon, more urgently now than ever before, to marshal our forces and prepare for a protracted counter-attack in order to salvage and reconstruct our nation. This is war, class war. We must have no illusions. We hail and applaud *Cheche Kenya*, a great pioneering summary and take up the challenge therein. It is our historic duty to stand up and refuse to simply go along. It is also our natural right to express ourselves, to disseminate ideas and to associate. These rights we will retake them, forcibly if necessary.

We, the *December Twelve Movement*, have chosen to make our contribution by starting the first truly revolutionary people's paper. Hitherto no paper has represented the wishes and activities of the poor and oppressed Kenyans correctly. Henceforth, we shall. Others must do whatever they can in order that a principled unity can be built based on concrete acts, *accomplished* and living experience gained, and not on dead words said or written.

December Twelve 1963 was the day most Kenyan masses united with the hope of a new national reality, a true independence. Unknown to them, this was not to be. It signifies to us a betrayal and the basis of a new, higher unity and a revolutionary rebirth.

This newspaper is dedicated to gathering, uniting, encouraging and protecting all those who would defiantly stand for our country's and people's true interests and who would sacrifice and fight towards our unity and victory. This is a serious political task and we solemnly dedicate ourselves and our abilities to it. We have no doubt that the overwhelming majority of Kenyans stand by this position.

This newspaper:

1. Firmly opposes the robbery of our national resources and wealth by imperialist interests, be they multinational corporations, banks or foreign governments. Kenyan wealth and labor must benefit Kenyans only.

Mwakenya: The Unfinished Revolution

2. Condemns in the strongest of terms the criminally corrupt and traitorous band of thieves who govern this country and who have allied themselves with U.S. imperialism to keep us perpetually down.

3. Is totally opposed to the presence on Kenyan soil of U.S. and any other military bases.

4. Supports all genuine, democratic and liberation movements fighting for people's self-determination in and outside Kenya.

This newspaper supports all genuine Kenyan organizations and individuals fighting any aspect of local or imperialist reaction and in particular:

1. Small farmers and producers working against government and "cooperative" theft and mismanagement.

2. Workers against IMF-enforced low wages and anti-strike controls.

3. The millions unemployed in their right to employment.

4. Small businessmen against foreign monopolies.

5. Indigenous professionals against fake expatriate "experts".

6. Teachers, students and pupils against irrelevant, authoritarian colonial education.

7. Committed intellectuals and journalists against official muzzling.

8. The poor and the landless in their demands for land reform.

9. All poor people against ever-increasing rents, prices and declining real incomes.

10. The entire dispossessed population against a corrupt, puppet government and its ever-repressive police rule.

More specifically and immediately, this newspaper will seek to raise principled debate, to raise political consciousness and awareness, highlight news that the foreign-run newspapers ignore and suppress, expose reactionary and imperialist plots and intrigues, protect and heighten our entire people's struggles, and generally work towards a *united* resistance in order to fight and overthrow imperialism and neocolonialism and achieve the long delayed true independence.

Pambana, June 1983. Nairobi.

Editorial

Release Political Prisoners Now!

The December Twelve Movement continues to support those who stand and sacrifice for the Kenyan people constitutional and democratic rights. We condemn in the strongest language the criminally corrupt, repressive and traitorous band of thieves who govern this country and who have allied themselves with the imperialists to keep the Kenyan masses perpetually exploited and oppressed. Their anti-Kenyan stance is clearly demonstrated by the continuing repression of innocent Kenyans through:

1. Detention and restriction for those who speak the truth and oppose foreign domination.

2. Kangaroo trials for the patriotic Kenyans.

3. Police brutality against workers, peasants and squatters.

4. Failure to prosecute corrupt government and cooperative swindlers of national resources (money, land and other property).

5. Detaining innocent Kenyans without trial, denying the workers the right of bargaining for their labor power and sanctioning redundancies to the benefits of the foreign monopolies.

6. Planned interference with the parliamentary and civic elections through barring, harassing and intimidating candidates and voters.

7. Establishing Anglo-American military bases on the Kenyan soil without the consent of the people of Kenya.

Mwakenya: The Unfinished Revolution

In the light of the above criminal denial of our people democracy and human rights, we, in the December Twelve Movement demand:

1. The immediate and unconditional release of political prisoners: Edward Oyugi, Willy Mũtunga, Kamoji Wachiira, Maina wa Kĩnyattĩ, al-Amin Mazrui, Mũkarũ, Koigi, Khamiwa, Kariũki Wang'ondu, university students and many others who are secretly and illegally imprisoned.
2. None interference with the coming general elections.
3. The immediate withdrawal of the Anglo-American soldiers and other military personnel from our country.

The December Twelve Movement appeals to all progressive and patriotic Kenyans to oppose the Moi dictatorship and its imperialist allies, to expose reactionary and imperialist plots against the people of Kenya and to heighten our people's struggles for democracy and socialism.

The December Twelve Movement has grown and continues to develop internally and externally as a people movement. The history of our anti-imperialist resistance is long and victory is certain.

Long Live Mau Mau!
Long Live the People's Struggle!
Pambana, Pambana! Pambana!

Pambana No. 2, July 1983

Pambana Stands for Unity

When the first of *Pambana* came out in May 1982, the people of Kenya and all freedom-loving people of the world received it with great joy. It filled Kenyans with hope and great expectations. It made them see that it was possible to change the prevailing oppressive conditions and create a better life for all Kenyans. This is what they had always looked forward to—an organ which would unite the poor and the exploited against the Kenyan ruling class and their foreign masters. Such a unity is what *Pambana* stands for.

Pambana united the poor and all those who love freedom and democracy; it united the workers and peasants all over Kenya; it united all the patriots in the civil service, the police and the army; it united students, teachers, lawyers, journalists, doctors, nurses, secretaries, mechanics, shop assistants and office workers. They all hailed *Pambana's* call for a relentless struggle against imperialism.

KANU in the Service of World Imperialism

Here in Kenya, the oppression of the people is systematically done on behalf of Euro-American imperialists by the KANU-led ruling class. The imperialists milk our country while watchdogs, the KANU-led regime rule over us like gods. These gods felt threatened by the unity and

Mwakenya: The Unfinished Revolution

consciousness created by *Pambana*. They responded by detentions without trial, imprisonment on trumped-up charges and indiscriminate torture of Kenyans. Anyone who dared to speak for democracy and constitutional rights was thrown into detention. Journalists, teachers, lawyers, workers, students, peasants were harassed mercilessly. They underwent brutal police interrogations. They were put into custody and prison because they dared to demand their democratic rights, they dared to oppose a one-party dictatorship and what is more they dared oppose the granting of military bases to the United States and British imperialists on Kenya soil, air and water.

The Kenyan comprador-ruling clique cunningly exploited the attempted coup of August 1, 1982 to kill thousands of innocent people, especially our young patriotic Kenyans, and to cow people into accepting the regime's murderous rule. The regime used the occasion to silence the voices of patriotic youth who sincerely believed in changes that would lead to democracy and socialism. For three continuous months (August, September and October 1982), the ruling clique and their army used to instill fear amongst the people. Moi's soldiers raped our women, robbed Kenyan peasants and workers of their property; snatched clothes, shoes, watches and radios from people traveling in *matatũ;* went into people's homes and took anything they wanted from innocent and unarmed people. They took the little that the workers had saved through sweat and blood. Thus the army clearly showed they were the enemy of the people. They behaved like the U.S. soldiers in Vietnam; the elders said that they behaved like the colonial British 'johnnies' during the British-imposed State of Emergency. The army, trained and groomed by the Americans and British, was mercilessly used against the people. We are totally opposed to these murderous brutes, going under the name of Kenya Armed Forces. We opposed an army, which guards the property of foreign capitalism and their comprador agents. But these soldiers are children of peasants and workers, and so when they use force against the people of their own class, it is like raping their own mothers.

Mwakenya: The Unfinished Revolution

There are no differences between the leaders of KANU and the leaders of neo-colonial regimes like Chile, El-Salvador, Guatemala, Honduras, Indonesia, Philippines, Pakistan, etc. these countries have military comprador regimes created by US imperialists to perpetuate the exploitation of workers and rob the wealth of these countries. In these countries, the struggle of peasants and workers to bring about democracy and socialism has reached a high stage. These people will surely defeat the fascist foreign-supported regimes as the peoples of Vietnam, Kampuchea and Nicaragua have done.

On August 1, 1982 the people of Kenya expressed their deep-rooted desire to change their condition of daily oppression by their attitude to the coup attempt. Thousands of people all over the country celebrated the announcement of the coup because it showed that it was possible to become free from oppression by the police, the administration, and City Council *askari,* and the whole government machinery administered by corrupt and unpatriotic officials; that it was possible to free themselves from the oppression of foreign lawyers, and some Kenyan lawyers too, who are the willing tools of the *mbwa kali* class. For thousands of hungry and unemployed, any change that would modify the prevailing conditions was welcome. This explains their enthusiastic reception of the news of the August 1 attempted coup.

Military-Backed KANU Regime Intensified Repression

The KANU government with its army attacked and tortured unarmed people. Thus the government and the comprador-ruling class exposed their true face as the enemy of the people. The authoritarian regime of Moi must repress all opposition with brutal force. How shall we ever forget the threats, the harassment and the torture against us by the Moi regime in 1982? The military-backed KANU regime has continued the oppression, this time under the guise of defending and upholding the constitution. Yet most Kenyan know the regime has no respect even for its own laws and constitution as shown by the kangaroo military courts, the

Mwakenya: The Unfinished Revolution

students' showcase trials and many political jailing and detentions. Biased judgments against workers in trade union disputes with foreign-own companies are the order of the day, while cases of corruption involving directors, managers, and senior civil servants are often dropped. Foreign judges (Europeans, Americans and British Asians) are highly paid rubber stamps. Unpatriotic Kenyan (African and Asian) judges and lawyers are also rubber-stamps who administer anti-people authoritarian laws. No! We cannot let ourselves be cheated by robbers and their laws! The whole world will not be deceived by the trumped-up charges against Kenyan patriots. We know that all those who are fighting for an economically and politically liberated Kenya cannot receive justice; there can never be justice under imperialism.

Culture of Theft and Bribery

Corruption has permeated through to some members of parliament, senior civil servants, senior army officers, and senior police, Criminal Investigation Department (CID) and Special Branch officers. These officers help in the cover up of corruption in land, food, oil, housing and all basic necessities. Even when patriotic journalists expose these practices, nothing happens to the culprits because those who are supposed to take them to court are equally involved in the same deals. Some journalists are even beaten up and newspapers threatened with banning. Thus the law protects the rich and oppresses the poor.

Bribery has become an integral part of the ruling culture. The police use guns and fierce dogs to extort bribes from innocent people. Most judges, lawyers and court clerks receive bribes. City Council *askari* shamelessly force old women who earn their living by hawking fruit and vegetables to give them bribes. It is impossible even to get free forms from government desk/counter clerks without a bribe. Of course, petty officials who take bribes to supplement their low incomes cannot be expected to act any different from their bosses. We believe that most of these will change their behavior once they realize that bribes will never solve their problems.

They will then join in the patriotic movement against imperialism and its comprador puppets.

Who Pays for it All?

It is the masses that are made to pay for all this corruption. Yet it is their sweat and hard work that create the plundered wealth. They are even forced to pay *harambee* contributions; hence their poverty increases daily. When the ruling clique say there are food shortages, they are busy smuggling out large quantities of maize; when they say there are shortages of petrol and oil, they are busy organizing motor races (safari rally); when they tell us we are overpopulated and hence no land for us, they and their foreign friends are busy grabbing thousands of acres of our best farmland; when they tell us there are problems in education and hence there are no teachers, books, equipment or enough classrooms for rural schools, they are busy lavishing high-cost education on their children. But when there is corruption in the importation and distribution of hospital equipment and medical drugs such that there is no medicine for the people, then they announce there is free medical care for all.

Thus for as long as a government is capitalist and is in the service of Euro-American imperialism, there cannot be equality between the rich and the poor in housing, education, health and in all other amenities. The equality preached by KANU is only in words at public meetings; in the Voice of Kenya news bulletins; in the *Kenya Times*; and in *Kenya Leo*. But the way we live is completely different from what they say and write about us. The poor still go hungry; pastoralists still suffer from hunger. Most school leavers are unemployed. Inequalities can never be eliminated unless the structure of society is completely changed.

Economy in a Shambles

For over year now, economic conditions for the majority of Kenyans have drastically deteriorated and yet big cars like Volvo, BMW and Mercedes and other luxury items continue to be imported by the comprador ruling

Mwakenya: The Unfinished Revolution

class. The comprador and their imperialist friends take away our hard earned foreign exchange. Whatever is left by multinationals after pocketing large profits is quickly taken out of the country into foreign banks. Multinationals, the World Bank and the IMF now plan the *development* of our country. But their main and primary objective is their own interests, not ours. Multinationals raise the prices of essential commodities at will, and so while their annual profits rocket, real wages plummet. The regime keeps on importing more and more expatriates as part of the 'aid' package deals to come and 'develop us' even as it jails very highly qualified Kenyans, who are already residing in the country and have never left it. Our country has now in effect been mortgaged to foreign creditors, when it has more than enough manpower to develop and run the country.

In 1981 our national debts to Europe and the United States amounted to Ksh. 205 billion (approx. US\$ 2,052,500,000), which is roughly equal to Ksh 2,032 per every Kenyan man, woman and child. Today, we have difficulties in repaying this debt. Although the debt was incurred by the compradorial ruing class to buy themselves a life of luxury, it will have to be repaid by the children of workers and peasants and all wage-earning Kenyans for many, many years to come.

History of Resistance

In spite of oppression, brutality, torture, threats, intensified spying and surveillance by regime agents, the peasants and workers, students and all patriotic Kenyans continue to oppose and fight oppression and all forms of exploitation. This is because Kenyan people are courageous and their history is one of heroic struggle against oppression.

Even though we were few at the time of British colonialism and we did not have much experience in fighting, we still fought the colonialists. We took up arms when we realized that the enemy could only be driven out through the armed struggle. Many battles at different times were fought by Kenyan nationalities against the colonialists and their Kenyan allies. The workers' movement was at the forefront in the struggle against colonialism.

Mwakenya: The Unfinished Revolution

All these culminated in the Kenya Land Freedom Army (KLFA) or Mau Mau armed against British colonial forces and their Kenyan friends (the *hũmungaati*). Even after 1958 many groups and revolutionary youth used underground newspapers to educate and mobilize the masses all over the country. Today, we of the December Twelve Movement (DTM) are following in the same tradition. Through *Pambana* we are trying to join together all the underground groups into one movement struggling against foreign and local oppression and exploitation. We want equality for all. Let us all now struggle in unity. We are many. We have the experience, education and courage from our own glorious history. Moreover, we know revolutionaries and workers of the whole world support us.

Rights not Privileges

Freedom of expression and the enjoyment of fruits of independence are the right of all Kenyans. Freedom is not something that is granted to us by the ruling class. It is our right by birth. But the regime has robbed us of this freedom. If a person takes twenty shillings from you and does not pay you back, will you demand it back? We cannot remain silent when our right to good housing, adequate food, decent clothing and education has been denied us by this oppressive regime. Twenty years after independence, we have been reduced to the position of beggars. Many commissions have been appointed to look into our living conditions, but all these are mere official cover-ups. Even parliament has not been able to change anything. We are still hungry, and we know that our children will suffer even greater hunger if we do not make the necessary effort, now, and sacrifice to change the present, brutal conditions.

Together We March Forward

The people of Kenya are on the move. They want to bring about real changes and make this country a better place to live in. The many protests by peasants and the strikes by workers all over the land are a crucial part of this struggle and we support them. There are many patriotic soldiers

Mwakenya: The Unfinished Revolution

in Tanzania and Uganda, many patriotic students overseas, and many patriots in exile who are joining hands with patriots within the country in the struggle for a revolutionary change of our lives. In the country there are patriotic soldiers, policemen and women who support this struggle.

So together we march forward ready to fight against oppression and fear in the land, and to weed out traitors and *humungaati* from amongst us. It has been our tradition, and it is this that gives us our identity as Kenyans. We must continue in that tradition and be com-mitted to the struggle like our past patriots among the Kisii, Akamba. Agĩkũyũ, Turkana, Pokot, Maasai, Giriama, Waswahili, Luhya, Luo people and many others who were killed fighting against colonialism. We must be committed like the KLFA/Mau Mau patriots who were killed before and after independence. Indeed we must be committed like the jailed and detained political prisoners (Maina wa Kĩnyattĩ, Willy Mũtunga, Edward Oyugi, Kamoji Wachiira and al-Amin Mazrui) and those patriots now forced into exile. We should know who they are and remember them. We must be committed for the sake of our country Kenya and the future of our children.

Compatriots, let us unite and defeat the comprador-ruling class. As long as imperialism reigns over us, it is our right and responsibility to liberate our country. It is our right and responsibility to write, publish and disseminate *Pambana* and to make sure it is read year after year. We shall continue to read and spread *Pambana* despite oppression, despite brutality and threats to our families and friends and despite the daily spying and surveillance by the Special Branch police. Our hope for our future lies in our history of struggle, in our patriotism and in the unity of all the exploited and the oppressed. *Pambana* will continue to voice the demands of all the protesting peasants, all the striking workers—all the defiant students, indeed of all the patriots who want to free in Kenya from the Euro-American imperialist stranglehold.

Pambana shall live and destroy all in the way of the struggle. The fire has been lit, the oppressed will turn the enemy to ashes and we shall march in unity singing: *Pambana! Pambana! Pambana!* Victory is ours.

Mpatanishi No 7, December 1983

(Mpatanishi was an ideological Journal of DTM)

Editorial

The Name Of Our movement

Now that the time has come when all the Kenyan progressives must address themselves to the question of the party programme, it is becoming necessary to have a name for our movement. We cannot indefinitely refer to ourselves as the "Movement", the "progressives" or just the "revolutionaries". Whereas we are not suggesting that these terms should not be used, we are suggesting we have a name that is more definite, scientifically correct and one that does not give room to opportunistic deviations from Marxism.

Our name, all by itself, must reflect our aims and objectives. It must also correspond to the nature of the struggle we are involved in at this point and time of our history. We are fighting for a socialist order and hence, ideally, our party should be called the "Socialist Party of Kenya". However, it is unfortunate that the name "socialist party" has long been adopted even by bourgeois parties that attempt to become a socialist party in theory, but not in a practical sense. Kanu, for example, is officially an African socialist party. Hence, Kanu uses the name of socialism to fight Scientific Socialism. It propounds a reactionary anti-communist ideology that denies any class struggle and its government even goes further to persecutes anybody thought to harbor scientific, socialist ideas. This

Mwakenya: The Unfinished Revolution

government stand was spelled out clearly by Nicholas Biwott in the *Daily Nation* of November 9, 1982. He stated: "The country is pursuing African Socialism and could not accept strange, far-fetched and unknown Marxist ideas which were not in keeping with Kenya today." We therefore, like the Kanu comprador bourgeoisie, should have no hesitations as to which name to choose for our movement. The name that will terrify the whole of the international capitalist bourgeoisie and their Kenyan puppets and will be capable of leading the whole Kenyan working masses along a socialist path. The name we have chosen for our movement is, the *Communist Party of Kenya* (CPK). That places Scientific Socialism as the basis of our movement, in a practical and ideological manner.

Long Live the Communist Party of Kenya!!
Long live Dedan Kĩmathi!
Long live Mother Kenya!

Mpatanishi No. 8, February 1984

Editorial

An Appeal To All Comrades

We recognize and continue to support the work of all organizations, groups and those individuals who oppose all undemocratic moves by the puppet government of Kenya. The DTM appreciates political activities by all its comrades, the DTM Branch of the University of Nairobi, the university students' body, the Committee for the Release of Political Prisoners in Kenya (London), Amnesty International and other progressive forces both local and international.

We are appealing to all our comrades (linked organizations, groups and individuals) to send their contribution through their links. Contributions in the form of letters to the editor, articles, money, etc. are welcome. Our Journal, *Mpatanishi*, continues to be the Central Organ linking all our forces both internally and externally, but our *Pambana* newspaper remains a mass paper. Please send your contribution before mid-March 1984 for our next issue.

Where We Stand and What Next?

Many comrades are aware that we have intensified our political activities throughout the country and in particular the urban centers. Our movement has grown and continues to expand both locally and abroad. We know victory is certain, but we cannot ignore the fact that our aims, objectives

Mwakenya: The Unfinished Revolution

and goals can only be achieved if we are thoroughly organized throughout our country, and have the ability and intelligence to arm our party cadres, verbally or in writing, with the MLM theory.

An historical examination of revolutionary movements reveals that many movements lag behind due to poor organization and the failure of revolutionaries to analyze situations properly at certain periods of the struggle, in order to ascertain the strength and stability of an impending movement, or a movement in progress. The December Twelve Movement (DTM) should not fall a victim of liberalism since we are aware of our strength and our shortcomings. We should always use organization as a weapon and analyze all situations concretely. In the light of these facts, we should take stock of our activities and analyze the political development in our country to determine our next step. It is a fact that knowledge is gained through practice, therefore, practice of being the mother of theory we must start from real situations for our guidance. Hence, the main concern for this article.

Historical Review

The Kenyan people have a long history of resistance to colonial and imperialist forces. They resisted the British forces for a long time during the invasion of our country. This resistance culminated in early fifties when the Kenyan peasants and workers took arms to fight the massive or better armed British forces and their local collaborators. The true history of this armed struggle is not taught in Kenyan schools because the puppet government does not want our children to know the truth. Students are taught only those ideas that do not challenge the status quo. Some scholars distort our patriotic history, while others who research and write the truth about the history of our people and their anti-colonial struggle are detained without trial, or thrown in the repressive Kenyan jails after going through kangaroo trials (e.g., Maina wa Kĩnyattĩ now is in prison after a kangaroo trial). And Ngũgĩ wa Thiong'o, the most progressive Kenyan writer, is now in exile because of his patriotic writing.

An examination of the history of our post-independence struggle reveals that we had for a long time acted as isolated groups, study circles, etc., until we organized ourselves as the December 12 Movement. The DTM is a united anti-imperialist front that aims at bringing together all democratic forces as a first phase of the general struggle towards Socialism. Examples of such a movement in history are: *The July 26 Movement in Cuba, Sandinista* in Nicaragua, *Farenabudo* in El Salvador, etc. Through such a movement, the democratic forces, mainly the workers, peasants and progressive intellectuals, are to be trained and prepared for a future communist party. The DTM aims at raising the fighting capacity of all the democratic forces. Hence, all progressive people should unite under this front in the struggle for democracy and against imperialism and its comprador allies. It is only after formation of such a front that we may enter the second phase of fighting under the communist banner.

Leaflet: J. M. Day of Solidarity
Don't Be Fooled, Reject these Nyayos
March 2, 1980

Kenyatta was intensely hated by most Kenyans because his regime worked hard to deprive us of our rights and to benefit a few individuals and foreign imperialism. The hopes of change for the better when he died have now been dished away by the indecisive, wavering conduct of his successors. A vague and undefined "nyayo" and a promised *glass of milk* must be dismissed by 15 years of looting and intrigues.

Nothing has changed. Things have gotten worse. Kenyatta, the master robber baron and the chief puppet of imperialism, is not dead. In countless ways he lives. His men, his class, his disciples, his cabinet, are in power today. Despite lies and cover-ups to the contrary, there can be no acceptable change if the following minimum demands are not addressed to:

1. Nullification of all government land deals since 1970.

2. Land ownership ceiling of 25 hectares for individual families (not co-operatives).

3. Maximum of one plot per family in urban areas.

4. Expulsion of foreign devils (experts) from redundant employment—to make room for Kenyan workers, technicians and university graduates.

Mwakenya: The Unfinished Revolution

5. Immediate firing of all known thieves of public wealth, their public trial and seizure of their loot and assets.

6. One man one job strictly—particularly for high political office.

7. Parliament must get back its constitutional powers.

8. Reduction of presidential power to ensure that the past semi-monarchical, autocratic feudal situation does not continue.

9. Public trial for JM's murderers. Only then will we correctly remember JM.

10. Till then no KANU (Kenyatta's party, minority party, etc.) on campus.

While the great majority of our people live in dire poverty, the dictator and his men arrogantly show off their loot and protect our principal enemies, the foreign imperialist dogs. This is unacceptable and we denounce it as "nyayos" to greater wretchedness and misery.

NO CLASSES FRIDAY: DEMONSTRATE OUR SOLIDARITY!
NEVER BE FOOLED!
NO KANU ON CAMPUS!
AVENGE JM!

Leaflet: Moi's Divisive Tactics Exposed

August 3, 1982

Fifteen long years of Kenyatta's undemocratic rule left neocolonial Kenya impoverished, depoliticized and disunited. He made way for Moi, Njonjo, etc. to misrule us. A rule of talk, talk, talk, and do the opposite. The nauseating demagogy which Moi and the traitorous clique around him employ to mask their unpopular rule has failed to hide the all-round suffering of the Kenyans. One notices the intensified pauperization of the Kenyan people, as evidenced in ever-rising unemployment, sky-high inflations (under the pretext of Harambee), to the already wealthy ones. This is what they call 'Love, Peace and Unity'. We have a different name for it: *Foreign Domination, Exploitation and Oppression.* Surely, only dreaming babblers can think otherwise. To be sure such conditions can only breed-justified hatred against these parasites. This is the background against which Nyayoism is unleashing untold suffering on the people of Kenya and consequently against which we must all coordinate our efforts to firmly expose and oppose it.

Moi has overthrown the constitution, replacing the parliament with an illegal outfit in the name of "leaders' conference" where anti-Kenyan intrigues are hatched. He has turned Kenya into an American and British military base, where Kenyan woman and men are murdered and their children eaten by Del Monte dogs. His foreign judges are then summoned

Mwakenya: The Unfinished Revolution

to shamelessly acquit the murderers. He has banned all democratic organizations and unions—leading to further depoliticization of what little his mentor, Kenyatta left.

Against this background Moi has found it necessary to invade and disorganize the university with his devious intrigues of divisive politics. And mind you, all this is coming from the chancellor himself. The university is now a living showroom where his divisiveness is displayed. His aim is to paralyze our solidarity with the Kenyan people. This would provide him with an organizational vacuum within which to intensify his repression. But this is bound to be short-lived as the Kenyan people are running out of patience with his unpopular rule.

His strategy is simple and heinous: collect academics and student stooges, bribe them and send them out as servitors or his collapsing rule. Notorious opportunists like Professor Ongeri and Professor Ongwany were the first to be dispatched to come and coerce Gusii students into a surreptitious loyalty-pledging errand to State House. Earlier on, Kalenjin students had been to a similar mission. This time the baseless pretext was that of consolidating ethnic Kalenjin rule. We know that Kenyatta tried this same trick in 1976. The vehicle for treacherous intrigues was then to be the Kikuyu Cultural Association. But he died regretting having tried to divide us along ethnic lines. The members of the International Student Association based at Kenyatta University College, under the patronage of the opportunist Dr Professor Ayot, were called to Nakuru to be bribed with Ksh. 60,000/- for their *services* rendered to Nyayo. The bootlicking Professors Senga and Maitha were also instructed to drag on eighty odd Kamba students into playing loyal to the babbling monarch. He paid them Ksh. 30,000/-. Following in their footsteps, John Okwanjo—MP for Migori and known CIA servitor to the US anti-Chinese movement, has been busy organizing students from his constituency to go and pledge loyalty to Nyayo. All these were supposed to take place secretly. But we have come to know about them from those who rejected Nyayo's divisiveness and came back to report. We still expect Arthur Magũgũ, the son of a notorious *hũmungaati,* will have his plan to lead Kĩambu students to State House frustrated.

Mwakenya: The Unfinished Revolution

How can we take Moi's twaddle about *love, peace* and *unity* seriously when, as we clearly see, on the one hand, he surreptitiously and secretly solicits ethnic loyalty from students, yet maliciously disbands national welfare organizations publicly? We have not forgotten Nyayo's China visit where he, with the help of the university authorities, hand-picked some of the stooges among us to accompany him. It has also come to light that many of these stooges are sons and daughters of powerful and wealthy rulers of this country.

Kenyans will remember that we resisted Kenyatta. More than ever now we must resist nyayoism and its foreign support. We demand, therefore, that,

1. The constitutional right of association of all Kenyans should be given back.

2. The reinstatement of the University Student Union should be speeded up.

3. Nyayo and Njonjo desist from dividing us by ethnicity.

4. The president should no longer be our chancellor.

5. American bases and murderers should leave Kenyan soil immediately.

6. The parliament should be free to assert itself within the framework of the supremacy of Kenya's constitution.

United Against Nyayoism!
United Against Foreign Domination!

What To Do When You Are Arrested

This document was secretly circulated by DTM on
the Kenyatta and Nairobi University campuses,
March 2, 1983.

Compatriot:

When approached by a policeman in uniform or in plainclothes you will either be called by your name or asked to identify yourself before being arrested. The following rights described are your basic constitutional rights, which you must insist on upon being arrested or in any way harassed by the security forces.

1. Ask for appropriate identification papers of the person arresting you. Take his name, force number, rank and name of his police station.

2. Try and inform a friend or relative or fellow employee of your intended arrest. Talk loudly to attract attention of others around you who can witness your arrest.

3. Ask the police officer the reason for your arrest and insist on the production of an arrest warrant.

4. If they come to your house, insist on an arrest warrant and a search warrant and immediately alert the neighbors to witness your arrest. Do not be afraid of the police, you are a Kenyan citizen.

5. If you suspect that you may be arrested, make arrangement with friends and relatives to keep regular checks on you at your place of work and residence.

Mwakenya: The Unfinished Revolution

6. If asked to accompany them to the police station or if called to the police station to assist in investigations, insist on a written order signed by the Officer in Charge of the station. Always inform friends, relatives or neighbors when called to a police station for any reason even if it sounds very interesting. Under dictatorship, police are thugs, criminals, terrorists, and murderers.

7. When at the police station you may refuse to answer any question except *giving your name, address and places of residence and work* unless your lawyer is present. Insist on a lawyer and keep in hand the names and addresses and house telephone numbers of two to three lawyers who you can call any time. Make arrangements in advance. If you do say anything—anything at all—it will definitely cause harm to your family, comrades, and friends, and most likely you'll just end up in worse trouble yourself. Of course, the police will tell you the opposite to get you to talk. Do not be fooled, police are not your friends; they are tools of the comprador state. They need the information—all you need to do is to be silent and firm.

8. If you are not brought to court within 24 hours after your arrest, your relatives have a right to ask a lawyer to make an application to the High Court ordering the police, CID, or Special Branch to bring you to court, either to be charged or released. It is therefore necessary to know who has arrested you and from which police station.

9. The name, address and nature of alleged offence of every person brought into a police station must be recorded on the Occurrence Book (O.B.), the large book lying on the counter as you enter a police station. Ask the police office if your name has been entered into the OB. If not, it would be difficult to trace you and you could be shuttled from one police station to another for a long time. Therefore, insist on OB entry of your particulars.

10. At the police station, refuse to sign anything. If you want to make a statement, write it yourself in ink and in your own handwriting and a language you understand best. Sign and countersign any cancellations or corrections

11. Force, threat, torture or inducement of any kind is illegal under the constitution. If forced to sign a statement, try and make a note on the

Mwakenya: The Unfinished Revolution

statement and near your signature that you are forced to make the statement. Also try not to put your real signature.

12. You must be brought to court within 24 hours of your arrest. Insist on this right. You may, however, be arrested on a Friday evening or Saturday when they can keep you in custody up to Monday morning.

13. If you have been beaten or forced to sign any papers and do not have a lawyer in court, then ensure that at your first court appearance you inform the magistrate of such treatment by the police. Do not let the magistrate or police prosecutor or prison guard interfere with your right to speak to court.

14. Never plead guilty to the charge, no matter what the inducement.

15. When at the police station, ask for a police bond. If they refuse, then ask for bail when in court. Bail is also a constitutional right. Argue your case for bail. Fight for your right. You have nothing to lose, but your chains.

16. At the police station, you have a right to keep quiet and say nothing. This also applies to your court appearances; you may tell the magistrate that you have nothing to say in reply to your charge until you have a lawyer. Ask for time to get a lawyer. It is your constitutional right to have a lawyer to represent you at your every court appearance, including the first court appearance.

17. At the police station you must be given a decent place to sleep, adequate bedding and food. If any of these are denied, immediately insist on reporting the matter to the Officer in Charge of the police station. Also ensure that you report this mistreatment to the court.

18. Always remember that under the Constitution you are innocent until proved guilty by a court of law after going through a full hearing and giving you an opportunity to be heard. Therefore, there is nothing to be afraid of. Insist on your rights as an innocent citizen. Be bold and courageous. The Court, magistrate, prosecutor, police and prison guards are your class enemy; face them without flagging, without fear. You are a Kenyan citizen.

Mwakenya: The Unfinished Revolution

19. Talk to fellow prisoners and learn from each other about your conditions and constitutional rights. Struggle together and organize with fellow prisoners to demand for your constitutional and human rights.

20. We repeat, do not be afraid of the police. Police brutality is illegal. If they try to mistreat you quote **Section 74** of the Constitution of Kenya which says: *No person shall be subject to torture or inhuman treatment or degrading or other treatment except lawful punishment ordered by the court.* Try and take the force numbers (written in steel on their shirt lapels) of your torturers and report them to your lawyer and the court.

No matter what happens, comrades—in prison or in grave—we must continue to oppose the comprador regime and its imperialist allies. It is the only hope of building a strong, revolutionary movement that will overthrow the neocolonial system in our country. Our aim is to create a socialist society, which looks after the interests of the workers, the landless, the unemployed and all other oppressed and exploited Kenyans. Together and united we cannot be defeated.

Mwakenya: The Unfinished Revolution

al-Amin Mazrui

Maina wa Kīnyattī

Edward Oyugi

Koigi wa Wamwere

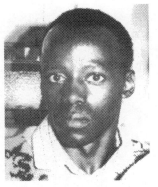

Karīmi Nduthu

Mwakenya: The Unfinished Revolution

Ngũgĩ wa Thiong'o

Kamoji Wachiira

Shiraz Durrani

Willy Mutunga

Abdilatif Abdalla

Part Three

Mwakenya Document, 1987 – 2001

The country just ushered in the new constitution which was promulgated today, August 27, 2010. The colonial Lancaster law is now out. As the party leadership and cadres know very well, the Kenyan working people are not going to earn its full rights both in politics and the economy without a struggle, new constitution or not. The exploiters—imperialists and their Kenyan allies—are determined to retain their illicit privileges through their organizations, institutions and coercive forces; the toiling masses have no choice, but to organize to seize the national leadership. This means war. We must prepare.

A. M.Remi, MKDTM cadre.

The Fundamental Goals and Objectives of Mwakenya

Mwakenya is the party of the proletariat. Its aim is to forge popular unity among the workers, peasants, pastoralists, progressive intelligentsia, and all the patriotic and democratic Kenyans on the basis of the following seven core principles. The first of these is: The Recovery of National Sovereignty and Integrity. The imperialist-client regime of Moi granted nuclear military bases to the USA in 1990 without the consent of the Kenyan people, and even without consulting parliament. The ruling neocolonial regime of Kenya, even to this day, continues to harbor Anglo-American and other foreign troops in our homeland. These are criminal acts and high treason against the Kenyan people. All patriotic, democratic and progressive forces in Kenya are united in their opposition to this. Mwakenya is committed to: **a)** uphold the principle of national sovereignty by building a genuinely independent Kenya, free from imperialist domination and foreign military base; and **b)** open discussion with our neighboring states with a view to declaring East African and the Indian Ocean a zone of peace, free from all foreign military presence.

Mwakenya: The Unfinished Revolution

The second objective is: The Building of an Independent and Integrated National Economy. Mwakenya believes that the Kenyan economy should serve Kenyans first and foremost. Kenya has rich fertile land and it must be able to feed its entire population. The strengthening of the home market and that between African countries is vital opposed to the current mentality that believes that a foreign western imperialist market is the only option for African countries. In practice this has meant Kenya relying more and more on the export of coffee and tea and tourist delights. Kenya has no control over the foreign market. It cannot dictate the prices of coffee and tea or of the goods it imports. A more important strategy and tactics are those that strengthen the home market; a strategy that works for national self-sufficiency in commodities and services that are vital to the economical survival of all Kenyans, if they are to survive in a foreign market; and in order to do this, Kenyans cannot look to the foreign market for supplementing goods and services, and not replacing them with the home and regional markets already in existence in Kenya.

Mwakenya, therefore, believes in the renegotiations of all unequal treaties, foreign investments and loans on the basis of equality and mutual benefits. It believes that there should be a clear programme for the protection of national capital against the unmitigated onslaughts of foreign capital. The policies of the International Monetary Fund (IMF), the World Bank (WB) and the North Atlantic Organization (NATO) are geared towards the promotion and protection of the interests of Western imperialist capital. Our Party believes in an industrialization policy geared towards basic self-sufficiency. Kenya's national capital must be involved in industrial ventures in the country.

Land reform is basic to Mwakenya's economic policy. There has to be a resettlement of all the landless Kenyans and insurance of adequate land for the poor peasants and pastoralists. Mwakenya believes in the integration of agriculture with the industry so that one sector does not develop at the gross expense of the other.

Mwakenya: The Unfinished Revolution

Mwakenya is concerned at the current tendency toward the development of mega towns like Nairobi parasitically feeding on the rural poor. The current influx of people into the major cities bespeaks of the underdevelopment of the countryside. But the key broad economic principle which sums up everything is the Party's belief in the promotion of industrial and agricultural policies, which will ensure that the exploitation of our human and natural resources are in the hands of nationals and that these nationals must put Kenya first.

The third objective linked to the first two is the establishment of genuine democracy because the Party believes that democracy is the correct basis of resolving contradictions in our society. It opposes the current criminal violation of human rights and the cynical disregard of all democratic freedoms by the ruling neocolonial regime and ongoing killing of citizens under the name of law and order. The Party would like to ensure the protection of human and democratic rights of all Kenyans, irrespective of race, ethnicity, gender, nationality and religious affiliations. Fundamental to these are the rights of association, assembly, speech, and communication, which will ensure the right of the people to hold different religious and intellectual beliefs and opinions. Free and fair elections would then be a natural outcome of these rights and principles, including the right to equality before the law; the independence of judiciary from the executive arm of the state; and the right to a fair and public trial.

The fourth principle is the establishment of social justice. Our party has always abhorred the present and ever increasing gap between the rich and the poor. Workers, peasant and pastoralists produce everything, but they are condemned to an ever increasing poverty and misery. The party believes in the improvement of the working and living conditions of all the working class people by ensuring adequate compensation for their labor and produce. The health and educational needs of the majority should not be left to tender mercies of the market forces, but rather the state must intervene in these areas. *Markets can never beheld into account of law or in a general election, but governments and the state can be held accountable.* It's the duty of the state to establish a medical system, which would ensure free and adequate medical care for all; an adequate public free and compulsory education for all; an adequate public transport system. Healthy and well-educated citizens are the basis of a healthy and educated nation.

All the patriotic, democratic and progressive forces in our country firmly oppose the present stranglehold of western transnationals on Kenya's economy.

The fifth objective is also closely tied to the third and fourth. Mwakenya stands for promotion of a patriotic and democratic national culture. The current neocolonial regime is completely enslaved to imitative Anglo-American bourgeois culture in schools, television, cinema, and theater, to mention just a few. When it comes to African culture and heritage, it is only interested in promoting the most backward elements of our pre-capitalist practices and attitudes, which includes discriminatory practices against women for instance. The result has been the domination of Kenyan life by a neocolonial culture of sub-servience, servility, meekness, sycophancy, and gratitude to charity, what Mwakenya describes as the begging culture of a puppet regime. That is why our party is committed to the goal of promoting a democratic national culture, borrowing from the stock of experience and revolutionary ideas of all our nationalities. It is committed to the teaching of the true history of our struggles, as a people, against the Portuguese, the Arab slave raiders, and the British colonialists and their indigenous collaborators. Allied to this was the need to promote positive democratic and progressive arts, books, theater, cinema and television of Kenyans—as well as Africans, in general, living in a world of people who may not view them as a culture that should be taken seriously. In order to enhance the images of our struggle, for example, and the construction of a civil human culture of mutual care and support, such a positive image must be promoted. Of particular concern is the position of African languages. Mwakenya stands for a national language policy that makes Kiswahili the official and national language of Kenya; the promotion of

Mwakenya: The Unfinished Revolution

the other nationality languages, which in our case means mostly African languages; and then English to enable Kenyans to negotiate their way in the international market place. Kenyans would then be trilingual. The ministry of culture and national heritage would be given adequate resources to ensure the success of this three-language policy.

The sixth objective, the building of a strong people's defense forces against attacks on Kenyan territory. Mwakenya believes that the present Kenyan army, in mentality, practices and outlook, is really a continuation of the British colonial army, which once fought against the Kenya Land and Freedom Army and other nationalist forces demanding independence. The party believes that it is impossible to build a just and democratic society using an army and police force built by the enemies of such a society. Mwakenya-DTM also abhors the current situation where the army and the paramilitary units are there simply to support the government in its anti-people practices. The national army is not and must never be a police force. Its duty is to defend the borders of Kenya, its integrity, and the people of Kenya against foreign invasions. Drastic re-education and re-orientation of the army and police is necessary to turn them into forces that are ready to fight for and protect gains of the national democratic revolution.

The seventh and last objective, the pursuit of an independent foreign policy should be a reflection and a strengthening of all the above positions. Mwakenya stands for the principles of the respect for the sovereignty and territorial integrity of other states; cooperation for mutual benefits; and the respect for human rights and dignity as contained in the United Nations Universal Declaration of Human Rights and other recognized rules and principles of international law. The party believes in a global order guided by the internationalism of the working peoples of Africa and the world. Arising from that is Mwakenya's belief in the unity of East Africa as well as the unity of the continent as a whole. A United States of Africa is the only way Africa and its people can really adequately negotiate their rightful position in the global community.

238

Kenya Democracy Plank
July 1991

Introduction

Since Mwakenya issued its *Democracy Plank* on July 11, 1990, everything that Moi has done in Kenya proves, more than ever, that its analysis and the demands are as valid and constructive now as they were then. Almost alone in the entire continent of Africa, Moi has adamantly refused to accept the call for democratic change. Instead he has caused more deaths and more detentions.

Since Saba Saba (July 7, 1990) Moi and KANU have blatantly instituted bogus treason and sedition trials against people standing up for the rights to organize, publish freely and meet freely to form political parties. Democratic-minded religious leaders have been murdered. Pro-democracy political organizers and lawyers have been hounded into detentions and framed for criminal offences, their homes and families have been attacked, newspapers have been banned, editors, journalists and printers terrorized, more Kenyans have been forced into exile, thousands of homes and businesses have been razed to the ground, and official corruption has boomed even as the prices of basic needs have soared. Obviously, it is Moi and KANU who should be tried for treason.

Moi and his cronies are fermenting civil chaos and ethnic strife. They have even called for ethnic confrontations and killings. They must be stopped before it is too late. Mwakenya calls upon the entire people of Kenya to be most vigilant against Moi's machinations, and in particular Moi's divisive tradition of *Bribe, Divide and Rule.* Factionalism among people and in organizations strengthens Moi and must be fought at all costs.

Kenyans must also be wary of Moi wearing a pretty new cloak to deceive us while continuing the same old abuses. Beware of the cornered hyena trying on the clothing of the lamb he has slaughter. In politics, bogus reforms are sometimes worse than no change at all. Moi cannot reform; he cannot be reformed or rehabilitated. Moi and KANU must move on in order for Kenya to move ahead.

We must not be deceived by Moi's declaration about everybody joining KANU and standing for elections. KANU is the problem. Nothing can be solved within KANU. The struggle for social change must continue. Let us avoid needless factions, and unite around the demands of the *Democracy Plank* to keep up the pressure for peaceful change in Kenya. The *Kenya Democracy Plank* is reissued to mark the first anniversary of Saba Saba, in memory of those who dared and the hundreds who fell.

Ngũgĩ wa Thiong'o
On behalf of MK Central Committee

Movement of Defiance

The current movement of defiance all over Kenya is an emphatic call for Moi and KANU to go. The various social forces—ranging from peasants, workers, the unemployed to the clerics, teachers, lawyers and a large section of the business community—are united in this. They have come to the position consistently held and maintained by Mwakenya –DTM over the last ten years: that the crisis in our country is primarily political. However, it manifests itself in all other spheres of national life. Workers will not be productive when the wages cannot even cover the sale of their labor. Farmers will not produce if they have no say in the marketing of their produce and the prices do not compensate for their investments and labor;

Mwakenya: The Unfinished Revolution

businessmen will not invest where there is little hope of political support of where the magnitude of government corruption makes it virtually impossible for national capital to prosper; students will not be able to learn if the teachers are constantly interrupted and cannot teach properly when the education system functions erratically, failing to produce highly skilled and highly intellectual students needed for the progression of the country, with so little reward at the end of it all; professionals will not be able to perform their duties creatively; and religious leaders will not be able to minister to the needs of their followers adequately when there is no free political environment in which to work in.

Moi's KANU

The party and the leadership to which Kenyans had entrusted their power, their money, their resources, their labor, and their hopes have betrayed that trust and completely failed us in the last twenty-five years. Instead of building, they have systematically dismantled structures and programs needed for development; instead of planting for a future harvest they have literally eaten up the very seeds needed for health and well being of our population of people; instead of inspiring our youth, they have sought to demoralize them, shutting them down mentally and spiritually; instead of healing minor differences, they have tried to bring about needless communal divisions; instead of nurturing life and progression, they have killed the very people they need for progression, along with their dreams of a better Kenya: Garissa in 1980, Wajir and Pokot massacres in 1984, Nairobi University 1985; Mworoto in 1990; and now the ongoing government atrocities that started with the assault on the pro-democracy rally of Saturday 7th July 1990. Government organized thuggery and death squads a la Latin America are now common in Kenya. Altogether there has been over six thousand killed by government agents since Moi came to power in 1978.

In order to thwart the growth of a united opposition movement, the regime has tried to divide Kenyan people on the basis of religion and

Mwakenya: The Unfinished Revolution

regions of origins. Fortunately, in these decades we have learned that we are one nation with a common history of struggle and a common future thanks to our experience of the last one hundred years, not least of which being the experiences of KANU's misrule. We have learned that we must protect our political gains and not stand idly while a tyrannical ruler erodes them and tries to divide us along any imagined crack or differences especially of "tribes"!

Demands for Thoroughgoing Changes

Everywhere across the Republic today the overwhelming majority of Kenyans are united in talking openly and loudly about the very decline of our country: the high price of basic necessities, the high unemployment, police harassment and brutality, corruption in all the national affairs, landlessness and the impoverishment of the vast majority. They are united in their expressed support of demands for thoroughgoing changes in government, in parliament, in the entire political process. They want changes in the commercial, farming, housing and employment policies. They want changes in the judiciary system, in the education system, and in such other services as health, transportation, and in many other things that affect their daily lives, including their personal security. Mostly they are talking about overturning KANU's illegitimate monopoly on power and the need for more political organizations and parties to challenge KANU's twenty-year stranglehold on the political process. In matatū, buses, market places, kiosks, churches, mosques, everywhere and despite countless police intimidations, people are discussing and renouncing single party tyranny and the constitutional distortions that KANU has forced down our throats over these years.

This is a period quite similar to the 1960s when, again, united and unfearing, Kenyans came together to fight for total independence. Then, as now, some opposed the demand and helped the colonial government. Mr. Moi and his party KADU supported British rule. Mr. Moi, for instance, is on record as saying that Kenya was not yet ready for independence. By 1966, the KANU platform that Kenyans voted to power and the independence constitution had become so subverted, so abused, that as they stand today they are a complete negation of our original expectations. By the 90s Moi had completely succeeded in negating our national independence and turned KANU into an instrument of personal rule. It is probably misleading to call the present day KANU a political party. It is more akin to the Mafia with Moi as the feared Godfather. Financial manipulation and thuggery and murders are its essence as now runs by Moi, Inc. the Godfather reaches for the gun whenever he hears the word *democracy* and *accountability* as voiced by opposition.

Opposition

Moi has correctly accused Mwakenya-December Twelve Movement and *Pambana* of leading the opposition since the beginnings of the 1970s. But it is Kenyans who have all along rejected Moi. In less than ten years since the December Twelve Movement daringly broke new grounds with *Cheche, Pambana and Mpatanishi* with their calls for a renewal of the democratic ferment, people from all strata have increasingly come forth to proclaim their interests and rights. For example, recently voters nationwide denounced the rigging of the 1988 party and general election; parents and students in all levels of education have opposed and decried the 8-4-4 confusion and mass failure; cash crop farmers, especially those who produce sugar, coffee, cotton, tea and cashew nuts, have been up in arms fighting to get fair returns; many clergymen have often spoken against the disappearance of democracy and the rise of authoritarian rule; students and many professionals have raised their voices against the erosion of human rights, the distortions in the constitution, the destruction of the environment and against a one man or party dictatorship; and finally, the entire country, and not just Kisumu and Nairobi, protested against the murder of Robert Ouko and denounced the clumsy "suicide" cover-up attempts by the government in the latest KANU style murder. In short, people have now rejected the culture of silence and fear. Hence the current democratic ferment and the united call for Moi and KANU to go.

Demands for a New Beginning and a New Direction

Quite naturally, the call for Moi and KANU to go has expressed itself in terms of a countrywide demand for a multiparty system. But the issues at hand are far broader than the question of just one or several parties. They have to do with the entire economic and political system. What the people want is no less than a new beginning and a new direction in all aspects of the national life. Mr. Moi responded to this countrywide demand by declaring war on the Kenyan people as can be seen in his unleashing the paramilitary forces against the thousands of demonstrators who are only expressing their democratic rights of free assembly. As the demonstrations spread across the whole country, the killings by the armed forces are increasing daily. Moi and KANU are leading Kenya towards pointless bloodshed.

We cannot sit idly by and helplessly watch Moi and KANU set up our country in flames. Mwakenya which has consistently opposed *nyayoism* and championed the cause of democracy, even in the days when others faltered or even worked for the regime, has once again accepted the request from the Kenyan people and even the challenge from Moi himself by coming with concrete proposals for the solution of the current political impasse. On 25th May 1990 Mwakenya issued a statement calling upon all the active progressive democratic and patriotic political organization, workers trade unions, peasants cooperatives, professional bodies, religious organizations, students societies, the business community, welfare and other nongovernmental interest groups to unite in a single force of action to pressurize Moi to resign. The call was answered loudly and clearly these last ten days especially since July 7, 1990. While it is true that the killings which have been mounting since the assault on the pro-democracy rally at Kamũkũnji in Nairobi on Saturday, July 7, 1990 by paramilitary forces are Moi's way of responding to the pressure, they point out even more so the urgency and the necessity of keeping up the pressure for him to go. So in the streets, in the marketplaces, in their workplaces, in the schools and colleges, in the churches and mosques, people have devised and will continue to devise ways of maintaining their defiance.

Mwakenya: The Unfinished Revolution

Mwakenya puts forward the following proposals first outlined in their statement of May 25th as a good basis for the solution of the current political impasse and the avoidance of further strife:

Moi and KANU Must Go

There can never be any compromise on this. A multiparty system cannot thrive as long as KANU continues its stranglehold on the judiciary, the administration, parliament, the mass media, and on other institutions. Moi and KANU have completely discredited the First Republic. By resorting to murder squads and organized thuggery, Moi and KANU have lost the moral right to rule.

The Present Parliament Must Be Dissolved

The current "National Assembly" is illegal because it came about through the queuing system by all Kenyans. The majority of Kenyans boycotted the so-called elections. This parliament has absolutely no legal mandate to make laws for Kenyans.

A National Conference Is Essential

The need for such a conference has been adequately articulated by a broad spectrum of Kenyans and particularly so in the Pastoral letter of the Catholic Bishops of Kenya on the current situation in the country. Delegates could come from religious bodies, professional associations, workers' trade unions, peasants' cooperatives, students' organizations, the business community, women's organizations, welfare and other non-governmental organized groups, Mwakenya and other democratic and progressive political groupings whether underground, inside the country or abroad.

Care-Taker Government or Administration

The national conference will appoint a caretaker administration whose duty is to draw guidelines and arrange election for a Constituent Assembly. The 1962 Lancaster House Constitution or the pre-1966 Constitution could be used as the legal basis for the election for such a constituent assembly.

There Must Be a New Constitution

The primary task for the Constituent Assembly is to draw up a new constitution for the Second Republic and to supervise the political process from the current dictatorship towards the second republic. The current Constitution, like the incumbent president, his government and his parliament no longer has any legitimate mandate and in many respects, they are illegal. The present Constitution is untenable because it has been tampered with so frequently and so illegally as to have made it lose the legal weight expected of such a basic document. It undermines the bill of rights, natural justice and basic civil rights. In particular, it underpins laws, which are undemocratic and completely unacceptable in a free Republic, for example, the Preservation of Public Security Act, the notorious Chiefs Act, and the recent powers given to the police to hold suspects for up to 14 days without charges. What Kenyans now want is a new constitution realized through a national consensus and resulting in the Second Republic, a constitution that guarantees that if they remove one tyrant, he will not be replaced by another even more vicious one.

There Must Be Checks and Balances on the Presidency

The Constituent Assembly will deliberate consultatively on the form of government that best suits Kenya today as we face the new millennium. It must ensure that presidential powers are reduced. Presidential powers at all times must be shared with a freely elected parliament. The president must never have any special powers to appoint or nominate members to parliament. His term must also be limited to two elected terms.

Free Multiparty Elections Must Be Held

The Constituent Assembly must allow a specified period for the formation and consolidation of political parties and then hold universal free and fair multiparty elections on the basis of a secret ballot and on guidelines that allow no discrimination on the basis of nationality, religion or gender.

All Acts That Discriminate Against Any Kenyan Nationalities Must Go

The recent presidential directives requiring the Somali nationality to carry special cards must be scrapped together with the state of emergency laws that still govern northeastern Kenya.

The Government of the Second Republic and Mwakenya's Draft Minimum Programme

Mwakenya issued a Draft Minimum Programme in 1987, which outlines the fundamental goals and objectives, which could form a reasonable basis for addressing our future in the building of a new free and democratic Kenya. Of particular note is Part Six of the programme, which among other things calls for:

- The recovery of national sovereignty and integrity.
- The building of an independent and integrated national economy.
- The establishment of a genuine democracy.
- Social justice for all classes and nationalities.
- The promotion of a patriotic and democratic national culture.
- The building of a strong people's defense force.
- The pursuit of an independent foreign policy.

For this reason we ask all Kenyans to study and discuss our Party programme and use it as the basis of judging any administration that may be entrusted with the work of national reconstruction. Any interim government or administration and even the government of the Second Republic must address themselves to Part Seven of Mwakenya's Draft Minimum Programme, which outlines the immediate political demands of most Kenyans.

Some Urgent Tasks

All the political prisoners must be free. There would have to be a proclamation of the rights of free speech, and freedom of association. There

The Immediate Tasks for all Kenyans

Mwakenya would like to draw the attention of all Kenyans to the fact that Mr. Moi will not simply disappear. He will in the short run turn even more vicious in a bid to cling to his personally lucrative dictatorship. A regime that is prepared to murder its own loyal Foreign Minister under the very eyes of the national and international community has lost all moral pretences. Moi must move on or be forced to move on. Mwakenya, therefore, appeals to all social forces and bodies whether religious, professional, politically active above or underground, internally or externally-based to come together and forge a practical alliance to establish a national resistance council for the decisive removal of the Moi-KANU regime.

Mwakenya also appeals to all the democratic minded elements in the armed forces and the police not to obey orders to fire on peaceful demonstrations by the people. This regime has lost all claims to political, legal or moral legitimacy. No Kenyan whatever his or her station in life has any moral obligation to obey the orders of a regime that has declared war on the very people it is supposed to be protecting.

Vigilance Against Power-Seekers and Warlords

During the changeover period, Mwakenya wishes to draw the attention of the people to the great danger of senseless coups by power-seekers and warlords. It has happened before at great costs and must not be allowed to happen unless they unite or relegate themselves to the people's wishes and the Democracy Plank. The danger of a reactionary military putsch still exists, as does a palace coup by Mr. Moi and his friends. There is also the danger of a foreign-backed rightwing take-over riding on the waves of this popular revolt and not addressing itself to the issues that have given rise to it. Such coups like Amin's in Uganda can solve none of the current problems. They are extremely destructive and they will delay or divert our national history. Mwakenya opposes this outright. It opposes any regime that might try to make the appearance of democracy look like the reality of democracy. So all Kenyans must renew the democratic ferment, support Mwakenya's *Democracy Plank* and the objectives of Mwakenya's *Draft Minimum Programme*.

With the current events of July, we Kenyans have reached a turning point in our history. These events are taking place in a world, which is changing rapidly. The whole world is talking about accountability to the people and indeed asking for the active participation in the national and international political process. Kenya and indeed Africa, in general, are no exceptions. The arguments that the existence of many nationalities in a single country is a barrier to democracy are not even worth examining. Is Africa going to ban its people merely because of their biological origins? The argument smacks of the old colonial and racist arguments that Africans were somehow not ready for independence. Kenyans have now started on the right foot in 1990s by banishing the culture of silence and fear imposed on us over the last thirty years or so. They have no alternative but to continue pressing their claims for democracy and the rule of law and justice. If the patriotic, democratic and progressive Kenyans unite they will have nothing to lose but Moi's reign of terror.

Finally, we ask the democratic forces in Africa, and the world, to support our just struggle for democracy and social change.

Mwakenya Purges Factional Clique
October 20, 1991

Many grave errors have been committed in the name of Mwakenya (MK) by a few individuals in the party to the dismay of the public, friends and supporters. Some of the devious activities and mistakes have now been traced back over several years. Other errors have consistently been part of their lifestyle and political practice. All these mistakes have caused tremendous pain and distress within the party and sown confusion and discord. After much discussion and prolonged debate within the party, the principle source of deviation has been identified and finally purged while further investigations are going on.

In issuing this announcement, the party recognizes and commends those who have struggled against this factionalist tendency throughout this difficult period and acknowledges the positions taken by:

- Those who are abused and hounded out of Mwakenya over years.
- People's organizations inside and outside country, which were shut out even when MK policy was to welcome dialogue.
- Exiles and other Kenyans abroad who were personally or collectively undermined.
- Our non-Kenyan friends and sympathizers whose trust in us was undermined.

Mwakenya: The Unfinished Revolution

Mwakenya will examine and analyze all the mistakes, deviations and abuses of authority by this factionalist clique. For the movement we wish to take full responsibility for their mistakes. We shall continue the rectification and healing process already under way. The party has always believed that active self-cleansing and self-criticism are essential for all organizations to stay healthy. It may have taken longer than we wished but the persistence has helped to resolve the problems. We extend our gratitude to the many fraternal groups and individuals who helped by exposing the reactionary clique through their publications even as we ourselves were struggling from within. We expect that those that were exposed were done in the spirit of helping Kenya's democratic revolution. Together we now face greater challenges to come forth boldly and create conditions for further closeness of all our democratic forces.

Perhaps the most virulent recent act of the purged faction was the publication, without authority or the least bit of consultation, of the so-called _Mkombozi-Mwakenya_ in November-December 1990. This spurious organ was released purportedly as the Organ of the Defense Forces of Mwakenya. (The very name was ascribed from an already existing publication). _Mkombozi_ is a departure from Mwakenya's well-known political line and spirit, which dates back to 1974. This, as articulated in our _Draft Minimum Programme,_ is the line of commitment "to the unity of all the patriotic, democratic and progressive forces, inside and outside the country, on the minimum basis of their opposition to the continued foreign domination of Kenya and of their commitment to struggle against the present neocolonial regime." In particular, _Mkombozi_'s line smacks of ultra-left adventurism and, in many instances, are clearly divisive. We therefore owe to members and friends of Mwakenya to explain this disparity between _Mkombozi_'s and Mwakenya's line:

1. In its column entitled, "No Short Cuts to Freedom," Mkombozi attacks externally based opposition organizations, accusing them of disunity, alienation from the realities of the Kenyan political scene, and a variety of negative personal attributes of some of their members. The Mwakenya leadership regards this as an extremely divisive

251

Mwakenya: The Unfinished Revolution

diatribe, which could feed right into the oppressive designs of the Moi regime. It is clearly in discord with the realities of externally based organizations. First, many of these organizations are hopefully *external wings of Kenya-based movements,* and they respond to the needs of Kenyan people as determined by those *internal* bodies. Under the circumstances, the issue of alienation of many external bodies from Kenyan realities does not even arise. Secondly, Mwakenya is aware that there are several externally based organizations—a situation, which creates the impression of disunity—and which Mwakenya has repeatedly deplored in the past. Mwakenya has always advocated an alliance of these forces and has supported efforts of other organizations seeking to form such alliances. Mkombozi fails to recognize that there have been, and continue to be, some unity conferences, which have precisely succeeded in building such alliances and cooperative strategies between some of the organizations. Mwakenya recognizes that the opposition organizations are made of people who have dedicated their lives to the cause of liberation of their beloved country. They have made many sacrifices at many levels—from familial to professional, from their freedoms of movement to their security of life. Any weakness or mistakes that have emerged, therefore, must be weighed against the much strength, the sacrifices that have been made and the successes that have been scored. Mwakenya would like to make it abundantly clear that it recognizes and respects the efforts of *all* people and organizations involved in the current struggle for democracy irrespective of differences in ideological inclinations. Our collective desire for political rights and freedoms, and for a better Kenya, is sufficient to bind us in our opposition against the Moi dictatorship and tyranny.

2. In another column, "What Must Be Done?", *Mkombozi* claims that "there are no shortcuts to our freedom and that no fundamental change can come about in neocolonial Kenya without the masses taking up arms and fighting to overthrow/ crush the existing system in order to establish a popular people's democratic power of self-government". Because of this, *Mkombozi* claims to support Mwakenya's determination to wage an uncompromising protracted people's revolutionary war using guerrilla tactics. In principle, Mwakenya finds nothing wrong

Mwakenya: The Unfinished Revolution

with armed resistance against tyrannical regimes. On the contrary, it believes that under certain conditions this may be the only path open to the people. Militant response to oppression is very much a part of our cherished history in Kenya. The violence of the neocolonial state against the very people it is supposed to protect is bound to breed counter-violence from the people at some point or another, if there are no genuine changes for the better. Indeed, the Kenyan people are being perpetually subjected to such extreme brutalities by the state that picking up arms may soon be their only alternative for self-defense and self-preservation. This is why Mwakenya stated quite categorically in its *Draft Minimum Programme* "amidst the current state of violence against the people, we want to reiterate to all the world, that Mwakenya has pledged to fight back by any means necessary." Mwakenya thus believes that armed struggle may be necessary, but has never advocated it as the only way forward. Nor has Mwakenya denied the role and importance of many other forms of protest expressing the interests of various social constituencies. We deem it highly irresponsible to advocate a situation in which haphazard or gratuitous violence will yet again provide Moi with the excuse to wreak unnecessary death and suffering on innocent people.

3. In another column, "The Controversy over Koigi's Return," *Mkombozi* presents "various versions of how and why Koigi returned to Kenya"— including Moi's and Koigi's versions. It then goes on to uncritically report the views of some unnamed political observers, claiming that Koigi returned to Kenya voluntarily believing that his arrest and imprisonment would boost his public image in Kenya and abroad. And in the event of the seemingly impending collapse of the Moi regime, Koigi would then come out of prison a national hero, which would facilitate his bid for the presidency, supposedly "his long cherished ambition". Mwakenya finds this *Mkombozi* line objectionable on two grounds: Firstly, there is no basis for giving equal weight to Koigi and Moi's versions of the circumstances that led to his arrest. Moi's entire rule has been founded on lies, cover-ups and disinformation. No public pronouncement of his can be taken at its face value or given any serious measure of credibility. Indeed, government lies have become established components of court proceedings on false

Mwakenya: The Unfinished Revolution

charges of treason and sedition to victimize people exercising their rights of expression and association for political change in Kenya. Mwakenya's position is that Koigi and others are innocent, and Mr. Moi is guilty of treason. Secondly, Mwakenya is not aware that Koigi has any ambitions to be the president of the country. But even if he does and chooses to bid for the country's presidency, it is within his constitutional right to do so as a citizen of Kenya. Mwakenya's defense and advocacy of the *fundamental right of every Kenyan* to contest every political office in the land, including the presidency, has been clearly articulated in its July 1990 *Kenya Democracy Plank.* Mwakenya also objects to Mkombozi's suggestion that the insecurity alarm raised by some Kenyan exiles is a mere hoax intended to pressurize the UNHCR to expedite their resettlement in Europe and Canada. These are Kenyans who have been hounded and forced into exile on account of their commitment to principles of democracy and justice. Given the Moi regime's record of arbitrary arrests, torture, imprisonment on false charges, detention and murder of political dissidents, there is no reason to believe that it cannot, and does not attempt to, organize the kidnapping and assassination of political exiles, especially those residing in neighboring countries. Moi has not been known to respect either domestic or international law, and in his present desperation, he is capable of committing virtually any crime against his critics. The insecurity of Kenyan exiles, therefore, is *very real.* And Mwakenya urges the UNHCR to facilitate their resettlement with utmost urgency. In fact, Mwakenya has consistently been urging the United Nations to recognize the fact that Kenya is a major refugee producing country and, therefore, member states should receive sympathetically Kenyans fleeing Moi's terror.

4. *Mkombozi* treats Mau Mau under a general heading, "Other People's Struggle". But *Mkombozi*'s analysis in no way represents Mwakenya's line. Since when did Mau Mau become, *"Other People's Struggle"*? The whole analysis undermines Mau Mau's achievements by claiming that it *lacked scientific revolutionary theory, organization and leadership.* Mau Mau had, in fact, central organs, leadership and strategies that were recognized even by the British war machinery. Recent research on Mau Mau has disproved this colonial and neocolonial point of view

Mwakenya: The Unfinished Revolution

of the movement. Throughout *Mkombozi*'s analysis Mau Mau is not seen as a development of different political and military tendencies at different stages of our history. And the aspect of continued internal *struggle* within Mau Mau is ignored. Obviously, then, it is not a lack of scientific theory on the part of Mau Mau that should cause concern, but its lack in *Mkombozi*'s own analysis of Mau Mau.

Mkombozi was a product of the factionalist clique that had emerged within the ranks of Mwakenya's organism. Factionalism creates divisions in a movement and weakens its internal cohesion. It has the same effect of dividing the Kenyans as it does needless splits among organizations that have similar goals and objectives. Factionalism among the people and organizations strengthens Moi's regime and must be fought at all costs. Mwakenya renounces *Mkombozi* unreservedly and reiterates that our former position on unity, alliances and political change in Kenya still stands as summarized in the *Draft Minimum Programme* of 1987 and *Kenya Democracy Plank* (1990). Since the very first issue of *Pambana* in 1982 we have advocated the right, indeed the urgent need, to protest for our democratic rights and to support the guarantees and freedoms enshrined in the original 1962 Constitution of Kenya. In *Kenya Democracy Plank*, Mwakenya has offered constructive proposals for resolving the very serious political impasse currently facing Kenya and for ridding us of Moi's and KANU's tyranny. *Mkombozi* ignores these proposals and disregards the current imperative of seeking unity of Kenya everywhere—inside and outside.

Mwakenya hereby renews its earlier call for broader-based alliances and action inside as well as outside Kenya. Only thus can we hope to move forward to defeat our common foe.

Note: David Kĩnyua and Kĩbacia Gatũ were the authors of Mkombozi-Mwakenya; they were expelled from the party in October 1991.

Mwakenya Internal Newsletter
February 1991

Comrades:

This communiqué is intended to bring you up to date on the outcome of the meetings of Mwakenya's Central Committee to reappraise the organization's position in relation to the political situation that is unfolding in Kenya.

1. The first major meeting took place on August 20-26, 1991 to discuss a variety of issues dealing with the movement's structure, organization, strategies and financial policy. Of central concern were the activities and conduct of a factional clique, which had seriously affected Mwakenya's operations, image and effectiveness for some time. After extensive investigations and discussions, committee members voted to purge the clique from the organization, with the affected parties retaining their freedom and right of appeal. To reduce the risk of factional tendencies developing in the future—a problem inherent in any political organization—Mwakenya resolved to strengthen its communication channels, and to restructure the decision-making apparatus to render it both more centralized and more democratic.

On Financial Policy:

It was agreed that: **a)** expenditure would be guided by a spirit of thrift, consultation, strict accounting, better record keeping and documentation,

Mwakenya: The Unfinished Revolution

and an even tighter system of checks and balances; and **b)** capital generation would be informed by the principles of self-reliance and self-sufficiency. Towards this end there will be, among other things: **i)** members' monthly due: 5% of net income for employed members; Kshs. 20/- for unemployed members residing in Kenya. The equivalent of $10 USD, for unemployed members living abroad. Contributions from members, friends and sympathizers are welcome. All dues, fees and contributions are to be forwarded to our central administration office in New York.

The minutes of this August 1991 meeting have now been reviewed and confirmed, and the resolutions and recommendations are being implemented.

2. Having consolidated Mwakenya's structures and organizations, the CC held another major meeting between the 27th and the 29th of December 1991, with one key item on the agenda: Does the present political situation in Kenya warrant our aboveground participation in the so-called multiparty electoral process? A comprehensive analysis of the situation led to the conclusion that the increasing number of opportunists who are positioning themselves in the forefront of the pro-democracy movement will, by all indication, lead us to a postelection continuation of Moism in all its fundamentl aspects, with or without Moi. Under the circumstances, Mwakenya resolved to remain underground and continue the struggle for the attainment of wananchi's aspirations and objectives as contained in its Draft Minimum Programme of 1987. However, as events keep unfolding, Mwakenya may decide to support one or more parties that have an explicit pro-people agenda above and beyond mere multipartism. Any decision reached over this matter will be immediately communicated to members and friends.

In the Meantime:

a) On October 20, 1991, Mwakenya released a statement to announce the purging of the factional clique mentioned above and to renounce the decisive, distorted, and adventurist political line contained in its unauthorized publication Mkombozi-

Mwakenya: The Unfinished Revolution

Mwakenya. In case, you have not seen a copy of this statement, please contact our administration office.

b) In response to popular demands, Mwakenya issued a reprint of its *Democracy Plank* in July 1991 in both Kiswahili and English. A few copies of the Plank are still available from Mwakenya's administration office. In the meantime a second reprint is in preparation. If you have any suggestion that you think should be incorporated in the reprint, please write to the administration office.

c) The spokesperson and coordinator of Mwakenya, Ngũgĩ wa Thiong'o, gave a keynote address at the First Conference of Umoja-Kenya, USA Chapter, which was held in Baltimore, Maryland, on October 19, 1991. The conference was extremely successful in terms of the number of participants, enthusiasm, organization, and the intensity and level of discussion. At the end of the conference the following resolution was passed: *Be it resolved the Umoja-Kenya (USA) supports the pro-democracy forces at home in Kenya in their demands for freedom for all political prisoners, for their call on the government of the United States of America to cease subsidizing the Moi-Kanu regime's reign of terror through military and economic aid. That Umoja-Kenya (USA) calls on other Kenyans to join hands with us in the fight for democracy in our country.*

d) Umoja-Kenya also held a well-attended public meeting on December 12, 1991, in London, to celebrate Kenya's Independence Day. In his address the chairperson, Abdilatif Abdalla, highlighted the betrayal of the aspirations of Kenya's freedom fighters by successive KANU regimes, and called upon all patriotic Kenyans to intensify the struggle for the true liberation of the country. "Our message to Kenyans everywhere" concludes the statement "is to continue with, and intensify the struggle against the regime, and not be fooled by its attempts to cut off a few branches of the rotten tree pretending that the rest

Mwakenya: The Unfinished Revolution

will reform. The entire tree is rotten and needs to be uprooted, as it will no longer bear anything. Let us tend to the new sapling that has begun to bear the first leaves, where our future of hope and progress lies." Mwakenya also sent a message of solidarity with U-Kenya in which it warned against opportunists, some of whom are now abandoning KANU and posing as reformed elements, who, in the heat of the pro-democracy movement, are preparing to substitute one form of Moism with another.

e) In January 1992, Mwakenya released a statement, in both Kiswahili and English, describing its official's position on the current situation in Kenya. In the statement Mwakenya cautioned against Moism continuing in the politics of our nation, and warned that "Moism without Moi is as dangerous as Moism with Moi".

In conclusion, we would like to reiterate, once again, that, given the current situation in Kenya, our struggle will have to continue being underground and protracted, and we must continue to abide by the strategies and methods of work that can sustain and promote a struggle of that nature.

Mapambano Yanaendelea!!
MK Central Secretariat
New York City

The Mwakenya Stand (1992)

Moism without Moi is as dangerous as Moism with Moi

This is a crucial moment in our history of struggle for democracy and social change. All Kenyans are united against Moi and KANU—in short, against Moism with Moi or Kanuism with KANU. As the national and international pressure for the Moi-KANU regime to go increases, we want to alert all Kenyans to the grave danger of the opportunists who only yesterday were happily participating in or defending KANU's programme of theft, robbery and repression. Some of these elements are now positioning themselves for leadership under the banner of a newly found zest for democracy. Kenyan people must scrupulously examine these people's history of service to the KANU regimes since 1963. We now must be even more aware of the danger of Moism without Moi and Kanuism without KANU. We say: Moism without Moi is as dangerous as Moism with Moi.

We Must Be Vigilant

We must remember how at crucial moments in our history we were robbed of what is ours; Kenyatta did it. Moi did it. The thirteen years of Moi's reign of terror resulting in the jailing of thousands on trumped up charges, in driving hundreds more into exile and into torture chambers, in the formation of death squads, and in large scale massacres of our people, is the horrendous price we have had to pay for lowering our guards. Today some forces in our country are celebrating simply because Moi, desiring to lure the Western donors into restoring the suspended aid, has said that Clause 2A, hastily passed in 1982 to turn Kenya into *de jure* one party state, has now been lifted. We are being told by some quarters that we need no longer be vigilant, that all we need to do is to beg Moi to register parties. Some people are even asking him to stay in power for six months to allow for all the relevant electoral details to be worked out—again by Moi and KANU or by the appointed agents. We are asking an assassin to stay around in our house and for him to work out the rules and terms of how we might share a corner in the house! The shepherds are being asked to let a hyena lead the herd to greener pastures!

We Must Never Lower Our Guard

We in Mwakenya see no cause for lowering our guards even for a second. We would like to remind Kenyans that Moi has a long tradition of wading five steps in the blood of repression and then, under internal and international pressure, retreating one step. Some people congratulate him, forgetting that he is already four steps in the sea of blood. When, for instance, in 1990 he was facing a virtual insurrection that culminated in the events of Saba Saba following the murders of Ouko and the Mworoto residents, he hastily appointed the KANU review committee to come out with reformist noises that were a clear insult to the political intelligence of Kenyan people. We Kenyans must remain suspicious of his apparent quick about turn, this apparent change of heart by a dictator who, only a few weeks ago on November 16, was prepared to kill Kenyans who defied him. We must mount more and not less pressure for the real democratization of our society and for the realization of social justice for the majority.

We Must Learn Our History

In this pursuit we must be prepared to learn from our history. The fact is that even before Moi's KANU was legalized into the only "legal" party in

Mwakenya: The Unfinished Revolution

the land in June 1982, Kenya had been a *de facto* one party state since the banning of KPU in 1969. In fact, it is the realization that repression would only intensify in the years to follow that made the democratic forces go underground under the umbrella of the WPK/December Twelve Movement. They set about producing literature of a democratic culture under the severe conditions of life underground and under constant surveillance from Kenyatta's, and later Moi's, secret police. How right we were! The decade that followed the banning of KPU also saw the banning of the Civil Servants Union, the University Academic Staff Union, the Students Unions, social and welfare societies, and even cultural organizations like the Kamĩrĩĩthũ Community Education and Cultural Center. Again, even before that fateful June 1982, the regime had already started detaining and imprisoning critical intellectuals including the academic staff and students at the universities. Even then more than five people meeting without a police license constituted an illegal assembly. The Public Security Act that empowered Moi to scrap all the democratic and human rights of Kenyans was still in force. Not a single member of parliament could hold a meeting in his or her constituency without permission from the district officers and chiefs who in any case had to chair all the meetings. All these repressive acts were in force long before the clause banning multipartyism.

Thus the years from 1982 to 1988, which saw Kenya move from a Moi-KANU dictatorship into a personal rule with KANU merely an instrument, only intensified a tradition. The 1988 fraudulent elections, the infamous queuing elections, merely formalized this personal rule. The United Movement for Democracy in Kenya and Mwakenya issued a ten point declaration in 1988 rejecting the legitimacy of the resulting government and parliament and reiterated our previous calls contained in Mwakenya's *Draft Minimum Programme* of September 1987 for Kenyans to unite in the struggle for genuine democracy and meaningful social change. We still stand by that declaration. Moi and KANU have not the slightest moral or political legitimacy. An illegal president through an illegal parliament and an illegal political party is ruling Kenya. They have more respect for the Western donors in Paris who all along have been their mainstay than to the

Mwakenya: The Unfinished Revolution

twenty five million Kenyans to whose demands for real change they have always replied with bullets and bayonets. Mwakenya has not the slightest intention of seeking registration under the Moi-KANU regime, for to do so would be according it a legitimacy it does not have. Our legitimacy is rooted in the masses of Kenyan people and not in the Moi-KANU dictatorship.

The Way Forward

This is the same dictator and his instruments of personal rule in which we are now being asked to entrust the management of change. The fact is dictator Moi will only manage change to prevent real change. We believe that there cannot be genuine free elections under the current regime. We ask all Kenyans to rally around the ten-point programme in the *Kenya Democracy Plank*. In addition, we must intensify our struggle for the following:

- All political prisoners including all those facing bogus treason and sedition charges must be set free immediately.

- The basic law must accord to all Kenyans the freedoms of assembly and of association without the supervision of the chiefs and district commissioners; that includes the right of free speech; and the right to organize trade unions, students' and youth associations and cultural and social organizations.

- All Kenyan nationals forced to flee must be free to return unconditionally, without penalty.

- Kenyan labor, resources and economy must benefit Kenyans first and foremost, free of interference from external control (if we cannot take care of Kenyans first, then there is no way we can take care of anyone else, refugees from other countries included—Kenyans must be first, our Kenyan house must be in order before we can substantiate the house of another national); for instance land which remains our basic resource must primarily be used to satisfy national needs, first, and that it shall be redivided among those who work for it.

Only a fundamental change in the economic, political and cultural direction and policies of the entire society to meet the needs of the majority can create the necessary ground for real democracy. These principles are

263

Mwakenya: The Unfinished Revolution

contained in Mwakenya's *Draft Minimum Programme* of 1987 and *Kenya Democracy Plank*. And real democracy is the only basis for meeting those needs. We must work for totally new beginnings. We believe that it is the duty of all the democratic forces and organizations to set the mechanism for a national conference of all the social forces actively engaged in the struggle for democracy and social change, without begging for permission from the KANU regime.

The Tasks Before Us: Defeating Moism With or Without Moi

The tasks for all the democratic forces in the country are now clear. First is the continuing struggle against the Moi-KANU regime. It is a murderous regime. It is dangerous to the stability and well being of all Kenyans. We must not slacken our efforts. We must say it loud and clear and indeed organize around the declaration: *Moi and KANU must go!* The right to organize and the right to choose are human rights and they are not dependent on the goodwill of Mr. Moi and his flock of parrots. Secondly, we must be doubly vigilant against opportunism that has no principal difference with the Moi regime except that somewhere along the line they had fallen out of favor. For such forces a chance to return to parliament and to some cabinet posts would satisfy all their newly found democratic idealism. Thirdly, we must forge a principled alliance of all the patriotic, democratic and progressive forces in Kenya to defeat Moism with or without Moi. It is only an alliance built on democratic principles that can root out Moism with or without Moi. Moism with Moi is dangerous for Kenya as Moism is without Moi. To the cause of rooting out Moism from our midst no matter under what other name and guise, we in Mwakenya and our allies, The United Movement for Democracy in Kenya (Ukenya), rededicate ourselves. The struggle continues! *Pambana* is still the key!

Long live Mwakenya and the United Movement for Democracy in Kenya!
Umoja wa Wazalendo ni nguvu yetu!

WHAT IS TO BE DONE?

Mwakenya and the Current Political Situation in Kenya
Discussion Paper No. 1. June 1992

Introduction

The political situation in Kenya has changed dramatically in the last three years. The position of the regime has weakened, both internally and externally since June 7, 1990—the Day of Saba Saba Uprising. The forces of opposition have gained overall. But this should not make us complacent as our position has not gone entirely our way and the regime has managed to force its way back into power and has divided some section of opposition. It is also necessary to be clear about the part played by WPK/DTM in the past. We have been in existence since 1974 and have consistently fought for the political and economic rights of the Kenyan people. We have maintained a principled stand throughout the present period as well. While the aboveground opposition looks for an explanation for its failure to make the most of the situation, we can look back with satisfaction and pride at the solution we had provided. Events have proved our position to be totally correct. At the same time, the people of Kenya feel betrayed. They responded to our various calls for action. The petty-bourgeois opposition did not understand the true nature of the regime and was carried away by their subjective hopes that Moi was about to give up power. They thus made incorrect political decisions and agreed to work with Moi, in the hope that the dictator will work towards his own downfall.

For our part, we have not done enough to explain our position as set out in the *Democracy Plank*, which has guided our actions throughout the period. At the same time we need to give more publicity *openly* to our position on the current situation and our plans for the future. We cannot openly discuss all our plans, nor reveal details of the intensive discussion going on within our various units. But an indication of our general position now seems necessary, particularly an explanation of our decision to remain underground when "democratic freedoms" are supposedly available in Kenya. Events have proved us right as the regime shows again its repressive character. There is however a political vacuum in Kenya today. The regime is continuing as if nothing has changed, the petty-bourgeois opposition is attacking the regime in small doses when people clearly demand a much more fundamental change. We have a clear political line, which has been shown to be correct. Of course, we do not expect reactionary, rightwing elements to accept it, nor will foreign forces for "democracy" support our line. It is entirely on us to give wide spread exposure to our programme, which alone can be accepted by the people and form basis for a meaningful change in Kenya.

This position paper explains briefly our position and contribution during this period of rapid change.

Movement from 1974 to 1990

From 1974 to 1990 our movement was the main political force that contained a systematic opposition against the rule by the KANU dictatorship. Our documents of this period show that we had a clear political position opposing the regime and its foreign backers. We continued organizing underground, spreading to working class areas and at the same time consolidating our support in rural areas. The reign of terror unleashed by the regime before and after the coup of 1982 and again in 1984-86 did some damage to our organization, including detention and imprisonment of some of our cadres

Mwakenya: The Unfinished Revolution

and exiling of others. Some even gave their lives in this period. The intense attack from the regime, and some incorrect organizational decisions led to weaknesses in our organization. One particularly difficult period was in 1985-87 when a large number of undisciplined people, including university petty-bourgeois academics and students were recruited into the movement, leading to many arrests. It was only the quick retreat into rearguard support areas that enabled us to survive this difficult period. We emerged with our center and main units safe.

We have faced other difficulties as well. Some corrupt elements as well as ultra-leftists remained within the movement and led to further damage. We managed to root these liquidators out as well. All these reverse as well as positive lessons of the 80s have in fact strengthened us and have given us greater ideological depth to face the 90s with a new confidence and courage. This assessment of our strength and courage proved correct during the events of the Saba Saba Uprising. One of the most important documents that we issued was the _Draft Minimum Programme_ (1987), which set out our long-term policy and in effect became the alternate path of development for Kenya. Its ideas and position have gradually become a part of our national demands for the future. The party document exposed KANU's programme as a neocolonial program, a shallow cover for corruption, pillage and plunder. Parallel with that, we rejected the 1988 fraudulent queuing elections, which the regime used to ensure it returned to power. We also rejected the legitimacy of the outcome of the "elections". People throughout the country demonstrated against the rigged elections, this mass movement helped to prepare people for the large-scale struggle of the 90s.

Saba Saba Uprising

On May 25, 1990 Mwakenya issued a statement calling upon all the active progressive democratic and patriotic political organizations, workers' trade unions, peasant cooperatives, professional bodies, religious organizations, student societies, the business community, welfare and other non-

Mwakenya: The Unfinished Revolution

government interest groups to unite in a single force of action to pressure dictator Moi to resign. The call was answered loudly and clearly in the Saba Saba Uprising.

The Saba Saba uprising marked a turning point in our recent history. The full record of the events and their significance are recorded in the Mwakenya's internal document. The events of about ten days starting July7, 1990 ended a dark period in our country. Thousands of people throughout our country defiled the KANU-Moi regime and took to the streets and participated in mass rallies and demonstrations against the hated, oppressive rule. Workers went on strikes; peasants took acts of defiance and resistance. The armed forces of the dictator were not sufficient to dampen people's demand for change. Large parts of the country slipped from the control of the regime as people took over local areas. Many police were attacked and killed. Police stations, government offices and property were attacked and destroyed. In some parts, such as working class areas of Nairobi, effective power came under the control of people. The regime was shaken by people-power. The people rejected the culture of silence and fear. Resistance was the order of the day. Change was what people demanded.

Mwakenya played an important part in the events of this period. We had a well-organized movement that quietly sprung into action. Years of underground existence had given us the experience to work quietly to guide and encourage mass popular movement towards active participation in the demand for change. Cadres intensified underground activities to encourage and activate people to take the path of open defiance. Many workers, peasants and other working people openly began to follow our guidance and began to defy the neocolonial authorities. Progressive elements of the petty-bourgeoisie followed the lead and challenged the bourgeois state in various ways. Many angry Kenyans, including NGO activists, lawyers, religious leaders, teachers, journalists, university students and academics took an open public stand for the first time. Some of these were later to forget the pioneering stand taken by our organization, our cadres, and as well as working people generally, which enabled them to speak out for democracy. They began claiming the full credit for the success of a *national* movement for resistance. The seeds of petty-bourgeois opportunism, which has become so obvious today, could be seen during this early period of change. Such people want to inherit the position of power in order to ensure that their class interests are safeguarded. Similar betrayal at the time of independence had seen the power slip from the hands of the class that had fought and sacrificed for Uhuru. It would be a folly to repeat the same mistake today.

Mwakenya's Democracy Plank

We issued the plank on July 11, 1990 during the Saba Saba Uprising. It set out the demands for peaceful change in Kenya. Our warning in the Plank has proved correct. The Plank states: "Mwakenya calls the entire people of Kenya to be more vigilant against Moi's machinations, and in particular Moi's divisive tradition of Bride, Divide and Rule. Factionalism among people and in organizations strengthens Moi and must be fought at all costs." The Plank sums up the significance of the Saba Saba Uprising:

> With the current events of July we Kenyans have reached a turning point in our history. These events are taking place in a world, which is changing rapidly...Kenyans have now started on the right foot in 1990s by banishing the culture of silence and fear imposed on us over the last thirty years or so. They have no alternative but to continue pressing their claims to democracy and the rule of law and justice. If the patriotic, democratic and progressive Kenyans unite they will have nothing to lose but Moi's reign of terror.

In the Democracy Plank we made it clear that the crisis in our country is primarily political. But we also made it clear that issues at hand are far broader than the demand for a multiparty system, than the question of one or several political parties. The real issues have to do with the entire economic and political system. What the people want is no less than a new beginning and a new direction in all aspects of the national life.

Mwakenya: The Unfinished Revolution

Multiparty Elections

The demand for change and end to the corrupt regime became a mass movement that could not be resisted. The foreign backers of the regime realized that they were in danger of backing the wrong side in the fast-changing situation; they began to play a double game. While openly calling for change, they quietly continued to back the regime, which had over the years enabled them to lay a strong foundation for maintaining their influence. Different foreign powers backed different forces so as to be in a strong position whoever emerged victorious in the end. The United States Ambassador, for example, became a "champion for change" in this absurd scenario, while the British continued to back the regime. The U.S. also backed some NGO petty-bourgeois groupings that were encouraged to join the opposition to Moi. Many of these were strong allies of Moi some weeks earlier, now suddenly becoming champions against Moi. They got open support from the U.S. Ambassador.

The forces that opposed Moi can broadly be grouped into two opposing class alliances: **1)** the petty-bourgeois groupings, which had internal contradictions within themselves and with Moi. They split into various smaller factions, each trying to get the largest share of state power and patronage. In essence, they differed little from the class interests represented by Moi and KANU, except they wanted *their* chance for power. They were not objectively opposed to Moi- KANU. In the final analysis, when Moi was ready to hand over vast fortunes in return for their support and loyalty, many of them were happy to rejoin KANU, having been assured of the slice of cake, which was all what they were really after. **2)** The second group was composed of various sections of the Kenyans left who broadly represented the interests of working people and rejected compromising with the Moi regime. But there were also differences among them, with different views on what their position should be in removing dictator Moi from power. Many felt the time had come for open political parties and in effect trusted Moi's word that he now believed in democracy. Some formed their own small, petty-bourgeois parties; others put their trust in FORD,

Mwakenya: The Unfinished Revolution

under Jaramogi Odinga's leadership, which had at one time seemed to possess power to overcome Mr. Moi's pro-imperialist forces. They did not make a correct analysis of the current political situation and what would be an appropriate response. They seemed to have been carried away by subjective wishes and not by the concrete situation. It is this failure of the broad left that allowed Moi to return to power by using dishonest means.

Facing increasing opposition from every side, Mr. Moi was forced to make some concessions or he would have been swept out of power. A very clever strategy enabled him to appear as if he was making a major change. He accepted that other parties could contest in elections, but at the same time ensured that only his party, KANU, would win. The Constitution was changed to make it difficult for any opposition presidential candidate to win. He also instigated violence using tactics borrowed from the racist South African regime practice of a "tribal" force to create a state of chaos and death in areas where he needed to win desperately. State power was used to ensure that Moi got maximum benefit and opposition parties isolated. Radio and television and press were used to ensure his message reached the people while blocking opposition news. When everything else failed, he used his state control over finances to print more money to bribe those who could be brought over to his side. Generations of Kenyans will end up paying Moi's election debts.

We have consistently called for a *principled alliance* with all the democratic, patriotic and progressive forces in Kenya. Alliance must be forged on principles that address themselves to the fundamental economic and political problems facing the majority of the population—the entire working and peasant populations. We must address ourselves to the issues of land, national capital, housing, health provisions, meaningful education, jobs, thousands of school leavers—indeed of the very neocolonial character of the regime, which given rise to our entire problem.

Mwakenya: The Unfinished Revolution

Current Situation and MK Position

Mwakenya's position on the current situation in Kenya was made clear in January 1992 in a publication entitled; *Moism without Moi is as dangerous as Moism with Moi,* which was later reprinted in the booklet, *The Mwakenya Stand* (1992). The points made are still valid today. The main point is "to alert all Kenyans to the grave danger of the opportunists who only yesterday were happy participants in defending KANU's neocolonial program of theft, robbery and repression.

Political Priorities for the 1990s
Discussion Paper No. 2.
March 1993

Introduction

As we plan our strategies for the 1990s, it is necessary to get our priorities correct. We need to be clear about the current political situation in the country as well as understand the strength and weakness of our own organization. Without such an analysis, we are in danger of taking decisions that may not be correct in the present period. This Discussion Paper attempts to set out our political priorities in the context of the current situation in the country. As we attempt new initiatives, it is important that all members and cadres discuss the issues raised here so as to arrive at a position that has been well discussed with input from all units and cells. It is proposed that following intensive discussions, points made by all will be incorporated into a new Policy Party Document, based on the following analysis.

Political Situation in Kenya

As set out in our Discussion Paper No.1 (Mwakenya Stand on the Current Political Situation in Kenya) there has been a dramatic change in the political position in Kenya since the Saba Saba uprising in 1990. Many gains have been made, but also there have been setbacks. Overall the

Mwakenya: The Unfinished Revolution

regime has managed to remain in power, although it is much weaker than before and faces daily attacks from people in every part of the country. Forces opposed to the regime lack a united position; they do not agree on what needs to be done during the current period. The regime has taken advantage of this paralysis and has continued to consolidate its position. The objective conditions are conducive to change, people are ready to take on the regime, but there is a lack of leadership that can guide the country during this period of change to remove Moi-KANU.

There is increasing disillusionment among the people with the aboveground opposition parties, many of which continue KANU policies and practices outside of KANU. Major parties remain representatives of petty-bourgeois interests and offer no hope for the country, which needs a fundamental change in the class basis of those in positions of power. Some other parties represent no more than individual interests. There remains a large popular support for change in almost every part of the country; for example, the people residing on the Coast, Central, and Nyanza areas, as well as in the north continue to demand change and are prepared to take action, including strikes, mass demonstrations, attacking government officials and property. Indeed, parts of the country, including parts of Nairobi city, remain under people's control where even the police fear going to. What is missing is a clear political guidance to turn all the goodwill and the local actions into an integrated, political, mass movement, which alone can push the dictator out. At the same time, it should be realized that the regime is not about to be toppled without intensive preparation, much sacrifice, and a clear political, ideological and military preparation. We cannot hope to see a change through the process of elections as was demonstrated during the last two general elections. Some people hope to change the position at the next elections. While we need to take advantage of every opening, we must not pin our hopes of any fundamental change while Moi remains in a position of power. Elections can be meaningful only *after* Moi has been sent packing through mass action guided by a well-thought-out political programme and an organized revolutionary party working in unity with all progressive, democratic and patriotic Kenyans. Perhaps the greatest

Mwakenya: The Unfinished Revolution

danger in the present situation remains Moi's ability to create chaos and intraparty fights that can lead to a state of civil war. He would rather plunge the country into a ravaged state of war than give up power.

Struggle in the past, out of necessity, had to be waged underground; and we are well prepared to do the same in the present. There is now a small opening for democracy. While we are organizationally able to function openly, our greatest need for aboveground work is finances. It was possible during the underground phase to be effective with limited funds. But without adequate funds it is almost impossible to do any political work aboveground. While the regime has unlimited funds from imperialist backers as well as from state machinery—note the use of such local sources as saving institutions and printing of new notes during elections—we on our part face even more difficulties because the sources that could have helped in the past are no longer available. It is thus imperative that we explore other ways of raising funds. No amount of correct political ideas and organizational strength can help if we do not have funds to be able to organize and function nationally. This should be our first priority.

It is therefore proposed that we prepare detailed work programs for the future, including finances as one of the most important items. The current Paper looks at the short-term plan from 1993-96. Future ones should project up to the end of the century and beyond. It is essential that we continue the practice of preparing annual work programs and prepare three and five year plans so as to focus on important tasks. Without this, we will drift from event to event on a daily basis, and in time we will lose our pioneering spirit, which has guided our practical and theoretical work since 1974.

The Short-Term Plan, 1993-1996

It is proposed that we look at different aspects of our work and prepare our goals over this period. These include political clarity, organizational matters, recruitment, strategy and tactics, and financial security during this period. The period up to 1996 should be used to consolidate our party and prepare for a new phase in our struggle, and ensure that we have a secure

Mwakenya: The Unfinished Revolution

financial base to be able to operate nationally. The decision taken recently to encourage external members to return home also needs to be consolidated. The target of change is our overall organization as well as each individual member who remain our strongest asset. In addition, various aspects of the short-term plan need to be studied in detail by all units and centers.

Political and Organizational Strategy

The new aboveground period will mean we must consolidate our links and alliances with other progressive organizations. While we have various formal and informal understandings with various opposition forces and have been influencing their policies and activities, we need to continue this process even further. Our cadres who are being released from detention and imprisonment should begin to be incorporated quickly back into our organizational structures. It is encouraging to note that it has been possible for externally based cadres to go in and out of the country over the last two years. This has enabled closer links between external and internal units. This process needs to be accelerated.

Nationally, it is obvious that there is a lot of disillusionment with aboveground opposition parties, as the promised changes did not materialize. We have had more and more people accepting our position as explained in our *Democracy Plank* and *Mwakenya Stand*. Many activists who had joined various opposition bourgeois parties are now eager to join us as soon as we begin emerging above ground. We shall need to be ready for this new influx of membership. Our membership recruitment policy should be simple and clear. Recruitment should be throughout the country and should cover all progressive, democratic, and anti-imperialist people who accept our *Draft Minimum Programme*. At the same time, our people have been active on different fronts—trade union, peasant cooperatives, professional and cultural organizations—all report a readiness among activists to join us when we come overground. Included here are the human rights and religious fronts in which we have played a significant part. It is essential that we are organizationally ready to accept new members from these fields. Such preparations should take place in all parts of the country.

Mwakenya: The Unfinished Revolution

Our aboveground Ukenya structures overseas are already being prepared for the new phase. It still is necessary to ensure that these changes are made in line with internal developments so that they develop hand in hand.

Military Preparations

It should be made clear to all members and cadres that our primary field is political and it is the politics that will determine the military strategy. We do not believe that the time has come for an armed stage yet. But we have to prepare for any eventuality for the future. As good fighters, generally, we have to be prepared in every field, including military. We should continue discussions already begun on training cadres and ensure, as many cadres as possible are able to undergo military training. This work should start as soon as possible.

Finances

As mentioned earlier, this will be our key activity from now onwards. Internal and external sources should be explored. The Treasurer's department should be expanded to undertake feasibility studies on local business and fund raising activities. Externally, friends should be contacted with a view to getting support in whatever forms available. Plans already worked out should begin to be implementing as soon as practical.

Conclusion

The period up to 1996 is one of consolidation and preparation for a new phase of struggle. We must understand that there is not going to be any short-term resolution of the problems facing our country. Just as we built a strong underground structure over a long period of time, we now need to ensure that while the underground remains strong, a new aboveground organization should be prepared, and equally as strong. Initially, this can be done by consolidating our links in democratic organizations of the working people in towns and in the countryside. Preparation for an open aboveground organization should also be worked out. With these changes the future of our organization looks bright.

Charter For Democracy In Kenya
Discussion Paper No. 3.
March 1996

Historical Background

As we mark the 32 Anniversary of our Independence, we would like to painfully remind Kenyan patriots that all the freedoms and democracy we fought and died for during and after the anti-colonial struggle have been completely swept under foot by the successive KANU regimes. These hard-won Kenyan birthrights have been totally eroded. Why?

Even as our post-colonial struggles forced the Moi-KANU regime to retreat, opportunists and reactionary opposition parties colluded with Moi and their external backers. They disguised themselves as people's deliverers, but were really thinking more about their individual power and the security of their ill-gotten wealth. They gave Moi a golden opportunity to rig the 1992 so-called "multiparty elections". Moi was totally rejected by the people—the majority voted against him and his regime was facing international isolation. It was these opportunists who helped the dictator wear the garb of a "democrat". Foreign handouts are now flowing into the country as usual, but not to the masse of Kenyan people; the official opposition has acquiesced in the rigging and in giving the regime legitimacy in the eyes of those who are not interested in genuine change.

Dictator Moi has already demonstrated a total disregard for human rights and life. He has murdered and continues to murder thousands of people in the Rift Valley. He has maimed and continues to maim thousands. He has internally exiled, as refugees, thousands of innocent Kenyans, of which many are representative of the drained brainpower of Kenya, culturally and intellectually. This cruel past time well rehearsed during decades of occupation of northeastern province, is now being extended to the rest of the country, particularly to the Rift Valley region and to the Coast. Since he took over power, Mr. Moi has killed over 10,000 Kenyans.

How Many More Must Die?

Compatriots!

How many more Kenyans will dictator Moi murder, maim, imprison and exile a la Renamo or Unita before we unite to stop him? How many more deaths will it take to prick the conscience of patriotic, progressive and anti-imperialist sons and daughters of our dear motherland? When will we take a principled stance and stand up to stop this national hemorrhage? We are lucky to have had a heritage of resistance. The spirits of Waiyaki, Koitalel, Me Katilili, Mũthoni Nyanjirũ, Kĩmathi, Pio Gama Pinto, Gen. Kago and other patriots who gave their lives for Kenya call upon us to take up our historical responsibilities in defense of the motherland. Now is the time to act.

Remember that our northeastern neighbor Somalia was turned into a human butchering field when Moi's friend, mentor and fellow dictator Siad Barre laid the foundation for civil strife in efforts to cling to power and continue plundering the country's wealth, even as Moi is busy doing the same in Kenya today. We believe it is time for all patriotic, progressive, democratic and anti-imperialist forces in the country to unite and act together. It is time to seize the historical moment and hour. We let it slip in 1982, then again with the queuing elections in 1988, and yet once more in 1992, this time with so-called "multiparty elections". All these failures have cost us dearly—the regime is responsible for over 10,000

Mwakenya: The Unfinished Revolution

deaths, and thousands of maimed, detained, tortured and exiled fellow Kenyans. Agents of the regime have wantonly destroyed personal property of thousands of our people. Millions are now without land or jobs, without any hope of getting either. The devaluation of the currency and circulation of illegally minted money—used to rig the elections and to bribe—have sent the prices and inflation soaring. Basic goods are beyond the reach of working people and even the middle class. Meanwhile, Moi and his sycophants keep accumulating more and more Kenyan wealth into their personal bank accounts overseas.

Compatriots! Do not fall into the trap of thinking as some opportunists do, that we will be saved from the clutches of the dictator by the goodwill of foreign "friends". They never have nor ever will. It is only our own actions that brought the regime to the brink of collapse in the past. The foreign "friends" joined in later to protect their own interests. Now as in the past, it is to our own actions that can bring about change. This is not to deny the importance of our overseas sympathizers who genuinely support our struggle in a true spirit of internationalism. We welcome their support. We also need to understand the current situation in the country. The dictator has found his way back into power. The "official opposition" has failed to provide any real opposition to the regime as our people expected them to. Nobody now expects them to provide any leadership. They are there to inherit the position of power from Moi. Let us not place our hopes for change in them.

Now is the Time for Unity

Therefore, now is therefore the time for principled unity of all proven patriotic, progressive, democratic and anti-imperialist Kenyans under the clarion calls that—Moi- KANU and the sycophants must go! This was the first demand made by Mwakenya in its publication, *Democracy plank* (July 1990) as a basis of meaningful change. The opportunists have not accepted these demands in their eagerness for personal power and their rush to enter parliament. This allowed dictator Moi to grab power once again. Let us

Mwakenya: The Unfinished Revolution

come together on the basis of Mwakenya's ten points, which can unify us in order to overthrow the dictator. We continue to be disunited at our own peril. Now is the time to take up a correct and collective principled stance. We cannot afford to be divided at this crucial period in our history. The country faces the danger of more years of dictatorship if decisive action is not taken. Once the dictator consolidates his power base through corruption, it will be more difficult to overthrow him.

The Call

We call for a principled unity of all proven patriotic, progressive, democratic and anti-imperialist, Pan-Africanist individuals and organizations to take a common stand for unity as a minimum prerequisite for united actions and efforts to dislodge the insatiable python from our midst. No democracy can be achieved as long as Moi and KANU remain in power.

We call upon all progressive individual Kenyans and organization to reaffirm that meaningful change can only be achieved through our own initiatives and organized and coordinated activities of mass actions like strikes, boycotts, demonstrations and other mass actions declared "illegal" by the illegal Moi regime. There is no doubt that given united action, we can bring about meaningful change through mass, organized, action. We proved this when fighting the British colonial occupiers during anti-colonial struggle. We proved this again after independence against Moi in the 1980s. We should therefore not continue to be divided by the self-seeking petty-bourgeois opportunists. History is on our side; we shall win if we are united.

Immediate Demands

As the first step, the Charter demands that all Kenyans should have the following rights:

- Freedom of Assembly
- Freedom of Association

Mwakenya: The Unfinished Revolution

- Freedom of Expression
- Freedom of Belief
- The right to life
- Freedom of Ownership
- The Right to Fight injustice
- The Right to form political parties
- The right to form trade unions
- The Right to contest elections
- The right to change the government

These rights should not only be enshrined on paper, but also translated into practice in everyday civic life. As a first step, oppressive laws such as the Preservation of Public Security Act and the Chief's Act should be annulled immediately. It will not be possible to achieve these immediate demands while Moi and his henchmen and women remain in power.

On Security

Moi's private army of thugs should cease immediately its murderous and wanton destruction and confiscation of property in the Rift Valley. The thug army should be charged with treason, as should Moi. There must be an immediate return of all the displaced people to the Rift Valley, Western Kenya and Coast province. Their property must be restored and they must get a proper compensation for loss of property and life from the vast looted funds accumulated by Moi and his fellow conspirators. An independent commission of inquiry should be set up to investigate the real perpetrators of these heinous crimes. Immediate action should be taken to stop the activities of this thug army from spreading to other parts of the country. It should be noted that these activities started after Moi claimed that multipartyism would lead to "tribal warfare". He has set out systematically to fulfill his own bloody predictions. It should be noted that people are still suffering from the effects of Moi's earlier activities in northeastern Kenya, at the coast and western Kenya. Similar tactics are even today intimidating working class people in Nairobi, Mombassa and other major towns. They all have the right to security of life and property. All those victimized have a legitimate right to compensation.

On Economy

Moi and KANU have distorted the economy to serve their own personal accumulation of wealth through corruption and looting. They have turned Kenya's national wealth into their private resource. They have allowed the national infrastructure to collapse. It is imperative that this trend be stopped immediately. All the wealth looted by the KANU gang should be returned to the national coffers. But the immediate question that must be addressed is that of land ownership. KANU has systematically deprived the people of Kenya of the very resource they died and fought colonialism for—land. Unless this question is settled in the interest of the people of Kenya, there can be no justice or peace in a country.

Parallel with that, the right to work and to social security must be guaranteed to all Kenyans. Workers should have the right to a living wage and the right to strike, if they have probable cause to do so. Productive public sector projects should be undertaken to increase employment. An end to corruption should free resources to embark on a major public works project. The economy should first of all be working in the interest of Kenyan people.

On Urban Areas

Local government services such as garbage collection, maintenance of roads, sewage and housing should be effective and efficient. The people have a right to withhold their rental payments, and challenge rate increases, if basic services are not provided. Adequate housing, healthcare and education are birthrights of all Kenyans.

Is Change Possible?

The real question is not if change is possible. Change is coming whether Moi likes it or not. The real question is what form the change will take

Mwakenya: The Unfinished Revolution

and whether it will be directed by working people and those who have the interest of the working people at heart. Moi will go all out to ensure that he and his friends are directing change. The third possibility is a total loss of control over the process of change. This could result from spontaneous, unplanned, acts by people driven to desperation in the absence of economic and political progress. Such chaos can also result from people on the "left" taking up individual acts of sabotage without mass support, adequate preparation, planning and direction. The danger in the current situation in Kenya is that Moi is driving the country to total break down of law and order. We must not allow him to do so.

In such a situation, our only hope is to ensure a unity of purpose, direction and action. The Charter for Democracy provides such direction. The alternative is too frightening to contemplate. Many may ask: How do we achieve the aims of the Charter? The answer lies within ourselves and the fervor with which we wish to find a peaceful solution. We do not need to depend on "permission" from Moi to start a debate among ourselves in small groups and circles about the Charter. Let us put the demands of the Charter at every forum we may be involved in. It will soon become the demands of all Kenyans. Let us organize conferences and meetings on implementing the Charter. Wherever there are Kenyans—inside or outside the country—there should be discussions on the Charter. In schools, in workplaces, trade unions, universities, among professional, social and other organizations, there should be a united call—the call of the Charter. Remember once an idea grabs a people, it acquires strength more powerful than all the armies that Moi controls.

Forging a New Unity through the Charter

All patriotic, progressive, democratic and anti-imperialist organizations of Kenya are invited to associate themselves with the Charter for Democracy in Kenya as a way to forge a new unity of all those opposed to the Moi-KANU regime. This may be our last chance to ensure peaceful, meaningful, change in Kenya. Let us recognize that our real enemy is Moi and the whole

Mwakenya: The Unfinished Revolution

gang of thieves calling themselves KANU. Our main struggle today is to remove them from power. Moi and KANU must go! Let us not fall into the trap of believing that they are all-powerful and we are weak. Remember our years of struggle to remove colonialism from Kenya. It was a long, hard struggle, which needed many sacrifices. But we persevered and won. Remember the glorious Saba Saba uprising of 1990. If we rise as a people, we can win. We are dying a slow (sometimes fast) death under KANU anyway. Let us die fighting so we can leave a bright future for our children. Our main weapon is our unity and a strong organization. Let us resist every move of the dictator. If each one of us resists, the combined force of all our resistance will be unstoppable.

The next step is to organize a national conference of patriotic, progressive, democratic and anti-imperialist forces in order to plan our future. Let us not be divided on the basis of nationality or region as Moi is attempting to do. Let us judge people and leaders on the basis of whether they are on the side of Moi or on the side of the people. History and the motherland call us to action. Let us seize the time. Mwakenya and its leadership are ready to unite on the basis of the Charter with other patriotic, progressive and anti-imperialist forces inside and outside the country. There is no victory without a struggle.

Circular No. 5: On Recruitment
August 1995

Dear Comrades:

For any party or organization that is living and active, recruitment is a basic necessity. It is through recruitment that new cadres are incorporated into the party and the party builds new cells and expands. It is also through recruitment that new ideas, fresh drive, new blood and initiative, sharing of the task are brought along. Stop recruitment and death of the party creeps in.

In our type of party (Communist Party), recruitment is so vital; it helps and replenishes our ranks to take on the most progressive stance and vigorously undertake our own replacement in that continuous process that keeps the banner of struggle alight. However, it is also through the recruitment that the enemy gets the chance to infiltrate the party and destroy it from within. Hence, the need to take utmost precaution is demanded without making any compromise or being sucked in by liberalism. It is a real balancing act, to get in as many as possible recruits, but not let in a single enemy agent or reactionary petty-bourgeois opportunist—to recruit but not be infiltrated. This is a dedicated task and most important task for the development of our party.

Our practical observation is that this vital task of recruitment has significantly stalled and almost grounded to the halt both at home and

Mwakenya: The Unfinished Revolution

abroad. We no longer hear of new recruits in our party circle, and this is most peculiar to us, as we have not had to deal with such, particularly as an issue of concern. But even outside our circle, among the liberal petty-bourgeoisie and the ultra-leftists, even among the workers, we are also hearing similar talks: *There is no underground movement in Kenya; Mwakenya is dead.*

Our feelings are that possibly the following are the major factors for our failures:

- Cadres do not know how to recruit.

- They are scared of the risk involved.

- They do not have time for this vital task. This is liberalism creeping in the party.

- They argue that there are no candidates at all for recruitment.

- They are confused by the multiparty scenario and do not see the differences between our party and bourgeois parties.

- They have lost ideological direction, discipline, commitment and dedication.

- They feel that everything is okay, if political gains are somewhat met.

Let us now discuss each one of the above factors:

1. *Cadres do not know how to recruit:* While this may hold true for the new inexperienced cadres, this is not true for the old experienced cadres. New cadres require discussions on the subject in their study cells, sharing experiences and knowledge. To train the new cadres how to recruit is the primary task of the party. But it must be emphasized that each cadre must bring new people into the party; otherwise the party will remain weak or will die.

2. *They are scared of the risk involved:* While fear always hangs somewhere in a cadre's life, it is this fear that we have to overcome and dare to try. We must go against the tide. A revolution is a serious business and cannot

Mwakenya: The Unfinished Revolution

be made by cowards and pretenders. When conditions change, we have to adjust accordingly and fit in with the changed circumstances. Our tactics and strategy also have to be adjusted. Arguably, it requires caution, courage, commitment, conviction and more time for critical examination, criticism and self-criticism, but by no means does it call for apathy and cowardice. Caution does not mean you stop recruitment or performing revolutionary work. It means more critical and conscious performance, and more courage and daring.

3. *They do not have time for this vital task:* It is possible they don't have time, but let us check it out. What could they be doing? We have made it clear, and we have discussed this issue repeatedly that the party work is priority. We need to discuss this issue again in our study cells. More time, more effort is needed of marking the candidates. Many have been banking on spontaneity, which is rare and liberal at best. Liberalism is the mother of compromise, opportunism and betrayal.

4. *They argue that there are no candidates at all for recruitment:* This is a liberal and backward argument, though some party members actually believe as if this were the truth. They forget that every Kenyan next to them is a possible recruit, a potential revolutionary, only that he has to fulfill certain conditions (determined by the party). Recruits are made consciously and critically by members. You can spend a lot of time talking to a possible recruit, but until you pinpoint, earmark and isolate a candidate for development, you will never have a recruit. Therefore, it is not true that there are no recruits around; it is you who is not looking for them and you need to discuss in your cell how to "look" for them. In building our revolutionary party, a lot will depend on recruitment of new members and the commitment and dedication of our party cadres.

5. *They are confused by the multiparty scenario and do not see the differences between our party and bourgeois parties:* There could be some truth in this as has been reported that some of comrades have deserted the party and joined the new bourgeois parties and NGOs. They have betrayed us and the party not from cowardice alone but also from personal vanity, from petty-bourgeois opportunism. But this only brings us to the fundamental question: How should we behave in the multiparty scenario? Our contention is that

Mwakenya: The Unfinished Revolution

nothing fundamentally has changed in the country; therefore, we must continue as before but take care not to be deceived by apparent "liberalism" of the multiparty era. In this case, cadres have to discuss new methods of work and at the same time draw a new strategy of recruitment. In fact, we can use the cover of multipartyism to broaden our party base.

6. *Cadres have lost ideological direction, discipline, commitment and dedication:* We would hate to believe this. Other indications do not support this thesis at all. But for the benefit of the majority of our cadres, it is advisable to resolute the following (as it is repeatedly stated by the party leadership). First, our struggle remains a protracted people's struggle using any means necessary and based on concrete reality of our country. We are a MLM party. Secondly, no fundamental changes have been made by the repeal of section 2A of the Constitution. The neocolonial system remains intact and the comprador bourgeoisie and their imperialist allies remain in power. Thirdly, recruitment is a continuous process as we move forward to overthrow the neocolonial state and build a democratic society. All have to question themselves: if we stop recruiting who will bring that change, who will continue with the struggle when we are arrested and imprisoned? Who will pick up the gun when we fall on the battlefield? Remember Che's famous words: "Wherever death may surprise us; it will be welcome, provided that this, our battle cry, reach some receptive ear; that another hand stretch out to take up our weapons and that other men come forward to intone our funeral dirge with the staccato of machine guns and new cries of battle and victory."

7. *They feel that everything is okay, if some democratic gains are somewhat met:* Some cadres could be misled into believing that a victory against a current regime is also a reason to no longer recruit new members, that demands and concerns have been met; when, in fact, nothing has been met until statistics state such for the poor, the homeless, the unhealthy, the landless, the uneducated, and so forth. It is hard to determine victory by the win of a political party, or that of a despised regime. The importance of membership, i.e., continued membership, is always needed to guard the masses, in a practical sense, and not in a rhetorical sense. It is easy to say what will be done, to/for the masses; but as old and new members, it is not that which we seek to hear about what will be done, opposed to that which we want to see that has been done. In order to be able to have that kind of power, in numbers, membership cannot be taken lightly, based on the whim of a win or a victory. To have numbers is power, because then it is hard to avoid the obvious, if everyone is watching, documenting, and addressing issues of concern, along the lines of a democratic nation that seeks to, first, take care of its own.

Seize the moment, seize the time, comrades!
The future of our country is bright.

Minutes and Reports
Minutes of Central Committee

New York,

May 28-29, 1995

Present: Joshua (recording), Kioko (chairing) and Hamisi.
Regrets: Achieng', Mkuki and Kimbo

Minutes of the April 1994 meeting were not tabled. To be tabled at next sitting.

The Administrative Secretary opened the meeting at 9:30 p.m. and explained London's continuing financial hardship and inability to raise ticket costs. Kimbo's reasons for failing to attend were noted. Hence, the meeting took place with only three members present. It was also noted that the meeting that had been planned for August or September 1994 did not materialize due to apparent lack of serious commitment despite agreement expressed at the April 19, 1994 meeting.

It noted that London had submitted documents and especially a set of agenda and comments for the meeting. These were most useful. National Coordinator (Karĩmi) had also submitted working documents and suggestions. The evening of the 28th of May was spent working out a structure and an agenda for structured discussions on the 29th. A combination of the London and New York notes provided the basis for the agenda, thus:

Mwakenya: The Unfinished Revolution

1. Pervasive Crisis within MK—state of MK and underlying causes of growing malaise:

   a) Overall direction of MK—re-appraisal of functions following political changes at home.

   b) Re-examining MK's primary objectives.

   c) Long-term strategy and work plan.

2. MK strength and membership:

   a) Projects, e.g., Okello's project, Ukenya publications (Tutashinda), etc.

   b) Finances.

   c) Work plan for the near future—debate on Reorganization and Restructuring.

   d) Pending and tasks unfinished as assigned to CC members.

I. MK in Crisis

The meeting started with a reminder that MK has not lived up to its own decisions taken as early as 1990 to hold a full Central Committee meeting and convene a national congress. The effect of this failure is that we have been overtaken and by-passed by many events at home. The CC has met several times and has not resolved in concrete action many outstanding problems and tasks. Today's CC meeting could, for various reasons including finances, only gather together three members, the lowest number ever for external. It was agreed that it is imperative for MK to address this state of affairs urgently and with resolution.

A discussion of the crisis afflicting the organization and the evolution of that crisis, followed. Firstly, up to 1990-91 MK was at the forefront of the political movement in Kenya with many path-breaking initiatives. Before that, in the 1980s, MK single-handedly kept the struggle alive when few dared to oppose the state and/or in many cases openly abetted the state. The recently formed opposition, dominated by old KANU rejects and former government ministers, soon took over the mass movement, derailed it, and then quickly killed it—at great cost to the long-nurtured democratic

Mwakenya: The Unfinished Revolution

movement and Moi's obvious glee. By standing on the sidelines at such a critical moment and allowing MK's leadership role to slip to such a dubious opposition, MK rapidly lost its place as initiator and vanguard. Other than providing useful early analysis and sharing this some then-leading lights in the incipient opposition, MK consciously refused participation in a movement it had "birthed". The basis of this refusal was outlined in the widely publicized statement entitled, *The Mwakenya Stand.* Since then, in contrast to the pre1990 period MK has offered neither new analysis nor initiatives to fit the totally new situation. Secondly, the current MK malaise results from important internal weaknesses with MK, especially the inability to analyze a new political and social reality and then adapt strategies and activities to fit. But external changes have also played an important role. Before 1990-92 internal dynamics, plus a relatively close link with the "living" situation in Kenya, propelled the organization forward. After 1991-92 developments external to MK (political changes in Kenya, new players, etc) had the effect of dampening the internal dynamics and slowing the organization; other external changes are related to the global collapse of the socialist states and the end of the so-called cold war. Compared to the confidence of the 60s and 70s, international socialism has undergone a crisis following the sudden death of the Soviets and their satellites and the continuing dominance of finance capital globally. There is also a lack of a coherent analytical ideological certainty to MK's membership and work. In brief, the vision created in the late 60s and successfully applied and re-enforced in the mass work of the 70s and 80s—a vision so useful in piloting a few dedicated cadres through to the 80s and building the basis of the abortive democracy movement—is now blurred and even under question. MK's ideological under-pinning needs re-examining and re-affirming. Obviously, this is a task for the whole membership and not for a partial Central Committee such as the one sitting today. (See under recommendations below).

Thirdly, the crisis in MK is, however, principally an internal one, which also needs thorough discussion, analysis and resolution. (It was, for example, mentioned that MK is vague and prevaricates on the issue

Mwakenya: The Unfinished Revolution

of power, any kind of power—a trail evident since the earlier days vs. University staff Union ceding leadership to others despite doing all the background work only to be sold out aboveground. This ambivalence on power includes state power. MK and its predecessor projected an image of "purists" working behind the scene to influence and inform power but not to be sullied by it).

Fourthly, before 1990 this approach worked incredibly well. Success after success were achieved by a few dedicated activists—university students movement, cultural movement and revolutionary drama, publications analysis and related mass work and political education; creating alliances with other sectors and individual MPs, journalists, etc.; recruiting and creating a network of structures that shook the state on several occasions; the highly effective London and overseas campaign to free political prisoners and for human rights and democracy.

Fifthly, in mid-1982, Moi's government attacked the DTM movement scattering and almost beheading it. At least five leading cadres were imprisoned or detained while a large number went into exile, where they organized a successful campaign. We had developed no effective in-country fallback plan for such an attack that was severe, brutal, unjust, and inhumane. Even after their release in the late 1980s, cadres were not able to regroup until 1990. The net effect was that new inexperienced members, (who should have been trained if such were to ever take place, as that of mid-1982), took up leadership within the country. In the vacuum that existed, pretenders came to the fore, distorted the organization and soon hijacked it at great cost in credibility among the exiled community. The DTM new leadership, which later changed the name of the movement to Mwakenya, resorted to sectarian leadership and organizational methods, which eventually led to internecine infighting, and backward mercenary basis of political work, thus alienating more friends and potential allies. Re-establishment of contact with elements of the DTM in 1987 meant assuming or inheriting all the liabilities, known and unknown, of the post-1982 Mwakenya leadership, both inside and in exile.

Sixthly, the social and political reality in Kenya is: **a)** a rapidly collapsing economy and growing impoverishment of all sectors of society, except the very connected to the state or robber-speculator circles, social institutions in total disarray unable to deliver any welfare services to the people (education, health, basic security or public services, etc.); **b)** an extremely hated KANU and its government still in power and consolidating its stranglehold on the society using all means, including buyouts, murder, ethnic cleansing and relocation of populations, a fracturing and increasingly unpopular opposition, which is unlikely to regroup in time for the 1997 elections—this is an almost assured return to power for Moi or some similar KANU or KANU-lie government until the year 2002, if no urgent and effective political actions are undertaken to arrest this trend; **c)** a disunited underground movement led by weakened organizations often led in exile; **d)** an enfeebled MK among them.

II. Strength and Membership

- London's position that MK has "no presence at home" is incorrect. There has been unbroken and continuous work carried out by cadres.

- After some discussion, the CC resolved that all Ukenya members be accepted as full regular MK members and arrangements made to inform them as per usual method.

- Although leadership inside Kenya is relatively new, it has already cleaned up the mercenary corruption inherited from the previous leadership of David Kĩnyua, Kĩbacia Gatũ, Warũirũ Mũngai and Mwangi Thuo and created a basis of trust to build on.

- In response to London's question, "How many external members can return or pay prolonged working visits inside?" Central Committee heard Hamisi's argument that "returning must remain the ultimate goal. There is a risk, however, of returning mechanically, removing individuals from a social base. Rather MK should encourage members to work where there are. Past experience with the Kangaroo (a cadre) episode shows that uprooting without appropriate structures and functions can be disastrous, and that economic survival is critical now that MK cannot commit to any support as a conditionality of their return before 1998." Brief visits inside are encouraged and have so far been very useful in maintaining links and exchanges. The visits to Dar in 1990-91 were enlightening and helped us evolve beyond the impasse created by the Dar clique. All visits inside, since 1992, by the Administrative Secretary (Maina wa Kĩnyattĩ) have been helpful for monitoring of work and progress. Where funds permit this must continue.

III. Role and Function of Spokesperson

All CC members have expressed dissatisfaction with the way the spokesperson position has functioned. London, specifically, asked for an examination of the role and the practice so far. Hamisi explained: Mandate of spokesperson was not adequately defined at the time it arose. The idea, initially, was found on the basis of, "half underground and half above". One immediate problem that arose was that the public saw the function as an individual, not as a representative of MK. The formal position of the Spokesperson no longer has any relevance, and may even be negative since it gives the impression that MK is one individual while also being confused with his image as a writer and cultural activist. The office of the Administrative Secretary has absorbed a lot of the previous coordinating work of the "spokesperson". MK should consider the practice of *ad hoc* spokesperson as issues (i.e., for specific issues). Hamisi asked to be released of the post. While the Central Committee notes that the Administrative Secretary is already the center of information dissemination and MK coordination, it is recommended that Hamisi continues in the current role until new structures are put in place, and functions/mandates are more clearly defined and approved.

IV. Projects

a) Journals and Periodicals (e.g. Tutashinda). London's proposal was noted and commended. Sweden's comment was also highlighted regarding past experiences with publications (*Habari, Kamũkũnji,* and *Mpatanishi*) and

MK's lack of continuity in this domain. Central Committee resolved that new journals and periodicals must not be started until restructuring has been completed. Mkuki will however be asked to continue preparing data for *Moi's Reign of Terror, Vol. No.* 2, from material provided by Inside and from elsewhere. Hamisi and Kioko will supply the structure for the database.

b) Language and Cultures Research Project: Updating the old *Nyota* idea with a language focus. Incipient grouping on this project already has been working informally since 1994. Central Committee approved this project and asked Kimbo to coordinate the project with CC. Principal source and actor to be Dr. Okello based inside. Hamisi is to facilitate and offer all necessary support on this task. Progress report must be presented at the next CC meeting.

c) Mkono: The highly anticipated *Mkono* (military) training last July and August (1994) failed due to: the link with *Mohammed* weakened and Achieng's loss of subsistence and base. While CC still sees the fundamental need for mkono given ever-worsening situation, the whole question needs a new thorough analysis and discussion along with the rest of the proposed reorganization. Meanwhile, Achieng is directed to analyze, briefly, for the next CC meeting—our experience with mkono thus far, the difficulties and successes of MK's mkono training policy, as well as providing proposals and suggestions for consideration.

V. Finances

The Administrative Secretary reported that while MK is not in any debt, there are virtually no funds to run the organization. The Secretary is instructed to prepare a financial report and send to CC members. Central Committee notes extreme delinquency of fee payments, and the heavy load borne by a few members in supporting MK organizationally, and financially. MK must aim to maintain a substantial fund in its account, in order to function properly, work, and support the home front. CC has recommended that the Secretariat send a letter asking members to begin paying their dues immediately, if the CC is going to function as a committee.

Mwakenya: The Unfinished Revolution

VI. Recommendations

As is evident above the meeting centered on the critical need for revitalizing MK and decided on MK-wide discussions on reorganizing and restructuring. The following are the recommendations to this effect: 1. MK to be reorganized with a definitive constitution, hence Centers and members are asked to discuss this issue and submit proposals to the Administration Secretary, as per work plan below.

2. A National Congress to be called to discuss and approve the new constitution.

3. Ukenya and MK to formally merge under the new constitution.

4. The National Congress to debate and recommend on modes of operation including the role of underground work.

5. Two CC members suggested change of name for merged organization.

6. There should be a thorough and ongoing discussion on the ideology guiding the reorganized MK, with an emphasis, particularly, on the role of MLM in future work that is in light of the current international situation. This should be carried out by the entire membership, and proposals and recommendations from members and centers are to be submitted along with other issues.

A special CC meeting should be held in December 1995 to study and approve recommendations and issue a work plan for implementation, dissemination to all members and centers.

Note: Joshua-Kamoji, Kioko-Maina, Hamisi-Ngũgĩ, Achieng-Abdilatif, Mkuki-Shiraz and Kimbo-al-Amin.

From Home Front:
Our Response to the CC Minutes
Nairobi, September 15, 1995

Comrades:

It cannot be said that things are easy for MK at the present. The reasons are both external and internal. In an effort to address this difficult situation, the following proposals are suggested:

1. *Attendance of Meetings*: There is an urgent need to re-emphasize the need for attendance of organizational meetings; members have to make a concerted effort to attend the meetings. The least excuse one expects is lack of finance. We feel that efforts could have been made by the London comrades to send at least one person. The same rigor should apply to all of the organization's meetings and tasks. We must declare total war against this vice; otherwise we might as well hang up our combat boots and go fishing or hunting.

2. *Role in the Current Political Situation:* The observation that MK has been sitting on the sidelines has been made before. There is some justification for such an observation. We will attempt to give several explanations. Firstly, it is our strong belief that the present situation in our country, where multipartyism is controlled by KANU and Moi, will not yield fundamental change, but at the same time MK has failed to provide an alternative. Secondly, we have failed to create a strong

Mwakenya: The Unfinished Revolution

leadership at home and abroad, which would influence the political trend in our country. We have left the stage to the reactionary petty bourgeois opposition parties and the neoliberal NGO groupings sponsored by Western imperialism. In fact, many Kenyans believe that MK is dead. Others think that FORD is an offshoot of MK. Thirdly, our political literature points to the correct path, yet we have no force to impose our condition. Fourthly, the previous MK leadership in the country under David Kĩnyua, Kĩbacia Gatũ, Mwangi Thuo and Warũirũ Mũngai almost destroyed the party through corruption and sectarianism. They were running the party as dictator Moi runs KANU. As a result of their mercenary methods of political work, the party sank into the boiling pot of organizational looseness and opportunism. It will take quite sometime to rebuild the party internally as well as to convince Kenyans that we are truly the party of national liberation, democracy and social justice—the party of workers and peasants.

3. *Vision and Ideology:* There is an urgent need to solve the ideological void in our organization. We must reaffirm our faith in Marxism-Leninism and Socialism, and at the same time we recognize the mistakes made by the Soviet Union and other socialist countries. We should study and analyze their mistakes in order to deepen our faith in Socialism. Our tactics and strategies can change or be modified, but our ideological tenet should not change. In theory and practice, we should take an anti-imperialist, anti-capitalist stance; we are Marxist-Leninists-Maoists. Consistent with that, we should study our society. A scientific and historical analysis of our society would mean that we begin to deal with the major historical tendencies and issues of concern, of various classes—their limitations and potentialities: how and why they move under certain political and economic conditions, and whose interests they represent. It would also help us to combat the politics of tribalism and narrow nationalism imposed on our people by the comprador bourgeois rulers and their imperialist backers.

4. Recruitment and Growth: To grow we must recruit. We must bring new blood in the movement. It is therefore the duty and responsibility of every member to bring a new member into the movement. Some members do not recruit; they don't think that it is their job to do so.

Mwakenya: The Unfinished Revolution

This elitist behavior must be vigorously combated within and the outside the movement. The following are our recommendations: a) those who are abroad should recruit from there. Every Kenyan is a potential revolutionary; b) there is a need to de-emphasize some areas as recruiting grounds. For example, a lot of focus on higher institutions of learning tends to alienate other fertile grounds like colleges, high schools, polytechnics, that we should be focusing on as well, given the fact that the talent outside of the university setting could be just as great, if not greater. Elements drawn from these places could have fewer elitist problems; c) there is a need to carry out our long-term and essential link with the peasantry and workers. To recruit peasants we must be active in rural institutions—schools, churches, and cooperatives and through person-to-person contact. For workers, we should join their trade unions and recruit them from within. There is also a fundamental need to organize a communist trade union, as in South Africa; d) we have few women in the movement. A positive way out is to deliberately contact progressive petty-bourgeois women in the various NGOs that address female issues. To broaden our base we have to work with them and in the process we may get positive and patriotic individuals among them. These are well-educated petty-bourgeois women and most of them live and work in the city. On the other side of the fence, there are working class women and they are easier to be recruited in the movement because of their class position in the society, but the problem is our organizational weakness—that we have not succeeded in creating a firm political base among working people and within the progressive petty-bourgeoisie; e) we must have two types of memberships: 1) Core membership and 2) General membership. The core membership should always be strong, committed and ideologically clear. This membership is composed of party cadres—the engine of MK; and f) we have to study, analyze and understand the role of NGOs in our country. It is a fact that they are imperialist agencies whose agenda is to sabotage and derail the national democratic revolution. They are enemies from within.

5. *Liberalism*: We must ruthlessly combat liberalism within the movement and among the membership; otherwise it will transform our movement into an amorphous, petty-bourgeois political party without structure,

Mwakenya: The Unfinished Revolution

ideology or discipline. It will open wide the gate of the movement to superficial and unstable characters.

6. *Overt Activities:* We are weak operating above ground or publicly confronting the neocolonial state. Our suggestion is that we continue the rejuvenation of the party underground until we are strong enough to face the oppressive regime and its foreign backers. Let's give ourselves the deadline of two to three years. This period will give us enough time to draw up our strategies and tactics and to build revolutionary institutions among the workers, peasants, pastoralists, and patriotic petty-bourgeoisie.

7. Mkono: We support the idea that our cadres should go for military training to prepare for the future. Mao teaches us, "Political power comes through the barrel of the gun".

8. Coalition and Alliance: Tactically, we have to form a united front with other progressive and patriotic organizations in the country in order to defeat Moism and to neutralize the reactionary opposition parties and the neoliberal NGO groupings. But we can only form a united front with other patriotic organizations if we are strong enough to defend our position; otherwise, we will lose our ideological identity, color and character and compromise our fundamental programme.

9. Finance: We are happy to note the commendable efforts by the external front to have a regular source of income. It is unfortunate that the burden has been falling on a few comrades. Here we need to emphasize the concept of self-sacrifice and commitment. Sacrifice means contributing even when things are bad for you. It means giving the organization/party first priority. It is sacrifice that will bring progress and make us a force in our country. As in other areas of our organization, there should be a spirit of emulation—which group or unit can raise the highest amount? We could even have "sacrifice" months where members exert themselves to the fullest to raise funds for our revolutionary work. The challenge is: If we cannot sacrifice financially, how can we sacrifice in other ways? The Mau Mau leadership taught us that a revolutionary movement must be based on self-reliance, self-help and self-sacrifice. It must build its own

Mwakenya: The Unfinished Revolution

independent financial and political institutions, and these institutions must be built among the workers and peasants.

10. Subsistence: Here at home, many excuses have been given for no-exertion in party work. One of these is lack of subsistence. It is commendable that more and more cadres found means of subsistence outside MK, but pursuing ventures of subsistence to the neglect of MK work is as harmful as total reliance on MK for subsistence. The point has to be made over and over—priority in all matters is MK work. Pursuit of means of subsistence is a basic means of enabling all of us the opportunity to perform the primary task of the party. Even our families should be part of our revolutionary work. With their support, it will enable us to serve MK with revolutionary energy and uncompromising commitment.

11. Constitution, Rules and Regulations: The organization must have a constitution, rules and regulations. And our DMPM (Draft Minimum Programme of Mwakenya) must be updated to keep up with the political developments in our country and the world. Apart from that, the language used in the Draft Programme is liberal, weak and vague; we should base our party programme on the DTM ideological line.

Karĩmi Nduthu
National Coordinator

Internal Memo

(For your eyes only)

Dear comrades:

During our last CC meeting, it was agreed that MK members, including the CC members, should pay an annual party membership due ($25 per person), and that membership will be terminated if a member fails to pay for more than three months. It is, therefore, the responsibility of members to forward their annual dues to the MK Central Secretariat. It was also agreed that we should continue with our monthly membership donations ($125.00 per person). You are also aware that the party branches/cells are required to donate $200 each, annually, to the party treasury.

Methods of work:

1. Secrecy and discipline must be maintained.

2. Collective responsibility and accountability is our strength.

3. Attend meetings of the cell/branch. Failure to attend more than three times, without an excuse, will result in an expulsion from the party. At every meeting a member should contribute $2.00.

4. Criticism and self-criticism should not be taken as a personal attack. However, criticism should always be constructive, positive and not negative. Otherwise, negative criticisms will create unnecessary

Mwakenya: The Unfinished Revolution

disunity within the party and among the cadres and general members.

5. Cadre or member should have the courage to raise questions, voice opinions and criticize ideological defects within the party at all levels.

Activities:

1. Sell our literature, buttons, T-shirts, etc.

2. Organize cultural activities twice a year (celebrate our national heroes on February 18th of every year).

3. Organize demonstrations against the Moi murderous regime in your community.

4. Form a coalition with progressive forces in your community. Create sub-cells and contacts around the party.

5. Cell studies must continue and be maintained. Intensify political education, criticize incorrect ideas, and combat liberalism within the cell or branch.

6. Recruitment. Every cadre must bring a new member (or members) to the party.

Democratic Centralism:

1. Democratic Centralism is our core principle and it basically means: **a)** the individual is subordinate to the party; **b)** the minority is subordinate to the majority; **c)** the lower level is subordinate to the higher level; and d) the entire membership is subordinate to the Central Committee.

2. Democratic Centralism must be carried on within the branch/cell so that members/cadres can understand its meaning and the concept of the united front. This way we can work with other Kenyan progressive organizations, without weakening our ideological stance or abandoning it altogether.

MK Central Secretariat

New York

April 15, 1996

Democracy and State Terrorism

Stop Moi's State Terrorism against the Kenyan People

The statement of Mwakenya at the 7th Pan-African Congress, Kampala, Uganda, April 3-8, 1994, read on behalf of the MK Central Committee by the current spokesperson, Ngũgĩ wa Thiong'o.

Mwakenya is profoundly honored to be part of this distinguished and historic gathering. We are here not only in the name of our organization, but also on behalf of many Kenyans with whom we have fought tyranny with these last several decades. On their behalf and on behalf of all the working people of Kenya, Mwakenya would like to thank the organizers for the timely convening of this 7th Pan-African Congress.

Today, as in 1945 in Manchester, we Africans on the continent, and in the African Diaspora, find ourselves at crossroads. Then, it was the aftermath of the Second World War, which had brought about profound challenges to the status quo. Today, the end of the cold war is equally challenging the status quo. Then, the challenges were against a colonialism, which threatened to intensify to help rebuild a shattered Europe. Today, the post-Cold War situation is one of intensified neocolonialism. Neocolonialism is not dead. It is precisely because it is not dead, that it now takes on features of re-colonization.

Mwakenya: The Unfinished Revolution

Our agenda today must deal, more than ever before, with the simple, but urgent, imperatives of survival with dignity. We must collectively determine to leave this week with the kind of single-minded resolve that two generations ago propelled our predecessors from Manchester to go forth and commit change. What they did against colonialism and for independence we must do against intensified neocolonialism and for national, continental and global liberation of our people. Pan-Africanism, by relying on our collective strength, provides us with the global vision that can guide our struggle for that liberation-economic independence and social justice. That liberation must mean the actual liberation of our lives. For Pan-Africanism is not, and must never become, an abstract ideal. Its material basis, its very subject and object are the African people themselves—real living people. Pan-Africanism would be nothing if it were not on the side of this dignity of even the lowest among us. African lives must be sacred to each one of us. That is why Mwakenya believes that in attacking and combating the external forces that now threaten recolonization, we must also as ferociously attack and combat those social forces within us that ally themselves with intensified neocolonialism. Slavery was not possible without the black slave drivers in our midst. Above all, we must be ruthless with any forces within and without that make the assumption that African lives are dispensable. Enshrined in our Pan-Africanist vision and practice must be the principle that it is the primary duty of any government, indeed the irreducible moral and political minimum, to protect the lives of its people. Any government that fails in this duty and treats its people as the enemy and the country as an occupied territory ripe for pillage and plunder, then such a government—whatever the shade of the color of their skin—loses all moral, legal and political legitimacy; and should be regarded as a pariah, an outcast, by all genuine Pan-Africanists. Take the specific example of my country, Kenya. Believe me, it grieves us most profoundly to have to take the example of a country whose people's profound connections with Pan-Africanism from Garvey to Manchester should have put it, under different circumstances, in the hall of fame of triumphant Pan-Africanism.

Mwakenya: The Unfinished Revolution

But today, Kenya is a tortured land. In 1945, our people were under a foreign power and occupation. They vowed to rid our country, of this foreign power and domination, and in less than 20 years, led by Mau Mau; and they did just that, only to be cheated out of their victory that was paid for in the form of torture, spilt blood, and death. Moi, who in 1954 at the height of the Mau Mau war for national independence, was a white settler colonial appointee to the then Legislative Council to help the British in mapping out ways of defeating Mau Mau armed resistance, has proved beyond any doubt the truth of the saying that "beware of the enemy within". Moi and his KANU have ravaged and fractured Kenyans along every minor crack one could either imagine or create. He has instigated regional civil wars, using his armed forces against Kenyans. In short, he has initiated the shortest sighted and vicious state terrorism in the land of Kĩmaathi and Mau Mau. We estimate from reports by human rights organizations, church-based accounts, and augmented by our own networks that since Moi initiated state terrorism in 1992 over 10,000 have been killed and over 500,000 displaced. Why has there been world silence? The reason is because it's the ordinary Kenyans who are being shot with bows and arrows and guns supplied to Moi's terror squads by the government. It is also because Moi is a darling of the West, particularly the British, who feel grateful for what he has done for them since 1954.

Moi and KANU did not just begin this terror in 1994. For instance, in 1984 there were massacres in northeastern Kenya against Kenyan Somalis and also against the Pokots. Indeed, according to a well-researched book, *Moi's Reign of Terror,* by the United Movement for Democracy in Kenya, between 1979 and 1989 Moi had already eliminated at least 6,000 Kenyans. However, while previous massacres were under a one-party state, and therefore met with denunciations from foreign governments and human rights groups all over the world, the current massacres are taking place under the protective umbrella of Moi's version of multiparty democracy. The registration of opposition parties under Moi's conditions has been more beneficial to the Moi-KANU regime that to the people of Kenya,

Mwakenya: The Unfinished Revolution

since it allows Moi to shout multiparty democracy to cover the sounds of gunfire and the cries of the tortured.

The seventh PAC is taking place in Uganda where state terrorism was practiced under the Idi Amin and Obote regimes while Africans on the continent and the African Diaspora, the largest in the world, watched, some even applauding Amin as a great Pan-Africanist. By our silence, we became accomplices of the Idi Amins, the Bokasses and the Barres of this world. If Pan-Africanism is to mean anything, it must be prepared to denounce all atrocities against the African people, no matter their racial, national or geographical origins. Mwakenya supports the call for the creation of a permanent secretariat. However, it is the hope of Mwakenya that when a permanent secretariat of the Pan-African Congress is established, it would have as one of its important components a human rights department. We want to reiterate that Mwakenya and the Kenyan people support every effort to bring African people together; to protect their lives and dignity; and to enhance their struggles for social justice and progress. It is only Pan-Africanism that is rooted in the struggles of all the working class peoples of Africa and the African Diaspora, rooted in their economic, political, cultural and psychological needs, which is best placed to become part of the living organ of Africa and all African peoples! In working tirelessly to defeat Moism and all its variants, we in Mwakenya shall be guided by that Pan-Africanist vision.

Long live the spirit of Pan-Africanism and may the 7th Pan-African Congress be the beginning of our victorious march over the forces of political and cultural degradation.

Moi: Stop Genocide and Disintegration
May 1, 1994

When in 1992 Mwakenya issued its statement, *The Mwakenya Stand* (1992), it declared that the movement will not seek registration under the Moi-KANU regime, because doing so will be giving legitimacy to an illegal government, which imposed itself on Kenyans by rigging the 1988 queuing-up elections. There were some who thought that we were either being unreasonable or were scared to face this repressive regime openly. But ours was a stand based on principles. We also warned our fellow Kenyans that no meaningful changes would take place as long as Moism and Kanuism—with or without Moi and KANU—are still in existence. Mwakenya has always believed that the Moi-KANU government could not be trusted in overseeing the democratization of our society. For Moi and KANU are themselves the problem. They both must go!

Two years earlier, in 1990, when most of those who are now in the registered opposition parties were working hand in glove with this repressive regime—and at a time when no apparent signs were in sight that Moi and KANU would be forced to accept multipartyism—Mwakenya published its *Kenya Democracy Plank*. In it Mwakenya set out ten demands and urged Kenyans to press for their implementation before rushing to seek registration for the political parties, let alone contest the last sham elections. Again based on principles, Mwakenya was of the conviction

Mwakenya: The Unfinished Revolution

that without a conducive, political environment—which we believe would have been brought about if those demands were achieved—no meaningful democratization would take root. Mwakenya pointed out the dangers of going into elections while Moi and KANU remained in power to manipulate them. How right we were!

In spite of all assurances that the elections would be free and fair, we saw once again how Moi and KANU rigged themselves back into power in December 1992. This was partly the consequence of opportunism displayed by the reactionary opposition parties, who rushed and contested the elections before the basic changes were made. We saw how Moi and KANU employed both old and new tricks. They amended the electoral laws to suit them. They appointed and refused to dissolve the electoral Commission that was biased towards them. They gave a short period for the registration of voters; and, as a result, millions of Kenyans were not registered. They cut off the opposition from many areas of the Rift Valley by declaring them, "KANU zones", and made it impossible for the opposition to propagate its policies by denying them permits to hold public meetings. KANU thugs prevented opposition candidates from presenting their nomination papers in time by kidnapping them. Finally, on the Election Day, KANU perpetrated many documented cases of irregularities through its agents. The result of such an election cannot be said to reflect the will of all Kenyans. It was a rigged election pure and simple. All patriotic Kenyans must reject it. Our stand remains that the Moi-KANU regime has no more legitimacy to rule now than it had before the 1992 elections. In fact, the majority of Kenyans voted against Moi and KANU. This is a government, which robbed the people of their power. Kenyans must not allow themselves to be misled by a few opportunists who, for their own personal gains, are campaigning hard for Kenyans to accept the results and leave Moi and KANU to rule in peace to the end of the term. Kenyans have already witnessed what Moi and his repressive and murderous regime can and will continue to do in the remaining years.

Moi and KANU have plunged Kenya into the worst crisis since Independence, threatening the very integrity of our dear country. Faced

Mwakenya: The Unfinished Revolution

with the increasing resistance from the masses, Moi and KANU have intensified the massacres and genocides, which they started way back in 1980 (Garissa) and 1984 (Wajir) where thousands of our fellow Kenyans of Somali nationals were mercilessly killed. We have warned before that Moi and KANU still have the capacity to instigate a civil war. They would rather see Kenya disintegrate than give up power. They must be stopped before it is too late!

With the support of the Western imperialist democracies, the Moi-KANU regime has unleashed genocide against defenseless Kenyan residents in Molo, Londiani, Burnt Forest, Enoosupkia, Laikipia, Kapenguria, Mombasa, Kwale and Bungoma. There has been a killing of nationals on a massive scale; there has been destruction of property, forced evictions, rapes and maiming. Murderous gangs trained, armed and mobilized by the Moi-KANU regime, have committed these criminal acts. As a result, tens of thousands of Kenyans have fled their homes and sought refuge in churches, public schools and even open fields. Not content with that, Moi's gangs pursue the victims even in refuge camps. For example, in Enoosupkia, those who took refuge in a local church were attacked, raped, maimed and brutally murdered inside the church. In Molo, the Moi regime has declared "security zones", which, in reality, are terror zones. Not only is the declaration of the so-called security zones illegal, but it has also denied Kenyans of their right to free movement. The media and international observers have not been able to document and expose the atrocities committed by Moi's terror gangs. Kenyans should not be deceived by official propaganda and disinformation that these are *"tribal clashes"*, when they are government orchestrated. Different nationalities in Kenya have lived peacefully together for thousands of years, without so much as a party or politician telling them what they can and cannot do; why, then, this sudden outbreak of wars against nationalities? The answer is that the Moi-KANU regime has instigated these "clashes" by putting into practice the old colonial policy of divide and rule to further its own interests of greed and exploitation of the land and people. Kenyans must refuse to be set against each other; we are not each other's enemies; nor should we

Mwakenya: The Unfinished Revolution

be pawns of a regime's need to justify their illegal activities. We must recognize our real enemy. It is the Moi-KANU regime. We must, therefore, forge a united, common, stand against it. We should also seriously ask those politicians going around the country preaching cooperation with this regime whether they want Kenyans to let Moi and KANU intimidate and kill them for another four years?

Kenyans should not, at any time, lower their guards in anticipation that this regime will change its ways. Let us not be deceived that just because the opposition parties have their members in parliament that they will be in a position to effect any fundamental changes. Because, in order to ensure that the representatives Kenyans elected do not achieve their objectives, the Moi-KANU government has manipulated the parliament. Even when Ntimama makes inflammatory and inciting statements from there, KANU's control of the House ensures that he is not censured. Moi even uses parliament to defend such unpopular laws as detention without trial. Outside parliament, Moi's treatment of the challenges from the opposition is no better. He has refused to register the Islamic Party of Kenya (IPK), the University Academic Staff Union (UASU), the Student Organization of Nairobi University (SONU '92) and several others. In addition, the regime has continuously denied some opposition parties permits so that they cannot freely assemble. The overall effect has been to deny these organizations their fundamental human rights of association and assembly.

What all the above proves is that Moi and KANU are still opposed to true democracy. In fact, Moi is on record saying that Western powers and financial institutions like the IMF and the World Bank forced pluralism upon him. During the Saba-Saba Uprising, the Kenyan people rose up against Moi and KANU. In order to preempt the real changes, which the Kenyan populace is struggling for, the imperialist forces instructed him to introduce multipartyism as a way of controlling the people's demand for a genuine change. The reality of the Moi-KANU rule is that it is leading the country into a total social, economic, political and cultural collapse. Health services to the majority of Kenyans have grounded to a halt. Educational standards are deteriorating fast, while it is becoming

Mwakenya: The Unfinished Revolution

more and more expensive for parents to educate their children. Prices of essential commodities are beyond the reach of the ordinary *mwananchi*; the economy is on a slippery slope. Moi and his small clique surrounding him are still extracting wealth from the economy, which has not yet recovered from the massive printing of notes to facilitate the Moi-KANU "election victory". *Wananchi* are now paying the price of this gross mismanagement of the economy. Once a self-sufficient country, Kenya is now faced with hunger and starvation. What all this boils down to is that no solution to the crisis facing Kenya today is possible while Moi and KANU remain in power. Every pressure should be exerted to dislodge them. We should not wait till the next elections, for they will behave just the same. We must not relax. We must not waver. We must not hesitate. We must intensify the struggle for a truly democratic and free Kenya. Doing otherwise will cost all Kenyans very dearly. For this regime will never cease to harass, jail, and kill patriotic Kenyans.

Mwakenya is a movement, which, for more than fifteen years, has been waging the struggle against repression; first, under the Kenyatta-KANU regime; and now under the Moi-KANU regime. Fighting for broad democratic changes, Mwakenya considers its patriotic duty to call upon its members and all democratic, progressive and patriotic Kenyans to do the following for the time being:

- Defy the Moi-KANU regime by all means necessary. Defy all repressive laws, which deny us our fundamental rights.

- Organize and fight without seeking permission from the regime. Students, teachers, workers, peasants, professional groups, women and religious organizations and groups should form whatever unions or associations that they consider necessary to promote their respective interests. Mwakenya salutes all those who have already taken defiant actions by calling for strikes, etc., like the Islamic Party of Kenya (IPK), matatũ operators, teachers, university academics and students, workers and peasants alike.

- Refuse to cooperate with the Moi-KANU regime, as it is an illegitimate one.

Mwakenya: The Unfinished Revolution

- Refuse to be manipulated by the Moi-KANU regime to butcher or cause harm to our fellow Kenyans.

- Reject the call for *Majimbo,* as this is a device used to further divide Kenyans. Those calling for *majimboism* are the very ones responsible for many of the problems now facing our country (Biwott, Ntimama, Shariff Nassir, Lolodo, etc.). And after all that they have done against Kenyans, they were awarded an award during the 30th Anniversary of Independence.

- Unite so as to effectively wage a campaign to remove Moi and KANU from power.

Mwakenya once again reiterates the call it first made in 1990 that the best forum for carrying out the peaceful, prosperous and democratic Kenya is through a national convention. Once again Mwakenya urges all democratic, progressive and patriotic Kenyans to form a principled and united front and hold the convention in spite of Moi's recent rejection of it. Meanwhile, all organizations and associations should start discussing this issue and come up with suggestions on how best to go about it. Nobody else, neither the foreign countries nor their ambassadors are going to liberate us, only ourselves. Finally, Mwakenya calls upon the police and other armed forces to desist from harassing and harming Kenyans struggling for their rights and justice. Mwakenya is reminding these forces that the Moi-KANU government is not going to be there forever. They should, therefore, be on the side of the people before it is too late.

Pambana! Pambana! Till Victory!
Our Unity is our Struggle!
A People United can never be defeated!

Assassination of Karĩmi Nduthu

September 7, 1996

Press Release

Mwakenya once again condemns the murder of the Secretary General of the Release of Political Prisoners (RPP) organization [and the National Coordinator of Mwakenya,] Karĩmi Nduthu, who was savagely murdered under suspicious circumstances on March 24, 1996. We hold the Moi regime responsible for the murder of yet one more innocent Kenyan, eliminated for his unswerving commitment to political change in Kenya. Only an independent, public, inquiry can establish the identity of his murderers.

Mwakenya also condemns the politically motivated charges against the 21 RPP members for daring to question the suspicious circumstances surrounding the murder of Karĩmi. We demand that the charges against the RPP activists be dropped immediately. We are asking all Kenyans to be vigilant. Do not allow the regime to use its one-sided "laws" and cruel prisons to deny us our rights to democracy and freedom. There can be no peace, no justice, and no democracy in Kenya until all political prisoners are released, until all basic rights are restored to the people, until we have an interim administration, which can allow free discussion about a new constitution, until we have a free and fair election. But Moi has to go. Moi can lead us only to national disintegration, chaos, disunity, poverty and death.

Mwakenya: The Unfinished Revolution

Moi has launched a war on all working people of Kenya. He has used his private army to massacre innocent citizens; he has created internal and external exiles; he has manipulated the Constitution to ensure his return to power in the next "elections;" he has created conditions for civil war in Kenya; he has stolen our land and national wealth. Moi must be charged with crimes against humanity. But let us remember that we won important victories during the Saba Saba uprising in July 1990 through our united action. Let us fight on in the same spirit until we have a government that answers all the needs of our people—economic and political. The spirit of Saba Saba is still with us.

Mwakenya calls upon the international community to support the people of Kenya in their struggle against the brutal dictator. But it is the efforts of Kenyans themselves that can bring true democracy. Mwakenya appeals to all Kenyans to unite and intensify the struggle to end the murderous Moi regime.

The Political History of A Patriot

An Extract from: *Karĩmi Nduthu: A Life in The Struggle.*

Karĩmi was born in July of 1961 to his parents—Nduthu wa Maathai and Wambũi wa Nduthu—at Karĩng'a in Molo division of Nakuru District. He was baptized in the Roman Catholic Church at Molo Parish and given the colonial Christian name, John.

In January of 1968, he joined Molo Primary School. During his primary education, he attended several schools necessitated by the frequent transfer of his father, who was a teacher. In 1975, Karĩmi sat for the Certificate of Primary Education ((CPE) at Gĩthima Primary School in Molo and later joined Molo Secondary School in 1976. He sat for the East African Certificate of Education (EACE) in 1979. He then joined Kapsabet Boys High School in Nandi District where in 1981 he sat for the Kenya Advanced Certificate of Education.

He took up temporary teaching jobs in Molo Township in 1982 and at Njabinĩ Girls Secondary School in 1983. In the short time that he taught in both schools he developed very close relationship with his students. The students loved him for his caring spirit and his fellow teachers respected him because of his dedication. His movement in the different parts of the country brought him face to face with the living conditions of the ordinary Kenyan and he was struck with one fact: that the living conditions of the working people in general and the rural peasants in particular were

Mwakenya: The Unfinished Revolution

basically the same no matter what part of the country they came from. At the same time he noted that the wealthy and the well-to-do, whatever their ethnic and regional origins, behaved the same towards the poor. He was determined to further his education so that he could acquire skills needed to help the people. He decided to take a degree course in engineering thinking that with the talk about technology being dominated by the West, he would be able to play a meaningful role in helping transform Kenya into a modern technological society.

So in September 1983 he was enrolled in the Mechanical Department of the Faculty of Engineering at the University of Nairobi. He immediately involved himself in student politics. For him engineering was part of society and he never took the safe position that the sciences had nothing to do with politics and culture. For him everything was related to everything else. He was particularly incensed by the fact students were not allowed to have a meaningful and well-functioning organization. The youth in Kenya were not allowed to form a nationwide body that could stand for their interests. Sometimes regional or ethnically based societies were allowed to function, but to Karĩmi this smacked of the politics of the colonial period when the colonial state would only allow the formation of ethnically based political organizations. He was elected a student leader. But many questions still clouded his mind: Why, for, instance, was it a crime for more than five people to meet without license? In the places he had been, at Molo, Njabinĩ, Nairobi, he had already seen family parties disrupted by the police because they had failed to secure a permit from the colonial chief or the nearest police station. It seemed to him that what was happening to the students reflected very much what was happening to the general society. Once again he took the position that students' politics were very much a part of the power struggles in society as a whole and the students had to play a part in it. He realized that no student was really free as long as the rest of the society was not free, and just as the rest of the society was not free as long as students were also enslaved. He wanted many students to see this vital connection between their struggles and those of the general society. He took his studies seriously and he was among the best in his class, however,

Mwakenya: The Unfinished Revolution

despite the University's acknowledgement of his exemplary academic performance and his outstanding character, he was among the students whose studies were interpreted in February 1985 when the government closed the university and expelled the student leaders. They did not want students who could think and ask questions—they did not want students with a political awareness.

It was during this period that he came across the underground literature of *Mwakenya*'s predecessor, The *December Twelve Movement* (DTM). He read the old issues of the organization's organs, *Pambana* and *Cheche*, and scales seemed to be removed from his eyes. It was as if *Pambana* and *Cheche* were articulating many of the thoughts, which had been forming in his mind. In one of its declarations published in Pambana, the DTM had stated that it firmly supported all genuine Kenyan organizations and individuals fighting any aspect of local injustice and imperialist aggression…He subsequently joined the *December Twelve Movement*. In so doing, he had exercised one of the most basic of human rights, the right to organize, but a right denied to so many Kenyans!

The *December Twelve Movement* was formed in the mid-1970s when Karĩmi was in primary school. The name *December Twelve* had been coined to suggest that Kenyans had to go back to the beginnings of the day the British conceded Independence to Kenya. The year 1963 the people of Kenya saw the climax of Kenya's struggles against the colonial state. Through Mau Mau the youth of the country had shed their blood to make that possible, while renegades like Moi were collaborating with the British on ways of crushing the nationalist struggle. But the years between 1963 and 1975, when the country was under the leadership of the first President, Jomo Kenyatta, Kenyans lost most of their democratic gains for which they had shed their blood and lives for. But the immediate post-independence period brought out the irony and contradictions of the post-colonial moment. All the forces associated with Mau Mau and Kenya's militant past were being edged out of power, culminating in the state organized assassination of the most important remaining symbol of past Mau Mau militancy—J.M. Kariũki, on March 2, 1975. The same period, on the

Mwakenya: The Unfinished Revolution

other hand, had seen a person like Moi move from a colonial collaborator, literally fighting tooth and nail to delay independence, to the position of Vice President and Minister for Home affairs. The police, who had arrested J.M. Kariũki in broad daylight at the Hilton International Hotel, were under the Ministry of Home Affairs.

Thus, by the mid-seventies, it was clear that with the crushing of Kenya People's Union (KPU), the jailing or silencing of progressive leadership within or outside the ruling party, Kenya had turned into not only *a de facto* one party state, but also a repressive dictatorship. The only way progressive elements among the youth could operate was through the underground. Hence, the birth of the *December Twelve Movement* with its organs: *Pambana,* and *Cheche*. The movement was so organized that even if the regime under Kenyatta or Moi were to strike at the center, sparks would fly out and reignite to make more fires for democracy. In that sense there was no way the movement could ever be crushed completely. This meant strict observance of security, secrecy and discipline among its members. But it also meant that if for some reason the center was hit, the various sub-centers, without the full knowledge of the operations of the whole, would take some time to regroup. This is precisely what happened in 1982.

Although the *December Twelve Movement* was not part of the coup attempt, despite the appropriations of its slogans of *Pambana* and *Cheche* by the jubilant supporters of the Air Force coup, the movement suffered from the indiscriminate attacks on anything democratic and progressive. A significant number of its key leadership was jailed with or without trial, certainly under any pretext. In 1982 one need not have been a member of an organization to get into trouble with the Moi dictatorship. Any person known, or suspected, of espousing a democratic position was an enemy of the dictatorship. The period after 1982 saw the takeover of the leadership of the movement by one of its sparks which now called itself *The Provincial Committee for December Twelve Movement*. This was the faction, which later transformed itself and the Movement into *Mwakenya* forming in the process alliances with other forces, which had not been schooled in the ideological traditions of the *December Twelve Movement*. Some of these

Mwakenya: The Unfinished Revolution

elements in turn took over the leadership of *Mwakenya* from 1985, soon after Karĩmi and other cadres had been recruited into the movement. This leadership made some crucial errors including the untimely calls for guerrilla warfare. The mistakes were to haunt the development of the movement until a principled struggle within the movement eventually led to the ouster of this leadership and the restoration of Mwakenya to the ideological path and methods of the parent body, the *December Twelve Movement.*

Karĩmi proved to be one of the most active cadres in the movement, always ready to give his body and mind to a cause he saw as helping in the creation of conditions for a new Kenya. It was while he was on a *Mwakenya* mission that he was arrested in July 1987. He was charged with sabotage activities against the dictatorship and he and his comrades-in-arms—Tirop Kitur and Kang'ethe Mũngai—were arraigned in court. Karĩmi never trembled, he never asked for mercy. Instead, he used the court to question the legitimacy of the Moi dictatorship. He argued that he was only obeying orders from the only political order he recognized as legitimate because it had its roots in the population and because it was actually fighting and struggling against a military dictatorship in civilian clothes. Sentence me if you may, he told the presiding judge in Moi's kangaroo court, but know that change, like death, is inevitable. In July 1986, Karĩmi was jailed for a period of fourteen years.

What the regime did not record was that in prison Karĩmi was to come into contact with the older members of DTM, like Maina wa Kĩnyattĩ, who were schooled in its ideological ways. At Naivasha, under the harshest of conditions, they turned the prison into an ideological institute, giving faith and vision and therefore hope to hundreds who had been jailed under the suspicion of being members of the underground. Many of them were not in fact members and quite often their political education begun at the "Kamĩtĩ-Naivasha Ideological Institute". *Mwakenya*'s literature was smuggled into prison. They kept in touch with the exiled elements of the *December Twelve Movement* who had regrouped in London under the Committee for the Release of Political Prisoners in Kenya. They thus let

Mwakenya: The Unfinished Revolution

others know that their cause was being waged in London and other capitals of the world. Karĩmi was one of those rare persons who led by example, and in Naivasha, he was held with great respect by the other prisoners. But for this he often suffered under the cruel arms of the prison warders. A poem written for him by Maina wa Kĩnyattĩ in May 1988 captures the spirit of revolutionary defiance.

Our Country or Death

(For Karĩmi Nduthu)

Alone in solitary confinement
Your hands are chained to the wall
The shackles around your waist
Behind the iron door is darkness
And the dogs are barking outside

Courage comrade
Even in solitary confinement
We must refuse to cede
We must not accept capitulation

Remember
The prison cell will not last forever
And coercion and torture cannot
Dampen the tide of revolution
We shall march from all directions
From the industrial centers
And beyond the great lakes
From the coffee and sisal plantations
Destroying everything which stands
Between us and liberty
We shall assemble at Kamũkũnji
To hoist the revolutionary flag

That is how Karĩmi felt, because in June when he was released, together with 15 other political prisoners, due to the pressure mounted on the government

Mwakenya: The Unfinished Revolution

by the Release of Political Prisoners (RPP) pressure group and mothers of political prisoners, he immediately joined the group to continue the struggle for the release of others and for the extension of the democratic space. He involved himself in the activities of RPP and was elected the secretary in 1993. Karĩmi was very active in fighting for the release of other political prisoners and fighting for democracy and good governance.

In all his work he was guided by the party's ideology, which he always saw as bigger than any individual office bearer. He remained faithful to his roots in the *Mwakenya*. He also read a great deal because he was always hungry to know what was happening in other parts of the world. Among the books he always kept at his side were Maina wa Kĩnyattĩ's book, *Thunder From the Mountains*, and Ngũgĩ wa Thiongo's novel, *Devil on the Cross*. But he also loved poetry particularly that of Abdilatif Abdalla. Karĩmi had found a kindred spirit. Abdilatif was a young KPU cadre when he was arrested in 1969 after writing and distributing underground literature, particularly the pamphlet, *Kenya Twendapi*, Kenya where are we heading to? In March 1969 Abdilatif was sentenced to three years in Kamĩtĩ Maximum Security Prison, but he never gave up his faith in the possibilities of a united democratic Kenya. In prison, Abdilatif had written poems of defiance and hope and which he later published under the title, *Sauti ya Dhiki*. A poem, *Siwati*, which Karĩmi always recited, is taken from this book.

The poem sums up Karĩmi's life and it was only appropriate that this was one of the poems read at his funeral in Molo. He never wavered in his commitment to the creation of a democratic and just society in which the wealth of our land and industry would go to enhance the lives of all the working people of Kenya. A first and necessary step for that was the creation of a path of a state controlled by the people. "We have chosen a goal and a path, and we have an obligation to work towards its success," he once wrote in a letter smuggled from his solitary cell to Maina wa Kĩnyattĩ who was also in solitary confinement. "We must fiercely combat vacillations and indecisiveness among us. It is our country or death".

He died for a democratic, just and fair society. He died for his country.

324

Murder of Bishop Muge

Press Release

The August 14 assassination of Bishop Alexander Muge is the further confirmation that:

1. The present KANU regime is rotten to the core, that it *cannot* be transformed from within, and that it must be rejected by the Kenyans in total.

Kenyans best remember Bishop Muge as a fearless critic of the Kenya government, of its human rights abuses, of its violence against the people it ought to serve, and of its pathological state of corruption. But after his wrangles with the regime following his exposure of the Pokot famine, Bishop Muge was persuaded into a change of strategy. Henceforth, he, like a good liberal, allowed himself to be drawn into its innermost circle, believing that in a new capacity, he would have a significant positive influence on the direction of Kenya's politics. But his short spell as an advisor and a confidant of the regime was enough to convince him otherwise—it was enough to convince him that the regime's political rot and moral decay are too deep, too pervasive to be salvaged from within, that it must be completely dumped lock, stock and barrel. True to his conscience, Muge took the courageous step of rejecting the patronage of the regime and taking the murderous bull by the horn. And that cost him his life.

Mwakenya: The Unfinished Revolution

2. The popular resistance in Kenya—from the more overt calls for democracy to the covert attempts by peasants not to supply their crops to Moi's processing industries—is increasingly forcing the regime against the wall. And like a trapped animal, it is bent on striking back with everything in its arsenal, from prisons to bullets.

While this violence is definitely a reaction to the unyielding resistance of the Kenyan people, it is calculated to intimidate the nation into silence and inaction. And as the resistance progresses we are bound to witness more incarcerations, more brutalities, more murders.

In view of these two factors, the only way we can immortalize the efforts of Bishop Muge, Kĩrĩma Nduthu and other pro-democracy advocates who have been brutally murdered by the Moi regime is:

To support the Mwakenya call of August 16, 1990 for:

a) A condemnation of the regime's persecution and assassination of pro-democracy advocates in Kenya.

b) A week of mourning from August 19 to 26.

c) A general strike in Kenya on August 24.

d) Continuation of efforts for the release of all political prisoners.

e) Continuation of the popular resistance for democracy and social justice. In his recent interview with the BBC, Reverend Peter Njenga declared that he was prepared to follow Bishop Muge's path to die rather than to yield to the tyrannical dictates of the KANU regime. As Kenyans, let us commit ourselves to the same: to follow the Muge-Njenga way whatever the cost.

f) To support Mwakenya's Democracy Plank of July 11, 1990, which calls for:

    i) Removal of Moi and KANU.

    ii) Dissolution of the present parliament.

    iii) Convening of a national conference.

Mwakenya: The Unfinished Revolution

iv) Creation of a caretaker government/administration.

v) Drawing up of a new constitution.

vi) Provision of checks and balances on the presidency.

vii) Holding of free multi-party election.

viii) Abolition of all acts of discrimination against any Kenyan nationalists.

In the meantime, we would like to remind the U.S. Government of our concern about its foreign policy toward the KANU regime in Kenya. The Kenyan people who have long been oppressed, violated and brutalized by the KANU regime will not accept the U.S.A's military interests in the Indian Ocean and in Kenya as a justification for its continued support of the murderous ruling regime in our country. Kenyans will not allow their human rights to be compromised by American's landing rights on their soil, as a result of the escalating crisis in the Persian Gulf.

Ukenya Center (USA)
August 15, 1990
Further Information:
Contact Maina wa Kĩnyattĩ: (Tel.) 718-291-6365
New York City

Ukenya (USA) Appeals to the International Community
September 25, 1990

Since Kenya attained its independence from Britain, over 27 years ago, Kenyans have witnessed their ideals, principles and expectations, for which they have shed their blood for during the anti-colonial struggles, being systematically shattered by the present Kenya regime. The rule of law has virtually collapsed. The judiciary has lost all semblance of independence, democratic institutions are in political decay, elections have been rigged en masse as a matter of routine, the press has been gagged, and periodicals, which have dared expose the truth have been banned. Freedom of assembly and association cannot be exercised, except for praising the dictator and his regime, and civil servants have become mere hand maidens for carrying out the wishes of the sole political party, KANU. There is widespread corruption and abuse of power. People have been imprisoned without charge or trial, and those who have been tried have often been denied legal representation; and political prisoners have been ruthlessly tortured and held under inhumane and degrading conditions. Fundamental freedoms of Kenyans have all been buried under a thick rubric of autocracy. Those who have tried to speak against these pervasive violations have been lampooned, booed into silence, imprisoned, tortured or murdered. In short, those in authority simply refused to concede that other Kenyans, outside of themselves, have any rights, whatsoever, except for those which Kenyans

Mwakenya: The Unfinished Revolution

are led to believe they have, such as the right to due process, if falsely arrested, which is a fundamental principal of fairness in all legal matters.

But now a fresh wind of change is blowing in Kenya. After years of decline, fear and silence, Kenyans have come out in unison to assume their responsibility of resisting repression and struggling for democracy and social justice. Protestors have been arrested, imprisoned and killed in their relentless pro-democracy campaign. At no time in Kenya's post-colonial history has there been greater unity of effort cutting across all boundaries of civil society, and greater consensus of opinion and political sentiments irrespective of ideological differences, about the direction of the country, than in the year 1990. Kenyans are now willing to sacrifice their livelihood, their security and even their lives in the cause of political and economic transformation in their beloved homeland.

Under the circumstances, how should the international community respond to this state of affairs in Kenya? There is no doubt that the struggling people of Kenya expect the international community to join them in their fight for democracy and social justice. They have vested their hopes in themselves as well as in the international community. They would like to see the international community align itself with the people seeking freedom and not with a brutal regime that has become notorious for its tyranny. To maintain political support for a government that is undemocratic and repressive in the extreme, to maintain economic support for a government that holds public accountability in contempt, that has made thievery an integral party of political bureaucracy, that consciously pursues wasteful economic policies, and to maintain military aid to a regime that turns its guns against its own innocent citizens, would be to undermine the moral, ethical, and political integrity of the international community in its efforts to build a better world—a just world. Such support of regimes like the present one in Kenya would erode the very foundations of the worldwide movement for democracy and liberty.

Ukenya (USA), therefore, appeals to the international community, to all nations and international agencies which have dealings with Kenya, to *stop* all political, economic and military support to the country, until the

Moi-KANU regime accedes to the wishes of the Kenyan people contained in the July1991 *Mwakenya Democracy Plank* (see p.151).

The Struggle Continues!
For further information contact Maina wa Kĩnyattĩ,
Tel. (718) 291-6365

Study is the Key in the Revolutionary Process

Levels and Handling of Contradictions
(Reprinted from Mpatanishi, December 1989)

Our study and practice teach us that life is never free from contradictions. This is a fundamental lesson whose implications must be examined at every stage of our struggle.

Our main contradiction is with imperialism and the comprador regime led by Moi and KANU. Imperialism uses the structures of neocolonialism to control our labor and resources. The regime runs the neocolonial state on behalf of imperialism. We are thus aware of who our main enemy is. We can therefore use correct methods of struggle against this enemy.

It would be incorrect to assume that the comprador regime and its imperialist backers are our only enemies. The enemy in also within us, representing their class interests among our ranks. Failure to struggle against this enemy will inevitably lead to failure overall. The experience of struggle at the very inception of our underground work, and subsequent to that, has shown the need for greater vigilance against the internal enemy.

This then is the second level of contradiction we face. It manifests itself as a contradiction among us. It is not, in essence, an antagonistic one and so requires an entirely different method of resolving it from that against imperialism. And yet, if not handled correctly, this contradiction

Mwakenya: The Unfinished Revolution

can become an antagonistic one and will objectively support our enemy. It is important to understand what this enemy among us is, how it manifests itself, and how to struggle against it actively and stubbornly.

Two such "internal" enemies can be mentioned. One is petty-bourgeois tendencies reflecting the outlook of that class. These manifest themselves in various ways including liberalism, individualism, subjectivism, lack of practice, undermining democratic centralism, lack of study, etc., a particularly dangerous manifestation is the use of correct forms of language, methods, ideas in order to defeat what we are trying to achieve. We need to be ever vigilant against this type of attack against us as they tend to lull us into complacency. Similarly, the correct form of criticism and self-criticism are used to attack petty, personal insignificant shortcomings under the guise of attacking fundamental issues. The result often is to divert our attention from struggling against incorrect ideas, practices, and issues of principle into never-ending petty, personal vendettas. Such actions undermine our very strength and render us easy to enemy attacks. It is important here to realize that these weaknesses objectively serve the interests of the enemy and weaken us.

One way of overcoming this tendency is to be ever vigilant and critical of these liberal tendencies in us and in those around us. It is then necessary to wage an active struggle against this reactionary tendency. Only then can we overcome these shortcomings and improve our practice and deepen our ideology.

The second danger to our movement is that of "ultra left" opportunism. This means moving faster than our current conditions demand. This happens when objective conditions have not been correctly analyzed, when subjective thinking outstrips objective reality. Such tendencies have surfaced once again among groups opposed to the regime. But their activities, if unchecked, are bound to result in some of them actually aligning themselves, consciously or unconsciously, with the dictatorship. We need to be on our guard against such tendencies gaining a foothold among us, within the organization. A possible method of countering such "left" deviations is to undertake more concrete investigations to understand the reality of our situation. At the same time a better understanding of theories and their application in practice would help in achieving a more balanced world outlook.

It is necessary at this time in our struggle that we understand correctly the various levels of contradictions facing us—those within our own ranks, those with others also opposed to the regime, and those with the comprador regime and imperialism. With a clearer understanding of these different levels and qualities of contradictions, we should be able to resolve qualitatively different contradictions with qualitatively different methods of resolving them. Having taken appropriate steps to handle the contradictions correctly, we shall march ahead confident in victory.

Liberal Tendency and Its Manifestations
(Reprinted from Mpatanishi, December 1989)

The method we have chosen to struggle against neocolonialism is to wage a war against every aspect of oppression and exploitation. This war is waged along different lines at different times depending on the concrete situation. The present stage can be described as preparation for the stage of armed struggle.

These preparations are carried on at various levels: political, organizational and ideological. These aspects can be identified not only inside the country itself, but outside as well. Recent developments here have seen the production of various documents setting out our ideological stand—the production has involved discussions to clarify our understanding of the MLM ideology. At the same time there have been developments, which have seen the emergence of new political and organizational forms to satisfy the needs of the particular situation facing us today.

While there is no doubt that substantial advances have been made, it is equally true that various weaknesses have come to the surface even as we were moving ahead. The most serious one is liberalism. The study of "Combat Liberalism" by Mao explains the theoretical and practical aspects of liberalism. The following points may help in a clearer understanding of the danger of liberalism and ways to deal with it.

Theoretical Aspects

We represent the class stand of workers, peasants and all working and democratic forces. Our ideology, Marxism-Leninism-Maoism, and our political programme reflect the needs of these classes. On the other hand, the enemy represents the class interests of imperialist bourgeoisie and native compradors. They too have their ideology and programme. In between stand the petty-bourgeoisie. This is a wide grouping ranging from upper, middle and lower strata, whose class interests are aligned with the proletariat at one level and with the enemy at the other level. Their vacillation reflects their own class contradictions.

Our great weapons against the enemy are a clear ideological stand, strong political organization, discipline and unity among our ranks. It is these very weapons, which are attacked by the enemy. Liberalism, a petty-bourgeois tendency, also attacks our MLM stand. Liberalism manifests itself in various ways:

- Lack of discipline; work not done, or not done on time, or not done properly; lack of punctuality and proper timing.

- Security not taken seriously; dismissing concern for security as "being afraid;" decisions on security not being implemented.

- Work assignment and commitment not taken seriously; allowances made for slackness in oneself and in others; information on important issues not distributed and kept as personal property.

- Becoming complacent about achievements in a one-sided way, not looking at shortcomings and at problems ahead.

- Putting an individual(s) before the organization in an attempt to make personal gain; taking organizational matters outside.

- Criticism not taken seriously, or taken as personal attacks, not as a means of resolving non-antagonistic contradictions and furthering unity in the organization; making criticism as personal attacks.

In essence, liberalism reflects the class interests of our enemy. It reveals a lack of practice with only verbal commitments made, but not put into practice. As a result, large projects are called for and small vital tasks are ignored, thereby preventing the overall work and organization from taking root. Liberalism shows a lack of understanding of the theoretical foundation of our struggle. If it persists over a long period of time, there is a danger of the whole organization been rendered ineffective. It is definitely not in the interest of the working people, but shows that the bourgeois influences are strong in our midst.

Combating Liberalism

Basically, it will be necessary to correct the liberalism tendencies in all its manifestations. It is important to understand what it represents and to struggle against it every time it arises, in every form, at every level in the organization. Particular attention should be paid to: **1)** criticism and self-criticism would be a regular feature of any level of organization. The only way to judge if criticism and self-criticism have been effective is through practice; **2)** improving one's practices, for liberalism results in preventing cadres from putting their theories into practice; **3)** undertaking the study of theory seriously and waging an active ideological struggle against incorrect ideas; **4)** finding ways (especially when one is away from the country) of being in touch with the masses of working people, being aware of their struggles and of being guided in our actions by their needs; and finally **5)** guarding against opportunism and against bureaucratic ways of working and thinking.

One of our main weapons in the struggle for the national democratic revolution is our organization. It is this very organization, which is threatened by liberalism. Liberalism is not something "outside there"; it is right within ourselves and is a reflection of the existence of classes opposed to us and our class struggle. In order to combat it, we need to struggle against that class. But first we need to struggle against it in our very midst, in our organization. Failure to do so could result in our demise;

Mwakenya: The Unfinished Revolution

and reflect our own class position whose material needs may be in conflict with our declared class interests. It is the duty of each one of us to correct tendencies to liberalism in ourselves and in each other, because if we don't our enemies will not come from afar, they will be the closest ones to us, with a greater hand in our impending demise as an organization. Only when we are vigilante enough to weed out those who are against us, can we really be said to be active and strong in the struggle for social justice in our country.

Study in a Circle
(Reprinted from Mpatanishi, September 1992)

To study is to endeavor to the acquire knowledge on a subject or an issue, a problem, an event by closely examining, investigating or scrutinizing it carefully, critically and in detail discovering and picking out the essential aspects for the purpose of applying the acquired knowledge in solving a practical or a theoretical problem. It is a method of solving the contradiction between theory and practice. This is a general definition. Farmers will study the mechanisms of farming in order to apply the knowledge acquired in improving their farming for better yields. Business people will strive to understand all the attributes of the business in order to succeed in business.

In our specific case, the principal aim of study is to have every member become both a student and a teacher who is both informed and articulate, who possesses all the prerequisite knowledge and ability to understand concretely the situation throughout the phases and changes of the entire struggle. We should never permit any of our members to become a blundering ignorance. From an understanding of the situation, we then should be able to improve our practice. There are three main methods through which study can be carried out:

1) **Research**: This can be research of theory or of practice. It can be conducted in two ways. First by becoming actively involved in

Mwakenya: The Unfinished Revolution

practice of production and protection of material wealth; the other way is through literature, written or oral, i.e., seeking knowledge through reading books, journals, periodicals, pamphlets, magazines, etc. This can also be done by undertaking investigations of other people's theories and practices.

2) **Analysis (thought process):** This involves picking an issue, a problem, a subject, then examining it critically within oneself, breaking it down so as to come out with its essential elements.

3) **Discussion:** This involves discussing with others an issue, a problem, a subject on essential and fundamental aspects.

From these stages it is then easier to apply the knowledge gained through research, analysis and discussion. It is only by applying this knowledge to practice that a problem can be solved—and this is the main reason for studying.

What is the Best Process of Study?

Let us first assume that one has a problem at hand. How does one go about undertaking study as it pertains to the given problem? The best way to go about is: **1)** reflect on your own—this is pondering over the problem, asking yourself what you know about it, i.e., history, development, present status, etc. Then identify areas that require further investigation; **2)** undertake research/investigation through: **a)** interview, questioning, observation, experiment, etc.; **b)** library research, literature, books, journals, and periodicals; **c)** compile the collected data in a systematic way; **d)** analyze/evaluate—on quantitative and qualitative aspects. Then draw inferences; **e)** discuss with others the fundamental and essential aspects needed to arrive at the inferences and draw conclusions. You now have an enriched theory relevant to the problem; **f)** apply the knowledge in solving the problem.

The most important task facing us today is to undertake political work among the masses (education, agitation, mobilization, etc.). In order to undertake these tasks effectively, members must elevate their political education, thus: **1)** raise their level of critical awareness; **2)** understand:

Mwakenya: The Unfinished Revolution

a) ideology—the system of ideas that guide us in the struggle; b) guiding policies—what are the policies of our movement that guide us in our activities? c) political theory—classes. Class societies, and class struggles; d) dialectical and historical materialism and the understanding of our social reality and the means of changing that reality; and e) prevailing political situation—what is the current political climate and how can we utilize it to advance our struggle.

What will Be Actually Studied?

The following guidelines are suggested as a way of conducting study:

Method A: Read the book, pamphlet, paper, etc. page by page together. Raise and discuss general questions, clarifying the difficult concepts. Then raise fundamental questions and discuss them, making references wherever appropriate. Summarize the outcome of the discussion in a brief report. This method is best for a person-to-person situation or in small groups where there is adequate time. It is a useful method during recruitment in the local community near you, but cumbersome in a study circle.

Method B: 1) Members should have the issue, the problem, the book, etc. in advance of meeting; **2)** They should have studied the problems, etc. thoroughly in their own time, noting general and fundamental questions, and also making initial attempts to answer them before the meeting; **3)** During the meeting, a person who should have been asked in advance should lead the discussion. All should raise and discuss the general questions and difficult concepts. Basic questions should also be answered: what are the basic issues and contradictions that have arisen? What is the background to the situation? Which factors are favorable and positive and which are negative? **4)** Raise and discuss fundamental questions, e.g., the ones that require further research. Further discussions can be held to understand the interrelationships and interconnections between different aspects of a problem. Understand objective reality and the subjective factors around a problem. Try to work out what practice is required to solve the particular problem. How appropriate is this solution, and for whom? Does it clarify

Mwakenya: The Unfinished Revolution

the interconnection between theory and practice in the field? How does it conform to or contradict policy? Are the people involved ready to adopt the recommended practice? If not, what steps can be taken? Write a brief and concise summary of the issues raised views expressed.

This is one of the best and most appropriate methods in a study circles with limited time and under difficult conditions. Circles/cells need to adjust their actual practice in keeping with their actual conditions. Study sessions on the whole should follow the same serious style used in other meetings. It should be pointed out here that complacency (i.e., being silently satisfied, and not participating, with the little we know, think we already know, or don't want to know) is a serious handicap to study, as it is to our practice. We cannot really learn well until we rid ourselves of it. We need to understand that learning is a continuous process. The attitude towards ourselves should be to be insatiable in learning, and towards others, to be tireless in teaching. When undertaking study, whether alone or in a group in a study circle/cell, we need to be guided by the saying "Nothing in the world is difficult for those who set their minds to it and keep on learning." Finally, always remember that studying a problem or an issue is never for its own sake; it is always done so as to improve our practice.

Conducting a Political Meeting
(Reprinted from Mpatanishi, September 1992)

A meeting is the coming together of a number of people at a particular time and venue for the purpose of discussion, deliberation, study, or for taking a decision. It is assumed that those meeting belong to the same organization and share a common, ideological, purpose. Here we shall look only at an underground meeting.

In order to conduct a meeting, certain guidelines are necessary:

- There must be a clearly defined purpose of the meeting.

- A day is chosen and an appropriate time set—both beginning and end.

- A venue is carefully chosen. This depends on the type of meeting, number of people involved, and security considerations (e.g., it is an underground meeting).

- For the purpose of discussion, there must be an agenda. Sometimes it is important for the people concerned to have copies of the agenda prior to the meeting, so that all can reflect on the issues. Generally, an agenda should contain the following: **a)** security; **b)** minutes of the previous meeting; **c)** reports (should be brief and concise); **d)** matters for discussion and decision; **e)** assignment of duties; **f)** any other business.

- Arrival: Time keeping is very important. If many people are involved, arrival and departure times should be set differently, and respected.

Mwakenya: The Unfinished Revolution

- There must be somebody to direct the meeting. This is the chairperson who represents the organization. There should also be a secretary to record minutes in codes if necessary. They should make particular record of tasks given, to whom and how they are to be undertaken. If conditions permit these tasks should be looked at again before the meeting closes.

- It is important to act upon the decisions reached at the meeting as soon as is practical.

- During the meeting: **a)** if presenting a report or leading a debate, one should focus on the fundamental points, avoid trivialities and verbosity. One must have reflected on the issues. However, there should be "created an atmosphere of free debate by hearing one to the end." Points of contribution should be focused, brief and concise— make concrete points; **b)** direct exchanges and rebuttals or person-to-person exchanges, clarifications and additions should be channeled through the chair; **c)** all should avoid haphazard interruptions that lack substance and clarity during a presentation. This distracts the speaker and results in time wasting. Note points to be raised then respond at the correct time. Listen patiently—it will be useful even with the masses; **d)** the chair must be respected. In turn, the chair must be non-partisan, maintain order, bring matters to attention, and bring debate to focus and seriousness. His ruling on matters should be final, but he should be criticized if he goes against democratic principles; **e)** for purposes of decision making on minor issues, the chair should listen to all views and decide along the popular and the most logical line in keeping with the overall objectives and principles of the organization. On major issues, debate should be carried out exhaustively and "Let a thousand schools of thought contend". Voting should be a final resort. The principles of democratic centralism must be followed. _Minority views must be given due consideration and listened to—they could be the correct ones_; and **f)** principled flexibility of mind should be followed in debates in order to understand and accommodate divergent views. Try to see others' point of view.

Mwakenya: The Unfinished Revolution

We stress that during meetings, discipline is very important and should be maintained throughout. For example, proper language use must be strictly followed—no ridiculing, no insults, no sarcasms, or any kind of rudeness should arise. Sexism, national Chauvinism and any form of social oppression must be avoided. There is no justification whatsoever for any of these in our type of organization.

Meetings should be short, concise, and to the point. If they have to be long and tedious, we stand to lose people, mentally; there should be short rest periods (breaks) to enhance efficiency. They should be conducted in a business-like manner. Depending on the venue, voices should be kept in normal conversational tones—shouting or screaming is not allowed, and serves no purpose, outside of aggravating those who are trying to, intellectually, decipher a shouting match that is out of control, but, equally, allow them to question the validity of the organization on a level of seriousness.

Initially, before experience in meetings has been acquired, people are faced with some difficulties. This is not surprising. But after a series of meetings, they develop a critical consciousness, a questioning attitude, skeptical and analytical minds, which enable them to avoid trivialities, minimize digression and focus on only the essential aspects.

Criticism and Self-Criticism

It has become evident in practice that cadres do not understand criticism and self-criticism. To some cadres, self-criticism is a method of "confession" one's mistakes and personal weaknesses to fellow comrades during sessions for that purpose.

Criticism is an admission that nothing is absolutely perfect and that there is always room for improvement. Due to changing circumstances we must learn to make corresponding changes in our methods, approach and attitudes to work. Failures to do so will lead to stagnation in our day-to-day work. We can only move forward and perfect our work by continuously evaluating our performance through criticism. We shall be able to identify

Mwakenya: The Unfinished Revolution

our strong and weak points, be able to devise methods of making changes and improvements in our methods of work and learn from each other to adopt ourselves to the changing circumstances; and without criticism one is surely to fail, because no one is pointing out your faults, if you have not acknowledge them, or that of the organization.

Self-criticism is recognition of the fact that our performance and work methods need continuous evaluation and improvement to avoid stagnation and degeneration. We should not be complacent or silent with our performance, and when our comrades criticize us, we should not see it as a personal attack. A continuous self-appraisal will help us understand whether we are making progress in whatever we do in life. Criticism and self-criticism is a weapon to combat liberalism and other human frailties.

When conducting criticism in the organization the following guidelines are useful:

- Criticism is geared towards helping comrades advance in tackling talks and problems.

- Criticism is a comradely act that should be conducted in a friendly and careful manner with respect, honor, and dignity.

- We must accept that people make mistakes, but we should always learn from past mistakes to avoid making the same mistakes in future.

- When conducting criticism we must adopt a format of well substantiated and tactful suggestions based on real and tested facts, and not on hearsay alone.

- We should look at the entire problem; analyze it from all angles to understand why it's viewed as a problem, and the contradictions involved in the problem.

- A one-sided approach where we only look at the negative side, ignoring the positive or tolerating praise, we defeat the purpose of criticism; whether the criticism is minute or significant, to ignore it for it to fester is dangerous to our existence.

Mwakenya: The Unfinished Revolution

- We should avoid and oppose the method of attacking and condemning or "finishing off" people with a single blow; to lose one member is one too many, for whom he/she speaks to after such a blow, will have a profound affect on future membership.

- Criticism directed to comrades should not be conducted in a rough manner and the comrade should not be treated as if he is an enemy; and if the criticism is serious and warrants only a few to address it, it should be done in privacy, out of respect, in order to grasp a full understanding of the matter at hand.

- We must never criticize a comrade with ridicule, personal attacks, sarcasm, insults and innuendos.

- Criticism should be conducted continuously as a duty. Criticize work done, analyze every situation and use past experiences to justify why the member is being criticized.

Strengthen the Underground!
Organization is the Key!

Some Basic Principles of Underground
(Reprinted from Mpatanishi, May 1993)

An underground movement is an organization whose members are not known to non-members and whose operations are conducted secretly to avoid detection by the enemy. It seeks to achieve its goals, aims and methods through a clandestine method. In our case, Mwakenya is an underground movement whose members and operations are not known to non-members. It operates as an underground organization to avoid detection and destruction by the enemy.

Practice has shown us that unless we operate clandestinely, we shall not be able to attain our goals and objectives. The regime will not tolerate our activities and will never allow us to propagate our programme openly. MK has been forced, therefore, to operate as an underground organization, due to the repressive environment that has been in existence in the country since attainment of flag independence. The neocolonial regime has never and will never allow pro-people opposition movements to operate freely in the country. It crushed the revived Kenya Land and Freedom Army, *Kĩama Kĩa Mũingĩ*, Kenya Land and Freedom Party and Kenya People's Union in the 1960s, declared a one-party state and silenced opposition even within KANU itself. Vocal KANU members have in the past been arrested, imprisoned, tortured or murdered for daring to question KANU's anti-people policies.

Mwakenya: The Unfinished Revolution

Even after introduction of a multiparty system and formation of new political parties, KANU has not changed or accepted that there is opposition in Kenya. It is still using state machinery to harass and intimidate the opposition, the press and the citizens. It is in light of this that MK has opted to continue operating underground.

For us to survive as an underground organization and in any order to achieve our immediate and long term goals and objectives, we must strictly adhere to the principles of underground organizations. Even with the most committed members, or the best programme we cannot succeed unless all members study and understand these underground principles and be guided by them in their day-to-day organizational work.

Below are some of the basic principles that guide underground organizations.

A. Discipline

Discipline is one's ability to conduct himself in accordance with the rules and norms of any given situation, e.g., in a social situation, in a political situation, etc.

Socially, we must be able to abide by the accepted norms and practices of our societies. That is the only way we can be able to operate within the people and gain their confidence and respect. If we fall below the socially accepted standards, people will abandon us. We shall not be seen as bearers of our people's culture of resistance, dignity and self-respect. We cannot be able to propagate the ideals and objectives of our movement or be able to set up organizational structures among the people if we fall below the standard set by our society.

In organizational matters discipline is our ability to operate within the organization and to understand and implement its programme, rules and policies.

Mwakenya: The Unfinished Revolution

A disciplined member:

Is guided by the programme of the movement.

a. Recruits in accordance with recruitment policy.

b. Keeps secrets of the movement.

c. Makes regular contribution to the movement.

d. Attends all meetings on time and takes his own notes.

e. Takes care of the movement's properties and documents.

B. Secrecy

The survival of an underground organization depends on its member's ability to maintain secrecy. The secrets of the movement include:

1) Who the members of the movement are?

2) The strategies of the movement.

3) Operations of the movement.

4) Organizational structure of the movement.

This information is not to be shared with a non-member or the enemy. A non-member who gets this information has no obligation to protect it and it will eventually reach the agents of the enemy. This will lead to the arrest of members, and this endangers the entire movement. A member, therefore, has a duty to not divulge any information, and to safeguard the secrets of the movement. The member must not do any act, which would lead to leakage of any secret of the movement.

A member must:

- Never talk about his/her association with the movement in front of non-members or strangers.

- Never pass a member's document to non-members.

- Never disclose the strategies and operations of the movement to non-members.

Mwakenya: The Unfinished Revolution

- Never disclose members of the movement to non-members.
- Never disclose the structure of the movement to non-members.
- Never disclose his/her organizational activities to non-members, etc.

If a member can maintain these secrets, there is no way the enemy agents will know about us and our activities. A member who cannot maintain these secrets must be, immediately, expelled from the organization. He/she is helping the enemy or is an agent-provocateur. In a word, he/she is a poisonous snake in our pot.

C. Democratic Centralism

Democratic centralism is a general organizational principle applicable to both open and underground organizations. Centralism means that there is a single central leadership; there are lower organs, which are subordinate to higher organs. In every organ the minorities are subordinate to the majority and the individual interests are subordinate to those of the movement. With centralism, a strong centralized organization emerges capable of planning and coordinating all activities of the movement. Without centralism there will be anarchy, each organ will be left to act on its own. There will be no central planning, and nobody will implement the programme, policies and strategies of the movement.

Cell Study Sheet
A Study of Political Economy
January 1979

I **Political Economy** is a study of the interrelationship between politics and economics and the power relations they express and produce. In order to understand the roots of neocolonialism and the class contradictions in our country, we must study (and study well) the political economy of our society. A scientific study of the political economy will tell us that changes in society are chiefly due to the development of the internal contradictions in society, that is the contradictions between social classes, between the productive forces and the relation between the old and the new.

II **Mode of Production** can be defined as the way in which people produce and exchange their means of life. Every society is based on a mode of production, which is what ultimately determines the character of all social activities and institutions. Simply, it is a stage in socio-economic development in society.

There are five modes of production known to humans, and they are:

a)   *Communalism*
b)   *Slavery-owning society*
c)   *Feudalism*
d)   *Capitalism*
e)   *Socialism.*

Mwakenya: The Unfinished Revolution

III Forces of Production consist of instruments of production, and people, with their production experiences and skills, who use these instruments. A labor force, with its experience and skill is part of the forces of production. In other words, the decisive productive force in a society is human itself—its live labor power. Simply, production requires that there be:

1. Human labor
2. Objects of labor
3. Instruments (tools) of labor

IV Relations of Production express relationship of humans to each other in the process of production:

1. Enter into mutual relations of one kind or another within production.

2. Cooperation and mutual help (socialism).

3. Domination and subordination (capitalism)

4. Transitional from one to another (from feudalism to capitalism, from capitalism to socialism, from socialism to communism).

V. Means of Production: All those means which are necessary to produce the finished product—including not only the instruments (which are part of the forces of production), but also land, raw materials, buildings in which production is undertaken, and so on. In other words, the objects of labor and instruments of labor together form the means of production.

VI. Production is the central aspect of human history

1. Human enters into relations of production that correspond to the stage of development of its material force of production.

2. The sum of the relations of production constitutes the economic structure of society.

3. On this economic foundation arises a legal and political superstructure. The mode of production thus conditions social, political and institutions.

4. Whatever is the mode of production of a society, such in the main is the society itself, its ideas and theories—its political views and social institutions.

5. Whatever is human's manner of life, such is his manner of thought.

VII. Evolution of Production

1. At a certain stage of development material productive forces come into conflict with the existing relations of production—the property relations.

2. An epoch of social revolution then begins: a) The change of the economic foundation transforms the entire superstructure; and b) The material transformation of society must always be distinguished from the ideological forms in which humans become conscious of this conflict and fights it out.

3. The clues to the study of the laws of history are not to be sought in men's minds, not in the views and ideas of society, but in the mode of production practiced by society in any given historical period. It must be sought in the economic life of society.

VIII. Surplus Value

1. The production resulting from labor is a very decisive force in the development of society.

2. The development of human society began when the labor of a family produced more than needed for subsistence and transformed this surplus into means of production: i) To the present, this surplus has been the possession of a privileged, capitalist class; ii) The coming social revolution will make this surplus the common possession of all society.

3. The surplus devoted to the means of production (capital) accumulates in the hands of the capitalists as profits: i) Profits are thus the surplus of product of human labor over and above the wages paid to the working class.ii) It is the quantity of labor, rather than wage, which determines value.

Mwakenya: The Unfinished Revolution

A case in point (simple mathematics):

A production worker works in a tire factory (Firestone Tire Factory of Kenya) on the night shift for eight hours. During this period of time he produces 5 tires, which are sold for Ksh. 3,000.00 each. He is paid Ksh.150.00 for his 8 hours of labor, per day. Expense for producing one tire is:

Worker's wage	=	Ksh.	150.00 a day
Rent	=	Ksh.	300.00 a day
Raw material	=	Ksh.	600.00
Misc. cost	=	Ksh.	160.00
Total Expense	=	Ksh.	1,210.00 per tire
Expense for 5 tires:	=	Ksh.	6,050.00
5 tires produced/sold	=	Ksh.	3,000.00 each
3,000.00 x 5	=	Ksh.	15,000.00
Expenses for 5 tires	=	Ksh.	6,050.00
Surplus value (profit)	=	Ksh.	8,950.00

The capitalists divide the profits (surplus value) among stockholders and executive salaries; the rest opens new investments, while the producer (worker) of all this wealth sleeps beside dogs and cats in a makeshift house, and his children eat from the garbage cans.

With the help of the Kenyan comprador ruler, the imperialist bourgeoisie takes finance capital produced by the Kenyan workers from one country to another and uses it to establish commercial enterprise for surplus of making more money—producing more surplus value.

IX. Kenyan Workers

There are different kinds of the Kenyan working people. These include: service workers, office workers, production workers in factories and industries, professional workers, agricultural workers, dockworkers, fishermen, etc. All of them sell their labor to the imperialist bourgeoisie and its Kenyan friends. The Kenyan working class is the most exploited

Mwakenya: The Unfinished Revolution

class of workers in the country. In fact, there is no difference between employed and unemployed workers in our country. The majority of them lives below the poverty line, and are victims of imperialist exploitation.

COTU as a control mechanism:

1. It acts as control mechanism against the working class people (the proletariat) who should be rebelling against imperialist exploitation and oppression in our country.

2. It leads workers to fight for economic issues, instead of leading them for the overthrow of the neocolonial state and the creation of a democratic society.

3. It is the most reactionary trade union organization in our country. It does not represent the working class interests. It is in the enemy camp. The comprador rulers and their imperialist allies use it against the working class interests. It must be smashed and replaced by a proletarian trade union with workers' control.

356

Part Four

Ukenya Documents

We want the world to know the truth about justice in Kenya and about the inhumane conditions and suffering we are subjected to daily. Most of us are under 24 years of age. The torture and brutality we have received should not be happening in a country that portrays itself as the most democratic in all of Africa.

Imprisoned University Students,
Kamĩtĩ Maximum Security Prison, 1982

Manifesto of Ukenya, 1987

Preamble

It has been over twenty years since Kenyans have watched their hard-won independence being mortgaged to foreign interests by the KANU regime of Kenyatta and Moi, under the cynical *philosophies* of "Harambee" and "nyayoism". Even our main seaports and airports have been turned into U.S. military facilities (for both conventional and nuclear weapons) to serve Western strategic interests, thereby seriously compromising our sovereignty, and threatening the security of the entire eastern region of Africa.

At the economic level, Kenya has been turned into a looters' paradise for transnationals and "aid" agencies thus continuously bleeding our wealth and national resources. Every year these foreign companies register an ever-rising rate of profits, while at the same time workers see a decrease in their wages. But the "commission fee" dished out to the ruling comprador clique centered on the presidency has created a small filthy-rich and greedy caste who have turned robbery and theft into a national creed. Corruption on a massive scale has seen national coffers looted, cooperatives robbed, parastatals paralyzed for private gain and funds in national institutions like social security and insurance siphoned off. This has resulted in the impoverishment of our society, turning many workers and peasants into paupers and beggars. The most productive land is in the hands of a few

Mwakenya: The Unfinished Revolution

Kenyan landlords and foreign companies, and has been turned over for production of cash crops for export at the expense of production of food for national consumption. Like in the colonial times, peasants are still confined to narrow strips of land or reduced to squatting, while still providing cheap labor under the most horrid, inhuman, conditions on plantations that are nothing short of slavery and exploitation. The amount an individual makes on these plantations is mere pennies in the capitalist world.

At the political level, the KANU regime has demobilized large sections of the people by monopolizing all political activities and crushing all patriotic and democratic initiatives. Political associations and organizations have been banned; the legal opposition party, KPU was banned as early as 1969 and its leaders were detained. Kenya has since been a one-party state; workers and peasants have no rights freely to organize and manage their own affairs; professional organizations, student unions, certain religious and welfare associations have been abolished. Indeed this unrepresentative KANU has now been decreed to be the supreme body even above parliament and judiciary. At the social level, a large section of Kenyans live under the most deplorable conditions deprived of adequate food, clothing and shelter. The gap between the rich and the poor in our country is one of the widest in the world. Thus, behind the façade of skyscrapers, deluxe hotels and mansions lies the bitter reality of some Kenyans sleeping in the streets in makeshift housing, (using boxes and raggedy tarps or whatever they can find), through extreme weather conditions; while others, who are not so lucky to have makeshift housing, die from malnutrition and hunger. But that is not all. Adequate medical care is the monopoly of the rich. The same applies to other social amenities, e.g., transportation and communications.

The educational system denies large sections access to schools, colleges and universities. It is geared towards producing men and women with an initiative aping mentality and a dependency complex. Foreign languages are promoted at the expense of national languages, including the all-Kenyan national language, Kiswahili. The entire educational system aims at making us look up to the western bourgeoisie for everything, while making us despise what is Kenyan, national and rooted in the people. Education is divorced from real production. All creative cultural activities

360

Mwakenya: The Unfinished Revolution

have been stifled by the KANU regime. Patriotic theatre and intellectual debates have been silenced with police batons and teargas. The aim has been to turn us Kenyans into mindless followers of presidential footsteps, whereby leading us to tyranny and neo-slavery. The "made-in-Hollywood" and "coca-cola" culture masquerades as the new "national" culture blindly aped by the *nouveau riche.*

The regime has been trying to crush the whole heritage of struggle whose highest peak was the Kenya Land and Freedom Army—Mau Mau—that had been the pride of all the struggling people in the world. But the spirit of resistance lives on. Temporarily by the short-lived euphoria of independence, it has since grown into well-organized national movements. The best known of these are the December Twelve Movement (DTM) with its newspapers, *Mwanguzi, Pambana* and *Mpatanishi*, and also Mwakenya with its organ, *Mzalendo Mwakenya.* In the face of increasing popular resistance, the KANU regime has escalated the repression against our people to new heights. Wholesale intimidations of the people, detention without trials, imprisonment through kangaroo courts, stripping of citizenships disappearances, torture, murder of students, execution of political prisoners, massacre of whole sections of the population—all these have created a climate of fear. This has forced many Kenyans into exile. Kenyan has been turned into a police state. Northern Kenya (the former Northern Frontier District stretching from Turkana to Lamu) for instance, is under a State of Emergency carried over from the colonial times. The present armed forces are instruments for the suppression of the population. Today Kenya is the classical neocolonial state.

A comprador class—a parasite—that is a subordinate ally of international capital, rules us. It is an overseer of imperialist interests in our country. These surrogates, *mbwa wakali* of the West are paid to suffocate the growth of national enterprises. In order to mask their shameless mortgaging of our country to imperialism and to maintain their minority rule over us, they sow seeds of discord, dividing us Kenyans into "tribal", racial and regional enclaves trying to make us believe that our problems exist because of this or that "tribe," race or region. (An example is the way that the Moi regime often deflects people's anger against its own corruption and mismanagement by inciting crude racism against Kenyans of Asian origin).

Mwakenya: The Unfinished Revolution

When this divide-and-rule policy fails and the resistance mounts, they use the police and the army to put us down. Thus the security apparatus, which should defend national interest and safeguard our rights, have become protectors of foreign interests against any internal threats. This class has marginalized the larger sector of the labor force in our country—women. This has meant that the woman carries the double burden of class exploitation as worker and peasant, and social oppression as a woman. By perpetuating negative feudal patriarchal (social, political, cultural and legal) attitudes and practices towards women, the comprador class has reinforced structures of underdevelopment inherited from colonialism. These feudalistic patriarchal attitudes and practices are indeed a barrier to women's meaningful participation in all aspects of our economic, political, social, and cultural life.

At the international level, this class has aligned Kenya with forces of reaction thus dishonoring our revolutionary heritage and the name of Kenya in the eyes of the world. This class is truly anti-national, anti-Kenya, anti-progressive and it is clearly the enemy of us Kenyans—workers, peasants, students, professionals, soldiers and all other patriotic elements must unite against it and its imperialist masters.

It is against this background of repression and resistance that we Kenyans living in Britain have come together and decided that we cannot stand idly by without taking a firm side in the struggle. After four years of intense debate and discussion on the situation in Kenya, we have taken the decision to form *Umoja wa Kupigania Demokrasia Kenya* (UKENYA). Ukenya is an anti-imperialist organization committed to struggle for democracy and the regaining of Kenya's sovereignty. We declared our total opposition to the present KANU-led neocolonial regime and our commitment to the dismantling of the neocolonial structures in all sectors of our economic, political, social and cultural lives. We support all the progressive and anti-imperialist liberation movements inside the country. We pledge to work hand in hand with these and with all the other patriotic, democratic organizations outside the country. United, we shall win, and a people-based democracy shall reign.

Mwakenya: The Unfinished Revolution

Objectives

Ukenya is fully committed to the restoration of Kenya's sovereignty and national integrity. Ukenya shall therefore strive for the unity of all patriotic Kenyans who are struggling against neocolonialism and hence are fighting for a national economy, a national democratic society; and a national independent culture, which reflects the diversity of the nationalities of Kenya. Towards the fulfillment of this, Ukenya shall be guided by the following broad and particular objectives.

Broad Objectives

Economic Objectives

We stand for:

1. The development of a national economy free from foreign domination and which is geared first and foremost to meeting the needs of Kenyan people.

2. The development of a truly national industrial base, which will lead to self-sufficiency and cater for local needs instead of the present situation where our industries are mere extension of Western transnationals. We shall struggle for an integrated economy where industry and agriculture will support one another. For instance, food production to meet the needs of all Kenyans must be our priority in land usage and planning.

3. The right of workers to gainful employment and the right of workers to a fair return for their labor. Therefore, we support the workers' struggle for higher wages, decent housing, adequate medical care, education and other basic social necessities. We support the workers in their struggle for the right to strike and picket, and for their right to engage in any forms of political struggle necessary to achieve the above and to liberate their labor from internal and external exploitation.

4. The right to own, as a peasant, pastoralist, or fisherman, adequate and productive land and other natural resources needed to survive; and to be granted a fair market value, whether it be on a domestic or on an international scale, for their produce. We, therefore, reject the present

Mwakenya: The Unfinished Revolution

situation, whereby the most productive land and other resources are concentrated in the hands of a few big landowners, both Kenyan and foreign.

5. We support the principle of land reform and redistribution, and we reject private ownership of large tracts of land.

6. We support the rights of peasants who struggle for land ownership, and their right to determine how the land is used. In addition, we support the peasants' right to have control over the disposal of their produce through cooperatives, or through any other form of association appropriate to their locality, culture and education.

7. We also support their right to decent housing, medical care, education and other basic social necessities needed for survival.

8. We support peasants' right to engage in any forms of political struggle necessary to achieve the above and to liberate their economy from external control and to liberate themselves from social oppression.

9. The alliance of workers and peasants of Kenya in their struggles.

10. The right of Kenyan people's struggles against the ever-spiraling prices of basic commodities.

11. The legitimacy of Kenyan people's struggles against the present corrupt, thieving comprador minority that continues to empty national coffers into its own private treasures at home and abroad, and uses public institutions and cooperatives to feed its never-ending appetite for stolen wealth.

Political Objectives

We stand for:

1. National democracy and freedom in Kenya.

2. The equality of all Kenyan nationalities in all aspects of our national life.

3. The equality of men and women in all aspects of national life.

4. The intensification of the struggle for the right of Kenyans, freely to express themselves, to organize, to form associations, to boldly state

Mwakenya: The Unfinished Revolution

their opinions without fear of persecution, to receive information without state interference and harassment. Indeed, it is the right of all Kenyans to form associations to express even their special self-interests as a group (e.g., women), for people's problems can only be resolved democratically, and not by presidential decrees and police boots.

5. The immediate abolition of the present Preservation of Public Security Act, whereby people are detained without trial, are subject to all forms of torture, denied access even to their families and to lawyers of their choice. Indeed we are opposed to the present judicial system whereby Kenyans in general are harassed and patriotic Kenyans in particular are punitively jailed on trumped up charges, or summarily executed.

6. The immediate abolition of all the state of emergency laws and regulations, which have been used to govern Northern Kenya since colonial times and which have seen detentions, torture and wholesale massacres of Kenyans in the north and destruction of their property.

7. The dismantling of the present military and armed police system used for the maintenance of neocolonial structures, for the defense of the propertied few, and against the majority of the people. We believe in the creations of a genuine People's Defense Force.

Social Objectives

We stand for:

1. The right of every Kenyan to adequate food, clothing, shelter and medical care.

2. The right of all Kenyans to free, compulsory and universal education, which will inculcate in the people a national consciousness, a national pride and one, which is opposed to all forms of parasitic values and to the domination of Kenyan life by foreign imperialist interests. While absorbing all the world democratic traditions, education should be geared to producing responsible Kenyans committed to the development of Kenya as a whole and who are responsive to the needs of the majority.

3. The development of a national transport and communications system that is geared to meet the advanced needs of the entire country, one that

Mwakenya: The Unfinished Revolution

is not governed by the government, such as, but not limited to, social networking, the Internet, or the use of cell phones.

4. The development of Kiswahili as the all-Kenya official and national language and also as the language of solidarity with the struggles of peoples of East and Central Africa. At the same time, we support the promotion of all Kenya's nationality languages.

5. The development of a national democratic culture rooted in our traditions of struggle and resistance to oppression and foreign domination. We support all patriotic movements in the areas of creative and performing arts, for instance in theatre, music and literature, without such we cannot heal as a nation, as a people.

6. The development of adequate leisure and sporting facilities for all Kenyans in all the regions, with an emphasis on the talent and continued health of all nationals, whether young or old.

Foreign Relations

We stand for:

1. The immediate removal of all USA military facilities and all other foreign presence from our soil. We reaffirm the sanctity of Kenya's sovereignty and territorial integrity.

2. The declaration of Kenya as a Nuclear Free Zone and the Indian Ocean as a zone of peace.

3. The realignment of Kenya's international links so as to establish and strengthen our support and solidarity with liberation movements in South Africa and Namibia, indeed with the liberation movements in Africa, Asia, Pacific, Central and South America, and the Caribbean. Particular Objectives

We stand for:

1. To work with Kenyans in Europe and elsewhere and organize ourselves into a united democratic resistance movement against neocolonialism in our country.

2. Establish working links with progressive forces and organizations of

Mwakenya: The Unfinished Revolution

Kenyans inside and outside Kenya.

3. Promote activities of democratic resistance in Kenya in cooperation with internal and external democratic movements towards a unified national resistance movement. This will be done with the clear knowledge and understanding that externally based movements can only get guidance from those internally based (i.e., those within Kenya) and therefore that those abroad will mainly play a supportive role.

4. Establish friendly links with existing Kenya solidarity committees in Europe, Japan, USA and any others that might be formed elsewhere.

5. Establish friendship with democratic forces throughout the world.

6. Engage in political, social and cultural activities, which promote the welfare of Kenyans and enhance the dignity of Kenyan people and their proud history of resistance.

From Kĩmathi to Mwakenya:
Resistance in Kenya Today

Speech delivered by Yusuf Hassan, Chairperson of UKENYA, on Wednesday, February 18, 1987. London. UKENYA was a front of Mwakenya abroad.

Kenyans and friends:

Ukenya has called this public meeting for all Kenyans and their friends to discuss the situation in our country today. At the beginning of the war for national independence, Dedan Kĩmathi, the leader of the Kenyan Land and Freedom Army (Mau Mau) said, "It is better to die on our feet than to live on our knees". Kĩmathi and his comrades-in-arms were fed up with just analyzing the situation. They decided to act in order to change it. This heroic decision signifies a very important fact. That, in the life of every human being, and every nation, there comes a time when that individual or nation can no longer tolerate any oppression. For us Kenyans, that time has come. It is now!

We have reached the peak of many years of repression in the hands of the unjust KANU regimes of Kenyatta and Moi. Since February 1986 hundreds of Kenyans have been arrested, some have been sentenced to long terms of imprisonment or detaining without trial and others have been intimidated, harassed and tortured. Among them are workers, peasants,

Mwakenya: The Unfinished Revolution

intellectuals, academics, teachers, students, writers, artists, civil servants, politicians and many other patriots. Others have been stripped of their citizenships. And many more Kenyans have fled into exile.

These patriots have been arrested because of calling for democracy; they have been detained without trial for demanding democracy; have been mercilessly tortured because of fighting for democracy; have been stripped of their citizenship for campaigning for democracy; and have been forced to flee their country and live in exile for lack of democracy in the country. In short, they are being punished because of their patriotism. But it is not only these patriots who are suffering. For throughout the country many more Kenyans have met with similar fate because of struggling for democracy and human dignity. KANU has become an instrument of mass oppression.

The KANU regime began to show its ugly face of repression as early as 1963. In order to cover its continued links with imperialism, the regime started to gun down those Kenyans who saw through its mask of nationalism and exposed its neocolonial face. I can cite several examples. But here I shall mention only a few.

We Kenyans will never forget the indiscriminate killings in northern Kenya during the war between government troops and the fighters of NFD liberation front in the years 1963-67. The official government report admitted to 6,000 deaths, but independent report put the figure at more than 20,000. We will never forget the 1969 Kisumu massacre where between 60 and 70 people were gunned down by Kenyatta's body guards, or between 300 or 400 Kenyans killed at Garissa in 1980; or the more than 2,000 killed in Nairobi and Nanyuki in 1982, or indeed the more than 800 who were killed in West Pokot in 1984. In 1969, the rightwing politician, Tom Mboya, was shot dead. And in 1975 the MP for Nyandarwa North, J.M. Kariūki was grisly murdered. The climax of these atrocities was the Wajir massacre in February 1984 when more than 1,000 civilians were killed by government troops. And on February 10, 1985 police invaded University of Nairobi students who were praying for peace and democracy. More than

Mwakenya: The Unfinished Revolution

12 students were clubbed to death. Kenyan patriots remember this day as Bloody Sunday.

These are only a few examples from a long list of repressive and cruel actions, meant to stifle the resistance of progressive Kenyans who want real independence. An important figure in these struggles was the patriot Pio Gama Pinto, who was also murdered on February 14, 1965, only a few years after the independence he had selflessly fought for. February is a very important month in the history of our struggles.

We have called this meeting in the month of February, therefore, in memory of all the Kenyans who have been harassed, tortured, imprisoned, detained without trial, exiled, and those killed in the struggle for democracy. But why the 18th of February? This is a significant day in Kenya's revolutionary struggle. Thirty years ago, today, the British colonialists hanged our leader, Dedan Kĩmathi wa Waciũri. Kĩmathi was the commander of the Mau Mau forces. For many years, and at different levels, Kenyan nationalities participated in the anti-colonial struggle. But the Mau Mau armed struggle was the height of that resistance, for the Mau Mau led the Kenyan national struggle to independence. In 1954 at a congress on the slopes of Nyandarwa, Kĩmathi was elected the first Prime Minister of Kenya. This action showed that independence is not something to be negotiated or begged for.

Kĩmathi was therefore seen as a big threat to British colonial rule. The British had already decided what kind of future Kenya should have. By 1967 they had begun to conspire and prepare their African stooges to take nominal power sometime in the future. By killing Kĩmathi, the British thought that they could extinguish the flames of political awareness fanned by Mau Mau. But the struggle continued, and in the end the British colonialists could no longer delay "granting" independence to Kenya. Nevertheless, in the 1962 Lancaster House talks, the British dictated the type of independence Kenya would have. They made sure that come the 12th of December 1963, their puppets would take over the leadership. That was the beginning of neocolonialism in Kenya under the auspices of

Mwakenya: The Unfinished Revolution

KANU. By neocolonialism we mean the control of our nation's wealth, the control of politics, and the control of our national culture by imperialists in collaboration with their local agents.

The independence gained on December 12, 1963 did not bring any fundamental changes in the economic structure. Our economy is still in the hands of transnationals and international finance capital. For example, 80% of our industries are controlled by foreign companies such as Unilever (British and Dutch), General Motors and Firestone (USA), ICI and Lonrho, and so on. Also just one British firm, ICI, controls 80% of Kenya's mineral resources. The Lancaster House constitution actually legitimized the colonial settlers' ownership of the land they had occupied by force in the colonial period. Kenyans were forced to buy their own land from some of these settlers. As if that was not bad enough, the KANU government had to borrow money from the British in order to buy out the white settlers. The total amount involved is estimated at more than 33 million British pounds. Although this deal benefited only handful of wealthy Kenyans, every single Kenyan continues to pay back the loan. Therefore we Kenyans were deceived not once, not twice, but three times. Firstly, the settlers robbed us of our land; secondly, we were forced to give them our labor; and thirdly, we were forced to borrow money to buy back our own land and pay the loans back with interest. Furthermore, large coffee, tea, pyrethrum and fruit plantations are still owned by transnationals. For example, the British company, Brooke Bond, alone, controls about 25% of all the tea grown in Kenya. The processing and distribution of agricultural chemicals and fertilizers are control by foreign companies. Virtually, all monetary transactions are in the hands of western financial institutions. For instance, two British banks, including Barclays Bank, control 50% of all finance capital in Kenya.

These foreign companies employ 70% of the entire work force in Kenya. It is the labor of these workers, who live on very meager wages, which is the source of the huge profits made annually by such companies. For instance, in the year 1977-78 foreign companies invested capital of about $10 million US Dollars. In the same period, they repatriated some

Mwakenya: The Unfinished Revolution

$23 million US Dollars in profits. A rough calculation reveals that these companies made colossal gains. The continuous repatriation of our wealth to foreign countries has resulted in the underdevelopment of the Kenyan economy. Therefore, the KANU government has to borrow more and more money from international financial institutions to keep afloat. As a result, Kenya's external debts increased annually. To illustrate, in 1964 Kenya's external debt stood at $86 million US Dollars. Ten years later this figure ha gone up to $312 million US Dollars and in 1985-86 it had reached $2 billion US Dollars and amounted to 45% of the Gross National Product (GNP). Loans and grants merely lubricate the machines of exploitation in the interests of foreigners and a small clique of nationals. A lot of these funds are used to buy weapons and instruments of repression. But the heavy burden of repayment has to be shouldered by Kenyan workers and peasants who have debts to bear for generations; even the unborn babies are in debt, and have a debt to bear from the past.

The only change that took place at independence was the replacing of British settlers with African overseers who have opened the doors of our economy to wider imperialist interests led by the USA. This class of African overseers is the main beneficiary of the looting of the masses by foreign interests. In addition to what they get from their role as middlemen, they have developed other corrupt schemes, e.g. Harambee and forced KANU membership drives, which have turned many of them into instant millionaires. At the same time the economic situation of the real producers of wealth worsens everyday.

Thus the main preoccupation of this exploiting class of African overseers has been to safeguard imperialist interest and to stifle every initiative by nationals to develop economically and advance politically and culturally. Today, the KANU regime has even handed over our country to be used by foreign military powers. Soon after independence the Kenyatta regime reached a "secret" agreement with Britain, which allowed the continued presence of British troops in Kenya. Also in 1980, the Moi regime signed yet another secret treaty with the USA imperialist regime, which allows the United States Air Force (USAF), and the United States Navy (USN)

Mwakenya: The Unfinished Revolution

military bases in Kenya. US warships, such as the USS Nimitz, pay regular visits to the Kilindini Harbour in Mombasa. These arrangements threaten not only the security of Kenya and East Africa, but also all of the countries in the region of the Indian Ocean. Another obvious danger is the cultural dislocation and moral corruption caused by the US Marine Corps (USMC) in several coastal towns, such as Mombasa and Malindi. The granting of military facilities to the US is a scandalous action, which places Kenya firmly into the reactionary camp of African countries. There is also the threat of dragging Kenya into US imperialist wars, which do not concern us at all, but puts all Kenyans in harms way, if a foe of the US is apt to strike the US on Kenyan soil, air or water. The sovereignty of our country has been mortgaged. In the international arena, Kenya has no independent voice. For instance, the Moi-KANU regime was told by the United States not to go to the 1980 Moscow Olympics, Kenya quickly obliged. Kenya also supported US aggression against Libya and the US invasion of Grenada. And in the Middle East, while paying lip service to the Palestinian cause, the neocolonial regime has continued its cozy relations with Zionist Israel through trade and security links.

At the social and cultural levels, the KANU government continues the colonial legacy of aping and promoting the social values of Euro-American bourgeoisie while at the same time trying to suppress all manifestations of a national, patriotic and democratic culture. Most films and plays shown at national theatres and Television, and songs and music broadcast on radio are those, which promote an Anglo-American way of life. But the arts, which portray the heroic struggles against injustice and tyranny, are banned. The destruction of Kamiirithu is a very good example. The entire educational system aims at making us look up to the western bourgeoisie for everything while making us despise what is Kenyan, national and rooted in the people. We have reached a stage where US imperialist "experts" plan most of our educational programs.

We have seen clearly the independence negotiated by KANU has not brought about any positive changes in our economy, politics and culture. On the contrary, the social conditions of Kenyans are worse today. Adequate

373

Mwakenya: The Unfinished Revolution

food, shelter, clothing and medical services are reserved for the rich. Corruption, openly led by the President himself, has become the guiding philosophy of the KANU regime. These stooges of imperialism have turned Kenya into a country of "20 millionaires and 20 million beggars", to borrow words of J.M. Kariūki .The failure of KANU to bring about any meaningful changes has disillusioned many Kenyans and the regime has resorted to force and threats in the recruitment of party members. Thus, isolated from the people, the KANU regime can only maintain itself in power through brute force. State violence against the people dates back to some few months after independence, when the KANU government deployed the army it had inherited from the colonial administration (Kenyan African rifles) to kill Mau Mau fighters. The government proceeded to ban all those parties which held similar views to those of Mau Mau, for instance, Ex-Freedom Fighters Union, Walioleta Uhuru Union and all other progressive organizations like the Northern People's Progressive party (NPPP). Unable to put up with the reactionary policies of KANU, the progressive elements in the party left it and in 1966 formed a new opposition party, Kenya People's Union (KPU). But three years later, the KANU regime banned KPU and arrested its entire leadership, including Jaramogi Oginga Odinga and Bildad Kaggia.

The KANU government did not stop at merely suppressing the opposition. In 1982 it changed the country's constitution and declared itself as the only political party in Kenya. Four years later, that is 1986; it took yet another step by declaring itself above parliament and the judiciary. Twenty-three years of KANU's repression had come of age. But this is only one aspect of Kenya's history. The other side of our history is the gallant resistance, which Kenyans have waged against 23 years of neocolonialism in our country.

Once again, the Mau Mau fighters were the first to realize that the independence they had fought for had been betrayed. In a book edited by Maina wa Kīnyattī, *Kenya's freedom Struggle,* a freedom fighter quoted had this to say:

Mwakenya: The Unfinished Revolution

We thought and expected that the land occupied by European would be distributed freely to us as a reward for our contribution to the liberation of Kenya. But to our dismay, our contributions were neither recognized, nor were we given the land. Instead, we were required by law to buy our own land from the same thieves who had stolen it from us, as if the price of blood we had paid was not enough. As you can see, we are still very poor; if anything, our situation has worsened. I lost my entire family, my small piece of land and now, after independence, I have to be content with being a farm laborer—earning Ksh.120 a month! The person who owns this farm was a hũmungaati, a killer of our people. So I am not satisfied at all. To be frank, I am very bitter.

The Mau Mau fighters did not show their dissatisfaction by words only, but some of them went back to the forests to continue with the war. But this time it was a war against neocolonial stooges. In 1964, for instance, it was reported that more than 200 Mau Mau fighters attacked government forces in Mĩĩrũ. By then neocolonialism had not shown itself up completely. Therefore many Kenyans, even the progressive-minded could not see the need for an armed opposition so soon after the new flag had been hoisted. That is why Mau Mau was easily isolated from the masses and thus defeated by the KANU regime.

It has taken Kenyans more than 20 years to realize that what the Mau Mau tried to do in 1964 was the only way neocolonialism could be rooted out. The April Issue of *Mzalendo Mwakenya*, the mass organ of the underground organization, Mwakenya, called for an armed struggle against the Moi regime. The ideological difference between the Mau Mau and Mwakenya is that the latter has fully analyzed and identified imperialism and its class allies in Kenya.

The struggle against neocolonialism from Kĩmathi to Mwakenya has been conducted at three levels. Let me look at them briefly:

Economic: Workers are in the forefront of this struggle. Although the trade union congress, COTU, is controlled by the government and its

Mwakenya: The Unfinished Revolution

leaders silenced through bribery and intimidation, and despite the fact that all strikes have been decreed illegal, the workers continue to demand their rights throughout the country. Since 1964 strikes have become regular phenomena. But the workers have intensified their fight and in recent years, strikes have become a matter of daily occurrence. For instance, in the month of July 1986 alone, more than 1,500 workers in different companies went on strike. Big companies like the Kenya National Trading Corporation, Firestone, Sanyo and others were affected. Peasants have also shown their opposition by action. For example, the peasants in Central Kenya and the Rift Valley region were uprooting their coffee trees in protest against the cash crop mentality of the KANU regime. In different parts of the country, thousands of squatters have occupied land owned by landlords, foreign companies and the state and members of cooperatives have held demonstrations against pilfering of their funds by government appointees. And peasant women have stood firm and continued to sell vegetables and fruits in urban markets in spite of police harassment. Petty merchants and local artisans have indirectly expressed their opposition by attempting to run an alternative economy to the one controlled by transnationals.

***Culture and Ideology*:** The cultural and ideological struggle is growing in strength in Kenya. Writers, musicians and other artists have tried to express in their works and ideological position consistent with the needs of peasants and workers. The works have often been inspired by the struggles of peasants and workers. Their works have given voice to the voiceless majority. We have many brilliant examples: *Sauti ya Dhiki* by Abdilatif Abdalla, who was arrested in 1968 and subsequently imprisoned in 1969 after writing a pamphlet entitled, *Kenya: Twendapi?* Historical works: *Thunder From the Mountains* and *Kenya Freedom Struggle* by Maina wa Kĩnyattĩ, who is presently in prison; the novels of Ngũgĩ wa Thiong'o, like *Devil on the Cross* and *Petals of Blood*; and the works of al-Amin Mazrui, like his play *Kilio Cha Haki*. There are others like Katama Mkangi and Micere Mũgo. Musicians too like Ochieng' Kabaselleh. But this cultural resistance has best manifested itself in theatre. The main symbol of this once again is Kamĩĩrĩthũ.

Mwakenya: The Unfinished Revolution

The underground patriotic and democratic writings between 1964 and 1984 showed great ideological awareness of imperialism and class forces at work in Kenyan society. A good example of this deepening awareness of imperialism is a book called *Cheche Kenya* published and distributed by the December Twelve Movement (later published by Zed Press under a new title, *In Dependent Kenya*).

Politics: Resistance has also heightened at the political level and has manifested itself in three ways: legal, underground organizations and exile-based democratic movements. Between 1966 and 1969, the political struggle was waged by legally accepted organizations, like the KPU. KPU campaigned vigorously for democratic rights, and took up the question of the ownership of national wealth, and took a stand against foreign interests in our country. By articulating the demands of Kenyan masses, KPU advanced the democratic resistance to a very high level. But the Kenyatta-KANU regime feared KPU's strength and support among the people so much so it kept on postponing the general elections. After the banning of the KPU, democratic opposition was led by university and secondary school students. Nairobi University and Kenyatta students' Unions played a big role in fighting for democracy and human rights, and opposing neocolonialism and foreign military bases in Kenya. The university students demonstrated in the streets, wrote leaflets, spoke in public student gatherings and in so many ways, helped expose the reactionary character of the KANU dictatorship. Even after some of them were jailed, their voices of resistance broke prison barriers and reached the ears of the world. In one of their protests smuggled from prison, they wrote:

We want the world to know the truth about justice in Kenya and about the inhuman conditions and suffering we are subjected to daily. Most of us are under 24 years of age. The torture and brutality we have received should not be happening in a country that portrays itself as the most democratic in all of Africa.

Because of the suppression of open democratic opposition and detention and imprisonment of political leaders, organized resistance went underground. One of the important movements in this underground

Mwakenya: The Unfinished Revolution

struggle was the December Twelve Movement (DTM), which took a clear, firm and committed stand against neocolonialism. Since 1982 its organ, *Pambana*, has made known its anti-imperialist philosophy. Because *Pambana appeared in Kiswahili*—language understood by most of Kenyan workers and peasants—it reached a wider audience among Kenyan masses. Such was the ideological impact of *Pambana*, that when in 1982 there was an attempted coup by the Kenyan Air Force (KAF), the soldiers and their supporters were shouting Pambana! Pambana! Pambana!

In 1985, the movement changed its name to Mwakenya (MK). Since then MK leadership has escalated the struggle against the KANU regime and its foreign backers to an even higher level. Mwakenya has instilled fear in the hearts and minds of those who lead the country today without the people's mandate. [It is interesting to note that there have never been any presidential elections since the Prime Ministerial elections of June 1963. Neither Kenyatta nor Moi ever tested their popularity through the ballot box.] The only three Mwakenya cadres who have been charged with sabotage activities were fearless in their conviction—and virtually turned the tables against the KANU regime and put the state on trial instead. Tirop argued that the real criminals were those responsible for the repressive conditions in the country. His comrades-in-arms, Karĩmi, proudly proclaimed, "I love Kenya. Truth has to be said. Change, like death, is inevitable." There are many heroes and heroines in our struggle. For instance, the consistency that Jaramogi Odinga has taken on many issues in our country has been exemplary. From colonial days to the present, Jaramogi Odinga has selflessly dedicated himself to the regaining of our human dignity and national self-respect. Despite his old age, he has shown us the resilience of a patriot. His opposition to USA military presence in Kenya, like his opposition to the theft of our national wealth has been unequivocal. The title of his book, *Not Yet Uhuru* was prophetic. Even religious leaders and lawyers have refused to tolerate the KANU government's repression in silence. Some have come out in the open and expressed their outrage against some of the despotic measures of the Moi dictatorship, such as the recent abolition of the secret ballot.

Mwakenya: The Unfinished Revolution

In recent years, the number of Kenyans fleeing into exile has increased tremendously. But these exiles have been organizing in different ways and places and have formed groups and movements, which continue to struggle for democracy and real independence in Kenya. For instance, there is the Kenya Anti-Imperialist front formed by Kenyan exiles in Southern Africa and the Organization for Democracy in Kenya in Sweden. Here in Britain, since the 1970s there have been various opposition groupings. KPU exiles formed themselves into a support organization and later the Kenya Democratic Alliance came into being. While in the US there have been groupings around Mkenya Ngambo and Kenya Yetu.

Since 1982 some of us began regular meetings and discussions on how best to campaign for the democracy in Kenya. Arising from these discussions and in response to requests from various individuals and organizations, we have decided to form Ukenya—Umoja wa Kupigania Democrasia Kenya (in English: Movement for Unity and Democracy in Kenya).

At this stage, I would like to thank all Kenyan patriots who have stood up for democracy. I also would like to thank individuals and organizations in Europe, Africa, US, Asia, Pacific and the Caribbean, who supported the struggle of Kenya people. Ukenya is an anti-imperialist organization, committed to the struggle for democracy and the regaining of Kenya's sovereignty. We declare our total opposition to the present KANU-led neocolonial regime and our commitment to the dismantling of the neocolonial structures in all sectors of our economic, political, social and cultural lives. Ukenya is fully committed to the restoration of Kenya's sovereignty and national integrity. Ukenya shall therefore strive for the unity of all patriotic Kenyans who are struggling against neocolonialism and hence are fighting for a national economy; a national democratic society; and a national independent culture, which reflects the diversity of the nationalities of Kenya.

Towards the fulfillment of this, Ukenya shall be guided by broad and particular objectives outlined in full in our Manifesto. Briefly then, Ukenya pledges to:

Mwakenya: The Unfinished Revolution

1. Work with Kenyans in Europe and elsewhere and organize ourselves into a united democratic resistance movement against neocolonialism in our country.

2. Promote activities of democratic resistance in Kenya in cooperation with internal and external democratic movements towards a unified national resistance movement. This will be done with the clear knowledge and understanding that externally based movements can only get guidance from those internally bases (i.e. those within Kenya) so that those abroad will, mainly, play a supportive role.

3. Engage in political, social and cultural activities, which promote the welfare of Kenyans and enhance the dignity of Kenyan people and their proud history of resistance.

4. Fight for the declaration of Kenya as a Nuclear Free Zone and the Indian Ocean as a Zone of Peace.

5. Establish links with other "Third World" anti-imperialist democratic resistance movements.

6. Support the liberation movements in South Africa and Namibia, indeed with the liberation movements in Africa, Asia, Pacific, Central and South America and the Caribbean.

7. Establish links with other "Third Worls" anti-imperialist democratic resistance movements.

8. Establish friendships with democratic forces throughout the world.

We in Ukenya are determined to struggle for a Kenya in which no person shall be harassed, intimidated, arrested, unaccounted for and nowhere to be found, tortured, jailed, detained without trial, exiled or killed—for holding opinions and views different from those in power.

In order to achieve our objectives Ukenya seeks the help and support of all Kenyans and all progressive and democratic-loving people all over the world.

Kenya's history is one of heroic resistance against forces of foreign occupation. We fought against the Portuguese; we fought against the Arabs, and in the 1950s we fought against the British. In each of these struggles,

Mwakenya: The Unfinished Revolution

Kenyan people have marked new heights in the struggles of Black people. Today, Kenyan people are once again poised to follow the lessons of their history. I've no doubt, as I stand before you that Kenyan people, African people, and indeed third World people, will win and usher in a new era of national democratic revolutions.

A People United Can Never be Defeated!
We Oppose U.S. Bases and All Other Foreign Military Presence in Kenya!
Victory to Ukenya: Down with Neocolonialism!
Support Democracy, Oppose Neocolonialism!
Pambana Ushindi ni Wetu!

Struggle For Democracy in Kenya

Special Report on the 1988 General Election in Kenya
Section One, June 1988

Preface

This special report is the first of a series of background material that Ukenya will be issuing to explain and document the ongoing democratic struggle in a country where the people's assertion of their right to organize, their right to assemble, their right to express their opinions and interests, is often met with police boots and bullets. In neocolonial Kenya more than five people cannot gather even for a family tea party or for funeral arrangements without a police license. The fascist ideology of Nyayoism—love the leader, make peace with the leader, unite behind the leader, without raising any questions—has been raised to the level of state philosophy. The philosophy best expressed itself during the last fraudulent elections where loyalty to the leader became the sole criterion of one's elective worthiness. The fact is that the Moi-KANU regime has betrayed everything that the Kenyan people have fought for and especially the ideals of the Mau Mau anti-colonial armed struggle of the fifties.

The bitterness that the majority of Kenyans feel at this betrayal is best summed up in one of the letters written by Robert Ngundo. It reads:

Mwakenya: The Unfinished Revolution

I am tried of being part of the silent majority. What is the use of being in the majority if we are silent about it? History will condemn us and the future generations will curse our memory for being passive witnesses to our downfall...I am tired of seeing patriots labeled as being in the pay of foreign masters. With this kind of negative reaction to any contrary views, we risk imparting to our children the fallacy that creativity, originality, innovation, change, can only be foreign, as all Kenyans think identically.

Kenyans are struggling for a democracy, which gives them total control of their economy, politics and culture. They are struggling for a Kenya in which the wealth of our country goes to benefit the majority and not the minority of thieves and robbers. UKenya fully identifies with that noble and heroic struggle.

Ukenya is an externally based organization formed in October of 1987 when a number of Kenyan resistance groups abroad came together under one umbrella. Ukenya wholly committed to the restoration of our national sovereignty, the building of a truly democratic society, and to the restructuring of the economy for the social progress of all Kenyans. Towards this end, Ukenya is pledged to continue opposing the minority Moi-KANU regime on the one hand, and to continue supporting Mwakenya and allied democratic and progressive forces inside the country, on the other.

Ukenya has constituent branches and contacts in Britain, Denmark, Sweden, USA and Africa, and a secretariat based in London. Ukenya will strive for *unity of action* of all democratic and progressive forces in Kenya, but on a principled basis. Ukenya therefore supports the Mwakenya's *Draft Minimum Programme* as the basis for real unity of all the forces committed to struggle for a new Kenya.

Introduction

On March 21, 1988 elections were held in Kenya. But this was an exercise in public deception as more than half of the members of the new parliament

Mwakenya: The Unfinished Revolution

had already been returned unopposed in the February 22 primary elections held by queuing. This new voting procedure, which requires KANU members to queue behind the photograph of the candidate of their choice, was introduction by Daniel arap Moi in 1987 despite nationwide opposition and condemnation. Moi had thus effectively killed the secret ballot as the democratic means of ensuring a measure of secrecy and personal freedom in casting a vote for a candidate even with the already restrictive one-party system. The results of the elections have been overwhelmingly condemned in Kenya and the legitimacy of the new government challenged by the underground resistance movement, Mwakenya and other democratic forces, in and outside the country.

As early as December 1987, Mwakenya, in a press release entitled, *Moi declares Unwarranted war Against Uganda*, had already started Kenyan people both to the timing of the elections—then a secret—and also to their fraudulent character. The statement reads:

> *As part of his tactics to divert the Kenyan people's attention from the real issue, and in a desperate attempt to diffuse the mounting internal opposition, Moi is secretly planning to call stage-managed early general elections in mid-February 1988. Parliament has already been recalled from recess to rubber-stamp constitutional changes to enable Moi to call early parliamentary and civic elections.*

In March of 1988, Mwakenya's publication, *Mzalendo Mwakenya* in a piece entitled, *The Moi-KANU Clique Continues to Crush Democracy in Kenya,* called on all Kenyans to continue boycotting the elections. On March 29, 1988 Mwakenya issued a press release, *Moi-KANU Regime has no Legitimacy to Rule Kenya* rejecting the legitimacy of the new Moi-KANU faction that has now assumed power after the electoral coup. We in Ukenya support Mwakenya's position as set out in these two statements. Ukenya takes the position that a legitimate government in Kenya can only emerge from the basis of the following eight minimum conditions:

Mwakenya: The Unfinished Revolution

1. The immediate nullifications of the last general elections.

2. The immediate restoration of the right to form, and join political parties, social and other democratic organizations of one's choice, and therefore the immediate stop to forced membership into KANU.

3. The immediate abolition of the electoral method of queuing.

4. The lifting of the present State of Emergency in northeastern Kenya and the immediate abolition of al the repressive laws and regulations imposed on the people of northern Kenya and other regions.

5. The unconditional release of all political prisoners in Kenya and the abolition of the notorious Preservation of Public Security Act.

6. The immediate stop of the arrests, harassments and intimidation, police brutality, torture, detention and murder of protesting workers, peasants, students and other patriotic Kenyans opposed to the Moi-KANU regime.

7. The immediate dissolution of the newly formed illegitimate Moi-KANU government imposed on Kenyan people.

8. The immediate withdrawal of all foreign troops from Kenyan soil and the cancellation of all secret treaties granting the USA and Britain storage facilities, as well as the use of Kenya's land, sea and air for any military maneuvers with nuclear or conventional weapons.

In the following pages, Ukenya sets out in detailed form, its analysis and documentations of the fraudulent elections characterized as they were by government inspired thuggery, violence, intimidation and police harassment. The analysis is meant to snow in documented form, to all Kenyans, and the entire international community, the minority and unrepresentative character of the Moi-KANU faction now in power. KANU as a party was already discredited in the eyes of Kenyan people. The previous Moi-KANU regime was a minority. What has now resulted is a minority of a minority regime representing no more than 13% of the population, a situation, which is inevitably plunging Kenya into a period of instability and chaos.

Mwakenya: The Unfinished Revolution

In presenting this document, we are asking progressive and democratic governments and forces in the world to understand our position, and why we Kenyan people have to struggle against this anti-Kenyan, anti-African and anti-people regime. We are also asking them to condemn and further isolate the Moi-KANU faction, and to support Mwakenya and allied democratic forces in Kenya. And lastly we call upon Kenyan people not to be taken in by any constitutional maneuvers and trickery designed to entrench Nyayoism either through Moi himself, or through one of his protégés now being lined up in the event of Moi being forced out of the scene through illness or through any other cause. No government formed within the framework of KANU and in particular on the basis of the results of the last fraudulent elections can have any moral or political authority to make decisions on behalf of twenty-two million Kenyans.

I. From a Colony to a Neocolony: Unique Features of a Kenyan Case

Kenya shares with all neocolonies certain similarities. The main one is the subjection of the economy, politics, and culture to foreign control and management. This is done through comprador bourgeoisie that had inherited power from the former colonial regime. In a neocolony, independence often brings no meaningful change in the pattern of ownership, control and management of land, industry, finance, commerce, trade, and the natural resources of the country. As international finance tightens its grip on the economy, the exploitation of wage labor intensifies. Economic and social misery is often the lot of the very majority who struggled and fought for independence and who are the main producers of national wealth. This has resulted in the political and cultural alienation of the ruling comprador bourgeoisie from the masses. This class has become rich out of all proportion to its contribution to production and it is totally removed from the reality of life for the majority. The contradiction between this ruling comprador minority and the masses is daily sharpening. To keep power, this class unleashes violence on the entire population through its monopoly control of the ruling party and the state machinery, including the armed

Mwakenya: The Unfinished Revolution

forces and the police. The army is not a tool for protecting the nation from external threat, when it relies on the U.S. and Britain for doing that; it is a means of protecting the ruling regime from the people, instead of for the people.

In such neocolonies, and particularly those in Africa, the only real change is the color of the personnel running the former colonial state. There is, however, another change. While the colony was more or less the monopoly of one imperialist nation, the neocolony opens its doors to wider imperialist interests. In such countries, USA, particularly after the Second World War, has become the dominant foreign power often determining the political policies and practices of the ruling regimes. Kenya, in this respect, has been no exception, and the ruling regime has given USA and Britain access to military facilities on the coast and the interior. But while it shares these features with other neocolonies, Kenya is unique in the sheer unbroken continuity between the form of the colony of yesterday and the neocolony of today. In the most vital nerve-centers of government—the administration, the judiciary, the police, the army, the very personnel; who used to serve the white settler colonial regime are the ones calling the shots, even today. The army is the best example. The present Kenya Army (KA) is the same Kings' African Rifles (KAR) that used to fight the forces of the Kenya Land and Freedom Army (Mau Mau) in the fifties. The present head of the Kenya armed forces, General Mohammed, was a soldier in the Kings' African Rifles. His predecessor, General Mũlinge, was with Idi Amin in the KAR, hunting Mau Mau freedom fighters in Mũrang'a district. The same pattern holds for many of the officials in administration—G.Karĩithi, Simon Nyachae, G. Kĩereinĩ, E. Mahihu, Isaiah Mathenge and many others who helped guide Kenya from a colony to its neocolonial photocopy. They were all highly ranked colonial civil servants.

But the most perfect example of this colonial continuity is Daniel arap Moi himself. He was a primary school teacher who found himself appointed to the colonial legislature in 1954 at the height of the intense Mau Mau struggle where he helped the white colonial settlers' scheme policies to crush the armed struggle. The white settler colonial regime

Mwakenya: The Unfinished Revolution

needed a black rubber-stamp and they found a perfect one in Moi. Later Moi became one of the leaders of the Kenya Democratic Union (KADU), which like Bishop Muzorewa's party in Rhodesia (now Zimbabwe) years later, was a class ally of the settler interests, which were fighting to delay independence. KADU joined KANU in 1965 and strengthened its right wing. Moi carries his colonial and settler mentors' ideology into KANU and the present structures of the regime.

The colonial era was characterized by the cyclical patterns of representing and resistance, more repression breeding more resistance. The same pattern has continued virtually unbroken into independent Kenya. This has now culminated in Kenya becoming a one-party, KANU dictatorship, on the one hand, and in the growth of well-organized and ideologically coherent underground resistance movements, such as Mwakenya, on the other. In offering new vision for a new democratic society, Mwakenya and the other resistance movements are generating and guiding popular support and hence posing the greatest challenge to a corrupt Moi-KANU regime. It is against that background of repression and resistance in neocolonial Kenya that the last fraudulent general elections must be seen.

II. Countdown to the Fraudulent Election

Kenya has been a de facto one-party state since the banning of the Kenya People's Union (KPU) and the subsequent imprisonment of its entire leadership in 1969. In June of 1982 the Constitution was changed, and without any debate in parliament, or indeed among the Kenyan people, Kenya became a de jure one-party state. Those who had attempted to voice opposition to this move, mainly university students were promptly locked up in jail or detained without trial.

In 1983 the powerful ultra rightwing Charles Njonjo, then Minister for Constitutional Affairs, was hounded out of Moi's regime amidst allegations that he was a traitor. Following a highly published, expensive and farcical public enquiry, Njonjo was given "presidential pardon", but kept in the political cold. Moi inherited his conservative ultra-rightwing

Mwakenya: The Unfinished Revolution

mantle. Since then, the regime has moved steadily towards a personal dictatorship for Moi, using a revived KANU. The regime resorted to forced KANU membership registration drives, in order to swell party ranks, but even more importantly, to enrich its coffers. Registration fees in 1987 were twenty shillings. Increasingly, the KANU registration drives have become an annual exercise in coercion. In desperate attempts to meet recruitment targets set by KANU officials, administration officials have used every means possible to force people to join KANU. In the town of Nanyuki, for example, civil servants were barred from entering their offices if they did not have KANU cards. Administration officials were posted at strategic points around council and government offices with instructions to turn away anybody who reported for work without a KANU card. The MP for Laikipia East, Charles Mũthũra told a KANU rally in Nanyuki that people, who had not enrolled as KANU members, should do so to avoid being questioned by the police. The acting District Chairman, Daudi Gĩthũmbĩ told the same meeting that KANU membership cards could even be used as official self-identification.

The regime also used a door-to-door campaign, which in many cases turned out to be another form of intimidating people, rather than a polite exercise at urging people to voluntarily enroll as party members. Many districts, including Eldama Ravine, Kilifi, Mombasa, Kiambuu and Nandi, adopted this intimidating strategy whose purpose appeared aimed at tracking down 'disloyal elements'. In South Nyanza, the District Commissioner Victor Musoga directed that nobody would be allowed to enter public market unless they were carrying KANU tickets. The order was extended to those who wanted to buy commodities in shops, and patrons intending to buy drinks in bars. In Mombasa, the chairman of the KANU branch, Sharrif Nassir, said that the branch would seek the cancellation of trade licenses of employers whose employees failed to register "so that we can determine who is loyal to the party and the president". In Eldoret town, the district officer Mtai visited the town's bus stop and forced 300 people to register as a condition, before they could board their buses. Later he went to bars and drinking halls and forced hundreds of people to register as

Mwakenya: The Unfinished Revolution

KANU members and threatened them with imprisonment if they refused. In Nakuru town, KANU youth wingers rounded up businessmen and women who had not closed their premises when a recruitment meeting was in progress. Their licenses were also confiscated. Throughout the country, there were numerous reports of police harassing those who did not have KANU cards on them, which bore similarities with the Kipande system that the British imposed on the Kenyan people during colonial rule.

Despite this forced membership of KANU, most Kenyans have shown their lack of support for KANU by the extremely low turnout at registration centers. In 1987, for instance, the registration drive began in March and was due to end in July, but the turnout was so low that Moi was forced to extend the registration to September. He was also forced to go round the provinces personally to force people to register. In a desperate effort to increase KANU membership and revenue, the regime combined voter registration with a KANU membership drive. Only four million registered as KANU members, a total of 6,091,798 people registered as voters, a figure which fell far short of the nine million targeted.

In a further attempt to strengthen his power and weed out people "disloyal" to him, Moi set up the feared KANU disciplinary committees in 1985. The members of the committee were Chairmen Okiki Amayo, Nathan Munoko, Burudi Nabwera, Jackson Angaine, Maalim Mohammed, Nicolas Biwott, Njenga Karũme, Sharrif Nassir, Moody Awori and Peter Ejore. They were Moi's running dogs. It is not surprising, therefore, that these people were returned into the front ranks of the regime unopposed, or through rigging. The committee had been formed to ostensibly instill discipline in party members. Through its deliberations, it transformed itself into an instrument of fear. In its 21 months' of existence, the committee had become the place where the fate of many a politician was determined. In 1986, Moi declared KANU to be supreme even above the parliament. The move was opposed throughout the country, and even Catholic bishops voiced their concern at what they said was a rapid move towards a dictatorship.

In a further move to stamp out all democratic opposition, however mild, Moi introduced the queuing system of voting. This move was opposed

Mwakenya: The Unfinished Revolution

throughout the country. Even the Law Society of Kenya and the National Christian Council of Kenya came out strongly and called for a public debate on the issue. But Moi refused by using KANU governing council and acting on the basis that KANU was supreme and above parliament, managed to impose the adoption of the queuing system. The queuing system revives British colonial practices, which also resulted in public intimidation to ensure the selection of chiefs loyal to the colonial governments. This countdown shows that the erosion of democracy was neither sudden nor accidental. It had been maturing over the entire period of Moi's leadership, particularly over the last six years. The actual elections saw the unfair and unjust involvement of the government, which resulted in several deaths. In one of the areas, policemen carted off a candidate, in handcuffs, whom Moi did not want around the voting stations, in an attempt to humiliate him publicly. In northeastern Kenya, where a state of emergency still prevails, police checked the voting intentions of the electorate, and turned away those who said that they would vote for candidates other than those favored by Moi. Even Moi's version of the secret ballot of March 21 was characterized by thuggery, violence and rigging. In Butere, for example, the ballot papers intended for Martin Shikukuu were later found in other constituencies.

Elections in Kenya have, since independence and even before that, always been fraudulent. But under Kenyatta, and in the first term of Moi's rule, there had been a semblance of constitutional legality about them. There were always attempts to camouflage the electoral fraudulence with the smokescreen of democratic verbiage about the sanctity of the secret ballot. But the last Nyayo elections have utterly abandoned all those pretences of legality, secrecy, democracy or decency and all pretences to fear of being caught red-handed.

III. Why the Elections were Held?

But why were the elections held at the time they were? Why did Moi, who already had enormous powers, find it necessary to introduce the controversial method of queuing, which could only expose him to the

Mwakenya: The Unfinished Revolution

world? Why did he choose the kind of cabinet that he did? There are three main factors: 1) Moi's own insecurity and instinct for personal survival; 2) national isolation; and 3) international isolation.

1. Moi's Insecurity and Instinct for Personal Survival

Moi is a primary schoolteacher of a poor peasant background. In the colonial days, education for the African was the route to making it as a relatively rich or well-off petty property owner. Intellectuals have always fascinated him even as he hates them. Today he surrounds himself with a few loyal academics. But he is always suspicious of them at the same time. Tired of one lot, he is prone to discarding them and acquiring a new lot. It is not an accident that his two vice-presidents have been former members of the academia. As a petty-bourgeois individual with a peasant background, he is in touch with the masses, particularly with the rural masses, but as a politician and a wielder of state power, he is in touch with the international bourgeoisie. Thus, as a primary schoolteacher in a rural community, he was in the service of the peasantry, but presently he is certainly in the service of the international bourgeoisie. One way of looking at Moi is as a feudal chief presiding over a capitalist state. Kenya is a kind of personal fiefdom with the nouveau feudal chief dispensing charity and "wisdom" to a "grateful" populace. In reality, his mentality is that of a thoroughly colonized petty-bourgeoisie, and certainly and completely alienated from the workers. But the key to understanding Moi's apparent erratic behavior is it does not lie in any well-thought out, coherent scheme of thought or philosophy. What gives seeming coherence to his actions are four things: a) a deep-rooted instinct for personal survival; b) a kind of religious belief in the power of money; c) his resentment against big nationalities; and d) a belief in loyalism, sycophancy and gratitude to the imperialist west. Let us analyze these four factors.

a) A Deep-Rooted Instinct for Personal Survival

Moi is the longest surviving member in Kenya's rubber-stamping parliament. He first entered those chambers in 1954 as a colonial

Mwakenya: The Unfinished Revolution

appointee. Thirty-four years on, from a colonial appointee to a neocolonial puppet president—that is a record. He has survived every crisis in post independent Kenya, always personally gaining from every such crisis— from the assassination of J.M. Kariũki murdered in 1975 and Tom Mboya, a rightwing, pro-imperialist poitician, murdered in 1969 to the struggle with Charles Njonjo after the 1982 coup, to the current electoral coup. For personal survival, *he can tell any lie, can ally with anybody, suddenly change alliances, can signal left or right, go to any church, often act spontaneously, or simple, or pompous, meek or arrogant and boastful, depending on his audience, time and place—he is nothing short of a chameleon that changes its colors to reflects its mood and ambience.* He has no loyalty to anybody or any principles outside himself. For Moi, the ruling maxim is neither permanent friends nor permanent enemies, but permanent personal interests. Note the different people he has closely worked with only to drop them later—Charles Njonjo, Mwai Kĩbaki, Julius Ole Tipis, Elijah Mwangale, Odongo Omamo, the late Stanley Oloitiptip, Simon Nyachae and G.G. Kariũki, to mention only a few obvious cases. Note also the way he has opportunistically tried to woo and even use leftwing opponents, only to later detain them.

Moi is a former *hũmungaati* loyalist who has quite comfortably used former fighters like late Kariũki Chotara to fight against the whole heritage of Mau Mau and its memory. Note also the way he has been using Warũrũ Kanja to fight against Mwai Kĩbaki. Warũrũ Kanja has a credible history as a radical nationalist. But his use to Moi is only in the struggle against Kĩbaki and he has now been rewarded with a cabinet post. Moi is a master at playing off one politician against the other by playing on their hopes and fears and petty-bourgeois ambitions, which he understands so well. Moi is definitely in tune with the petty-bourgeois consciousness prevailing in a dependent capitalist state.

b) A Kind of Religious Belief in Money

Moi has infinite faith in the power of money. He acts as if people carry price bags on their foreheads. Anybody can be bought off with money or hints of better things to come. Dishing out money is his major organizing political principles, to those whose loyalty he seeks. He delights, for instance, in inviting selected university lecturers for tea at the State House and at the end, giving them small bags of money "for petrol on the way". His appetite for money is also insatiable and there is no business, however, small—from taxis, petrol stations, to be big business like shares in transnational companies, transport, construction, real estate, land acquisition—that he will not enter, either alone or in partnership with others; and he has been known to use the orders of detention to imprison business associates with whom he has fallen out with. In anticipation of the oil discovery, he long ago formed an oil company. He has made one of his closest business aids, Nicolas Biwott, the Minister for Energy, his oil company friend. In the same way he has placed his protégé, Professor George Saitoti, a complete political nonentity until Moi picked him, as Minister for Finance. With people beholden to Moi placed in charge of the Ministry, and more crucially into the Central Bank of Kenya. Moi can ensure the smuggling out of foreign exchange into foreign accounts for himself and his friends without the restraining hand of those with professional integrity arising from a measure of political independence.

But it is through the Harambee system of public charity—that he is able to openly collect money from peasants, workers and civil servants. He has even formed dubious charity organizations as a vehicle for collecting money. Moi has made corruption in public life, a way of life in Kenya. But his appetite for money has ironically made him fear those who have it. What he cannot understand is the integrity and commitment of the young Kenyan people who have refused, and who are refusing, to be bought with money, or with hints of partnerships in theft, and robbery in public.

c) The KADU Roots of his Resentment Against Big Nationalities

Moi acts as if he has a deep-rooted fear of the big nationalities, particularly the Gĩkũyũ and the Luo. This suspicion emanates from his days as an ally of the colonial settler regime, which had always seen the two nationalities

Mwakenya: The Unfinished Revolution

as a threat because of the large working class forces that stood behind the two. The settler inspired KADU of which Moi was a leader tried to base itself on the small nationalities, playing on "tribalistic" suspicion, which had been engineered and always fanned by colonial settlers as part of their divide and rule tactics. Moi's tactic has always been one of presenting himself either as a victim of the big nationalities, or as the savior of the smaller nationalities depending on the situation prevailing at the time, gracing the world of diplomacy as cautiously as he can, without choosing either side, but giving the impression of doing so. He therefore tries to build a broad alliance, hostile to the big nationalities, by presenting himself as the champion of minority nationalities, or by playing off one nationality against the other, in the tradition of the same divide and rule tactic of colonialism. Where genuine patriotic leaders in Africa are trying to work for the unity of their nations, Moi thrives on disunity.

At times, Moi has also used anti-Asian sentiments to try and distract Kenyans from problems. At other times, he has used external threats, all created by himself, as the case of Uganda in 1987 as a way of trying to get unity of Kenyans behind his rule. When he was Kenyatta's vice-president, and even after becoming president, he would often project himself as an innocent, almost helpless victim of other people's machinations and he would win some sympathy. Creating or exaggerating a threat has become part of his political style. What, of course, Moi does not say or show is that he is basically a champion of the interests of the top five percent of each of the nationalities and that what he is playing off are the fears and hopes and sensibilities of the various elements among the top five percent of the different nationalities, big or small. The poor Nandi, Gĩkũyũ or Luo, Somali or Luhya, Kisii or Maasai peasants are all in the same boat: They are victims of the Moi-KANU regime's alliance with foreign interests against the real interests of the Kenyan people. The workers, no matter from what region, are exploited in the same way by the neocolonial system. (Note that historically there is no nationality in Kenya called "Kalenjin". The name was a *creation* of Moi in his anti-Kenyan attempt to unite the native nationalities of the Rift Valley region against the rest of the Kenyans.)

d) Loyalism, Sycophancy and the West

Moi's rise to the top was not through any alliance with the struggle of Kenyan people, but through his alliance with the settler British interests in the colonial days and the West in the neocolonial days. Loyalism, sycophancy and servile allegiance to the West have given him rewards of money, power and leadership. That is why even today his belief is not in the capacity of the Kenyan people to change their destiny and hence change themselves, but in the capacity of western interests to change Kenya and Africa. That is why to please the West, he can, for instance, harbor Mozambique National Resistance/Resistencia Nacional Mocambicana (MNR/Renamo) bandits in Kenya. He is always a ready and willing tool of for the USA and Western ruling circles. Another aspect of the same was his sycophancy and loyalism to Kenyatta, which yielded big results—he inherited the power of the country. Acts arising from love of Kenya, or loyalty to Kenyan and African people are to him Communist subversion. He therefore tends to trust only the qualities of loyalism, sycophancy and yesmanship from those who are around him, whether it be the MPs, councilors, students, civil servants or cabinet ministers. By the same token, he is insecure vis-à-vis of people with integrity, be they students, teachers, MPs, artists, patriotic nationalists, like Oginga Odinga, or workers and peasants.

But while a consideration of Moi and the forces that have shaped him is important in understanding the man's behavior, it is important to realize that the reason why Moi felt it necessary to call general elections when he did, it was because of the national and international isolation his regime has been facing over the years. Both resulted from the regime's increased repression of democracy, its massacre of whole communities, its torture, and imprisonment and murder of political opponents, say, its utter disregard for the human and democratic rights of Kenyans. This together with massive corruption, economic mismanagement and the fact that wealth of the country and served foreign interests has in turn given rise to well organize, and justified, resistance.

2. Resistance causes Moi's National Isolation

When Moi came to power in 1978 the oppressive KANU regime had already been discredited in the eyes of the Kenyan people. But Kenyatta was largely successful in preventing a united front of democratic forces opposed to his rule through a combination of the stick and the economic carrot. He frequently used the General Service Unit (GSU) and the military against the people. He banned opposition and jailed those who posed any meaningful challenge to his rule. However, this was combined with the fact that with independence came an end to racial barriers (color-bar) to land and property ownership and acquisition, access to jobs in the administration and private sector, and these had given him a frontier within which he could maneuver. Unlike Moi, Kenyatta possessed a charisma that only got stronger during his early years, when he was the symbol of anti-colonial nationalism. Moi inherited all the contradictions of the Kenyatta regime, without the advantages of his mentor. He did not have the wisdom, or the charm needed for respect as a serious leader of the people. He stepped into power with a discredited colonial past, without a national or party consensus behind him. Lacking as he did in any real support at the national level, he faced one opposition after another, culminating in the 1982 coup attempt. His preoccupation before and after the coup attempt has been: how to stay in power. But while managing to neutralize his opponents within the party, he has created powerful factions against him within KANU. This opposition within KANU was finding a focal point in Kibaki. Then, there is always the older patriotic nationalist tradition symbolized by Oginga Odinga, which by its very existence and continuity in such patriotic people has always exposed Moi's colonial collaboration with Kenya's enemies. But the greatest threat to Moi's regime came from opposition of a very different kind and outside the party. Moi had started his rule by assuming that Kenyatta-style banning and threats would be sufficient to silence opposition. But the events preceding the 1982 coup attempt showed that organized underground resistance had arrived on the postcolonial Kenyan scene.

From the December Twelve Movement to Mwakenya, the underground resistance has stood firmly on the side of workers' struggle against their

Mwakenya: The Unfinished Revolution

economic exploitation and political oppression; peasants' in their struggle for land and for fair returns for their produce; students in their struggle for relevant education; the national capitalists in their struggle against Euro-American based transnational and finance capital; all the unemployed in their struggle for the right to gainful employment, in short, on the side of the struggles of the exploited and oppressed majority against a thieving, anti-people minority regime of KANU and Moi. Mwakenya-DTM, for example, acknowledges that, "The major clamor and movement for change (in Kenya) comes from the people themselves. They have the material base—production—to make their clamor for social change felt and heard".

Mwakenya has undertaken a study of these forces clamoring for change in Kenya, thereby revealing the source of its own strength. The study entitled, *Kenya: Register of Resistance 1986* examines the various sectors of the Kenyan people against the Moi regime. The *Register* detail lists as strikes involving over 42,000 workers spread over 44 towns. All these were strikes from the industrial proletariat, ranging from the strike by 5,500 textile workers throughout the country to the strike of 400 workers of the HZ construction company in Eldoret. The *Register* details strikes by plantation workers' strike, peasants' resistance throughout the country, resistance by the lower petty-bourgeoisie and the progressive intelligentsia. The *Register* draws various conclusions from the resistance it documents. These include the fact that "there was a strike every month throughout the year" and that "in most cases, police, GSU or the army had to be used to quell the resistance". This resistance continued into 1987. For example, 1987 saw a total of 109 strike incidents. It was the industrial proletariat that led in the strikes. The manufacturing sector as a whole had 76 strikes, which involved 85,711 workers.

At the same time there emerged a new manifestation of popular rejection of the KANU regime's policies. Mass demonstrations in major towns faced armed police and para-military forces and made political demands. For instance, in October and November of 1987, over 4000 people of Muslim and other faiths took part in big demonstrations in Mombasa. They attacked the government provincial headquarters, destroyed government

Mwakenya: The Unfinished Revolution

buildings and vehicles, and attacked the main police station, which was forced to close for the first time in its history of more than sixty years. Then they engaged in running battles with the police throughout the night, using urban guerrilla tactics. They even attacked one of Moi's loyalists, an assistant Minister, Sharrif Nassir. Similar street demonstration took place in Nairobi where 3,000 students of the University of Nairobi took to the streets to demand the release of twelve of their colleagues detained by the police as a result of their strong advocacy of student demands. December of the same year saw 8,000 employees of the City Commission of Nairobi (the city council is yet another victim of Moi's crushing of institutions) went on strike and demonstrated through the streets of Nairobi. By 1987, then, the Moi regime was facing stiff opposition and resistance from four broad fronts: a) the workers and peasants and small producers; b) Mwakenya and other progressive movements in the country; and c) the institutions, including churches, mosques, professional bodies and patriotic nationalists; and the rightwing in two factions: 1) the liberal wing within KANU; and 2) the conservative wing outside KANU.

a) The workers, peasants, and small producers

This was because of the widespread unemployment; the ever rising prices of food and essential commodities; the naked corruption led by Moi who had become one of the richest presidents in Africa; and, of course, the general police harassment and brutality, imprisonments and widespread massacres. The workers and peasants and the general public were the recipients of underground literature from Mwakenya and other underground forces. All this has culminated in widespread strikes and public demonstration, some of which are mentioned above.

b) Mwakenya and other progressive movements in the country

Mwakenya has summed up the democratic mood of the underground resistance under its slogan, *Ni Haki Kupigania Haki* (It is our right to struggle for our rights). One of the rights denied to Kenyans is the right to organize. Mwakenya has been organizing and spreading throughout the

Mwakenya: The Unfinished Revolution

country. It has continued the process of unifying formally and informally, progressive and democratic forces inside the country. It has continued to issue its mass publication, *Mzalendo Mwakenya*. At the same time, it has issued its *Draft Minimum Programme* and *The Register of Resistance*. The *Draft Minimum Programme* is one of the most important documents to emerge in the post-independence period. It concretely places the current struggles in the context of the history of Kenya, gives brief glimpses of the rise of progressive movements in Kenya and sets out demands that can be the basis of unity and the foundation of a new Kenya. Proclaiming "the way ahead is through struggle". The *Draft Minimum Programme* states Mwakenya's belief that the "National Democratic Revolution (NDR) is the minimum step towards the eventual transformation to realize a state of economic, political and cultural *Uhuru* for all Kenyan people". Mwakenya sets the resistance of Kenyan people today in the context of the famous saying of Kimaathi: "Fighting against oppression is the duty and responsibility of every patriotic Kenyan". For its own part, Mwakenya pledges, "to struggle for real freedom, real independence, real liberation and real changes in the lives of the toiling masses of our country".

While Mwakenya and other progressive forces were spearheading the struggle against the comprador Moi regime, patriotic Kenyans abroad were also organizing. Encouraged by Mwakenya's example of principled resistance, seven of these groups came together during the October Unity Conference in Kenya, with branches in Europe, USA and Africa. The success of Mwakenya and other underground resistance movements in Kenya in exposing the sellout character of the Moi regime and its anti-people lies has been such that by 1987 people were turning more and more to the underground literature for the truth about what was happening inside the country. Today underground literature has become a way of life and the Moi-KANU regime is completely powerless to stop the production and the spread of this literature, which exposes the regime's weaknesses on a mass scale. Mwakenya has made it very clear, however, *that, it is the neocolonial system imposed on Kenyans that is to blame and not just the character of Moi.*

Mwakenya: The Unfinished Revolution

c) The Institutions including the Churches, Mosques, Professional Bodies and Patriotic Nationalists

The most serious indication of the widespread character of opposition was the stand taken by the church, since for a long time; this had been Moi's natural constituency. Prominent church leaders like Bishop Alexander Muge, Rev. Gĩtarĩ, Rev. Henry Okullu and Rev. Timothy Njoya opposed the deteriorating human rights situation and often called for an end to undemocratic practices. The Catholic Church, for instance, issued a statement denouncing KANU's assumption of a totalitarian role. The Law Society of Kenya also voiced its concern over a number of illegal practices of the regime, as did the *Nairobi Law Monthly* with its special issue on human rights. A few patriotic MPs continued voicing their opposition to certain aspects—like the stealing of public funds and the government inspired illegal export of foreign currency. All these mounted their dissent, adding their voices to those of older nationalists like Oginga Odinga, Masinde Muliro and to those of populist, democratic minded MPs like Martin Shikukuu, Mwachofi, Koigi wa Wamwere and Abuya Abuya.

d) The Rightwing Factions Within and Outside KANU

This falls into two factions: First was the liberal rightwing faction within KANU. This came from the likes of Mwai Kĩbaki, Kenneth Matiba, Charles Rubia, Kĩmani Nyoike, Odongo Omamo, Paul Ngei and others. These were only a faction within the regime. It is not that they were opposed to the neocolonial system, but they could clearly see the implications of the deteriorating human rights situation and the implications of the regime's worsening international image. Their resistance was more passive rather than active. They believed in the same neocolonial system. Then there was the conservative rightwing faction, mostly outside KANU. This was associated with Charles Njonjo and his allies. Njonjo had been thrown out of KANU and, therefore, denied a forum within the opposition, which could manifest itself openly. The gradual convergence of these forces and particularly the patriotic, democratic and progressive forces was actually isolating the Moi-KANU regime nationally. The unanimity of these voices

Mwakenya: The Unfinished Revolution

was clear, for instance, in the condemnation of the queuing system, the method devised by Moi to ensure the 'election' of only those who had demonstrated blind loyalty to the Moi dictatorship.

Thus, by 1987 the activities of Mwakenya and other democratic and progressive forces in the country were really succeeding in isolating the regime and exposing it for what it really was—a minority comprador regime which sold out Kenya to US-led imperialist interests. They had exposed the Moi-KANU regime's claim to represent the people of Kenya. In the face of national isolation, the regime sought to hoodwink world opinion and the domestic masses by the so-called general elections of February 22 and March 21, 1988.

3. Resistance Causes Moi's International Isolation

Since 1982 the Moi-KANU regime has been exposed through human rights organizations, like the London based Committee for the Release of Political Prisoners in Kenya and similar ones in Africa, Japan, Europe and USA. This has resulted in the regime being perceived differently by its traditional image-makers in the West. Its massacres, tortures and murders of opponents could no longer be written-off as if the world didn't care, and it was just an in-house Kenyan problem, but nobody else's problem, and definitely not the western world's problem—what goes on in the home, stays in the home! But the winds of change were changing rapidly, through those who were liberal enough to question the number of students imprisoned without probable cause, the professors who dared to challenge the status quo, the working class people who questioned their wages and working conditions, and the untold people who were, simply, just missing. The climax came in 1987 with the publication of Amnesty International's report: "Kenya: Torture, Political Detentions and Unfair Trials". The most humiliating event was the failure of the Scandinavian tour by Moi, which had to be cancelled at the last minute for fear of the massive demonstrations awaiting him there. Moi had, personally, invested a lot of time and money in this visit because the Scandinavian countries have a good reputation

Mwakenya: The Unfinished Revolution

in the field of human rights. A good reception there would have diffused the public humiliation he suffered in Washington in March 1987. The Moi regime has always valued its image in the West, for that is where its main support comes from. By the end of 1987 even the British press had started criticizing the KANU regime over the human rights record. The Moi regime felt so concerned as to buy glossy advertisements in several major newspapers and magazines including *Time Magazine*. It became very paranoiac about them, even the mildest criticism over the BBC, and kept on making formal protests. The regime's anger was reserved for the Kenyan exiles abroad whom it saw as being responsible for its worsening international image by their exposure of democratic and human rights abuses. The formation of Ukenya in October 1987 added to the regime's anger and frustration.

The release of nine people in February of 1988, who had been detained without trial, was meant to buy back a bit of its previous image in the West. It was meant to cover up the fact that there are over a thousand political prisoners who have been jailed through the kangaroo court system, and also the fact that death in custody and massacres by the armed forces is routine. It was not only in the West Moi's isolation increased. Kenya used to have a positive image in Africa and in the socialist world because of the achievements of the Mau Mau freedom fighters in their struggle against colonialism. The KANU regime under Kenyatta basked in this reputation in the early years. However, by the time Moi took over its internal and external policies its reputation began to decline, and isolation by various governments was inevitable; others who had supported Moi's government as well, were also leery of having too closed of a relation with it.

Kenya, under Moi's regime, should be identified as a state that too willingly opened Africa to the US and other Western strategic and military influences. Its territory is being used to destabilize African countries that are attempting an independent political and economic system. The bandit Renamo agents use Kenyan soil as their base for coordinating their propaganda against the Mozambican people. Uganda's peaceful

Mwakenya: The Unfinished Revolution

development is being threatened by Moi regime's activities. Progressive Africa has always been ashamed of Kenya's record in affording Israel and South African regimes the use of its soil for their anti-people activities in Africa. Again, when he was the chairman of the OAU, Moi shamelessly used his position to further US interests and acted against another OAU member state, Libya.

At a time when progressive Africa is struggling to establish its independence from all foreign interferences, Moi's regime stands condemned as facilitating British and US military presence on African soil. In order to win support, Moi has even allowed US nuclear presence in Kenya in secret treaties hidden from Kenyan people; treaties that should have been transparent to the people who had every right to know about something as serious as this.

Summary

The general elections were therefore called earlier than they were scheduled for—for the following reasons:

a. To consolidate the basis for personal dictatorship under the fascist ideology of Nyayoism.

b. To blunt and diffuse the internal opposition by the oppressed classes led by Mwakenya.

c. To blunt or diffuse the liberal rightwing opposition largely rallying around Mwai Kibaki. In other words, Mwai Kibaki was beginning to be seen as a liberal alternative to Moi—very much the way Moi himself had been as a liberal Christian alternative for Kenyatta.

d. To diffuse or blunt revolt growing among the institutions, especially the churches and mosques and other religious organizations as well as other patriots, democratic and progressive forces.

e. To restore the regime's democratic credibility in the West. One of Kenya's assets as a reliable ally of US-led imperialism was its unblemished history in the militant struggle against colonialism and in the postcolonial image of stability and democracy.

Mwakenya: The Unfinished Revolution

The results of the elections, and the government formed after, conforms more to the Nyayo ideal of being surrounded by a "choir of parrots". Nyayoism is a fascist ideology of "follow the leader peacefully, love the leader, and unite behind the all knowing leader, without any questions. With the last elections Kenya has moved from the state of a one-party bourgeois dictatorship to a state of a one-man dictatorship. Even if Moi, through illness or through the Constitution, were to be replaced by any member or members of his new "choir of parrots" the situation would not change. The following is an excerpt of Mr. Moi's "famous" speech on his return from Addis Ababa on September 13, 1984:

Ladies and Gentlemen...I would like to say, while here with you, that for progress to be realized there should be no debates as to what is required is for people to work in a proper manner...I call on all Ministers, assistant Ministers and every other person to sing like parrots. During Mzee Kenyatta's period I persistently sang the Kenyatta (tune) until people said: this fellow has nothing [to say] except to sing for Kenyatta. I say: I did not have ideas of my own. Why was I to have my own ideas? I was in Kenyatta's shoes and therefore, I had to sing whatever Kenyatta wanted. If I had sung another song, do you think Kenyatta would have left me alone? Therefore you ought to sing the song I sing. If I put a full stop, you should also put a full stop. This is how this country will move forward. The day you become a big person, you will have the liberty to sing your own song and everybody will sing it.

III. Moi Suffers Defeat after Election "Victory"

The regime never achieved the aims it set out to achieve. These have been analyzed above. In fact, far from diffusing the opposition, the elections have further fuelled it. The regime now faces: 1) Continued National Isolation; 2) Continued International Isolation; and 3) Instability and continued resistance ahead.

Mwakenya: The Unfinished Revolution

1. Continued National Isolation

The *Washington Post* of February observed quite correctly that an exceptionally large number of voters took the elections as an opportunity to vote against the system by staying at home. It was just one of the ways of expressing the unpopularity of the regime. Moi also thought that by appointing Josephat Karanja as his vice-president, he would be strengthening himself by getting rid of the liberal rightwing challenge from the Kĩbaki alliance. Instead, this has further weakened the regime, for Karanja has absolutely no political constituency outside Moi himself. Karanja brings into the cabinet, and government, a long history of authoritarian confrontation with popular forces, while he was the vice-president of the University of Nairobi. In fact, in the process of consolidating a personal dictatorship, Moi has weakened himself by fuelling the very opposition he had hoped to diffuse.

The last hope for democracy under the Moi regime has been killed. The government-induced death of the secret ballot has finally removed any deception that things could be changed within the system. There has been increased support for Mwakenya and its alternative vision for a new Kenya as contained in its *Draft Minimum Programme*. The rightwing coalition (KANU/KADU) held together by Kenyatta's skillful manipulations has, under Moi, been split three ways. Firstly, there is the Moi/Karanja/Biwott faction. Secondly, there is the Kĩbaki liberal rightwing faction, and finally the rightwing faction outside KANU ousted with Charles Njonjo. Added to this opposition is the continuing pressure from the institutions, especially the churches and mosques, as well as other long standing nationalists.

The fact that the fraudulent elections provoked instant protest from those who had taken part in them, and others, who had rejected the whole exercise, was proof that things were changing in a big way. The following are just a few incidents, which took place nationwide: a) In Butere, Kakamega, 2,000 people defiled armed police and the district commissioner's order and continued their protests against the election results, which had ensured the "defeat" of the populist, rightwing leader,

Mwakenya: The Unfinished Revolution

Martin Shikukuu; b) In Eshiataala Market, Butere, 3,000 voters refused to obey government officials and police orders to disperse after an election rally had been banned by the administration. They insisted that Shikukuu be allowed to address them. In further defiance of government directives, they organized a three-kilometer march. Again in Kakamega 7,000 people demonstrated against the government because the candidate they supported was deprived of the parliamentary seat. They rejected pleas from the police and government officials to disperse; c) In Taveta, 4,000 angry voters organized a four-kilometer long demonstration in protest at the false election results announced by government officials. They had announced the 'victory' of Mwacharo Kubo who is favored by the administration. The popular leaders—Nthenge Lukindo and John Mūnene were declared 'defeated' although they received more votes than Kubo. The demonstrators threw stones at the government officials and forced the closure of offices and shops. Protest activities spread throughout Taveta. Fierce battles raged between the protesters and the armed police who had to get reinforcements from the whole province. The paramilitary General service Unit had to be called. Fearing that the example of the Taveta people might spread throughout the country; the government imposed a news embargo between Taveta and the rest of the country. The police killed a sixty-six year old man. Over one hundred people were arrested and detained in Voi. Ten people were admitted to the hospital with police inflicted injuries, d) In Kībera, Nairobi, voters from Langata constituency demonstrated in the streets against the election results. Philip Leakey "won" in Langata having secured 1,590 votes out of a total registered KANU membership of 55,659 in the primary queuing elections. In the general elections, he managed 5,409 votes out of 39,339 registered voters. Leakey has been appointed Assistant Minister for Wildlife. A large number of people in Kisumu defied a heavy downpour and baton yielding police and formed a procession through the town in protest at election irregularities, and finally e) in Kiambuu, voters defied threats from armed police and challenged election results. Out of seven constituencies in Kiambuu, six had no elections as candidates were returned "unopposed" after other contestants were eliminated by Moi's

407

Mwakenya: The Unfinished Revolution

queuing system and fraudulent election practices. Four out of the six "unopposed" MPs were subsequently appointed to ministerial posts.

Generally, the elections were the most massive rejection of a regime even within its own terms. For example, when it was clear that Moi did not want a particular candidate, e.g., Paul Ngei in Kangundo, Mwai Kĩbaki in Ũthaya, Masinde Muliro in Kitale and Kenneth Matiba in Mbiri, the turnout of voters was extremely high. Otherwise, voter turnout was the lowest in the history of Kenya. In Nairobi, for example, which traditionally has always had a very high turnout, only about 6% of registered voters actually turned out to vote?

2. Continued International Isolation

The conduct and results of the elections have exposed the Moi regime. The democratic cover and pretence have been shattered beyond repair. The fact is that it is a minority regime; national resistance will further damage this international image in two ways: 1) being a minority regime, Moi's regime can only remain in power through its western backers. It follows from this that it will have to make even more concessions to these foreign interests as it has done in the past particularly in 1980 when it secretly granted military facilities to USA. This will inevitably result in its further isolation from progressive and democratic forces and governments in Africa and the Third World. The more aligned to the West, the more the regime becomes isolated in African and the Third World affairs. No African government can *willingly* cooperate with the South African regime and still claim to be in tune with the interests of Africa; and 2) the regime's minority position and the increasing resistance against it will increase. Already in April of this year, there were reports of massacres in Turkana in northwestern Kenya (see *Mbiu ya Kenya.* vol. 1 no 3, 1988). More of such violations will cause increased international isolation even in the West. Moi has taken all the stereotypes of a Third World dictator, a la Marcos, Duvalier and Pinochet and now he awaits their fate.

Mwakenya: The Unfinished Revolution

3. Instability and More Resistance Ahead

The stage has now been set for a long period of instability for the simple reason that the new Moi-KANU regime will be governing a basically hostile population. Mwakenya and other democratic forces have challenged the legitimacy of the new regime. Mwakenya and UKENYA have issued conditions under which a democratically legitimate government can emerge. The Mwakenya statement containing the conditions is being read everywhere, and is the basis for questioning the legitimacy of the regime from grassroots level upwards. When the Moi-KANU regime found that the issue was being taken up, with more and more religious leaders and other institutions coming out openly in opposition to the electoral coup, Moi banned all public discussion of the new system.

The regime has finally been cornered. Ahead lies a period of instability and chaos brought about by the desperation of the Moi regime faction. That chaos and instability would be accentuated should Moi due to ill health or constitutional manipulation be replaced by members of his rightwing faction, Biwott/Saitoti/Karanja/Nabwera, etc., or any other product of the fraudulent elections. On the other hand, in the national resistance, which is daily gathering momentum lays the hope for a new democratic Kenya.

Conclusion

Ukenya proclaims that there can be no democracy and peace in Kenya except through the unity of all patriotic, democratic and progressive forces within and outside the country on the basis of the fundamental goals and objectives listed by Mwakenya in their *Draft Minimum Programme* of September 1987. These include: 1) the recovery of national sovereignty and integrity; 2) the building of an independent and integrated national economy; 3) the establishment of genuine democracy; 4) the establishment of social justice for all classes and nationalities; 5) the promotion of a patriotic and democratic national culture; 6) the building of a strong people's defense force; and finally, 7) the pursuit of an independent foreign policy.

Mwakenya: The Unfinished Revolution

Ukenya maintains that no amount of fake elections and whitewashing can hide the ugly nature of the oppressive minority regime in Kenya. Mwakenya has shown the way ahead with its proclamation: "Change like death is inevitable". The change in Kenya today will blow away the minority dictatorship and usher in a National Democratic revolution led by Mwakenya and other revolutionary forces. This is the will of the people. The people are once again taking history into their own hands. They proved their might in the days of the Kenya Land and Freedom Army (KLFA). They are doing so again.

Long Live Kenyan People's Resistance!
Long Live the Unity of the Kenyan People!
Umoja Wetu ni Nguvu Yetu!

The Struggle Continues

Speech delivered by Abdilatif Abdalla, Chairperson of the United Movement for Democracy in Kenya, at the 7th Pan-African Congress, Kampala, Uganda, April 3-8, 1994.

The Chairman
Distinguish Delegates
Brothers and Sisters in the Struggle

On behalf of the United Movement for Democracy in Kenya—an externally-based Kenyan organization formed in October 1987 as a result of the merger of seven political organizations based outside Kenya—I take this opportunity to salute the Secretariat and the organizers of the 7th Pan-African Congress for having made it possible for all of us to assemble and deliberate on issues which affect us all. We also wish to express our thanks and gratitude to the people and the government of the Republic of Uganda for facilitating the holding of this historic Congress on the soil of Uganda on the eve of the 21st century.

We also take this opportunity, Mr. Chairman; to thank the international community for the solidarity and support our movement has received in these last seven years. The United Movement for Democracy in Kenya was formed with two main objectives in mind: **1**) to expose to the world the repressive and dictatorial nature of the Moi-KANU regime, which the

Mwakenya: The Unfinished Revolution

Western world used to present as most stable, the most developed and the most democratic country, particularly in the Eastern African region, and **2)** to organize, sensitize and involve Kenyans living abroad in the struggle for democratic and meaningful changes for all our people in Kenya.

The concerted efforts of the patriotic Kenyans in the country and international community forced the regime to hold what we regard as sham elections in December 1992. What has to be made very clear is that regime did not so after being ordered by the imperialist forces, apparently in order to pre-empt the real changes which the people of Kenya have been fighting for all these years.These elections, therefore, were meant to hoodwink the world into believing that the regime has restored democracy, but brothers and sisters, nothing substantial has changed. What we have in Kenya now is an electoral dictatorship. In actual fact, things have gone from bad to worse. The regime continues to deny Kenyans their basic freedoms of assembly, of association, of movement, etc. For example, even today it is illegal in Kenya for more than five people to assemble without a license from the government. This old, colonial law which was used to make it difficult for Kenyans to fight for their freedom is still in force today 30 years after Kenya got its independence! Even when the license is issued, it's no guarantee that the regime will allow the meeting to take place. Just last month, the 27th of March to be precise, the regime's repressive forces forcibly dispersed the people gathered at the open-air eye clinic in Limuru to receive free medical treatment. This clinic was organized by a charitable organization for those poor Kenyans who cannot afford the exorbitant fees charged at the hospitals. On the same day, a Christian congregation was dispersed from church premises by a heavily armed so-called anti-riot (but themselves very riotous) police immediately after the service.

Innocent Kenyans continue to be killed through state-sponsored terrorism throughout the country, particularly in the Rift valley and the North Eastern provinces and in the coastal area of Mombasa. This ugly situation is turning thousands of Kenyans into refugees in their own country. Hundred others continue to flee the country into exile. Equally, the regime continues to deny university academics and students their right

Mwakenya: The Unfinished Revolution

to form their associations. There are more examples, which I could give were it not for the constraints of time.

Despite all the above, however, I feel proud to report to this august assembly of fellow activities and strugglers that the struggling people of Kenya are not just agonizing and lamenting on the outcome of those sham elections, but they continue to organize and mobilize in their different capacities to prepare for the day when they will bring about the changes they want, and not the changes which the imperialist powers, the IMF and the World Bank want. These patriotic Kenyans are led in this struggle by MWAKENYA (Union of Patriots for the Liberation of Kenya) which has been consistent in the struggle for more than a decade and a half now, and which we in the United Movement for Democracy in Kenya support.

And here Mr. Chairman is where we make our special appeal. Whereas in the past we have appealed to the international community in general, we are today making a particular appeal to you brothers and sisters in the Pan-African Movement in the African continent and in the Diaspora, for your support in the Kenyan people's struggle to bring about genuine democracy and the resoration of their dignity and sovereignty. For our struggle is your struggle as well. As the veteran Pan-Africanist, Ambassador Dudley Thomson, said yesterday when quoting the Cuban revolutionary and philosopher, Jose Marti, "We either save ourselves together, or we disappear together."

Those of us who are in the same struggle against neocolonialism and imperialism should not feel guilty in helping one another. Why should we feel so when the imperialists feel neither shame nor guilt when helping their agents who are ruling most of our countries in Africa? Let us pull down these artificial geographical and psychological borders, which instill in us false identities and prevent us from joining each others' struggles.

Brothers and sisters, our appeal to this Congress is based on the historical role of Pan-African movement, which gave our country, Kenya, moral and political support during our first liberation struggle against colonialism, particularly after the 1945 Pan-African Congress in Manchester, UK. We

Mwakenya: The Unfinished Revolution

need a similar support now (if not more) in our second liberation struggle against the forces of neocolonialism and imperialism.

Finally, we appeal for unity of purpose amongst all Pan-Africanists in our struggles to liberate our peoples the worldover from the stranglehold of colonialism and imperial-ism, led by the United Stats of America. It can be done! Let us do it! Imperialism is not invincible. What we need is to have the right attitude.

In conclusion, we of the United Movement for Democracy in Kenya join Mwakenya in appealing to you brothers and sisters to denounce and expose all manifestions of state-terrorism and the denial of democratic rights of the Kenya people by the Moi-Kanu regime.

We, in our part, assure you that we will keep on struggling for what we believe to be right, no matter the consequences. For as Dedan Kĩmathi, the legendary leader of the Kenya Land and Freedom Army (the Mau Mau) once said: "It is better to die on our feet than live on our knees".

Thank you for your patience.

Part Five

We March Forward

The people who forget their struggle and their history are people who have no awareness of their destiny.

Evo Morales

The Harare Declaration

Make 2001
The Year of Renewal and Coordination

A Special committee of Mwakenya met from January 4-7, 2001 in Harare, Zimbabwe. After vigorous discussion of the political development in Kenya and the rest of the world, it produced the following declaration:

We evaluated the balance of social forces from 1992, the year when the Moi dictatorship reluctantly struck down "clause 2A" it wrote into law in 1982 and which forbid the formation of political parties, to the present when the same dictatorship is trying to manipulate the movement for a new democratic constitution first called for in our party document, *Mwakenya Plank* (1991) into a mechanism for enshrining Moism even without Moi. We noted and welcomed the fact that since 1992 the culture of silence and fear identified in the party's documents—*Pambana, Cheche* and *Mpatanishi*—has been broken. The numbers of newspapers, journals and radio stations that carry voices other than those of the dictatorship have increased. Our people have become increasingly bolder and more outspoken in their demands for their economic, political, cultural and human rights. Our party can justifiably take pride in the central role it played in the struggles that led to the multiparty concession of 1992. Even this was not achieved without sacrifice. From the foundation of our party in

Mwakenya: The Unfinished Revolution

1974 to the year of the multiparty concession in 1992, the Moi dictatorship tortured, jailed, exiled, detained and even killed many party members in the course of their struggle against the dictatorship. The harassment did not end with the concession but continues to this day. The cold-blooded murder of one of our leaders, Karĩmi Nduthu, on March 24, 1996 is still fresh in our minds.

We must remind ourselves that the sacrifice was not for superficial changes. It was for the empowerment of the people, which means their control of the state, their right to land, water, air, electricity, jobs, houses, schools and medical care and to security in their homes, in the workplaces and in the streets. The multiparty concession did not, nor was it meant to, bring about these changes. Instead, more peasants have lost their land, the jobless have multiplied, hundreds of school and college graduates walk the streets, the employed live on meager wages with an ever-decreasing purchasing power, and the gap between the rich few and the poor majority has become wider and wider. In many cases, even the primary right to life and security has been taken away. The state policy of divide and rule through ethnic cleansing has turned thousands into refugees in their own country. Any state of whatever political persuasion that deliberately initiates, carries out or even abets in the killings of any section of the population loses any legal and moral legitimacy because it has in effect declared itself an enemy of the people.

During the same period the international scene changed drastically. At the beginning of our party in the 70s, the Cold War was in full bloom, but the year of the concession, the Cold War in its old form had ended, the Soviet Union and Eastern European socialist governments had collapsed, and the forces of imperialist globalization had picked up speed. The changed international situation left the USA as the only superpower in the era of globalization. These forces have affected Kenya, like many countries in Asia, Africa and South America, adversely. Imperialist globalization has made the Kenya state too weak to control the flow of finance capital in and out of the country, but strong enough to suppress the people when they try to organize against the dire effects of that globalization. Before

Mwakenya: The Unfinished Revolution

the global capital, the state is meek, mild and helpless, but before its own people it is arrogant, boastful and always ready to unleash the army against the population. While upholding the rights of foreign capital to pillage the natural resources and labor of the nation, the dictatorship brazenly tramples upon the human rights of Kenyans to organize how, where, when, and what these capitalist want to pillage. Multipartyism in effect has become a colorful camouflage of an IMF-Word Bank police state.

The globalization and worsening national situation have a meeting point in the comprador dictatorship that presides over the Kenyan state and quite naturally the national resistance has taken the concrete form of a struggle for constitutional reform and democratic accountability. While applauding the patriotic efforts made by religious institutions, opposition parties and civic groups to come up with a new constitution we also reject the assumption underlying some of these efforts that the dictatorship, which has fostered corruption, looted the nation, massacred our people and finally surrendered the decision-making about the economy to IMF and the World Bank, can somehow become a trusted partner in the reform process. No shepherd can ever trust a hyena to lead the flock to greener pastures or even negotiate with a hyena on the best way to the greener pastures.

Our stand as expressed in our 1992 document, The *Mwakenya Stand,* in which we called for intensified struggle against Moism with or without Moi, still remains. The accused cannot preside over the case against him. The Moi dictatorship cannot be the referee and the judge of the most effective constitutional path to end its misrule. We said it then and we say it again, *the dictatorship must go* as a pre-condition for genuine constitution reform and all the democratic forces should unite to work for the ouster of the dictatorship. We must never beg or bribe the dictatorship to move. The dictatorship must be removed to make it possible for Kenyan people to move on, and to move forward. For us the struggle for a new constitution must not be an end in itself, but part of the struggle for a state controlled by the people and for genuine changes in the economic, political and cultural life of the working people of Kenya. This can only be brought about by

Mwakenya: The Unfinished Revolution

the united power of Kenyan people. This *united power* cannot come about through pious hopes, good intentions and appeals to reason. There is only one way—intensified organization. We agree with the slogan of the 7th Pan-African Congress, held in Kampala, Uganda, on April 3-8, 1994: *Organize! Don't Agonize.* This has always been our position. It is still our position.

In the past, particularly in the '80s and 90s, the all-pervasive and paralyzing culture of silence and fear made it necessary for us to keep on highlighting the crimes of the regime through leaflets and pamphlets and other publicity generating activities at home and abroad. The success of this sometimes made some party members believe that leaflets and press statements were the only method of struggle and at times the production and distribution of leaflets became the main activity of the party. The success of the party was judged on whether it has produced a leaflet or not. The absence of a leaflet on whatever is current was often seen as the death of the party. While the phase of our struggles may have demanded it, we must recognize that leafleting cannot be a substitute for real organization to carry out an effective programme of actions. We must, however, not minimize internal difficulties the party has gone through. Communication between the CC, the various organs of the party, and the entire membership has not been regular and this has led to some confusion, with some members feeling adrift and not connected like separate limbs without a head or even a body. We may not issue a public statement, but surely members deserve to know and debate the position of the party on the party itself and on the national and international scene.

Following this review of the party, the nation and the international situation, the Special Committee resolved to shift emphasis from publicity generating activities and concentrate on reorganization. The Special committee has called the year 2001 the year of Renewal and Consolidation through organizing in order to connect:

- The party with people
- Leadership with members
- Ideas with action (through mutual interaction of ideas and action)

Mwakenya: The Unfinished Revolution

The party can realize these ends by: **1)** establishing lines of clear and regular communications between the various organs of the party; **2)** strengthening and deepening the relationship between the internal and external wings of our party; and finally **3)** making, deepening and strengthening concrete links with the working people through organizing around grassroots (local) needs and actions.

It was resolved to:

- Clarify the name of the party and call it Mwakenya-DTM, so as to reflect correctly the history, continuity and the main streams that have gone into making it. Hereafter, the party will be referred to as Mwakenya-December Twelve Movement (MKDTM).
- Hold regular members' conference.
- Strengthen leadership at all levels.
- Intensify the education of members in theory and practice.
- Intensify the recruitment of new members.

While the other parties' scramble for parliament and the State House and they become variations of the KANU ruling party, we strive to organize our parliament in the grassroots and our State House in the organized Kenyan people. We noted with pride that though there have been difficulties since the 90s of the twentieth century, internationally, nationally and even within the party, the setbacks have not deterred the MKDTM cadres and they continue to recruit, study, organize cultural activities and highlight issues of human rights abuse. Our party has survived and enters the new decade, the new century and the new millennium with more determination. But while noting the continuing hard work and commitment of our MKDTM cadres, the CC appeals to all members not to rest on the laurels of mere survival and successes of specific activities. Guided by our vision as stated in our party documents—*Pambana, Cheche Kenya, Mpatanishi* and *Draft Minimum Programme*—let us all resolve to adopt and successfully make the year 2001 as the Year of Renewal and Consolidation through organizing our people for a real National Democratic Revolution.

Don't Agonize; Organize.

422

Part Six

Without a revolutionary party, without a party based on the Marxist-Leninist theory of revolution and the Marxist-Leninist style of revolution, it's impossible to lead the working class to victory.

Chou en-lai

The Party Study Guide

Organizational aspects

People in our country would like to see the ruling alliance of imperialism and the comprador bourgeoisie under the repressive neocolonial KANU regime overthrown. Indeed many people would welcome the successful completion of the National Democratic Revolution (NDR) as the most minimum basis for the socialist reorganization of our society.

However, some people think that these changes can come about without political organization and sacrifice. Many petty-bourgeois intellectuals even think it is beneath their dignity to join a political organization, and particularly one that talks about workers and peasants. Some others are willing to join some form of political organization. However, when such people talk of organization, they mean different things.

There are those who will join an organization only if it does not interfere with their jobs: their family life, their social life, etc., in short, if it does *not make demands on them, if it does not inconvenience them, if it does not require them to obey rules and collective decisions, or carry out tasks.* They would like to feel that they belong to an organization. Their work, their family, their social life, their friends, come first; politics and organizational demands come second. Others think of organization in terms of the old pre-independence petty-bourgeois organizations that were based on *platforms and parliaments.* They would like to organize the masses, but they themselves don't want to be organized. The masses are a platform

Mwakenya: The Unfinished Revolution

for entry into parliament. Our experience with the present pro-democracy parties is a great lesson.

The following readings notes concern those who would like to join an organization that is truly a detachment of the working class and the peasantry—an organization whose members are wielded together by unity of will, unity of action, unity of discipline, and unity of ideology. Under the prevailing police state in Kenya, such an organization can only exist through the strictest observation of the rules of *discipline, secrecy and security.* And it must be underground.

Under the above heading, the following to be noted:

A. Organizational Principles: Unity of theory, Practice and Discipline.

Readings:

1. Lenin, One Step Forward, Two Steps Back.
2. See summary in A History of the CPSU (B). (Chapter Two: Section 4)

B. Democratic Centralism:

Readings:

1. See A History of the CPSU (B). Chapter Two: section 4. Item 5.
2. Mao Tse-tung, "The Role of the Chinese Communist Party in the National war in Selected works of Mao Tse-tung: Section on Party discipline.
3. Fundamentals of Marxism-Leninism, 1963.

C. Criticisms and Self-Criticisms

Readings:

1. Mao, "Combat Liberalism".
2. A History of the CPSU (B). Conclusion. Item 5.
3. Mao, "On Correcting Mistaken Ideas in the Party", Selected works, Vol.1.
4. Fundamentals of Marxism-Leninism, 1963.

Mwakenya: The Unfinished Revolution

Notes:

1. If an organization and its members put "politics first", then all the other things will fall into place.
2. Practice, Theory, Practice: that should be the aim of study.
3. Lenin tells us: "Without a revolutionary theory, there can be no revolutionary movement".
4. Mao writes: "Theory becomes a material force as soon as it has gripped the masses".
5. MLM theory is not a dogma, but guide to action.

Readings:

1. History of the CPSU (B). Conclusion. Item 2.
2. Mao Tse-tung, "Reform our study" in Selected Works, p.198.
3. Amilcar Cabral, Unity and Struggle:

   a) Party Principles and Political Practice
   b) The Weapons of Theory

D. How Society Develops: Dialectical and Historical Materialism

Mastery of the laws of the development of society and particularly the law of class struggle is crucial in a party that aims at leading the working class and peasantry against the imperialist-comprador alliance with its machinery of spreading ignorance among the people. The ruling bourgeois class does not want people to understand how society works; how it came to be; and how it can be consciously changed for the life-enhancement of the working people and society as a whole. If people were to understand how society works on paper, then it would be harder to cheat and steal from them; because most contracts, treaties, measures, and laws are designed to steal from the people; and are written in a way that is too advanced for the uneducated, which is apt to confuse and aggravate them, rather than to help them.

Mwakenya: The Unfinished Revolution

There are two world outlooks or conceptions of the world or ways of interpreting things: Materialism or Idealism:

Materialism- is not a dogmatic system. It is rather a way of interpreting, conceiving of, explaining every question. It believes that there is nothing but matter in motion. It is opposed to Idealism, Liberalism and Spiritualism.

Idealism- is a belief that there are forces outside of matter or the individual that control and affect an organism. Idealism is inseparable from superstition, belief in the supernatural, the mysterious and unknown; it is nothing more than clericalism. In other words, idealism supposes that everything material is dependent on and determined by something spiritual; whereas materialism recognizes that everything spiritual is dependent on and determined by something material.

Two laws on the development of things: on the development of society, of matter of any organism: Metaphysics and Dialectics.

I. Metaphysics—see things as:

1. static
2. one-sided
3. isolated
4. repetition
5. in abstraction from their conditions of existence
6. in abstraction from their change and development
7. in separation one from another, ignoring their interconnections and interrelations
8. fixed and frozen, ignoring their change and development

Notes:

1. Such change as there is can only be an increase or decrease in quantity, or a change of place.
2. Cause of any change is not inside things, but outside them—the motivating force in external.

Mwakenya: The Unfinished Revolution

3. Capitalist exploitation, competition, the individualist, the ideology of a capitalist society—the oppression of humanity can still be found in ancient slave society, the feudal society and, therefore, will exist forever unchanged.

II. Dialectics—see things as:

1. constantly changing
2. many sided
3. interdependent and interrelated
4. interconnected
5. moving from a qualitative stage to another

Notes:

1. Things are constantly changing, growing or dying, increasing or decreasing. This is an extremely important concept. Capitalism, for example, appears to be a very powerful economic system, but is a dying system.
2. Things are interdependent—each thing in its movements is interrelated with and interacts on things around it. In order to understand a thing— like society or the role of women in society. We should study it internally and its relations with other things.

III. Things are Many Sided—the Unity and Struggle of Opposition

1. The internal dynamics of all phenomena or things have forces, which oppose each other or struggle against each other or are in contradiction with each other. This struggle of opposites or contradictions is what causes that thing to grow or decay.
2. At the same time, the very existence of these opposing forces in a single entity (their unity) makes up the very essence of that thing. For example:

    a. Positive and negative

    b. Life and death

    c. Slaves and owners

    d. Feudal lords and serfs

Mwakenya: The Unfinished Revolution

  e. Capitalists and workers

  f. Men and women

3. The cause of any change or development should be seen as a result of its own internal and necessary self-movement. The cause of the development of thing lies in the contradictory nature of things. There is internal contradiction in every single thing, hence its motion and development.

4. Changes in society are due chiefly to the development of the internal contradictions in society that is the contradiction between classes, between the productive forces and the relation between the old and the new.

5. It is the development of intensifications or opposing forces, which push society forward and give the impetus for the supervening of the old society by the new.

IV. Historical Materialism

1. Historical materialism is the result of application of materialism and dialectics to the study of human society; consequently, it rests on the general philosophical materialist world outlook.

  a. It gives the answer to the fundamental question of philosophy: The relationship between social being and social consciousness.

  b. It recognizes that social being is objective reality independent of social consciousness. In either case, it is consciousness, including social consciousness that it regarded as a more or less faithful reflection of objective reality.

  c. It discloses the connections between the various aspects of social life; it shows, for instance, the interconnection between the economic system of society and the political institutions and ideological forms arising on that basis. In contrast to the particular social sciences, it deals with the development of society as a whole.

V. The Laws of Historical Materialism are General in a Twofold Sense:

1. They operate in all or in some of the socio-economic formations.

Mwakenya: The Unfinished Revolution

2. They give expression to the relationships between the different spheres and aspects of society as an integral organism.

Readings:

1. See Chapter 4 of A History of the CPSU (B).
2. Mao, Selected works Vol.1:
   a. On Practice
   b. On Contradiction
3. Maurice Cornforth, Historical Materialism
4. Maurice Cornforth, Dialectical Materialism

Note: Dialectical and historical materialism constitute the theoretical basis of communism, the theoretical foundations of the Marxist party, and it is the duty of every active member of our party to know these principles and hence to study them (Lenin).

E. Classes in Society

Definition: Classes are large groups of people differing from each other by the place they occupy in a historically determined system of social production, by their relation (in most cases fixed and formulated in law) to the means of production, their role in the social organization of labor, and, by the dimensions of social wealth of which they dispose and the mode of acquiring it. Classes are groups of people one of which can appropriate the labor of another owing to the different places they occupy in a definite system of social economy (Lenin).

Readings:

1. Lenin, A Great Beginning, Vol. 29
2. Marx & Engels, The Communist Manifesto
3. Mao Tse-tung, "Classes in Chinese Society", Vol. 1.
4. Fundamentals of Marxism-Leninism
5. Kwame Nkrumah, Class Struggle in Africa.
6. Amilcar Cabral, The Struggle in Guinea (pamphlet)
7. N.C.G. Mathema, The Philosophy of the working Class
8. Ngũgĩ wa Thiong'o, Devil on the Cross (novel)

Mwakenya: The Unfinished Revolution

9. Maina wa Kĩnyattĩ, Classes and Class Struggle in Kenya
10. Dialego (1978), Philosophy and Class struggle

F. Imperialism

Lenin teaches us:

1. Imperialism is moribund capitalism.
2. Imperialism is the eve of the social revolution of the proletariat.

No study of our situation, no revolution in our society today can really succeed without our party understanding imperialism (not as a slogan), but as capitalism at a certain stage in its growth. Today Africa is a product of imperialism and the struggles of the people against it. We can distinguish three stage of imperialism in Africa:

1. *Slave Stage*: Millions of the African people were forcibly taken to Europe, Asia and the Americas to work as slaves on plantations and factories. The people who were taken were young men and women, between 15-30 years of age. The most productive age in any society. Africa has not recovered from this savage trade and mass killings of those who refused to be enslaved.

2. *Colonial stage:* The occupation of Africa by Western imperialisms. European missionaries worked side by side with imperialism to uproot African history, culture and heritage. The struggles of the people against colonial occupation led to *Independence.*

3. *Neocolonial Stage*: The struggles of the people against a neocolonial economy will lead first to National Democratic Revolution and then to social transformation, i.e., the building of Socialism. The success of socialism will lead to communism.

Readings:

1. Walter Rodney, How Europe Underdeveloped Africa
2. L. Leontyev, "Basic features of Imperialism" in A Short Course of Political Economy, 1968.
3. Lenin, Imperialism: The Highest Stage of capitalism.
4. Nkrumah, Neocolonialism: the Last Stage of Imperialism.
5. Jack Woodis, What is Neo-colonialism?

Mwakenya: The Unfinished Revolution

Rodney's book and Lenin's book are the basic texts. Leontyev's article is an excellent piece. Nkrumah's and Woodis's books have useful data relevant to Africa.

G. The National Question or the Question of Nationalities

Joseph Stalin formulated the major Marxist definition of a nation in 1913. He writes:

1. A nation is historically constituted, stable community of people, formed on the basis of a common language, territory, economic life, and psychological makeup manifested in a common culture.

2. A nation is not merely a historical category but a historical category belonging to a definite epoch, the epoch of rising capitalism. The process of elimination of feudalism and development of capitalism is at the same time a process of the constitution of people into nations.

It is important to study this question historically. The problems and solutions to the national question when nations were emerging from feudalism (Western Europe) are slightly different from the same for nations emerging from feudalism in the era of imperialism (Russia and Eastern Europe), or from those of nations emerging from imperialist colonialism and neo-colonialism (Africa, Asia and Latin America). This reading can help the party cadres to understand the politics of *tribalism* and the forces behind it, and how to combat both of them. It is also important for the party cadres to comprehend the concepts of self-determination, multipartyism, ethnicity and *majimboism* and their implications on our multiethnic country.

Readings:

Stalin, Marxism and the National Question. See also other articles by the same author in the different volumes of his collected works. But the above is the basic text.

1. Leontyev, A short Course of Political Economy.
2. Lenin, "Rights of Nations to Self-determination".

Mwakenya: The Unfinished Revolution

H. The Religious Question

It is very important to study this question in order to distinguish both the radical progressive traditions in Christianity and Islam and the reactionary, backward looking traditions in both religions. Karl Marx forcefully argues that religion is the opium of the masses. And Kaggiaism—a religion founded by Bildad Kaggia in Kenya—contends that, there are two Gods: the God of the oppressor and the God of the oppressed. Kaggiaism and the Mau Mau leaders are on the same page on this issue.

The South African Communist Party on religion: Million of South Africans, including black workers, subscribe to various religious beliefs. The South African ruling class and its allies, like oppressors elsewhere in the world, have always tried to use religion as a tool to control and instill passivity and resignation among the working masses. With the development of the liberation struggle there has emerged an interpretation of religious doctrines, which is in the interest of the struggling people. Moved by a profound rejection of oppression, countless religious leaders and believers have taken up the battle against the colonial system. Many are to be found within the ranks of the liberation movement and the people's army. The ideology of the South African Communist Party (SACP) is based on scientific materialism. But we recognize the right of all people to adopt and practice religious beliefs of their choice. We work for the involvement of all anti-apartheid forces in the common struggle for freedom and democracy. There is common ground between the immediate and long-term perspectives of the party and a theology of liberation that identifies with the poor and oppressed. In actual struggle, this bond has grown and must be further strengthened.

Readings:

1. Marx and Lenin: on Religion.
2. Castro, Fidel and Religion, 1987. This is basic text.
3. Marx & Engels, The Communist Manifesto.
4. Islam and African traditional religions should be studied by the party

cadres. They are major social forces in Africa. The party cadres should also study the historical development of Christianity, its positive and negative impact in Africa, and particularly in Kenya.

5. The Path to Power: Programme of the SACP as adopted at the 7th Congress, 1989.

I. The Woman Question

In a capitalist society and other oppressive societies the female worker suffers under *exploitation* as owner of labor power and *social oppression* as a woman. She is punished, instead of being rewarded, for her role in the reproduction of the human race.

Readings:

1. Engels, The Origin of the Family and the Sate (basic text)
2. Thomas Sankara, "The Revolution Cannot Triumph Without the Emancipation of Women" in Thomas Sankara Speaks, 1988.

J. On the State and State Apparatus

A state, according to Maulana Karenga (1993), can be defined as the totality of institutions, which facilitate governance and insure social control. Within the general framework of these functions, two sets of institutions stand out as most definitive. These are the institutions of dominance, i.e., coercion (army, police, courts, prisons, etc.) and institutions of political socialization (the educational system, the media, religion, parliament and other structures used to advance and consolidate the ideas and values of the ruling class. In our country (Kenya), the institutions of dominance are used to consolidate the neocolonial system, to strengthen the comprador-imperialist alliance and to reinforce the imperialist exploitation and oppression of the majority of our people. In this respect, the liberation of our people will not be possible without the state and its apparatus in the hands of the people. Neocolonial armies, police, judiciary, parliament, NGOs, etc., can never be instruments of people's power. Coup d'états,

Mwakenya: The Unfinished Revolution

multiparty system, bourgeois parliament and constitutions can never bring about the revolutionary change in Kenya. The social transformation of our country can only be brought about by a proletarian party with its base in communism. With this in mind, the Mwakenya-DTM leadership is firmly convinced that with total devotion, commitment, sacrifice and endurance in our struggle, we shall accomplish the task and achieve the national democratic revolution.

Readings:

1. Engels, The Origin of the Family and Private Property.
2. Lenin, State and Revolution.
3. Nkrumah, Neocolonialism: The highest Stage of Imperialism
4. Lenin, Imperialism: The Highest Stage of Capitalism
5. Maulana Karenga, Introduction to Black Studies
6. Amilcar Cabral, Unity and Struggle

K. Historical Aspects

It is very important to study the development of other organizations and parties, which have brought Socialist transformation in history.

Readings:

1. A History of the CPSU (B), 1938.
2. Red Star Over China (for glimpses into a history of CPC. See also various works of Mao on the Party and Revolution). Read also revolutionary literature of: Cuba, North Korea, Albania, Vietnam and the History of the Communist Party of South Africa.

Note: China has transformed its socialist economy into a free market economy. Eastern European states are semi-neocolonial and semi-capitalist states. Under perestroikaism the Soviet Union has broken into nation-states. Each of them, including Russia, has adopted a capitalist model of production. On this issue, read Joe Slovo's article, "The Nature of Socialism" in *The African Communist*, No.124, 1st Quarter 1991.

Mwakenya: The Unfinished Revolution

L. Africa

To understand the history, geography, natural science and politics of our continent and its islands is important. Particularly, we should study the successes and failures of armed struggles—in Kenya, Algeria, Guinea-Bissau, Mozambique, Angola, Namibia, Zimbabwe and South Africa—against colonialism and neocolonialism.

Readings:

1. Frantz Fanon, The Wretched of the Earth. Read sections:
   i. The Pitfalls of National consciousness
   ii. On National Culture.
   iii. Concerning Violence
2. Cabral, Unity and Struggle (chapter on: National Liberation Culture).
3. Cabral, Revolution in Guinea.
4. Museveni, Articles and Speeches.
5. Sankara, Thomas Sankara Speaks.
6. Babu. Africa Socialism or Socialist Africa.
7. Ben Turo, Africa: What Can Be Done?
8. Samora Machel, The Tasks Ahead: Selected Speeches of Samora Machel
9. Kwame Nkrumah's writings.
10. Sekou Toure's works
11. Maina wa Kĩnyattĩ, Kenya's Freedom struggle and Mau Mau: a Revolution Betrayed.

M. South Africa.

Readings:

1. The African Communist (Quarterly).
2. The Red Flag in South Africa (a popular history of the Communist party 1921-1990).
3. F. Meli, A History of the ANC: South Africa Belongs to Us.

N. Kenya

There are some who are proud, instead of ashamed, of knowing nothing or very little of our own history—ignorant of their own country. Some people can only relate tales of ancient Greece and other foreign lands (Mao Tse-tung).

For an organization such as ours, no amount of study of foreign revolutionary situations and successes can ever substantiate the knowledge and seriousness of our situation. Those of us, who have been brought up in a colonial and neocolonial environment, are always looking outside ourselves for a study and solution to our problems. Theory comes from practice; therefore studying our own concrete realities will give us the theory and knowledge to differentiate what works for Kenyans today and in the future, when addressing neocolonialism, in a practical sense. Already we have a rich history of a disciplined working class organization under Cege Kĩbacia, Makhan Singh, and Fred Kubai, Mau Mau movement under Bildad Kaggia, Fred Kubai, Isaac Maina Gathanju, Stanley Mathenge, Enoch Mwangi and Eliud Mũtonyi, and armed resistance under the leadership of Marshal Dedan Kĩmathi. The Pambana Press (1970-2001) has produced an enormous amount of the theoretical material rooted in the Kenyan experience. The Kenyan experience of organization, resistance and struggle should be the starting point of our revolutionary reading. Only from that fundamental basis the international experiences in places like the Philippines, North Korea, Peru, Cuba, Vietnam, Nicaragua, Palestine, Angola, Mozambique, Guinea-Bissau, etc., can enrich our own. We can learn and understand their failures and successes.

Readings:

I. General History

1. Makhan Singh, History of Kenya's Trade Union Movement to 1952
2. Oginga Odinga, Not Yetu Uhuru
3. Bildad Kaggia, The Roots of Freedom
4. Mũgo wa Gatherũ, Kenya: From Colonization to Independence, 1888-1970

Mwakenya: The Unfinished Revolution

5. Wanyĩrĩ Kĩhoro, The Price of Freedom
6. Maina wa Kĩnyattĩ, History of Resistance in Kenya, 1884-2002

II. Writings of KLFA Fighters

1. Barnett & Njama, Mau Mau From Within.
2. Gucu Gĩkoyo, We Fought For Freedom
3. M. Mathu, The Urban Guerrillas
4. Ngũgĩ Kabiro, The Man in the Middle
5. Warũhiũ Itote, Mau Mau General
6. K. Mũchai, The Hardcore
7. H.K. Wachanga, The Swords of Kĩrĩnyaga
8. J.Wamweya, Freedom Fighter
9. G. Wachiira, Ordeal in the Forest
10. Kourugo wa Kĩragũ, Mwarimũ and Gĩtungati kĩa Mau Mau (unpublished manuscript). This volume can be found in Mau Mau Research Center, Nairobi.
11. Nyakĩyo Waikũmbĩ, Ndaarĩ Mũtitũ Kũrũĩra Wĩyathi (unpublished manuscript). The document can found in Mau Mau Research Center, Nairobi.

III. Mau Mau Detention Writings

1. J.M. Kariũki, Mau Mau Detainee
2. Gakaara wa Wanjaũ, Mau Mau Writer in Detention
3. Waititũ wa Kĩnyattĩ, A Detention Notebook (Unpublished manuscript). The document can be found in MMRC, Nairobi.

IV. Critical and Ideological Literature

1. Ngũgĩ wa Thiong'o's works
2. Shiraz Durrani, Kĩmaathi: Mau Mau's First Prime Minister.
3. Maina wa Kĩnyattĩ, Mau Mau: The Peak of Nationalism in Colonial Kenya
4. Maina wa Kĩnyattĩ, Thunder From the Mountain

Mwakenya: The Unfinished Revolution

5. Maina wa Kĩnyattĩ, Kenya's Freedom Struggle;
6. Maina wa Kĩnyattĩ, Mau Mau: A Revolution Betrayed
7. Al-Amin Mazrui, Kilio Cha Haki

V. Prison Writings, 1970-2002

1. Abdilatif Abdalla, Sauti ya Dhiki
2. Ngũgĩ wa Thiong'o, Detained: A Writer's Dairy
3. Maina wa Kĩnyattĩ, Kenya: A Prison Notebook
4. Maina wa Kĩnyattĩ, Mother Kenya: Letters From Prison
5. Maina wa Kĩnyattĩ, A Season of Blood: Poems From Prison
6. Maina wa Kĩnyattĩ, Mwaki Ũtangĩhoreka
7. Koigi wa Wamwere, Justice on Trial

VI. The WPK/DTM-Mwakenya Underground Press

Every party member must read these following documents:

1. Cheche Kenya (produced and distributed by the Workers' Party of Kenya. Reprinted by Zed Press (London) under a new title: InDependent Kenya.
2. Kenyan Students Against Imperialist Education
3. Mwanguzi, Pambana and Mpatanishi
4. The Draft Minimum Programme of Mwakenya
5. Kenya Democratic Plank
6. The Mwakenya Stand
7. Karĩmi Nduthu: A life in the Struggle

Men make their own history. But they do not make it just as they please. They do not make it under circumstances chosen by themselves, but under circumstances directly encouraged, given and transmitted from the past.

— (Karl Marx).

Central Secretariat
January, 2001

Mwakenya: The Unfinished Revolution

REQUEST TO READERS

The Mau Mau Research Center (MMRC) would be glad to accept any monetary donations for continued research, as well as your opinion of this book, its content and design, and any suggestions or comments you may have for future publications.

Please send all your suggestions, monetary donations, or comments to:

Mau Mau Research Center
P.O. Box 746-00200
Nairobi, Kenya.
Email: info.mmrc@gmail.com

Printed in the United States
By Bookmasters